D1548505

The figure of the puritan has long been conceived as dour and repressive in character, an image which has been central to ways of reading sixteenth- and seventeenth-century history and literature. Kristen Poole's original study challenges this perception, arguing that, contrary to current critical understanding, radical reformers were most often portrayed in literature of the period as deviant, licentious, and transgressive. Through extensive analysis of early modern pamphlets, sermons, poetry, and plays, the fictional puritan emerges as a grotesque and carnivalesque figure; puritans are extensively depicted as gluttonous, sexually promiscuous, monstrously procreating, and even as worshipping naked. By recovering this lost alternative satirical image, Poole sheds new light on the role played by anti-puritan rhetoric. Her book contends that such representations served an important social role, providing an imaginative framework for discussing familial, communal, and discursive transformations that resulted from the Reformation.

KRISTEN POOLE is Assistant Professor of English at the University of Delaware.

RADICAL RELIGION FROM SHAKESPEARE TO MILTON

Figures of Nonconformity in Early Modern England

KRISTEN POOLE

WITHDRAWN

CAMBRIDGE
UNIVERSITY PRESS

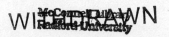

PUBLISHED BY THE PRESS SYNDICATE OF THE UNIVERSITY OF CAMBRIDGE
The Pitt Building, Trumpington Street, Cambridge, United Kingdom

CAMBRIDGE UNIVERSITY PRESS
The Edinburgh Building, Cambridge CB2 2RU, UK   http://www.cup.cam.ac.uk
40 West 20th Street, New York, NY 10011–4211, USA   http://www.cup.org
10 Stamford Road, Oakleigh, Melbourne 3166, Australia

First published 2000

Printed in the United Kingdom at the University Press, Cambridge

Typeset in 11\12.5pt Baskerville   [CE]

A catalogue record for this book is available from the British Library

Library of Congress cataloguing in publication data
Poole, Kristen.
Radical religion from Shakespeare to Milton: figures of nonconformity
in early modern England / Kristen Poole.
p.   cm.
Includes bibliographical references and index.
ISBN 0 521 64104 7 (hardback)
1. Puritans – England – Controversial literature – History and criticism.
2. Dissenters, Religious – England – Controversial literature – History and criticism.
I. Title.
BX9334.2>p66   1999
285.'.9'0942–dc21   99–37800   CIP

ISBN 0 521 64104 7 hardback

To my parents,
David and Marilyn Poole,
and in memory of my grandmother,
Elvera F. Poole

So great . . . is the audacitie of those which lacerate the fames of Puritans, & with so much confidence doe they vent their obloquies, that they which know the falsity thereof, & easily perceive that that same aspersions are more truly due to the Authors and raisers of them, yet they are dazeled, and driven to some doubtfull admittance thereof. Neither could this audacity be so prevalent amongst the vulgar, but that Scholars . . . are now become the most injurious detesters & depravers of Puritans, having taken up in Pulpits and Presses, almost as vile and scurrilous a licence of fiction and detraction, as is usual in Play-houses, Taverns, and Bordelloes.

Henry Parker, *A Discourse Concerning Puritans. A vindication of those, who uniustly suffer by the mistake, abuse, and misapplication of that Name* (1641), 2

Contents

Illustrations

Acknowledgements

Early modern pamphlets frequently tackle questions of religious identity through the form of a dialogue: a curious character, often traveling, encounters a bizarre range of individuals with whom he disputes, banters, ponders, drinks, and converts. On the journey to this book, I have had the good fortune to share the company of many who have guided my steps, prompted me to question, pointed me in new directions, lightened my load with friendship, and transformed my vision of the landscape.

But for Heather Dubrow, I would not have begun the trek. Haphazardly choosing a course to fulfill an undergraduate distribution requirement, I found myself in Heather's classroom; this happy accident put me on an unexpected path. An inspiring teacher, compassionate scholar, and generous mentor, Heather has provided me with guidance ever since.

The book first took shape at Harvard University, where a group of faculty and graduate students created a culture of vibrant intellectual camaraderie. As much for their formal feedback as for provocative comments over coffee, I am grateful to Doug Bruster, Carolyn Dever, Marjorie Garber, Scott Gordon, David Hillman, Stephen Greenblatt, Roland Greene, Carla Mazzio, Curtis Perry, Libby Spiller, Kathryn Schwarz, Marc Shell, Scott Stevens, Doug Trevor, and Eric Wilson. Leo Damrosch provided valuable comments that tempered some of my more hyperbolic claims. Jennifer Carrell sustained me throughout with her imaginative readings, her sane perspective, and, most importantly, her friendship. I spent a year researching this project in Oxford under the supervision of Nigel Smith, whose vast knowledge of seventeenth-century pamphlet literature helped me to navigate a daunting field of text, and whose timely suggestions pushed the dissertation to unexpected points.

The thesis was steered by the unholy alliance of Jeffrey Masten and Barbara Lewalski. Jeff read an onslaught of chapter drafts with an unfailing sense of good humor and generosity. Barbara directed the dissertation in a way that kept me in step with her rigorous scholarly expectations while still allowing the freedom of my offbeat improvisations. Her unbounded joy of Renaissance literature made an arduous process exciting, and her professional dedication and integrity have provided me with a model I can only hope to emulate.

The project was deeply influenced by my participation in a National Endowment for the Humanities Summer Institute, "Religion and Society in Early Modern England," directed by David Cressy and Lori Anne Ferrell. A Folger Institute seminar, "Tudor Historiography," led by David Kastan, was also inspiring; David continually challenges my ideas and makes them grow.

Along the way, I have benefited from the comments and suggestions of Joan Bennett, Bryan Crockett, G. Blakemore Evans, Tom Freeman, Matt Greenfield, Jay Halio, Ann Hughes, Mat Morrison, the infinitely patient Barbara Mowat, Tom Olsen, Gail Kern Paster, Michael Schoenfeldt, Andy Shiflett, Luke Wilson, and a very helpful anonymous reader at *Shakespeare Quarterly*. My graduate students have forced me to look at familiar texts in unfamiliar ways. I have also received valuable responses and bibliographical tips from audience members at conferences of the Modern Language Association, the Shakespeare Association of America, and the Renaissance Society of America. Tom Hamill kindly provided his research assistance in the unwieldy task of checking all my quotes. The staff at the Bodleian, British, Cambridge University, Huntington, and Newberry Libraries have been pleasantly helpful; the staff at the Houghton and Folger Shakespeare Libraries have been cheerfully tolerant. Without the financial support of a Jacob K. Javits Fellowship, a Mellon Dissertation Fellowship, traveling fellowships from Harvard University, and a General University Research grant from the University of Delaware this book would not exist as it does. A version of chapter 1 first appeared in *Shakespeare Quarterly* 46 (1) (1995), and a subsequent version was reprinted in *Shakespeare and Carnival: After Bakhtin*, ed. Ronald Knowles (London: Macmillan Press Ltd. and New York: St. Martins Press, Inc., 1998); variation of chapter 4 will be published in *Form and Reform in Renaissance England: Essays in Honor of Barbara Kiefer Lewalski*, eds. Amy Boesky and Mary Thomas Crane (University of Delaware Press, 2000). I am grateful for permission to include these chapters here.

At Cambridge University Press, I was honored to have Patrick Collinson read an initial draft of the manuscript; the present book records my debt to him not only through innumerable citations of his scholarship, but also through the silent testimony of chapters re-written and re-conceived in response to his insightful comments. The suggestions of "Reader B" were also perceptive. The unflappable Josie Dixon was an ideal editorial guide, and Ann Lewis made her way through a haze of early modern orthography with a keen eye and a steady humor.

For their encouragement, criticism, and quirky wit, I am indebted to Lois Potter and Julian Yates, my colleagues at the University of Delaware. Jonathan Grossman graciously read the entire manuscript in the eleventh hour, and his keen and incisive observations substantively contributed to the final revision in the twelfth. Barbara Silverstein's reading saved the book from some of its less successful logical leaps.

The book's dedication only begins to acknowledge how much I owe my parents, David and Marilyn Poole, who fostered creativity and curiosity, and who unquestioningly supported and encouraged journeys into the unknown. I would also like to recognize the influence of my grandmother, Elvera F. Poole, and my aunt, Jean Fletcher Schmidt, models of strong-minded women. And, although they can't read, it seems unfair not to honor the contributions of Cleo and Floh, who always keep things in perspective.

Through many years and over many miles, Martin Brückner has been my companion. He has shared in my fits of enthusiasm, suffered my sloughs of despond, and read, many times, every word. He has critiqued and edited, structured and sustained. Always, he makes me laugh, and he inspires.

Note on the text

In all quotations of primary sources I have kept original spellings, except for standardizing long "s." In citing titles of pamphlets and sermons, I have also standardized fonts and capitalization. For sixteenth- and seventeenth-century texts, the place of publication is London unless otherwise noted.

Introduction: deforming Reformation

> In these preposterous times many vices are predominant, but amongst all the whole brood of vices, there is none so great, there is none grown to that height, ther's none so leprous as this of Puritanisme, the errours of which Sect . . . I will plainly Anatomize and lay open to the view of all men.
>
> David Owen, *The Pvritanes Impvritie: or the Anatomie of a Puritane or Separatist* (1641), 1

In 1646 John Benbrigge delivered a sermon entitled *Gods Fury, Englands Fire. Or A Plaine Discovery of those Spirituall Incendiaries, which have set Church and State on Fire.* With rhetorical zest, Benbrigge vents his anguish over what he perceives as the dissolution of society, and hurls accusations at the religious sectarians whom he considers to be the source of this disruption: "Such was their hypocrisie in all they did . . . [that] their *Reformation* was but a greater *Deformation*, and that opened yet wider the Flood-gates of their *Desolation*" (sig. A2ᵛ). Benbrigge was far from alone in his assertion that religious radicalism had perverted the English Reformation – a movement which in the previous century had fostered a sense of national unity[1] – into a source of ecclesiastical and civil destruction. In the same year as Benbrigge's sermon, the presbyterian Thomas Edwards chides Parliament for their failure to quell the disruptive force of schism:

> You have, most Noble Senatours, done worthily against Papists, Prelates and scandalous Ministers, in casting down Images, Altars, Crucifixes, throwing out Ceremonies, & c. but what have You done against other kindes of growing evils, Heresie, Schisme, Disorder, against Seekers, Anabaptists, Antinomians, Brownists, Libertines and other Sects? . . . You have made a Reformation, and blessed be God who put it into your hearts to do such things, but with the Reformation have we not a Deformation, and worse things come in upon us then ever we had before? were any of those monsters heard of heretofore, which are now common among us?[2]

I

On the very brink of victory, a century-long process of ecclesiastical struggle was seemingly being undermined by a rabble of misguided zealots. Where Edwards longs to see a gloriously unified national church, he finds division and monstrosity.[3]

Sixteenth- and seventeenth-century orthodoxies stressed unity and universality: one nation was dependent upon one church. The body politic and the body of Christ were to be coterminous, integral, entire. One reformist tract, called *The Fortresse of fathers, ernestlie defending the puritie of religion* (1566), emphatically proclaims the centrality of the church: "There is *one* word, *one* Scripture, *one* Baptisme, and *one* death of Christ, *one* Father, *one* Religion, & *one* Charitie, *one* Sacrament of tha[n]kes giuing, *one* laing onne of handes, and *one* discipline, & *one* consent of the Ministers . . . To conclude, all thinges that are ordained, to the buylding or profitt of the Chirch, we must haue all those as *one* thinge" (sig. A4^{r-v}, my emphasis). Throughout the subsequent century, this call to unity was taken up by writers of strikingly diverse ecclesiastical perspectives; while those arguing for episcopacy and those advocating presbyterianism, for example, may have differed in their conception of church government, there was no question but that there could be only one church.[4] Sermons and pamphlets repeat, mantra-like, variations on Paul's letter to the Ephesians: "There is one body, and one Spirit, . . . One Lord, one faith, one baptism, One God, and Father of all, who is above all, and through all, and in you all" (4: 4–6).[5]

But lurking behind these repeated and insistent articulations of religious hegemony is the specter of religious difference. "*A perfect union in the same minde and judgement?*" asks an incredulous John Brinsley in his tract on religious schism. "Alas! nothing lesse. What multiplicity of divisions are here to be found? *Tongues* divided: *Hearts* divided: *Heads* divided: *Hands* divided: *States* divided: *Church* divided: *Cities* divided: *Towns* divided: *Families* divided: the neerest *Relations* divided."[6] Religious sectarianism shattered the ideal of Protestant unity. At the end of the sixteenth century, as ecclesiastical reform became the subject of national debate – and as Scripture became increasingly accessible to an increasingly literate public – new ideas about spiritual community challenged the primacy of the established church. Separatists such as the Brownists formed their own congregations, arguing the need for segregation of the godly and the ungodly; the mystical Family of Love practiced outward conformity while secretly belonging to their own alternative spiritual community; semi-separatist Baptists claimed a dual loyalty to their parochial church and to their own private, voluntary congregations. Conceptions of religious community became numerous and complex, contradictory and fluid.

This multiplication and confusion of religious identities destabilized systems of order and confounded traditional social and ecclesiastical categories. In early modern literature, this confusion was frequently given the label "puritan." As contemporaries recognized, the term "puritan" was used as "an Epithite of reproach" and a "scornefull Nick-name."[7] While modern historians have tended to apply "puritan" to those advocating reform from within the boundaries of the established church, in the first half of the seventeenth century the term most often designated those who sought to separate themselves (in varying degrees) from the dominant ecclesiastical community. Contemporaries most often employed the term as a derisive synonym for "schismatic." Oliver Ormerod, in his pamphlet *The Picture of a Puritane* (1605), defines "Puritanes" as "a Schismaticall and vndiscreete companie," "peeuish and peruerse Schismatickes," and "factious leaders."[8] This common stereotype is succinctly expressed in the title of Giles Widdowes's *The schysmatical puritan* (Oxford, 1630), and even in the title of John Geree's sympathetic *The Character of an old English Pvritane, or Non-Conformist* (1646).

As early as the 1590s, when the term "puritan" was gaining common currency, authors began to question its exact definition, and debates over the word's significance continued throughout the seventeenth century. One author writes in 1642, "if any man shall propound that old Quære, *What is a Puritan?* We may resolve the Question, and describe him . . . after this manner: A Puritan, is one of the pestilent party, the very plague of the Church and Commonwealth, . . . one that breathes nothing but sedition and calumnies."[9] Other definitions appear more specific; Widdowes contends that "A Puritan is a Protestant Non-Conformist."[10] With nonconformity itself covering such a range of beliefs and practices, however, even this seemingly pointed definition is far from clear. "Puritan" described all those who were divided from the central church body. The expansion of the term finds a parallel in that of its correlate "round-head"; one seventeenth-century author writes, "There hath beene a great noyse and rumour about the appellation and name of Round-heads, such that this riddle was never dissolved, nor none by him ever named, who or what particular sect was the intended Round-head, therefore it must, shall, and can be not otherwise intended and meant, but that [it applies to] all sects, as Papists, Brownists, Anabaptists, Separatists, Cavalliers, and whatsoever else are not with, or [are] any way against the true protestant Religion maintained by the King, Parliament and State of this Kingdome."[11] "Puritan" was equally capacious, unsettled, and indicative of subversive impulses.

In recent years, "puritan" – "the P word," as Patrick Collinson calls it[12] – has once again sparked heated discussion among historians; scholars have proffered almost antithetical definitions for the term and lamented its classificatory impotence. The word is so fraught that an introductory definition of "puritan" has become a standard generic feature of early modern historiography.[13] The difficulties with the term arise from the conflicting purposes of modern historians and early modern authors. The aim of the historian, to speak broadly, is to give shape and narrative to a synchronic and diachronic field of events. Historians thus require a terminology for expressing the period's diverse devotional practices, reformist impulses, ecclesiastical agendas, and spiritual desires; "puritan" has been stretched and contracted to serve as a useful label for categorizing various individuals and ideologies. By contrast, the aim of many early modern authors was to express a profound sense of shapelessness, to convey the chaos of transforming and disintegrating communal categories, to paint a muddled world picture. The historian's need for "puritan" as a useful category jars, therefore, with the seventeenth-century author's need to represent taxonomic crisis. Widdowes observes, "Concerning the name (*Puritan*), it is ambiguous."[14] To the historian, such ambiguity seems to demand clarification; to the early modern author, however, this very ambiguity becomes the word's value, and its significance.[15]

"Puritan," as it was used in pamphlets, poems, and plays, did not label a particular type of person; rather, in its early modern literary usage the term most often signified social elements that *resisted* categorization. In a culture loudly proclaiming the need for religious uniformity, "puritans" were the mutable, the indeterminable, the unlocatable; they seemingly incorporated pluralities, oppositions, and binaries. They were at once Protestant, Papist, and Jew; repressive killjoys and wanton libertines; of foreign origin and dangerously, subterraneously domestic; the sacred and the obscene. Ormerod begins his *Pictvre of a Puritane*, paradoxically, by declaring the very impossibility of drawing such a picture:

the painting of a *Puritane* is so hard and difficult, as that the ioynt skill of *Apelles, Pyrgoteles, Praxiteles,* and of al the cunning Painters in Saint *Chrysostoms* time, will scarce reach this object.

For as *Proteus* changed himselfe into diuers shapes, & appeared sometimes like a flame of fire, sometimes like a Bull, and sometimes like a terrible Serpent: so the Puritane changeth himselfe likewise into diuers shapes, & appeareth sometimes like a Protestant, sometimes like a Papist, & some-times like an Anabaptist. (sig. A2^v)

The word "puritan" invokes compromised and sliding categories, is metamorphic and inherently contradictory. From the late sixteenth through the mid-seventeenth century, English literature exhibits an uneasy fascination with certain cultural figures that indicate the disorder of things: cross-dressed women, masterless men, "noble" savages, and hermaphrodites, among others. The puritan is one of these figures. As a representational category, the puritan registers the anxieties surrounding socio-ecclesiastical structures in flux.

Throughout early modern discourse, from *Coriolanus* to *Leviathan,* ideals of civil order were expressed through the common and even hackneyed trope of the body, with the monarch as the acknowledged head and subjects serving as various limbs and organs. So too ideas of ecclesiastical order were given physical form, as the church was depicted through explicitly corporeal descriptions. In one such example, church "members have [Christ] for their Head, from whom by their joynts and synewes, they take their growing . . . for these members are so thorowly joyned as they are called *Flesh of his flesh, and bone of his bone,* Ephes. 5.30."[16] To survive, conservative authors argued, this body must function organically. The author of *An Alarum: . . . Discovering the Danger of Sectaries suffered: and the necessity of Order, and Vniformity to bee Established* (1646) writes:

consider in nature; is there any disorder or disunion in the Members of one body? They are many members, but all make one perfect body . . . much more should the Members of the spirituall body be one, that there should bee no schisme in the Church; Christ is the head of the Church, every Christian is a Member, the Church the body, the head hath not many bodyes, but the body hath many Members and by many Members, the body is made perfect. (6)

Although composed of many individuals, the larger ecclesiastical corpus ideally presented a model of integration, as the many bodies merge into one.

This vision of corporate perfection was corrupted by sectarians, who, in the eyes of orthodox authors, transform the body of Christ into a grotesque figure. "And those make Christ yet more monstrous, that setting up so many Independent Churches . . . which they call each, severally the mysticall Body of Christ, [they] do make Christ a head that hath so many bodies," declares one author.[17] These numerous separate congregations do not join together to form a larger, coherent ecclesiastical body, but, like an inverse hydra, share Christ as their head. Another author reverses this image, warning that radical claims of spiritual individualism, and the dissolution of proper hierarchical order, lead to a body of Christ whose trunk is covered with organs and extremities:

as in the body the most usefull members thereof, the eyes, the ears, the tongue, the hands, the feet would not onely be uselesse, but make a confused deformity, if they were every one annexed immediately to the grosse of the body, and not joyned by the mediation of some noble limb: the eyes, the ears, and tongue, by the head; the hands, by the arms, and the feet, by the legs: so would it be in the Church Catholique, if every particular Member should hold it self immediately to depend on it, and not on the noble and mediating limb of his particular Church.[18]

Proper ecclesiastical organization, like the skeletal framework of the human form, maintains the structure of the church body; once removed, this body collapses upon itself in "confused deformity."

In early modern literature, these concerns about the corruption of the larger body of Christ were frequently channeled into representations of individual sectarians: the puritan body itself became a site of deformation. George Spinola observes, "I have not found such strange, exotick, forrain, ridiculous deformities, and non-conformities of parts in the Faces and Limbs of any kinde of Men, as in those which at this day are familiarly called the Sectaries and Separatists."[19] Spinola envisions a body whose confused and contradictory origins result in an indeterminate form: "From his dislike of Episcopacy results his love of Presbitery, and from those two together, such a miscellaneous Impression is made in the blood, that any thing begot of that is very likely to look monstrous scurvily . . . Certainly, it must needs prove a thing of doubtfull Interpretation, of a Priest-and-Minister Face, of a Secular and Ecclesiastick Head and Shoulders" (sig. A3ʳ). Elsewhere, the puritan body is presented not so much as a hybrid, a melding of antitheses, as a composite of sectarian divisions. Thomas Edwards blazons the body of an Independent, demonstrating how it is "made up and compounded" of diverse sectarians, as a variety of errors "[meet] in the same persons, strange monsters, having their heads of Enthusiasme, their bodies of Antinomianisme, their thighs of Familisme, their legges and feet of Anabaptisme, their hands of Arminianisme, and Libertinisme as the great vein going thorow the whole."[20]

This emphasis on physical monstrosity led to a vogue for literary anatomies of the puritan body.[21] The pamphlet from which I have taken my epigraph, *The Pvritanes Impvritie: or the Anatomie of a Puritane or Separatist*, indicates the tenor of these tracts; when puritans were not being portrayed as physically monstrous, they often appear with bodily margins that are impure, compromised, and porous. In *The Anatomy of the Separatists, alias, Brownists, the factious Brethren in these Times: wherein this seditious Sect is fairely dissected, and perspicuously discovered to the view of the World* (1642), John Taylor initially caricatures the Brownists thus:

ye may know them by their frequent and far fetcht sighes, the continuall elevation of their eyes, their meager physiognomies, solitary countenances, sharp noses, by the cut of their hayre, made ever with the top of their prick-eares . . . yee may further discerne them by their broad hats and narrow rufs, which they usually weare, the putting of their gloves under their girdles, and the folding of their hands one within another. Indeed they are painted Sepulchres, whited walls, whose Religion consists in frequent fasting, and longer prayers. (2–3)

Such is the image of the puritan which has descended into our day. Eyes upturned, hands piously folded, denying bodily appetites in favor of extended prayer: these are the makings of a Malvolio, a Jonathan Edwards, an Arthur Dimmesdale. But Taylor continues:

They are much addicted to prayer and fasting; for they frame a long Babel-like prayer, made up with hums and hawes; and though they affect fasting well, yet they love their flesh better. They much delight in private conventicles, and secret and obscure places, in which voluptuous wantonnesse has her meeting, where the Spirit enlightens the understanding to see a sister in the darke: though they are superciliously rigid and censorious, yet they seem very charitable, for rather then their sisters shall want food, they will fill their bellies, and rather then they shall be naked, they will cover their bodyes. Brothers they are, but not of the blade; for they cannot endure our Cavaleers; yet they are lovers of the sisters of the scaberd. (2–3)

The puritans' purity is thus revealed as a sanctimonious façade, as the fast is replaced by the flesh, conventicles become wanton, and acts of charity such as feeding and clothing the poor become transformed into bawdy puns on sexual intercourse. The rigid exterior belies a libidinous interior, and charity becomes code for fornication.

Within the context of early modern literature, the figure of the puritan is thus frequently represented through the lens of the grotesque. Mikhail Bakhtin's classic description of the grotesque body – "It is not a closed, completed unit; it is unfinished, outgrows itself, transgresses its own limits. The stress is laid on those parts of the body which are open to the outside world, that is, the parts through which the world enters the body or emerges from it, or through which the body itself goes out to meet the world . . . the open mouth, the genital organs, the breasts, the phallus, the potbelly, the nose"[22] – typifies the puritan body as it is portrayed in drama and pamphlet literature of the late sixteenth and seventeenth centuries. Jonson's Zeal-of-the-Land Busy is continuously eating; the puritan women in Middleton's *A Chaste Maid in Cheapside* gorge themselves on sweetmeats and become drunk; a "zealous brother" in the pamphlet *The Anatomy of Et cætera* (1641) can barely speak through his drunkenness: "Nay, *said Roger*, hic-up, if you go to that, hic-up, you are as arrant a knave, hic-up, as my selfe" (5). Mistress Purge from *The Family of Love* is unabashedly sexually promiscuous, and has a purgative effect on the bowels of those around her; Falstaff and Hudibras have excessive, protruding bellies; and the sharp nose is a regular feature of puritan physiognomy.

If the puritan body is portrayed as grotesque, puritan gatherings are often cast in terms of the carnivalesque. Such representations emerge from the self-enclosed, often clandestine nature of sectarianism. For mid-sixteenth-century reform-minded Protestants such as John Foxe, the one, true church consisted of the small cells of believers who were forced underground by a corrupt ecclesiastical structure. By the late sixteenth and seventeenth centuries, however, mainstream Protestants viewed private enclaves of the self-declared elect with a wary eye; the secret gatherings which preserved true religion during the Marian period of papist oppression were one thing – the separatist impulses which destabilized a peaceful Protestant church were another. Such communities became transformed in the minds of many into a dangerous (or tantalizing) underground of sects engaging in a bewildering array of often bizarre religious and social practices. In literary portrayals, sectarian communities are "hot, private, lusty, and promiscuous meetings,"[23] where the "time was spent in drunkenness, uncleanness, blasphemous words, filthy songs, and mixt dances of men and women stark naked."[24] Schismatics are depicted gathering in the tavern, the field, and the fair,[25] and their activities revolve around drinking, eating, and orgies as much as preaching and praying. They "delight . . . in gluttony and drunkennesse, chambering and wantonnesse."[26] Thus in *Bartholomew Fair* Dame Purecraft, Busy, and Win Littlewit enter the fair of the title; in *The Family of Love* Mistress Purge meets her co-Familists in a secret, darkened den of iniquity; and in *1 and 2 Henry IV* Falstaff – who, as I discuss in chapter 1, was readily identified by his audience as a proto-Protestant martyr – finds his home in the tavern. In the 1640s, these accusations were illustrated through numerous woodcuts depicting the sectarians' alehouse conventicles, as well as some of their other deviant pastimes (see Figures 1 and 2).[27]

As is evident from Taylor's description, inherent to satiric portraits of the puritan is a binary structure: impurity is most sensational when juxtaposed with purity. This dualism is a fundamental aspect of most religious satire. Martin Luther was portrayed as a grotesque body in sixteenth-century woodcuts; ascetic monks are displayed as overindulgent in Rabelais's Gargantuan world; moralizing televangelists are uncovered as sexually voracious in today's yellow press. In current literary criticism, however, this duality of the puritan's image has largely been lost, as the carnal aspects of this representation have been stripped away. Pared into a one-sided figure of repression, The Puritan plays a crucial thematic role in readings of early modern literature and culture. In modern scholarship, Malvolio has long stood as the puritan posterboy; his strict adherence to regulations, his concern with social borders, and his condemnation of festivity place him in direct opposition to the irreverent and riotous world of Sir Toby Belch.

This somber, ascetic persona is required to maintain an interlocking series of binarisms which has long been inscribed in historical and literary accounts of the period. "Puritan" (and its more common adjectival form "puritanical") has been posited as the antithesis to that which is generally valued by literary critics: puritan v. wit, puritan v. theatre, puritan v. cavalier, puritan v. festivity – perhaps underlying all of these, puritan v. erotic desire. In sum, scholars have employed "puritan" as part of a dichotomous construct which has conceptually organized early modern literature, politics, and society. While postmodern theories of language have destabilized many conceptual and linguistic relations which were once thought to be the most fundamental (male/female, for example), in critical discourse "puritan" often continues to serve as a

A
SVVARME
OF
SECTARIES, AND
SCHISMATIQVES:
Wherein is difcovered the ftrange prea-
ching (or prating) of fuch as are by their Trades
Coblers, Tinkers, Pedlers, Weavers, Sowgelders,
and Chymney-Sweepers.

By JOHN TAYLOR.

The Cobler preaches, and his Audience are
As wife as Moffe was, when he çaught his Mare.

Sam: How

Printed luckily, and may be read unhappily, betwixt
hawke and buzzard, 1641.

Figure 1 Title page of John Taylor's *A Swarme of Sectaries, and Schismatiques* (1641)

A Brown
Dozen of Drunkards:
(Ali-aſs Drink-hards)

Whipt , and ſhipt to the Iſle of Gulls :

For their abuſing of Mr. *Malt* the bearded ſon, and *Barley-broth* the brainleſſe daughter of Sir *John Barley-corne.*

All joco-ſeriouſly { Wine-drunk,
deſcanted to our { Wrath-drunk, { ſtaggering Times.
{ Zeale-drunk,

By one that hath drunk at S. Patricks *Well.*

London : Printed by *Robert Auſtin* on *Adlin-hill.* 1648.

Figure 2 Title page of John Taylor's *A Brown Dozen of Drunkards* (1648)

foil, that against which the radical and transgressive can best be seen. (This tendency is perhaps strongest in the United States, where the notion of the "Pilgrim Fathers," the traditional high school set piece *The Scarlet Letter*, and even the holiday of Thanksgiving – despite its pervasive gluttony – contribute to a cultural legend of puritanical national origins.)

Flattening the representational image of the puritan, if allowing for a comprehensible schematic of the period, results in a literary anachronism. If modern and postmodern critics have tended to emphasize the puritans' retention at the expense of their indulgence, early modern authors were most likely to highlight quite the reverse; if contemporary culture has come to identify as "puritanical" those opposed to the transgressive, sixteenth- and seventeenth-century culture often used "puritan" to signify transgression. In early modern literature, it is the drunken, gluttonous, and lascivious puritan who predominates. While the killjoy Malvolio is today often identified as the archetype of the literary puritan, he is but one type, and in the minority at that.[28] Throughout early modern drama and pamphlet literature, Malvolios and Tribulation Wholesomes are out-numbered by the likes of Zeal-of-the-Land Busy and Hudibras. To lose sight of this mode of representation is to lose sight of an important vehicle through which English men and women envisioned, explored, and confronted the social, theological, and discursive issues raised by radical Protestantism.

The cultural attention to sectarians in the late sixteenth and early seventeenth centuries far outstripped the direct threat they posed; the number of sectarians before the turmoil of the 1640s was small, and many of these came from the relatively powerless lower classes.[29] Of the various sects which came under attack, many were minuscule and invisible to the public eye, and some of the obscure groups listed by pamphleteers were probably nonexistent, the fictional products of active imaginations. Some historians have argued that with negligible political influence and only a tiny membership, the radical sects did not have a significant cultural impact.[30] But the vast quantity of pamphlet literature addressing the issue of sectarianism argues to the contrary. Conceptually, if not physically, religious sectarianism was a considerable cultural force in early modern England. While sectarians themselves may not have always published their ideas, the tenets of religious radicalism were extensively disseminated by the alarmed authors who wrote against them.

In a period of social transformation marked by rapid demographic growth and mutating economic structures, the established church became a touchstone of communal stability and continuity; writing against religious difference served as an important means of affirming traditional ideas of social and political order.

For early modern authors, the interlocking system of family, church, and state served as a powerful ideological paradigm. As Francis Dillingham so succinctly phrased it, "A family . . . is a picture of a Common-wealth," and "families should be Churches" (sig. H3ᵛ); Dillingham's own title, *Christian Oeconomy. Or Houshold Government* (1609), suggests how thoroughly these three concepts were intertwined. Religious radicalism – with its emphasis on the individual conscience and its arguments for voluntary religion – threatened these conceptual social foundations. The phenomenon of religious nonconformity spurred English men and women to contemplate and interrogate the basis of their familial, parochial, and national communities, bringing questions concerning the organization of church and state into the alehouse and home. At stake in discussions of sectarianism and separatism lie far-reaching implications for the relationship of the individual to the community; the grounds for political authority; the autonomy of the individual conscience; the right to participate in public discourse; and the right to determine one's own religious society.

The social and ecclesiastical issues raised by religious separation were frequently linked to issues of speech: coterminous ecclesiastical and social boundaries were largely demarcated through discursive means. Within the established church, the minister in the pulpit proclaimed an authoritative biblical interpretation and voiced the monarch's proclamations. The recitation of the liturgy from the Book of Common Prayer reinforced and reaffirmed the unity of the Commonwealth. King James's authorized Bible provided a sanctioned and regulated version of the Scripture. A system of licensing provided a means of monitoring printed religious beliefs. By contrast, radical religion, with an emphasis on the individual conscience and a disregard for orthodox discursive boundaries, seemed to create an anarchical Babel. The sanctity of the pulpit was undermined by itinerant lecturers and unlettered tub preachers delivering sermons in public squares, marketplaces, and street corners; the formal, rhetorical style of the sermon itself was replaced by modes of ecstatic prophesy. In their rejection of the Book of Common Prayer, religious radicals seemed to replace the bounded, controlled, and uniform text of the state with the uncontrolled outpourings of men (and, even more shockingly, women) from diverse social strata. The dissemination of unlicensed religious texts such as the Familists' illegally imported tracts in the 1570s, the Marprelate tracts of the late 1580s, and the flood of pamphlets in the 1640s were significant indications of the authorities' inability to control not only the printing press but the spread of radical ideas.

Flowing over normative rhetorical boundaries and collapsing traditional textual order, sectarian modes of speech and writing were in themselves viewed as monstrous. The grotesque puritan body thus functioned as a means of representing not only socio-ecclesiastical deformations, but the interrelated issues of discursive deformity as well. Throughout early modern literature, puritan characters' corporeal transgressions (such as overeating, drunkenness, promiscuous sexual behavior, and nakedness) are repeatedly allied with their discursive and rhetorical aberrations (extemporaneous prayer, tub preaching, illicit publishing, and so forth).

The aims of this book are twofold. First, I wish to illuminate a sixteenth- and seventeenth-century literary tradition that has long remained obscured or ignored; through studying various images of the grotesque puritan, I hope to question one of the central paradigms that has long informed the ways in which we have conceptually structured early modern literature. Second, I mean to argue that fictional puritans functioned as a means of representing the social and discursive repercussions of radical religious nonconformity. The book is organized around a series of figures and images which recur throughout sermons, pamphlets, poems and plays from approximately the 1570s to the 1660s. While the trajectory of the book is roughly chronological, beginning with the Marprelate tracts and concluding with Samuel Butler's poem *Hudibras*, it provides a history of representation rather than social history, and in some chapters I have culled examples from a broad temporal field. I have retained the word "puritan" as a wholly representational category signifying a religious nonconformist or schismatic, the term's predominant usage in the literary sources I examine; when discussing actual historical practices or individuals, I have tried throughout to indicate more specific religious identifications (such as presbyterian or Baptist; "conformist" indicates one who supports the established, episcopal Church of England).

The book begins with the advent of the stage puritan in Shakespeare's Falstaff. Recognized by original audiences as a manifestation of the Lollard martyr Sir John Oldcastle, Falstaff grew out of the Marprelate controversy and especially the anti-Marprelate performances which lampooned puritans in grotesque terms. The introduction of Falstaff marks the origin of an early modern mode of representing religious nonconformity, one which gives shape to the rhetoric of anti-sectarian pamphlets. The tradition of the "puritan bellygod" which begins with Falstaff continues with Zeal-of-the-Land Busy, the subject of chapter 2; leading his band of followers into the fair, where he attempts to withhold himself from society even as he gorges on the communal pig, Busy dramatizes the dynamics of religious semi-separatism and the politics of unlicensed preaching. Chapter 3 focuses on accounts of the notorious sect the Family of Love, and the ways in which the sect's alleged sexual promiscuity registered various modes of discursive deviance; the licentious Mistress Purge in the early seventeenth-century play *The Family of Love* embodies the consequences of such sexual and textual abnormality.

Chapters 4 and 5 turn to the prolific pamphleteering of the 1640s. Chapter 4 considers images of swarming as a means of registering the perceived chaos resulting from sectarian claims to liberty of conscience, and examines how Thomas Edwards, one of the most vocal opponents of sectarianism, attempts to restore social order through rhetorical means in his *Gangræna*. The subsequent chapter concentrates on images of monstrous genealogies as a means of illustrating the conflict between the proliferation of radical text and the origins of authority; turning to Milton's antiprelatical tracts, I consider Milton's strategies in transforming the bishops' own anti-sectarian discourse into an attack on episcopacy. Chapter 6 explores how figures of the naked sectarian – both the fictional Adamites (reputed to worship in the nude) and real Quakers (who, in their own words, went "naked as a sign") – manifest the pursuit of the perfect, Edenic language; the textual history of these naked sectarians resonates throughout Milton's creation of Adam and Eve in *Paradise Lost*. The book concludes with an Epilogue on *Hudibras*, a text which at once marks the grotesque puritan's apotheosis and denouement.

CHAPTER I

The puritan in the alehouse: Falstaff and the drama of Martin Marprelate

In the early fifteenth century, a pious, innocent man was put to a most gruesome death – at least, that is the story according to his sixteenth-century chronicler, the Protestant bishop John Bale. A faithful follower of John Wyclif and an avid reader of the Scriptures, this gentleman was a "moste valyaunt warryoure of Iesus Christ" (Figure 3) who courageously battled that Whore of Babylon, the Roman Catholic church:

In all adve[n]terouse actes of wordlye manhode was he ever bolde, stronge, fortunate, doughtye, noble, & Valeau[n]t. But never so worthye a conquerour as in this his present conflyct with the cruell and furyouse frantyck kyngedome of Antichrist. Farre is this Christen knyght more prayse worthye, for that he had so noble a stomake in defence of Christes Verite agaynst those Romyshe supersticyons, than for anye temporall nobylnesse eyther of bloude, byrthe, landes, or of marcyall feates.[1]

Against an onslaught of hostile questions from an archbishop and his henchmen, those "spyghtfull murtherers, ydolaters, and Sodom-ytes," the Christian knight firmly stood his ground, bravely defend-ing the opinions he had gleaned from the Gospel concerning the material substance of the eucharist (merely symbolic), the sacrament of confession (invalid), and the efficacy of pilgrimages (pointless). But alas, the "bloud thurstye rauenours" that were his opponents sentenced him to death, and not a pretty one at that. The faithful prisoner, bound "as though he had bene a most heynouse traytour to the crowne," was carted from the Tower to St. Giles Field and a new pair of gallows. There he fell to his knees, praying "God to forgeve his enemyes." Standing, he "behelde the multytude" and exhorted them "to folowe the lawes of God wrytten in the scripturs," and to be wary of teachers that are "contrarye to Christ in theyr conuersacyn and lyvynge." Finally, the unfortunate was hung in "cheanes of yron and so consumed a lyve in the fyre,

16

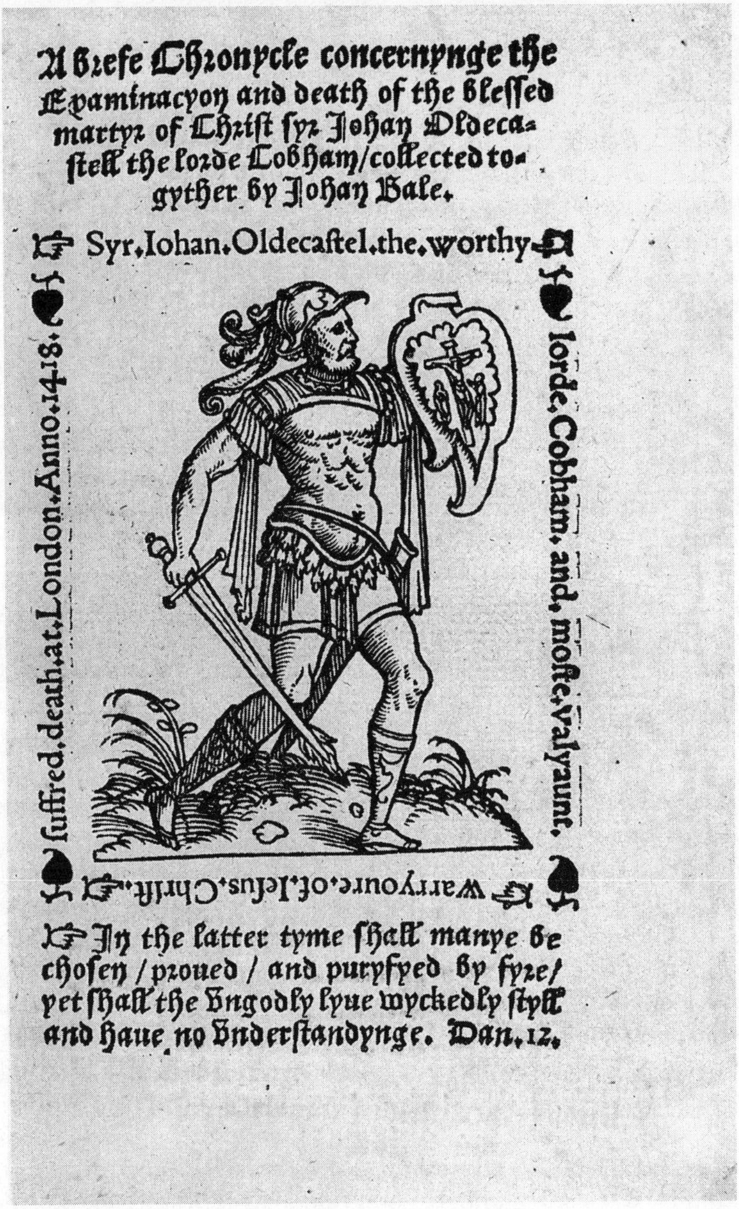
A brefe Chronycle concernynge the
Examinacyon and death of the blessed
martyr of Christ syr Johan Oldecastell the lorde Cobham/collected to-
gyther by Johan Bale.

Syr.Iohan.Oldecastel.the.worthy.
lorde.Cobham.and.moste.valyaunt.
warryoure.of.Iesus.Christ.
suffred.death.at.London.Anno.1418.

In the latter tyme shall manye be
chosen / proued / and puryfyed by fyre/
yet shall the vngodly lyue wyckedly styll
and haue no vnderstandynge. Dan.12.

Figure 3 Title page of John Bale's *Brefe Chronycle concernynge the Examinacyon and death of the blessed martyr of Christ syr Johan Oldecastell the lorde Cobham* (Antwerp, 1544) praysynge the name of God so longe as his lyfe lasted. In the ende he commended his sowle into the handes of God, and so departed hens most Christenlye."[2]

The subject of this account was Sir John Oldcastle, Lord Cobham, reputed leader of a Lollard insurrection in 1414. Bale clearly hopes to establish Oldcastle as an early martyr of the Protestant Reformation, proclaiming that Oldcastle had "a tryum-phau[n]t Victorye ouer his enemyes by the Veryte which he defended," and that he "dyed at the importune sute of the clergye, for callynge vpon a Christen reformacyon in that Romyshe churche of theyrs, & for manfullye standynge by the faythfull testymonyes of Jesu."[3] John Foxe, Bale's friend and former housemate,[4] incorporated this version of events in the 1563 edition of his martyrology *Actes and Monumentes*, with Oldcastle's death graphically illustrated in a woodcut (Figure 4). This hagiographic depiction drew sharp attacks from those who adhered to the fifteenth- and early sixteenth-century image of Oldcastle as a devious heretic and traitor. In response to such criticism, Foxe added a thirty-page "Defense of Lord Cobham" in his 1570 edition, a gesture which at once increased the Lollard's popularity and highlighted his controversial status. Oldcastle became a prominent cultural figure in Elizabethan England, his trial and death subsequently recounted in Stowe's *Annales*, Holinshed's *Chronicles*, and elsewhere, and his antics drama-tized in the anonymous play *The Famous Victories of Henry the Fifth*.[5] For some, Oldcastle was a schismatic rebel who betrayed his friend and king Henry V;[6] for others, he was the valiant martyr we see in Bale's account, a courageous force of proto-Protestant reform.[7]

In his own story of Henry V, Shakespeare again put Oldcastle on the stage – in the form of Sir John Falstaff. Shakespeare's audience readily identified Falstaff as a representation of Oldcastle. In early performances of *1 Henry IV* the character appears to have actually been called "Oldcastle," and even after he was re-dubbed "Falstaff" extensive historical and literary evidence indicates that the public did not quickly forget the character's original and "true" identity.[8] The name "Oldcastle" was retained for private (including court) performances, and many seventeenth-century authors indicate that "Falstaff" was widely understood as an alias for the Lollard leader.[9] ("Falstaff," it should be noted, was itself a name with Lollard connotations.[10]) In *1 Henry IV*, Hal addresses Falstaff as "my old lad of the castle" in their very first exchange (1.2.41), although the oft-

The deſcription of the cruell ᴄMartyrdome of
ſyr Iohn Oldecaſtle Lord Cobham.

Figure 4 The martyrdom of Sir John Oldcastle, as depicted in *The First Volume of the Ecclesiasticall history contaynyng the Actes and Monumentes of thynges passed in euery kynges tyme . . . Newly recognised and inlarged by the Author John Foxe*, 2 vols. (1570), 1:762.

quoted Epilogue from *2 Henry IV* – "Oldcastle died martyr, and this is not the man"[11] – vehemently protests the association of Falstaff and Oldcastle.

This defensive epilogue not only indicates how extensively audiences did equate the two, but also suggests the need for a public apology. While critics have traditionally assumed that the name-change took place in order to placate the outraged Elizabethan Lords Cobham, it is just as likely – if not more so – that the playwright found himself needing to appease disgruntled members of a nationalistic audience who considered Oldcastle an important early hero of the English Reformation.[12] Post-Falstaffian representations of Oldcastle frequently seek to remedy the knight's battered image. *The First Part of the True and Honourable History of the Life of Sir John Oldcastle, the Good Lord Cobham* (1599), as the title suggests, redeems Bale's Oldcastle from Falstaff's fleshy sins; the Prologue again asserts that the Oldcastle–Falstaff transformation was common knowledge: "It is no pampered glutton we present, / Nor aged counsellor to youthful sin, / But one, whose virtue shone above the rest, / A valiant martyr, and a vertuous peer" (ll. 6–9).[13] Written by Michael Drayton, Anthony Munday and others, this play was commissioned by the savvy theatrical entrepreneur Philip Henslowe, who obviously calculated that the popular demand to see Oldcastle restored as a heroic martyr was great enough to be profitable. The urge to recuperate the image of the pious Lollard was also illustrated in John Weever's hagiographic poem *The Mirror of Martyrs, or The life and death of that thrice valiant Capitaine, and the most godly Martyre Sir Iohn Old-castle knight Lord Cobham* (1601). The need for such ardent counter-representations testifies to Falstaff's popularity as well as his infamy.

The early modern desire to restore Falstaff's righteous Lollard origins has found an analogue in recent scholarly desires to recover Falstaff's original identity. Seeking to purify Shakespeare's text from the coercive influences of the censor, prominent editors have rein-stated Falstaff's original name of "Oldcastle."[14] This decision has led to a profusion of critical debate and meditation on topics ranging from editorial protocol to the theatrical dynamics of fictional character.[15] But these discussions have largely left unanswered crucial questions about Shakespeare's depiction of a well-known Lollard: why, contrary to so many of the contemporary representa-tions, did Shakespeare take the figure of this "noble Christen warryour" and mold him into the Rabelaisian, gluttonous coward of the Henriad? Conversely, why did he deviate so far from the alternative tradition of depicting Oldcastle as a bellicose heretic, a serious martial threat to king and state?

Some critics maintain that "Shakespeare simply blundered"[16] – that he more or less picked a name out of a historical hat, a name which happened to have unfortunate political consequences. Others assert, more plausibly, that Shakespeare intended to satirize the Elizabethan Lords Cobham (Sir William Brooke and his reputedly less competent son and successor Henry) related by marriage to the Lollard Oldcastle.[17] Neither of these answers seems satisfying. The notion of the playwright innocently and ignorantly choosing the name of a figure who had become hotly contested as a cultural icon by competing religious/political factions does not seem likely. And while Elizabethan and Jacobean gossips seem to have reveled in the Falstaffian portrayal of the Lord Cobhams' namesake, thus far scholars have established no clear motive for personal parody; rather, there were strong reasons to avoid conflict with William Brooke, then Lord Chamberlain and in control of the theatres.[18]

In this chapter, I aim to demonstrate that the conversion of Oldcastle into Falstaff was neither haphazard nor a local moment of satire; nor was it, as some critics have supposed, a "profoundly original . . . representation" or a "daring and provocative inspira-tion," an innovative departure from the stereotypical image of religious reformers.[19] Rather, I will argue that Falstaff – in all of his sack-swilling glory – both catalyzed and epitomized the early modern representation of the stage puritan. The years immediately preceding the creation of the Henriad witnessed the extended and rambunc-tious pamphlet warfare known as the Marprelate controversy; origi-nating with the illicit anti-episcopal pamphlets of the pseudonymous "Martin Marprelate," this textual phenomenon evoked widespread public mirth and official outrage. Borrowing from Marprelate's own comic and often grotesque style, a bevy of hired authors fired back, attacking Martin in satirical pamphlets and often violent theatrical performances. Dramatizing the historical persona of Oldcastle, a renowned reformist leader, Shakespeare followed the pattern that the anti-Martinists had established for representing religious dissent. In the process, Falstaff assumes the characteristics of Martin Marprelate himself, reproducing Martin's irreverence for established authority and bringing the dynamics of religious controversy into a burgeoning sphere of public print culture.

The Marprelate tracts grew out of frustration over a stagnating process of ecclesiastical reform. In the late 1580s, "popish" vestments and ceremonies were still an integral part of the English church, and in 1583 the conservative John Whitgift had been appointed Archbishop of Canterbury. As the desired reforms became more illusory, individuals such as the popular twenty-four-year-old preacher John Penry began illegally publishing attacks on the bishops and nonpreaching (often nonresident) clergy. The church authorities felt the sting of these attacks and appointed John Bridges, Dean of Salisbury, as their spokesman. But his *Defense of the government established in the Church of Englande for ecclesiasticall matters* (1587), a large quarto volume containing 1400 pages of "lumbering orthodoxy," did little to stop the flow of antiprelatical attacks.[20] Early in 1588 Penry sallied forth with the *Exhortation*, a scathing assault on the bishops, and in April of the same year the young John Udall challenged the episcopacy with *The State of the Church of England laide open*. The printer for many of these pamphlets was Robert Waldegrave, whose printing press was finally seized and destroyed in the spring of 1588.[21]

According to legend, during the chaos surrounding the destruction of his press Waldegrave managed to escape with a box of types hidden under his cloak.[22] Armed with these types and a newly acquired press, Waldegrave was able to help launch the guerrilla pamphlet warfare of Martin Marprelate. In October of 1588, Martin's first clandestine tract *The Epistle* exploded onto the scene, quickly circulating in and around London. Intended as an introduction to *The Epitome* (a critical summary of John Bridges's work), *The Epistle* hailed the "terrible priests" in a riotously irreverent and comic tone, a stark contrast to the stodgy pedantry of Bridges's *Defense*. Martin Marprelate (a pseudonym for one or more undetermined authors, most likely including Penry, Udall, and Job Throkmorton[23]) informs his readers from the first that he must play the fool, since that is the appropriate response to Bridges's text: "Because I could not deal with his booke commendablie, according to order / vnless I should be sometimes tediously dunsticall and absurd."[24] In a subsequent tract, *Hay any worke for Cooper*, he asks, "The Lord being the authour both of mirth and grauitie / is it not lawfull in it selfe / for the trueth to vse eyther of these wayes?" (14). Martin recognizes the public's apathy regarding ecclesiastical controversy, and seeks a means to attract their attention: "perceiuing the humors of men in these times . . . to be giuen to mirth. I tooke that course" (*Hay*, 14).

While the text bursts with laughter ("Ha ha ha," "Tse tse tse," "Wo ho how"), the attack on the bishops is ominously real: "All our L[ord] B[ishops] I saye / are pettie Popes / and pettie vsurping Antichristes" writes Martin in *The Epistle* (8). Marprelate's chief weapons are ridicule and insult. Rather than confute the authority of an episcopal church government through biblical analysis (the standard approach of most reform-minded authors), Martin endeavors to mar the prelates with more personal smears. He laments that "we haue so many swine / dumbe dogs / nonresidents with their iourneimen the hedge priests / so many lewd liuers / as theeues / murtherers / adulterers / drunkards / cormorants / raschals / so many ignorant & atheistical dolts / so many couetous popish B[ishops] in our ministery: & so many and so monstrous corruptions in our Church" (*Epistle*, 33). To illustrate his claims, Martin relates the personal foibles of bishops and ministers with unmitigated zest and extensive poetic license; he promises, "In this booke I wil note all their memorable pranckes" (*Epistle*, 41).

Geoffrey Jones, a pastor from Warwickshire and a regular at the local alehouse, became an exemplary victim of Martin's witty, sarcastic narration. Once, while frequenting the alehouse, Jones flew into a rage (Martin speculates that Jones had either been asked to settle his account or had lost money gambling) and "sware he would neuer goe againe into it." "Although this rash vow of the good priest" was much to the dismay of the alewife, Martin informs us that "the tap had great quietnes and ease therby / which coulde not be quiet so much as an houre in the day / as long as Sir Iefferie resorted vnto the house" (*Epistle*, 42). Jones soon repents his vow of abstinence, but is hesitant to break his oath; "And so he hired a man to carie him vpon his backe to the alehouse / by this meanes he did not goe / but was caried thither / wherevnto he made a vow neuer to go" (*Epistle*, 42). Not only do Martin's cynical comments on this compromise mock Sir Geoffrey, but this episode serves as an allegory for the bishops' manipulation of scriptural loopholes.

Martin inflicts the greatest harm on the clergy by simply not taking them seriously; for him, nothing in the episcopacy is sacrosanct. He openly scoffs at Archbishop Whitgift (whom he hails with such names as "John Cant," "Dumb John," and "Don John"), and claims that Dean Bridges has been playing "the fool . . . in the pulpit" (*Epistle*, 43). He mocks the bishops' mitre with parodic titles such as "my horned Masters of the Confocation house" (*Epistle*, 5), and provides them with helpful, moralistic "true" stories:

Olde doctor Turner . . . had a dog full of good quallities. D. Turner, hauing inuited a B[ishop] to his table / in dinner while called his dog / and told him that the B. did sweat. (You must think he labored hard ouer his trencher.) The dogg flies at the B. & took of his corner capp (he thought belike it had bene a cheese cake) and so away goes the dog with it to his master. Truely, my masters of the cleargie / I woulde neuer weare corner cap againe / seeing dogs runne away with them. (*Epistle*, 43)

With this one tale, Martin inflicts more damage to the bishops' image than tomes of biblical exegesis could ever have accomplished. Now the bishops not only had egg on their faces, but cheesecake on their heads; who could take them seriously? Here, as elsewhere, Martin proves himself a master of timing. With this ridiculous image of dog, priest, and cheesecake before us, Martin immediately asks the bishops a pointed and sobering question: "May it please you . . . to tell me the cause / when you have leysure / why so many opinions & errors are risen in our Church / concerning the ministerie?" (*Epistle*, 43–44). The question becomes rhetorical. The bishops, represented as buffoons, are disempowered and cannot respond.

Martin's charm comes from what Christopher Hill termed a "witty, rumbustious, savage and extremely effective colloquial style."[25] Martin writes in a vivid, informal first person; he is part reporter, part neighbor, part preacher, part gossip. *The Epistle* contains abundant anecdotal accounts of the bishops' travesties, from not paying their bills to stealing cloth to bowling on Sundays. He claims to be gathering rumors and the sentiments of parishioners, printing such "reports" in their own words. Martin even plays the comedian and does impersonations; here he mimics the Bishop of Gloucester preaching on St. John, coming to "the very pithe of his whol sermon": "Iohn / Iohn / the grace of God / the grace of God / the grace of God: gracious Iohn / not graceles Iohn / but gracious Iohn. Iohn / holy Iohn / holy Iohn / not Iohn ful of holes / but holy Iohn" (*Epistle*, 47).

For twelve months, Martin harassed the bishops in his hit-and-run style. The infuriated authorities organized large-scale hunts for the underground Marprelate press, but always arrived just after it had moved on. *The Epistle* was followed by five equally lively tracts, and the persona of Martin was joined by his sons, Martin Jr. and Martin Sr., who engaged in fraternal bickering after the younger brother took the liberty of publishing one of their father's manuscripts which he had "found" lying under some bushes, dirty, crumpled, and only partially legible.[26] The Marprelate tracts were enormously popular. "England falles a Martining and a marring," complains one pamphleteer;[27] Martin, on the other hand, chuckles, "I haue bene entertayned at the Court: Euerye man talkes of my worship. Manye would gladly receiue my bookes / if they coulde tell where to finde them" (*Epitome*, sig. A2^r). Martin's tactic of using humor to foster widespread ecclesiastical debate had paid off; the tracts, according to Hill, soon became "the biggest scandal of Elizabeth I's reign."[28] Hill observes that "Martin's rude, personalizing style appealed because it was subversive of degree, hierarchy and indeed the great chain of being itself. The shocking thing about his tracts was that their rollicking popular idiom, in addition to making intellectuals laugh, deliberately brought the Puritan cause into the market place."[29]

Not everyone, of course, found this an endearing quality: the bishops were confounded and the queen was not amused. Following the publication of *The Epitome*, Richard Bancroft preached against Martin Marprelate at Paul's Cross, and Thomas Cooper, Bishop of Winchester, wrote *An Admonition to the People of England* (1589) defending the episcopate and providing scriptural authority for the bishops' large incomes.[30] Such counterattacks merely became fuel for Martin's fire, and he entitled his next pamphlet *Hay any worke for Cooper* (an echo of the common London street cry, "Ha' ye any work for the cooper?") in the Bishop of Winchester's honor.[31] When paternalistic "admonitions" failed to quench Martin-mania, the tracts were categorically outlawed. Legal measures proved equally futile, however, and even the Earl of Essex allegedly pulled a Marprelate tract from his cloak, waved it before his queen, and demanded "What will become of me?"[32] Martin reveled in the mischief he was causing; Martin Senior tauntingly mimics the Archbishop of Canterbury, having him lament to his servants, "No warning will serue them; they growe worse and worse . . . I thinke I shall grow starke madde with you, vnlesse you bring him [in]."[33]

After futile attempts to take the Martinists by force, sermon, or dense theological prose, the bishops finally hired mercenaries who could challenge Martin on his own ground: John Lyly, Robert Green, Anthony Munday, and the young Thomas Nashe (Penry's former associate at Cambridge). These new arrivals studied Martin's style, learned to imitate it, and for the next six months pamphlets were furiously hurled back and forth. Colorful insults flew, and each side lampooned the other with zeal and relish. New personae entered the scene (Mar-Martine, Pasquill, Marphoreus, Cutbert Curryknave, and Plaine Percevall the Peace-maker) as the pamphlet warfare took on a plot of its own. Characters made personal challenges to other characters and formed alliances. At one point rumors even filled London that Martin was dead; *Martins months minde, that is, A Certaine report, and true description of the Death, and*

Funeralls, of olde Martin Marre-prelate (1589) reports, "some say hee was taken by the Sp[aniard]s and burnt in the Groyne" (sig. E2ᵛ). The "Groin" was the English name of a battle site in Essex's military expedition to Cadiz, but the possibility of military heroism is quickly deflated by bawdy humor; Lyly writes, "But soft *Martins*, did your father die at the *Groyne*? It was well groapt at, for I knew him sicke of a paine in the groyne."[34] (Martin's "sons" capitalized on these rumors. In *The iust censure and reproofe of Martin Iunior*, Martin Junior laments, "I weene not, if my father should be hurt, either at the Groine, or at the suburbes of Lisbone" [sig. A2ʳ], while the Arch-bishop of Canterbury is quoted as saying, "He died at the Groine, as they saie? Naie, heele be hanged ere heele die there. He is in some corner of England, lurking and doing mischiefe" [sig. A4ᵛ]. Martin later reappeared in another pamphlet to assure his readership that he was alive and well.) Martin was soon portrayed on the stage and became the target of broadsides; Mar-prelate was attacked by Mar-Martine who in turn came under fire from Marre Mar-Martin. *Antimartinus* (1589) took up the cause in Latin. The controversy became so prominent that even Gabriel and Richard Harvey and Francis Bacon joined in the pamphlet battle.[35]

   The anti-Martinists amplified the grotesque undertones of the Martinist tracts. Martin Marprelate, according to Neil Rhodes, originated the grotesque comic prose of the 1590s.[36] Throughout Martin's writing, the prelates, those "Carnal and sensles beastes," "monstrous and vngodly wretches," revel with their "bo[o]sing mates" in a world of social madness and hierarchical inversion. Martin blasts, "horrible and blasphemous beastes / whither will your madnes growe in a while / if you be not restrained?"[37] In the anti-Martinist tracts, elements of the carnival grotesque become explicit and predominant, as Martin's own rhetorical strategies are turned against him with full force. Lyly specifically invokes Martin's strategy: "for whatsoeuer shall seeme lauish in this Pamphlet, let it be thought borrowed of *Martins* language" (*Pappe*, sig. A4ʳ). Anti-Martinist authors portray Martin as "the Ape, the dronke, and the madde":[38] he copulates, vomits, drinks, gorges himself and gives birth. In *An Almond for a Parrat* (1589) Nashe overtly asserts he will attack the puritan "Hipocrites" by "imitating... that merry man Rablays."[39]

   In the anti-Martinist pamphlets, Martin becomes the Bakhtinian grotesque body *par excellence*, the archetype of Bakhtin's description: Martin's form "discloses its essence as a principle of growth which exceeds its own limits only in copulation, pregnancy, childbirth, the throes of death, eating, drinking, or defecation. This is the ever unfinished, ever creating body, the link in the chain of genetic development, or more correctly speaking, two links shown at the point where they enter into each other."[40] Nashe and Lyly depict Martin and his "neast" as a swarm of monstrous, intertwined beings; death, birth, sex, and bodily functions coexist. Martin's birth, as described by Nashe, becomes a defecatory process of Gargantuan proportions: "thinke that nature tooke a scouring purgation, when she voided all her imperfections in the birth of one *Martin*."[41] Elsewhere, Martin epitomizes the grotesque merging of birth and death. In *A Countercuffe given to Martin Junior* (1589), the self-proclaimed cavalier Pasquill responds to the rumors of Martin's death, "If the Monster be deade, I meruaile not, for hee was but an error of Nature, not long liued: hatched in the heat of the sinnes of *England* . . . The maine buffets that are giuen him in euery corner of this Realme, are euident tokens, that beeing thorow soust in so many showres, hee had no other refuge but to runne into a hole, and die as he liued, belching" (I: 59). This simultaneity of dying and hatching recurs in Lyly's description of Martin in *Pappe with an hatchet*:

I sawe through his paper coffen, that it was but a cosening cor[p]se, . . . drawing his mouth awrie, that could neuer speake right; goggling with his eyes that watred with strong wine; licking his lips, and gaping, as though he should loose his childes nose, if he had not his longing to swallowe Churches; and swelling in the paunch, as though he had been in labour of a little babie, no bigger than rebellion; but truth was at the Bishoppes trauaile: so that *Martin* was deliuered by sedition, which pulls the monster with yron from the beastes bowells. When I perceiued that he masked in his rayling robes, I was so bolde as to pull off his shrowding sheete, that all the worlde might see the old foole daunce naked.[42]

A man in a coffin, feigning death yet childlike, giving birth through his bowels, masquing in a shrouding sheet: this, to many, was a sixteenth-century image of the puritan.

Such caricatures were soon translated onto the stage. While the texts for these theatrical entertainments have not survived (if they ever existed[43]), both Martin and his foes repeatedly and pervasively allude to the popular anti-Martinist lampoons which played in private and public theatres.[44] In *The iust censure and reproofe of Martin Iunior*, Martin Senior writes that "the Canturburie Caiphas, with the rest of his Antichristian beasts, who beare his abominable marke,

were content in a maner to turne his purposes from a serious matter,
to a point of jesting, wherewith they would haue onely rimers and
stage-players . . . to deale" (sig. A2ʳ). In *Theses Martinæ*, Martin Junior
writes of "the stage-players, poore seelie hunger-starued wretches"
who "for one poore pennie . . . will be glad on open stage to play the
ignominious fooles, for an houre or two together. And therefore,
poore rogues, they are not so much to be blamed; if being stage-
players, that is, plaine rogues . . . they in the action of dealing
against Maister Martin, haue gotten them many thousande eie
witnesses, of their wittelesse and pittifull conceites" (sig. D2ᵛ). These
"conceites" – by Martin's own account extremely popular – appear
to have been, in the words of Charles Nicholl, "coarse, sensational
performances, full of violent antics."[45] An especially brutal staging
by the boys of Saint Paul's probably caused the company to be shut
down in 1589.[46] Pasquill writes in *A Countercuffe* of "the Anatomie
latelie taken of [Martin], the blood and the humors that were taken
from him, by launcing and worming him at *London* vpon the
common Stage."[47] In another performance described in *The Returne
of . . . Pasquill*, a battered and scratched character named Divinity is
brought forth "holding of her hart as if she were sicke, because
Martin would haue forced her" (1:92). Unsuccessful in his rape
attempts, Martin then "poysoned her with a vomit which he
ministred vnto her." In addition to accounts of actual performances,
the anti-Martinist pamphlets also invited audiences to imagine
Martin as the subject of dramatic representations.[48]

The city magistrates and church authorities who commissioned
the vicious anti-Martinist attacks had sought to disarm Marprelate's
subversive, carnivalesque appeal; like a public execution, the
pamphlets and performances were intended (borrowing a phrase
from Michel Foucault) to "reactivate power."[49] The attempt failed.
Made a "*Maygame* vpon the *Stage*," Martin is "*drie beaten*, & therby his
bones broken, then whipt that made him winse"[50] – but within this
"*Maygame* vpon the Stage" Martin also appears cross-dressed as
Maid Marian, with a cloth covering his beard.[51] Thus even as he is
made an object of ridicule, Martin plays a central role in a
traditional festive ritual. The "many thousande" who flocked to the
anti-Martinist performances begin to resemble not so much a jeering
mob seeking retribution for Marprelate's affront to ecclesiastical
authority as a crowd of carnival celebrants enjoying the antics of a
lord of misrule.

By placing Martin Marprelate on the stage, however vicious the representation, the anti-Martinist authors merely replicated the role that Martin had created for himself within his own writings. The Marprelate tracts, as Ritchie D. Kendall has discussed, are inherently theatrical, full of dialogue, scene changes, and asides to the audience. Kendall writes, "The theatrical world Martin Marprelate creates in his satires is vibrantly alive with a kaleidoscopic assembly of colorful characters, shifting settings, and varied incidents . . . Keeping this maddening host of plays and players in check is the master of ceremonies, Martin Marprelate himself. Never in the course of his work does the satirist's persona surrender his claim to the center stage."[52] Thus, as Raymond A. Anselment observes, Bancroft's decision to license anti-Marprelate plays "unwittingly played into Marprelate's hand by making the basic fiction of the satires a reality."[53] The anti-Martinist authors are frequently self-conscious about Marprelate's carnivalesque, theatrical role. The author of *Mar-Martine* accuses Marprelate of copping jokes from the famous Elizabethan clownish actor, Richard Tarleton: "These tinkers termes, and barbers iestes first *Tarleton* on the stage, / Then *Martin* in his bookes of lies, hath put in euery page."[54] Similarly, the anti-Martinist persona Marphoreus has Martin "confess" that his "fond phrases" were learned "in Alehouses, and at the Theater" (*Martins months minde*, sigs. F1^v–F2^r).

Having mastered his trade in the theatre and the alehouse, Martin cannot himself be easily subdued through carnivalesque attacks; rather, even within anti-Martinist pamphlets offering scathing satire, he continues to act as a carnival center. In *Martins months minde*, a text which clearly aims to sound Marprelate's death knell, the author ridicules the reception of Martin's pamphlets, scornfully depicting a riotous tavern scene with a Marprelate tract serving as the evening's attraction:

[Martin], together with his ribauldry, had some wit (though knauish) and woulde make some foolish women, and pot companions to laugh, when sitting on their Alebenches, they would tipple, and reade it, seruing them in steede of a blinde Minstrell, when they could get none, to fiddle them foorth a fitte of mirth.[55]

This lively vignette provides a glimpse into early modern reading practices, as we see an illegal pamphlet being read aloud to a ribald crowd, Martin's anti-episcopal tirades serving as a viable substitute for musical entertainment. As an attempt to dissuade an audience from reading Marprelate's tract, however, the scene proves a poor disincentive. The seduction of this scenario, with the warm camaraderie of the "pot companions" and the hilarity of the "fitte of mirth," overwhelms its satiric purpose.

Through his initial carnivalesque pamphlets, Martin Marprelate had seized a rhetorical terrain that could not be wrested from him, since descriptions of his tactics inevitably reproduced them. Even the anti-Martinist authors are not immune to Martin's charm. Lambasting Martin's opinions and scoffing at his prose style, authors such as Nashe and Lyly nonetheless display a sense of affinity with him, and they begin to blur the distinction between the satirizer and the satirized.[56] "Even as he attacks Martin," writes Evelyn Tribble, "Lyly inadvertently implies a sort of fellowship with him; momentarily they become two ruffians drinking together."[57]

The authorities who had orchestrated the anti-Martinist attack looked with horror on the turmoil they had created. Rather than quelling public desire for Marprelate's writings, the anti-Martinists had spurred the popularity of the offending Marprelate tracts and had produced an appetite for all things Martin; rather than eliminating him from the cultural landscape, they had made Martin ubiquitous. The anti-Martinist theatrics themselves were "to the greate offence of the better sorte," as John Harte, Lord Mayor of London wrote to Lord Burghley.[58] The Privy Council soon sent a letter to the Archbishop of Canterbury, the Lord Mayor of London, and the Master of the Revels requesting strict censorship of the theatre, and in 1589 the theatres were closed due to the nature of the anti-Martinist performances. The Council wrote to the archbishop that "there hathe growne some inconvenience by common playes and enterludes in & about the cyttie of London, in [that] the players take upon [them] to handle in their plaies certen matters of Divinytie and State, unfitt to be suffered."[59] By initially sanctioning the assault on Martin Marprelate, the authorities had in fact only furthered Martin's very aim of making the intertwined issues of "Divinytie and State" a point of discussion in an emerging public sphere.

Marprelate did not succeed in his attempts to overthrow the bishops (although, significantly, his legacy was resurrected in the 1640s when episcopacy was abolished[60]). But Martin did demonstrate, in a highly public and dramatic way, the limits of authoritative discursive control. Religious nonconformity had long revolved around contested textual and verbal forms. The Lollards, for example, with their emphasis on literacy, the vernacular Bible, and secret study groups, had challenged the ecclesiastical authorities' privileged relationship to sacred text. While the early Lollards had circulated copied texts and translations of the Bible, the introduction of the printing press enabled the wider dissemination of dissenting literature; the later Lollards were increasingly associated with the underground dissemination of books and the posting of illegal broadsides.[61] From the beginning of the sixteenth century, authorities feared the subversive implications of print; in 1531 the Bishop of London forbade the reading of thirty books, among them several Lollard texts – including *A boke of thorpe or of John Oldecastelle.* Throughout the 1530s and 1540s a stream of illicit religious texts, many of them Lollard, justified the church's fears of underground printing.[62] For the rest of the century, religious dissent was associated with an uncontrollable flow of small illegal texts, easy to transport, easy to conceal, easy to destroy. The widely circulated Marprelate tracts flagrantly transformed the authorities' nightmare into a reality.

The Marprelate tracts not only represented the threat of hidden textual infiltration, but also exploded the very boundaries of orthodox discursivity. Martin's rejection of traditional ecclesiastical hierarchy, as Tribble notes, finds a parallel in the printed form of the texts themselves, which play extensively with the authorial relationship between center text and marginalia.[63] The profoundly subversive nature of these tracts was duly observed by the authorities, even by Queen Elizabeth herself. Tribble writes: "In her proclamation [against "Schismatical Bookes"] Elizabeth characterizes the pamphlets as attacking the bishops and the church as a whole 'in rayling sort and beyond the boundes of good humanitie.' 'Beyond the boundes': these words sum up the nature of the Marprelate threat. The pamphlets enact a grotesque breaking of the boundaries of the text and of conventional ecclesiastical discourse."[64] For Martin's opponents, then, not only his body, but his body of text was perceived as grotesque.

Though intended to suppress religious dissent, the anti-Martinist attacks ultimately revealed the fragility of orthodox discursive control. The bishops and city magistrates eventually did suppress the Martin phenomenon, suspending their own hired pens, seizing the Marprelate press, torturing the printers, and executing suspected Marprelate author John Penry.[65] (Significantly, the authorities also turned their wrath on separatist leaders Henry Barrow and John Greenwood, indicating the degree to which Marprelate contributed to fears about religious sectarianism.) Martin Marprelate's legacy, however, continued to thrive long after the silencing of the tracts and sensational stage manifestations. Martin surfaces again in popular texts such as Nashe's *Pierce Penilesse* (1592),[66] and his traces can be seen in passing literary references. Indeed, this irreverent fictional spokesman for the reformist cause remained a vivid cultural figure for the next fifty years. Most importantly, the Marprelate controversy spawned a new mode of representing religious zeal. In both textual and theatrical representations, religious nonconformity was now portrayed primarily through the images and language of the grotesque.

Six or seven years after the Marprelate tracts were silenced, Shakespeare's Oldcastle took the stage. Oldcastle was already a familiar theatrical character from *The Famous Victories of Henry the Fifth*, a play which was popular enough to merit repeated performances and printings for over three decades (1585–1617).[67] Oldcastle was also well-known to Elizabethan audiences through the texts of Bale, Foxe, and historiographers such as Raphael Holinshed *et al.* These various and varied accounts of Oldcastle contain numerous biographical details. Bale, for instance, describes Oldcastle as an intellectual who wrote religious tracts calling for a "reformacion." Holinshed tells how Oldcastle spent several years in hiding, constantly evading his pursuers; borrowing a tale from Walsingham's *Historia Anglicana*, Holinshed relates how Oldcastle was once tracked down by the authorities and only narrowly escaped, leaving in his wake a stash of subversive books. Walsingham records how Oldcastle promised that he would be resurrected a few days after his death, a promise which, as Annabel Patterson suggests, was perhaps "even at the time only a metaphor for the vitality of his own legend, for the iterability of the great tales from the distant past of resistance and nonconformity."[68]

As an intellectual reformist writer associated with illegal tracts who was pursued by the authorities and constantly on the run until he was finally tracked down and killed, Oldcastle begins to resemble Martin Marprelate. Martin, too, promised a resurrection of sorts: "For the day that you hange Martin / assure your selues / there will 20. Martins spring in my place" (*Hay*, 20). Even Marprelate's enemies were quick to commend this resilience; when the Martinist tracts resumed after a short silence, one pamphleteer proclaimed, "Welcome Mayster *Martin* from the dead, and much good ioy may you haue of your stage-like resurrection."[69] The legend of Oldcastle and the story of Marprelate thus share striking structural similarities. Patterson observes Holinshed's fascination with Oldcastle's fox-like "capacity to slip through the government's fingers," and comments that "the most obvious reincarnation of Oldcastle's elusive spirit at the end of the Elizabethan era is neither Shakespeare's 'old lad of the castle' nor the defensively disengaged Oldcastle of the rival play, but the irrepressible Martin [Marprelate], whose persona survived the destruction of his secret presses in the country, to reappear half a century later."[70]

Shakespeare's Falstaff, however, is a literary creation that does "reincarnate" elements of both Oldcastle and Martin Marprelate. (Falstaff also clearly has genetic links to a host of other literary traditions and characters, such as the *miles gloriosus* and the Vice figure of earlier morality plays.) While Shakespeare does not rely upon the agile, elusive Oldcastle of Holinshed's account, he does draw upon one of Oldcastle's personality traits as it is described even in Bale's hagiographical narrative; there, Oldcastle admits "that in [his] frayle youthe [he] offended the (lorde) most greuouslye in pryde, wrathe, and glottonye, in couetousnesse and in lechere."[71] In addition to Oldcastle's propensity for gluttony, Falstaff incorporates Martin Marprelate's role as a lord of misrule, who "together with his ribauldry, had some wit (though knavish) and woulde make some foolish women, and pot companions to laugh, when sitting on their Alebenches." Shakespeare's portrayal of a famous Lollard thus interweaves elements of Oldcastle's history with Marprelate's characteristics, merging together these two notorious reformist leaders.

Not only does Falstaff assume Martin's general personality traits, but within the texts of *1 and 2 Henry IV* we detect more specific resonances of the Marprelate controversy. The Marprelate phenomenon was so politically explosive, and the suppression of both Martinist and anti-Martinist authors so extreme, that direct and sustained invocations of Martin would have certainly invited the censor's wrath. Yet a few possible allusions to the anti-Martinist tracts glimmer in the background of Shakespeare's plays. Act 2, scene 4 of *2 Henry IV*, for example, contains a number of lines which seem to resonate of the controversy. The Prince's observation "Look whe'er the withered elder hath not his poll clawed like a parrot" (256–57) is suggestive of the anti-Martinist *An Almond for a Parrat* ("elder" being a term frequently used for describing a hierarchical position within separatist congregations); similarly, Doll's exclamation to Falstaff, "Alas, poor ape . . . let me wipe thy face" (213–14), echoes the title of one popular anti-Martinist pamphlet, *A Whip for An Ape*, a text which appears to have inspired earlier stage representations of Martin Marprelate.[72] Pistol's earlier question, "Fear we broadsides?" (178) is also intriguing in this context. Taken on their own, such references may not appear rich in significance. The rapid succession of these lines in one scene, however, suggests a running gag. Most interesting is Quickly's question to Falstaff, "Are you not hurt i' th' groin?" (207), after he has drawn his sword on the warring Bardolph and Pistol. The line does not seem justified by the skirmish that precedes it, and Doll (who has just spoken to Falstaff to commend his valor) makes no mention of the possibility that he could be wounded; Quickly's comment receives no response from the other characters. It is possible that this gratuitous line invokes the anti-Martinists' claim that Martin Marprelate had been killed at the Groine, and is added only as a winking intertextual reference for the amusement of the audience.[73] In addition to such possible glimpses of Martin within the text of the play, the original performances of *1 Henry IV* may also have invoked the Marprelate controversy through the casting of Will Kemp as Falstaff – the same actor likely to have portrayed Martin in the anti-Martinist theatrics.[74]

These connections between Falstaff and the Marprelate controversy are admittedly speculative; but a more thorough and sustained comparison can be made through Falstaff's consistent speech patterns. Modern editions of the Henriad (such as the Arden, the "New" Arden, the Riverside, the Folger, the New Variorum, the New Shakespeare, and the New Cambridge Shakespeare) all acknowledge Falstaff's theatrical origins in the character of Sir John Oldcastle from the *Famous Victories of Henry the Fifth*, and critics have often commented on Falstaff's "puritanical" characteristics and habits of speech. J. Dover Wilson noted that "traces of Lollardry may still be detected in Falstaff's frequent resort to Scriptural phraseology and his affectation of an uneasy conscience," and that the passages on repentance, "together with the habit of citing

Scripture, may have their origin . . . in the puritan, psalm-singing temper of Falstaff's prototype."[75] Alfred Ainger, one of the earliest twentieth-century critics to discuss the Falstaff–Oldcastle connection, similarly observed, "What put it into Shakespeare's head to put this distinctly religious, not to say Scriptural phraseology into the mouth of Falstaff, but that the rough draft of the creation, as it came into his hands, was the decayed Puritan? For the Lollard of the fourteenth century was in this respect the Puritan of the sixteenth, that the one certain mark of his calling was this use of the language of Scripture, and that conventicle style which had been developed out of it."[76]

Falstaff does indeed quote extensively from Scripture; of the fifty-four biblical references identified in *1 Henry IV,* twenty-six are his.[77] He quotes indirectly from Genesis, Exodus, 1 and 2 Samuel, Psalms, Proverbs, Matthew, Mark, Luke, 1 and 2 Corinthians, and 1 Thessalonians. The parables of Dives and Lazarus and the Prodigal Son in particular, as Ainger notes, "seem to haunt him along his whole course" (*Lectures and Essays,* 142). In addition to biblical allusions, Falstaff's speech is also rich in sixteenth-century godly jargon. He speaks of his "vocation" (*1HIV* 1.2.101–02) and repeatedly mentions the "spirit," a cornerstone of radical theology of the "light within" (as opposed to the conformist emphasis on ecclesiastical authority). In both Parts 1 and 2, Falstaff makes references to psalm singing, a key element of the sixteenth-century puritan stereotype.[78] He wishes he "were a weaver" so that he "could sing psalms" (*1HIV* 2.4.130) (weavers, who often sang at their work, were particularly notorious for their reformist psalmody), and later claims, "For my voice, I have lost it with hallooing, and singing of anthems" (*2HIV* 1.2.188–89). (Ainger points to the puritan in *The Winter's Tale* who "sang Psalms to hornpipes.") Critics have also commented on Falstaff's repeated allusions to salvation by faith alone, and his death-bed reference to the Whore of Babylon, "the customary Puritan term for the Church of Rome."[79]

Modern literary scholars are not the only ones to note these reformist speech patterns; Falstaff's companions also appear to identify him as a man of religion. Hal, who prides himself on his chameleon-like ability to speak to various social groups in their own languages, repeatedly uses biblical idiom when speaking to Falstaff/ Oldcastle. In their very first scene together, Falstaff and the Prince engage in an exchange rife with religious language.

FALSTAFF: But Hal, I prithee trouble me no more with vanity. I would to God thou and I knew where a commodity of good names were to be bought: an old lord of the Council rated me the other day in the street about you, sir, but I marked him not, and yet he talked very wisely, but I regarded him not, and yet he talked wisely, and in the street too.

PRINCE: Thou didst well, for wisdom cries out in the streets and no man regards it.

FALSTAFF: O, thou hast damnable iteration, and art indeed able to corrupt a saint: thou hast done much harm upon me, Hal, God forgive thee for it: before I knew thee, Hal, I knew nothing, and now am I, if a man should speak truly, little better than one of the wicked. I must give over this life, and I will give it over: by the Lord, and I do not I am a villain, I'll be damned for never a king's son in Christendom.

PRINCE: Where shall we take a purse tomorrow, Jack?

FALSTAFF: 'Zounds, where thou wilt, lad, I'll make one; an I do not, call me villain and baffle me.

PRINCE: I see a good amendment of life in thee, from praying to purse-taking.

FALSTAFF: Why, Hal, 'tis my vocation, Hal, 'tis no sin for a man to labour in his vocation.

(1.2.79–102)

Falstaff's repetitive speech patterns typify those of the reformist stereotype, and his concern with the distinction of the "saints" and the "wicked" reflects the language of the late sixteenth-century separatists. Hal's responses, which paraphrase the books of Proverbs, Matthew, and Acts of the Apostles, mimic and engage with Falstaff's own biblical style. Later, however, Hal becomes exasperated with Falstaff's religious jargon, and refuses to play along: "Is she of the wicked? Is thine hostess here of the wicked? Or is thy boy of the wicked? Or honest Bardolph, whose zeal burns in his nose, of the wicked?" (*2HIV* 2.4.324–27). ("Zeal," of course, being another godly byword.) This rhetoric is neither incidental nor a moment of local humor, but a consistent characteristic of this fallen Lollard.

Falstaff's religious associations, then, are pervasive and unmistakable. Most critics noting his tendency to speak in biblical idiom and godly jargon have assumed that Falstaff is actively mocking the zealous reformers. They comment that Falstaff himself is a self-conscious satirist making "jibes at the Puritans," that his part "involves Puritan posturing," and that "his 'religiousness' is a joke at this stage of his life."[80] Several editors have shared this opinion. Samuel Hemingway, who edited *1 Henry IV* for the New Variorum Shakespeare, maintains that "in mimicry of the Puritans Falstaff here uses one of their canting expressions" (a reference to his use of "the wicked"), and that "Falstaff here repeats in ridicule another Puritan shibboleth" (a reference to his use of "vocation"), to cite two examples.[81] A. R. Humphreys, editor of the New Arden edition of the Henriad, also observes that Falstaff uses "frequent Puritan idiom," or more precisely, that he "mimics Puritan idiom."[82] Humphreys asserts that in his godly speech patterns Falstaff devises "Puritan parody" and "parodies . . . mealy-mouthed Puritanism."[83] Critics frequently agree that Falstaff speaks in a "parody of liturgical language," that he "is given to parodying Puritan preachers," and that his lengthy speeches often smack of the "scriptural style of the sanctimonious Puritan."[84]

It is difficult, however, to reconcile Falstaff's religious identity with such explanations of deliberate parody. How can an audience perceive Falstaff both as a representation of Oldcastle, and as a character who mocks reformist religion? This seeming incongruity has puzzled scholars, who have long relied upon a notion of the puritan as a fun-hating, dust-breathing fogy.[85] This figure is clearly in opposition to the bacchanalian character of Falstaff. Taken as polar opposites, any "puritan" speech in the mouth of Falstaff must thus be considered insincere, ironic or parodic. But this oppositional relationship is built upon a false premise; the apparent incompatibility of these two roles emanates from anachronistic assumptions about the early modern image of the "puritan." As we have seen, in the wake of the Marprelate controversy the predominant image of the stage puritan was that of a grotesque, carnivalesque figure. While the dour (and most often hypocritical) moralist was one species of puritan representation, the carnal and grotesque figure was far more prevalent. Falstaff, more so than Malvolio, epitomizes the predominant late Elizabethan expectations for a stage puritan.[86]

Falstaff does not, therefore, parody the self-styled saints in a determined, willful way. Rather, Falstaff – in and of himself – is a parodic representation of a "puritan." (Indeed, his very name, "False staff," could be read as a spin on such godly names as More Fruit, Faint Not, Perseverance, Deliverance, etc.[87]) In Shakespeare's portrayal, Falstaff/Oldcastle becomes an object of playful ridicule – much like Martin Marprelate in the anti-Martinist theatrical performances (although Falstaff's treatment is certainly more benign). The discrepancy between Falstaff's gluttonous lifestyle and the more abstemious conduct expected of a reformist leader becomes a basis for satire that runs throughout both parts of *Henry IV*.[88] Similarly, the distinction between the belligerent religious leader of historical accounts and the coward of the Henriad is just as obvious a source of satire. Falstaff is emptied of Oldcastle's dangerous qualities, and is even written out of the Scroop–Grey–Cambridge plot, in which Oldcastle was implicated in accounts such as Holinshed's.[89] Instead, Falstaff is made the object of practical jokes and the consistent butt of humor.

But just as Martin Marprelate maintained his role as comic center even as he was being lampooned and ridiculed, so too Falstaff, as a parodic representation of a reformer, becomes the lord of misrule. Martin's manner of heckling the bishops and kicking away their pedestals (reducing Cooper to a cooper), enables him to taunt them as equals. Martin explodes sanctioned hierarchies and pieties; it is this leveling tendency that makes him so threatening, and so appealing. Falstaff, too, respects neither hierarchy nor social order, and in his irreverent jests he assumes a voice – and a role – similar to that of Marprelate.

Falstaff's speech itself reverberates with Martin's own grotesque, carnivalesque tone. The banter between Falstaff and Hal often resounds of Marprelate's fictional dialogues with the bishops, or the taunting exchanges between Marprelate and his textual opponents such as Cutbert Curryknave or Pasquill.[90] Falstaff hails the Prince as his "dog" (*2HIV* 1.2.145), "the most comparative rascalliest sweet young prince" (*1HIV* 1.2.78–79), and "a good shallow young fellow" who "would have made a good pantler, a would ha' chipped bread well" (*2HIV* 2.4.234–35). He also hurls such tangy insults as "you starveling, you eel-skin, you dried neat's-tongue, you bull's pizzle, you stock-fish" (*1HIV* 2.4.240–41) and tells Hal to "hang thyself in thine own heir-apparent garters" (*1HIV* 2.2.42). Twice Falstaff even threatens treason: "By the Lord, I'll be a traitor then, when thou art king" (*1HIV* 1.2.141); "A king's son! If I do not beat thee out of thy kingdom with a dagger of lath, and drive all thy subjects afore thee like a flock of wild geese, I'll never wear hair on my face more" (*1HIV* 2.4.133–36). In addition to mocking the Prince, Falstaff lacks all respect for the Lord Chief Justice and undermines the very code of chivalry ("honour is a mere scutcheon") that was to become so central to the way nostalgic Elizabethans viewed Henry V; in Part 2 he boisterously sings, " 'When Arthur first in court' – Empty the jordan. – 'And was a worthy king' – How now, Mistress Doll?" (*2HIV* 2.4.33–35), intermingling allusions to the legendary paragon of chivalry with references to chamber pots and prostitutes. In Falstaff, as in Martin Marprelate, social and discursive order are undermined and overturned.

Falstaff thus plays the role of satirist even as he is the object of satire. Bakhtin draws a useful distinction between modern satire and the satire of carnival: "The [modern] satirist whose laughter is negative places himself above the object of his mockery, he is opposed to it . . . The people's ambivalent laughter, on the other hand, expresses the point of view of the whole world; he who is laughing also belongs to it."[91] From this ambivalent position, Falstaff reproduces a fundamental dynamic of the staging of Martinism. These burlesque performances provided Shakespeare not only with a performative model for representing puritans in terms of the grotesque, but also with a vivid example of the staging of satire and the use of the carnivalesque. Falstaff, like Martin, inhabits a pivotal position from which he is able to toy with the boundaries of orthodoxy and subversion. The duality as satirist and object of satire that lies at the heart of the Marprelate controversy is largely a function of the social and discursive boundaries Martin and his adversaries begin to erase. In his irreverent attacks on the bishops, Martin challenged ecclesiastical hierarchy and the traditional borders between laity, clergy, and episcopacy. The anti-Martinists, too, inevitably played with, rather than policed, the boundaries they were assigned to defend. The tantalizing appeal of the Marprelate controversy is located along this quivering border between the authoritative and the subversive, the orthodox and the heretical.

This same play at and with social boundaries infuses the Henriad with much of its dramatic energy. These plays, *1 Henry IV* in particular, are largely driven by Hal's flirtation precisely with this border between authority and subversion. Like the anti-Martinist authors (or, like the bishops and magistrates who hired the anti-Martinist authors), Hal enters into the terms of carnival subversion, represented and embodied by Falstaff, while still maintaining his position of authority. The danger, however, is that the tension between these two positions might prove stronger than Hal's ability to control and define his own situation, that the boundary distinguishing the role of the Prince from that of the reveler could snap

before Hal can orchestrate his glorious return to orthodoxy and
filial duty – his "reformation," as he puts it (*1HIV*, 1.2.208). In Act 3,
scene 2 of *1 Henry IV*, King Henry explicitly warns his son of the
dangers of slipping over this line, lamenting that Hal "hast lost
[his] princely privilege / With vile participation" (ll. 86–87). Henry
advocates a strict division between community and king. Describing
Richard II's fall and his own rise to power, Henry prides himself on
not becoming "stale and cheap to vulgar company"; instead, he
kept his "person fresh and new . . . like a robe pontifical" (3.2.41,
55–56). By contrast Richard II, "the skipping King" (l. 60) in
Henry's version of events,

> Grew a companion to the common streets,
> Enfeoff'd himself to popularity,
> That, being daily swallow'd by men's eyes,
> They surfeited with honey, and began
> To loathe the taste of sweetnesse . . .
>   . . .
> So, when he had occasion to be seen,
> He was but as the cuckoo is in June,
> Heard, not regarded; seen, but with such eyes
> As, sick and blunted with community,
> Afford no extraordinary gaze,
>   . . .
> Being with his presence glutted, gorg'd, and full.   (3.2.68–84)

By "mingl[ing] his royalty with cap'ring fools" (as Henry says of
Richard [l. 63]), Hal risks losing himself in the bowels of the common
people, risks being absorbed and swallowed so that the distinction
between the crowd and the Prince is no longer recognizable.

The Henriad thus reenacts issues of discursive and political
control presented by the Marprelate controversy. This breakdown of
hierarchical division described by King Henry is what Oldcastle
threatened in leading a mob against the king, and what Marprelate
proposed in seeking to pull down "robe[s] pontifical." Within the
Henriad, Falstaff assumes a voice and role similar to that of Martin
Marprelate, becoming a swelling carnival force that threatens to
consume Hal's "princely privilege." The ever "glutted, gorg'd, and
full" Falstaff virtually embodies the removal of social, hierarchical
boundaries: Falstaff becomes the community which can, through
jest, ingest its leaders. His rotund, expansive figure, emblematic of
carnivalesque festivity, potentially signifies absorption and loss of

social distinction. Like Martin, Falstaff thus challenges the very hierarchies that constitute the structure of church and state. And like the anti-Martinists, Hal confronts Falstaff's festive social force by engaging in its own terms, for a time reveling in the playful contest of insults. But ultimately the Prince, like the London magistrates before him, discovers that the boundary between authority and subversion is too fragile to be long toyed with in this way, and that hierarchies cannot be restored while the discursive play continues: Falstaff has to be banished just as Martin's press has to be crushed and the anti-Martinists have to be suspended.

In the anti-Martinist productions, the audience is obviously intended to be ridiculing and laughing at the abused Martin; but, as in the anti-Martinist tracts themselves, the legacy of Martin's popular appeal overwhelms the pressures of satire, and the audience finds itself in the position of laughing with the target of the attack. Similarly, the translation of the martial Oldcastle into the comic Falstaff seems to require mocking laughter, but even as a butt of satire Falstaff exudes such inviting carnival energy that the audience engages with him: he is, in his own words, "not only witty in [himself], but the cause that wit is in other men" (*2HIV* 1.2.8–9). For a short time, the audience becomes Falstaff's "pot companions," and they too are "fiddled forth" into mirth – subversive laughter often at the king's expense. It is this wit that draws the spectators into "vile participation" with a historical figure who led an army against the king. From the position of the satirized, both Falstaff and Martin Marprelate entice the audience to join their carnival revelries. The spectators simultaneously laugh at and with subversive forces, are simultaneously disapproving and participating: this is the play of the play.

The character of Falstaff helped to give shape and form not only to the image of the puritan, but to the very concept of "puritanism" as a category of religious dissent. In his essay "The Theatre Constructs Puritanism," Patrick Collinson remarks that "it is a remarkable fact that the word 'Puritan' hardly ever appears in the thousands of pages written against those we call Puritans in the 1590s";[92] yet around the turn of the century the term achieved currency, and the "puritan" emerged as a cultural and theatrical category. Speculating on the possibilities of "art anticipating life," Collinson contends that "it may have been the stage-Puritan who invented, or re-invented, the Puritan, and not the other way around" (164). Collinson claims the Marprelate controversy as the moment "when, where and why the stage-Puritan made his entry" (167) and then turns his attention to Ben Jonson's *Bartholomew Fair* for the further dissemination of this image. *1 and 2 Henry IV*, however, mark an earlier and crucial stage in this figure's development. Falstaff, Shakespeare's notorious and widely recognized rendition of a Lollard, established a model for the grotesque, carnivalesque puritan which would predominate for decades to come.

Even as art anticipated life, art retrospectively changed history. For many contemporaries, Falstaff quickly became fact. John Speed was alarmed at how quickly the theatre could re-form history; in 1611, Speed attacked the Jesuit Robert Parsons's *Treatise of three Conversions of England* (1603), contending that the "author of the three conuersions hath made *Ouldcastle* a Ruffian, a Robber, and a Rebell, and his authority taken from the *Stage-plaiers*."[93] Shakespeare's gluttonous fictional character quickly became inscribed in the popular imagination and in historical accounts. With his extended appearance in Foxe's *Actes and Monumentes*, Oldcastle clearly gained cultural stature; with his appearance in Shakespeare's Henriad, Oldcastle clearly gained weight. In Stowe, Bale, Foxe, Polydore Vergil, *The Famous Victories of Henry V,* and his numerous other pre-Henriad appearances, Oldcastle is never described as corpulent (despite his confession of youthful gluttony). Yet by 1604 the Lollard appears to have become as synonymous with obesity as, say, Falstaff; in *The Meeting of Gallants* a character inquires, "Now *Signiors* how like you mine Host? did I not tell you he was a madde round knave, and a merrie one too: and if you chaunce to talke of fatte Sir *John Old-castle*, he wil tell you, he was his great Grandfather, and not much unlike him in Paunch."[94]

The tendency to view earlier historical accounts of Oldcastle through the lens of Falstaff has informed literary criticism as well. Ainger, in his early examintion of Falstaff's Lollard origins, performs acrobatics of logic to justify Shakespeare's representation of Old-castle. In this influential essay, Ainger proclaims that "there seems to have been always a tradition (likely enough a true tradition) that [Oldcastle] was *very fat*" (original italics) – a statement which is oddly supported by a footnote acknowledging "I am not aware of any reference to Oldcastle's fatness earlier than 1597, the date of Shakespeare's play."[95] Lacking such evidence, Ainger concocts his own, describing how a wandering friar could have used Oldcastle's confession of youthful gluttony to demonstrate the failings of Lollardy; here, Ainger's imagined commentary of the friar by a "villager's fireside":

'Why, my friends, you have but to look at him to see the effects of his wicked life. *What does that great fat paunch mean?* What *can it mean* but one thing – a career of gluttony and drinking of old sack and canary' . . . We can imagine Oldcastle's old enemies using this kind of language . . . and we can understand how, as the story was told over and over again . . . it would depart more and more from historic truth, and get the ludicrous incidents, real or fictitious, more and more accentuated . . . Just so the fat knight Oldcastle would be sure to be made as ridiculous as possible for popular presentation; and at the time when Foxe printed his famous work there is good reason to know that there was current a popular conception of Oldcastle as a bloated old sensualist . . . Let me quote two or three passages from writers of the seventeenth century in proof of this. (original italics)[96]

Ainger's description again concludes with anachronistic proof: the "good reason to know" that Foxe was confronting a popular image of a "bloated" Oldcastle is provided by decidedly post-Falstaffian references. In all, Ainger devotes four pages to this question, "*What does that great fat paunch mean?*"

Asking the same question of Martin Marprelate, we might find an answer from Lyly, who writes of Martin's "swelling in the paunch, as though he had been in labour of a little babie, no bigger than rebellion" (*Pappe*, sig. E1^r). Martin Marprelate, by his own admission, is a source of endless reproduction; as his enemies claim, he "will spawne out [his] broyling brattes, in euery towne to dwell."[97] Martin's pamphlets, and his followers, seem to proliferate wildly. Falstaff, too, assumes a pregnant form, as Valerie Traub has argued.[98] Falstaff's "womb" (*2HIV* 4.3.22), like Marprelate's belly, becomes at once a site of voracious consumption and endless reproduction.[99] By inflating Oldcastle into Falstaff, Shakespeare created a character who embodies the seduction and the subversion of radical religion. At the center of the tavern world, Falstaff, for a time, is a figure of popular religion. While Falstaff (like Shakespeare) does not directly engage in the issues of ecclesiastical governance raised by Oldcastle and Marprelate, Falstaff's consistent reformist idiom reminds us of the consequence of religious discourse in the alehouse. The Marprelate tracts realized the possibilities of print culture in religious debates, and testified to the role of polemical literature in the simultaneous development and exploitation of an emerging public sphere. Having entered the tavern, the Marprelate tracts create communal laughter among those "sitting on their Alebenches." Martin's foes derided this popular appeal. In *A Friendly Admonition to Martine Marprelate, and his Mates* (1590), Leonard Wright comments, "Alasse, *Martine*, I pittie thy want of discretion, who in publishing thy unprofitable and immodest conceites, breaking the unitie of the Church, hindering the course of the Gospell, & disquieting the peaceable state of the realme: hast set thy selfe uppon an open stage, in the view of the whole world, to bee scorned, hated, and detested for euer" (sig. A2^r).

But even those who detest him are not immune from the effect of Martin's "publishing." In a later passage, Wright again expresses his disdain for Martin's method of alehouse dissemination. The marginal note, however, is telling: "whereby (though against theyr wils) the people are broght by experience to know and feele, that pub like reading (in some measure) is preaching" (sig. A4^r). Wright admits what many are intuiting, that public reading usurps the privilege of the pulpit, serving as an alternative forum for spreading religious and political opinions. Even when it is mere "pub like reading" (in the wonderful anachronism created by this orthographic rendering of "public"), the discussion of religious reform in the tavern created the beginnings of what Jürgen Habermas has deemed the "public sphere."[100] This sphere would more fully emerge in the mid-seventeenth century, when, in the words of one contemporary, "Religion is now become the common discourse and Table-talke in every Taverne and Ale-house."[101] Over the course of the Henriad, Falstaff withers and dies as a force of carnival communality. As a rotund vision of religious discourse taken into the alehouse, however, Falstaff was quickly resurrected, and his sons multiplied. Through Falstaff, "certen matters of Divinytie and State" were taken out of the pulpit and played upon the stage, becoming matters of "common discourse."

CHAPTER 2

Eating disorder: feasting, fasting, and the puritan bellygod at "Bartholomew Fair"

My little beagle,
. . .
For news here we have none but that we fear ye shall think us all turned Puritans for such a feasting night as was made upon Friday last in this town, wherein I assure you it chanced well that the Act of Parliament against drunkenness is not yet passed, otherwise the Justices of Peace had much work ado here at that time.

> King James to Robert Cecil, 23? January, 1606[1]

For many walk, of whom I have told you often, and now tell you even weeping, that they are the enemies of the cross of Christ: Whose end is destruction, whose God is their belly, and whose glory is their shame, who mind earthly things.

> Philippians 3: 18–19

Strolling across the early modern stage and through the archives of early modern pamphlet literature is The Bellygod. Rotund and gluttonous, this figure frequently appears, however fleetingly, in polemical religious literature, as authors of diverse persuasions hurl the insult of "bellygod" at their opponents. In the mouths of reformers, the slur implies the greed and gourmandizing excess of the Catholic clergy or corrupt English bishops. John Bale uses the word to describe the Lollard Oldcastle's inquisitors, as he proves "what beastlye blockeheades these bloudye bellyegoddes were"; Martin Marprelate asks a vicar, "And art not thou a monstrous atheist / a belly God / a carnall wicked wretch / and what not."[2] George Buddle writes, "as *Cato* in *Plutarch* complaineth of the Bellie-gods of Rome in his time; the same might truely haue been spoken of the *Epicurisme* of the *Mannichæans*, and may be truely verified at this day of the Romish Clergie, making their bellie their god, and their glory their shame."[3] The "many-benefice-gaping mouth" of Milton's "canary-sucking, and swan-eating" Prelate is just another manifestation of the bishops' tendency to "set themselvs up two Gods instead, *Mammon* and their Belly."[4]

"Bellygod" was also used to scorn the reformers themselves. Thomas Nashe identifies "puritans" as "Hipocrites and belli-gods, that deuoure as much good meat in one of [their] brotherly loue meetings, as would wel-nye victuall the Queenes ships a whole moneth."[5] When aimed at those who purported to be seeking not only a pure church but a purified lifestyle, the word takes on particular resonance, as the corpulent figure belies claims of physical restraint and discipline. Throughout anti-puritan literature, excessive physical appetite overwhelms religious and spiritual concerns: in Thomas Overbury's character sketches assembled in *A Wife* (1616), a "Precisian" is one who "conceiues his prayer in the kitchin, rather then in the Church."[6] The figure of the bellygod can provide visible testimony of the moral reformers' hypocrisy, or can exemplify the alleged consequences of antinomianism and unbridled carnal desires.[7] As an early modern literary character, the puritan bellygod also serves to illustrate the impulses of religious separatism, or more specifically, the ambivalent social dynamics of semi-separatism. It is this function I will be discussing here.

At the end of the sixteenth and the beginning of the seventeenth centuries, England witnessed the flourishing of a separatist tradition.[8] Dismayed at the lack of thorough ecclesiastical reform, and increasingly driven by a desire for segregation between the godly and the ungodly, individuals began to join self-selected, self-withdrawn "covenanted communities." These congregations huddled in London, exiled themselves to Amsterdam, and eventually even sailed to America. In the 1590s, separatist ideas found spokesmen in Robert Browne, Henry Barrow, and John Greenwood, whose printed pamphlets drew furious rebuttals. Diehard separatists could be readily identified; boarding a ship and setting off in search of the new Canaan, for example, provided a strong hint to one's neighbors. Semi-separatists, on the other hand, were more difficult to label. Murray Tolmie has discussed the emergence of a culture of Jacobean English men and women who, although conformists, enjoyed going to hear lectures outside of their parish, gathered for saintly conversation at the homes of friends, and conducted domestic religious instruction by reviewing sermons or reading the Bible with their children and servants – devout practices which some perceived as verging on separatism.[9]

This ambiguity as to what constituted religious sectarianism made it a particularly resonant topic in early modern literature. The extreme separatists who actually left the geographical boundaries of England's shores did not greatly destabilize traditional categories of nation and church; from the perspective of those in England, these emigrating separatists largely removed themselves from immediate configurations of social identity. Semi-separatists, however, profoundly (if often subtly) challenged normative social categories and undermined the integrity of the family/church/state paradigm. Although gathering in their own selective religious communities, they continued to interact with the greater community, and often even considered themselves full members of the established church. As Tolmie notes, many who are labeled "semi-separatist" by their contemporaries or later historians would have refuted the claim, perceiving themselves as godly supporters of the national religion.[10] Such is the case with Malcontent, a character in Henoch Clapham's *Errovr on the Right Hand* (1608); a dissenting presbyterian, Malcontent nonetheless conforms to the national church, and he condemns separatism even as he refuses to participate in communion. This duality perplexes his acquaintance Flyer, who pointedly demands of him, "Are you a member of the Church of England, yea or no?" Malcontent replies, "A member I am, but no *Ordinarie* member" (4). In his consternation and outrage at this ambivalent response, Flyer articulates sentiments which were shared by his more conservative countrymen, fictional and otherwise: "O monstrous hypocrisie . . . Was it euer heard of in the Bible, that a man should be a member and not a member of a Church . . . If this be not a Babel, a Confusion of men and manners, what then can bee?" (5). Semi-separatists thus inhabited a dual identity – at once integrated into greater society while practicing religious self-segregation. This ambivalent identity was repeatedly described in terms of "paradox."[11]

As the outlines of the church body grew increasingly indeterminate and paradoxical, the figure of the bellygod stepped in to give visible shape to this confusion. The puritan bellygod, I will argue, is a literary image that embodies the social contradictions of semi-separatism, the various paradoxes of communal participation and withdrawal. These issues of socio-religious separatism are inextricable from issues of discursive variance; semi-separatism was marked largely by participation in discursive practices which took place beyond the formal borders of the central church (such as hearing non-ordained itinerant lecturers, engaging in domestic post-sermon analysis, etc.). These interrelated and even coterminous issues of religious and discursive separatism are captured in the bellygod's expansive, dilating corporeal form. This figure (which, as I discussed in chapter 1, was first put on stage in the form of Shakespeare's Falstaff) makes another theatrical entrance as Zeal-of-the-Land Busy in Ben Jonson's *Bartholomew Fair*. In this chapter, I will examine the figure of the puritan bellygod as it appears in popular seventeenth-century pamphlet literature. I will then consider how Busy – in his contradictory desires to remain separate from the impure community of the fair while indulging in its gastronomic pleasures – dramatizes the social paradox and the discursive implications of religious semi-separatism.

Christianity, like many other religions, depends upon food rituals to enact and reinforce communal boundaries: the sharing of the eucharist celebrates the community's cohesion, while periods of fasting can invoke a meditative spiritual solidarity. In the sixteenth and seventeenth centuries, however, competing notions of Christian community positioned these rituals as points of strife and contention. Contested ideas of the eucharist transformed the physical architecture of church buildings into the site of an ideological wrestling match; altar rails came down and went up and came down again, and the altar itself was replaced by a communion table, the geographical positioning of which became the subject of rancorous debate among parishioners. Such debates over interior décor implicitly addressed the relationship of ecclesiastical authority to lay congregations, just as arguments over the ceremony of communion touched on the very nature of congregational community. The orthodox viewed communion as an affirmation of universal membership in a national church, while separatists and semi-separatists saw the need for discrimination – the sacrament was perceived as defiled and its symbolism undermined by the promiscuous mingling of the godly and the wicked. Clapham's Malcontent, for example, announces, "as for the sacrament of Communion, I neuer meddle with it; because *Righteousness* can haue no fellowship with unrighteousness" (4–5).

Like communion, the fast also became the source of ideological discord. In the sixteenth century, the Roman Catholic significance of the fast (sharing in the suffering of Christ, a form of *imitatio Christi*) was replaced by a Protestant emphasis on humiliation, the contemplation of one's own spiritual powerlessness.[12] Within the Protestant ranks, however, diversified notions of the fast began to emerge. Richard Hooker, the premier spokesman for the established church, stressed the collective fasting days of the Christian calendar and minimized the importance of private fasts. The issue of fasting was not of central concern for orthodox writers; for the godly, however, the fast assumed great personal and social significance. The historian Tom Webster discusses the function of the fast in defining group identity: "Fasts represented one way in which voluntary religion aided the mutual recognition of the godly, one way in which communities could be formed and maintained among people divided by distance" (*Godly Clergy*, 68). The private, solitary fast also intensified a sense of distinguishing oneself from mainstream society, since "the isolation and discipline taken on voluntarily when others were about their worldly affairs must [have] been a particularly sharp process of identification and separation from the ungodly" (69). For contemporaries, the godly fast was thus perceived to be (and in many ways was) a ritual of social withdrawal and spiritual separation.

Seventeenth-century commentators depict nonconformist fasting practices as anti-social and anti-authoritarian. In *The Picture of a Puritane* (1605), Oliver Ormerod creates a dialogue in which an Englishman and a German discuss the religious sectarianism of their respective countries:

THE ENGLISHMAN: Shew me . . . how the *Anabaptists* did spend their time at their priuate conuenticles?

THE GERMAINE: They spent it not in a Gluttony and drunkennes; but in fasting, in praying, and in humbling of themselues: And by these their Hypocriticall fastes, they seduced many of the vulgar sorte.

THE ENGLISHMAN: . . . Though the keeping [of fasts] without the knowledge & authorizement of the Magistrate, bee a [di]minishing of his authoritie, by preuenting his decree, and controuling (as it were) his gouernment; though it be a preiudice against him, . . . though it argueth an affectation of singularitie, . . . yet it hath beene an ordinary thing with our Sectaries, to keepe such extraordinary fasts, wherunto the authorizement of the Prince was not had.   (9)

This exchange clearly indicates the social isolation and political subversion associated with religious separatism. The Anabaptists and the English sectaries retreat from the public world into their "private conventicles," enclaves which reject the larger communal governing systems. This self-segregation is made all the more threatening in that it is not signaled by belligerent anti-authoritarian acts; rather, the sectaries ensure their "singularitie," even while surrounded by a host of authoritative structures ("authorizement," "controul," "gouernment," "Magistrates" and "Princes"), through passivity and inaction. The practice of *not* eating, virtually impossible to police, reclaims a sense of personal somatic autonomy that directly undermines the power of the body politic.

But while Ormerod initially attacks the sectaries' tendency to fast without the authorities' permission, he soon reveals an even more aggressive form of gastronomic protest through the violation of state-decreed periods of fasting. Some of the very hottest sort of Protestants abhorred what they saw as the perpetuation of Catholic traditions and rituals. ("I hate *Traditions*," exclaims the separatist Ananias in *The Alchemist*; "They are *Popish*, all!" [3.2.106–07]) Among these remnants of perceived papist evils was the prohibition against eating meat on Fridays or during Lent, a regulation which was endorsed (in part to provide economic support for the fish trade) by English secular and religious authorities from the reign of Elizabeth to that of Charles I.[13] In addition to their aversion to all things popish, the zealous sometimes protested the principle of obligatory fasting, contending that neither the civil government nor the central church had a right to determine periods of fast, but that such times must be chosen by individuals or by congregations.[14] Fasting at self-determined moments and rejecting national fasts, such religious dissenters soon gained a reputation for their own idiosyncratic dietary habits.

As Ormerod's dialogue continues, the Englishman relates:

I heard of a nation of men . . . *[who] when their King had intended a feast for the honour of his country, they on the contrary side proclaimed a Fast,* . . . And I know a societie of men, who in the time of Lent, were wont to eate Flesh-meate seauen daies in the weeke, though out of Lent but fiue daies. I thinke they did it for no other end, but onely to crosse the authoritie of that power which inioyneth vs to abstaine from Flesh-meate at that season of the yeare . . . To conclude, they will euer be in an extreame: for when we Feast, they will Fast, & when wee Fast, they will Feast. (20–21)

The sectarian desire to "crosse the authoritie of that power" through obstinate, counter-cultural eating practices is an image that pervades seventeenth-century literature. In *The Schismatick Stigmatized* (1641), Richard Carter echoes Ormerod's accusation: "When we fast they will feast. And againe, when we feast they will fast. They will nibble on a red Herring on Christmasse day but feast liberally on good-Friday . . . carping at every thing but pleased with nothing but with Schisme, Faction, and Rebellion" (3).[15] Religious nonconformity is portrayed as an impulse to fall out of step with the unifying liturgical calendar of contemplation and celebration. "For since our Religion is justly opposite to theirs; why should we agree with them in any thing?" proclaims one fictional sectarian. "If they fast on Good-Friday, what day is fitter for our feasting? If Christmas day be their Festivall, why is it not fittest for our working-day? . . . Their Lent should be our Carnevall."[16]

Schismatics, as the Englishman notes, must "euer be in an extreame": this extremity is manifest in the swelling borders of the puritan body itself. John Taylor describes a puritan gathering:

but I haue often noted, that if any superfluous feasting or gurmondizing, panch-cramming assembly doe meete, the disordered businesse is so ordered, that it must bee either in *Lent*, vpon a Friday, or a fasting day: for the meat doth not relish well, except it be sawc'd with disobedience and contempt of Authority. And though they eate Sprats on the Sunday, they care not, so they may be full gorg'd with flesh on the Friday night.

> Then all the zealous Puritans will feast,
> In detestation of the Romish beast.[17]

By feasting during times of state-imposed dietary restrictions, the puritan community locates itself beyond social boundaries or outside of social order. The puritans become "superfluous." The "panch-cramming," "full gorg'd" puritan body, extending beyond normative corporeal bounds, reflects this political transgression. As a subversive social force, the puritans even corrupt the domestic sphere; Taylor imagines the consequences of a puritan entering the home of Jacke a Lent:

He hath a wife named *Fasting*, as leane as himselfe, yet sure I thinke she is as honest as barren: but it were very dangerous for an Epicure or a Puritan to haue a bastard by her, for there were no other hope, but that the father of the brat (if it should proue male) would tutor it in all disobedience against both *Lent* and *Fasting*: for although *Lent* and Abstinence be but forty dayes endurance, yet to these valiant men of their teeth it seemes forty yeeres, for they put the Letter (*e*) into the word *Fast*, and turne it into *Feast*. (*Workes*, 114)

The ascetic household is exploded from within by the puritan; not only would such a character encourage filial disobedience for Mr.

and Mrs. Lent, but Fasting herself is transformed from a lean, barren figure of repressive control into an inflated figure of illegitimate pregnancy. As a force of transgressive excess, the puritans even expand discursive boundaries. The additional "e" which overflows the bounds of "fast," transforming it into "feast," parallels the expansion of the puritan body; the word and the body dilate, transformed from signifiers of purity and restraint to signifiers of uncontrolled, Epicurean appetites.

The Pictvre of a Puritane is in fact framed by the equation of puritans and epicures. The text begins with a prefatory letter addressed "To all Fauourites of the Puritan-faction," in which Ormerod relates a strange Persian tradition. The Persians, as he tells it, "kept in their Houses, the picture of an Epicure, sleeping with meate in his mouth, and most horribly ouerladen with wine, that by the viewe of such an vgly sight, they might learne to eschew the meanes of the like excesse." Ormerod states that he has created his own *Pictvre* in imitation of this didactic method. The implicit parallel between the picture of an epicure and the picture of a puritan immediately establishes a potent and graphic context for Ormerod's text. Meat hanging where a tongue should be, a body filled with wine to the point of being "ouerladen," the epicure – like the factious puritan – is a figure of compromised and grotesque somatic boundaries. Where we might have expected Tribulation Wholesome, we are greeted by a puritan Sir Epicure Mammon.

The puritan thus becomes a bellygod. Jonson's pairing of the insatiable Sir Epicure and the separatist Wholesome in *The Alchemist* presents one possible configuration of the traditional battle between Carnival and Lent, in which the fat, greasy form contends with the lean, self-denying figure of his adversary.[18] More commonly, however, it is the puritan characters who seem to play the role of Carnival. Falstaff's Sir John Paunch, for instance, takes on Hal's John of Gaunt. Less sustained representations appear elsewhere on the stage, as is the case with Master Ful-Bellie, the puritan minister in *The Puritan, or, The Widdow of Watling-street* (1607), whose name says it all. In Middleton's *Inner Temple Masque, or Masque of Heroes* (1619), the nonconformist Plumporridge steps forth to proclaim his loathing of the Lenten fast:

> With any Fasting Day, persuade me not;
> Nor anything belongs to Ember week;

> And if I take against a thing, I'm stomachful;
> I was born an Anabaptist, a fell foe
> To fish and Fridays; pig's my absolute sweetheart,
> And shall I wrong my love, and cleave to saltfish,
> Commit adultery with an egg and butter?[19]

John Taylor draws extensively on purported anti-Lenten puritan sentiments throughout his prolific pamphlets. Of Jacke a Lent, Taylor writes that "a Dogge, a Butcher, and a Puritan, are the greatest enemies hee hath" (*Workes*, 118). For "The Great Eater of Kent," Taylor claims "Of all things, hee holds fasting to be a most superstitious branch of Popery, . . . he hates Lent worse then a Butcher or a Puritan" (*Workes*, 147). Sectarians "in generall are Arch-enemies to Lent, Saints Eves, Ember weeks, Fast dayes, and Good Fridayes."[20]

But while fat puritans, in their gluttonous overindulgence and opposition to Lent, are structurally positioned in the role of Carnival, this casting is not that simple. Although the puritan bellygod assumes the external appearance of a Bacchanalian god of mirth, his (or, in rare instances, her) physical excess does not signify carnival communality so much as it signifies social isolation.[21] Indicative of counter-cultural fasting and feasting, the puritan bellygod becomes a paradoxical signifier. Just as the word "feast" continues to contain "fast" (to reverse Taylor's word play), so too the puritan bellygod, assuming a grotesque, Epicurean outward form, continues to contain impulses of self-withdrawal.

The puritan bellygod thus incorporates the battle of Carnival and Lent, simultaneously serving as an emblem of both. (The name of one sectarian character from *The Family of Love* – "Dryfat" – epitomizes this ambivalent identity.) Indeed, the very word "bellygod" in many ways constitutes a paradox. The *Oxford English Dictionary* supplies only two definitions for "bellygod," both current in the sixteenth and seventeenth centuries: (1) One who makes a god of his belly; a glutton. (2) A god presiding over the appetites (e.g., Bacchus). While the excess involved in making a god of one's belly and the excess exemplified by the Bacchanalian bellygod may seem, outwardly, to be part of the same phenomenon, in fact these two bellygods are not entirely compatible, and can even be at odds. The first definition ("making a god of the belly") implies an extreme egocentrism and a turning inward; the second ("a god presiding over the appetites"), as the symbol of the feast, seems to demand abandoning the self in order to become fully integrated into the community. It is not merely the individual, but the society at large which (at least temporarily) abolishes normative social boundaries and codes of conduct in order to become more fully integrated and united. The first usage thus invokes anti-social isolation, while the second suggests a highly communal intermingling. The bellygod thus holds an ambivalent status, signifying at once festive unity and anti-social withdrawal.[22]

Ben Jonson, himself a notorious, self-styled bellygod, was fascinated by the interplay of religious and social identities.[23] Jonson repeatedly explored the nuances of religious difference, and considered how individuals of diverse ecclesiastical perspectives interact within a common social milieu. *The Alchemist* (1610), for example, presents a veritable smorgasbord of various religious characters. The setting of the play is Blackfriars, an area specifically identified as "puritane" (1.1.128);[24] from the beginning, the swindlers of the play are intensely self-conscious about their incompatibility with their "sober, sciruy, precise neighbours, / (That scarse haue smil'd twise sin' the king came in)" (1.1.164–65). Within this context of implicit religious conflict, characters repeatedly allude to more extreme forms of radical sectarianism. The names of John of Leyden, polygamous leader of the Muenster Anabaptists, and Hendrik Niclaes, the Dutch leader of the Family of Love, are both invoked as insults (3.3.24; 5.5.117). The alchemical tricksters even use the language of religious separatism in their own squabbles; Subtle's momentary mutiny is described in terms of "faction" (1.1.156), and Dol threatens, "I shall grow factious too . . . and quit you" (140–41). Schism is avoided when Subtle promises, "I'll conforme my selfe" (153). With the entrance of Tribulation Wholesome and Ananias, we encounter actual religious separatists. Although Subtle initially refers to Ananias as his "Anabaptist" (2.4.20), his subsequent description is more accurate: "This fellow is sent, from one negotiates with me . . . for the *holy Brethren* / Of *Amsterdam*, the *exil'd Saints*: that hope / To raise their *discipline*, by it" (2.4.28–31). Tribulation, a "very zealous *Pastor*" (2.5.51), and his deacon Ananias are not sectaries so much as members of an English separatist congregation, self-exiled in Amsterdam and adhering to a presbyterian ecclesiastical structure; they identify themselves as "seruant[s] of the *exil'd Brethren*" (2.5.46) and "we of the *Separation*" (3.1.2). Ananias's desire for self-segregation of the saints is so strong that he seeks to avoid any intercourse with the wicked, arguing that "the *sanctified cause* / Should have a sanctified *course"* (3.1.13–14). Tribulation assures Ananias of the necessity for economic commerce with the ungodly, since "The children of perdition are, oft-times, / Made instruments euen of the greatest workes" (3.1.15–16).

Bartholomew Fair (1614) presents something of an inverse image of *The Alchemist*. Rather than portraying a group of rascals in the midst of the reformed, this play presents a small band of self-styled saints voyaging into the heart of commercial and social exchange at the fair. *Bartholomew Fair* also provides a far more complex and sustained interrogation of the relationship between the godly and the ungodly, examining the friction and intersection of the two. The interplay of these cultures is explored most fully through the character Zeal-of-the-Land Busy, an elder and a "prophet" in a loosely defined religious sect. Literary critics frequently label Busy a "hypocrite," one whose pious pontifications jar with his indulgence in carnal pleasures. As a puritan bellygod, however, Busy does not simply represent a character whose restrained outside belies his carnal inside; rather, he embodies competing desires, containing both simultaneously. Busy's attempts to segregate and to integrate himself at the fair, his endeavors to fast and to feast, position him as the social nexus of the play. Theories of carnival dynamics tend to focus on the processes of reversal and inversion, assuming a polarized social structure. In their modification of traditional Bakhtinian models, Peter Stallybrass and Allon White argue that "Hybridiza-tion, a second and more complex form of the grotesque than the simply excluded 'outside' or 'low' to a given grid, produces new combinations and strange instabilities in a given semiotic system. It therefore generates the possibility of shifting *the very terms of the system itself*, by erasing and interrogating the relationships which constitute it" (original italics).[25] As a semi-separatist, Busy too "produces new combinations and strange instabilities" in the system that defines religious identities and structures. Through his alimentary practices of restraint and indulgence, he conflates categories and confuses definitions of religious community.

Busy arrives at the Littlewit household, home of Dame Purecraft, her daughter Win-the-fight, and Win's husband John Littlewit, in the vague capacity of suitor/spiritual advisor. The family is part of a larger organized group of the "party-coloured brotherhood" (5.2.52), in which Busy is an "elder" (66); Dame Purecraft, by her own admission, is an "assisting *sister* of the *Deacons*" (55) who exacts

money from her suitors and serves as a devious matchmaker for the
economic support of the "poore *elect*" (59). While this group seems to
have a clear sense of membership and internal hierarchy, they are
not presented as strict separatists; they are not compared to the
brethren of Amsterdam, but to the puritan "feather-makers i' the
Fryers, that are o' [their] faction of faith" (5.5.85–86).[26] These
"party-coloured" puritans thus exhibit separatist impulses, creating
and safeguarding their own select community, even as they continue
to be a part of the greater society around them.

This ambivalent social identity is put to the test when John and
Win Littlewit crave a trip to the fair. Littlewit urges his pregnant wife
to simulate an uncontrollable yearning: "long to eate of a Pigge,
sweet *Win*, i'the heart o'the *Fayre* . . . Your mother will doe any
thing, *Win*, to satisfie your longing" (1.5.154–56). Upon hearing that
her daughter is consumed by a desire to eat pig, Dame Purecraft is
instantly alarmed: "Looke vp sweet *Win-the-fight*, and suffer not the
enemy to enter you at this doore, remember that your education has
bin with the purest, what polluted one was it, that nam'd first the
vnclean beast, Pigge, to you, Child?" (1.6.5–8). The language of
purity and violation intensifies when Purecraft exclaims, "O! resist
it, *Win-the-fight*, it is the Tempter, the wicked Tempter, you may know
it by the fleshly motion of Pig, be strong against it, and it's foule
temptations, in these assaults, whereby it broacheth flesh and blood,
as it were, on the weaker side, and pray against it's carnall prouoca-
tions" (1.6.14–19). As the Tempter introduces the idea of pig into
Win's head and penetrates Win's body with "fleshly motion," he
compromises not only Win's own bodily margins, but threatens the
integrity of the spiritual "family" in which she has been raised.

Win's cravings are instantly transformed into questions of communal solidarity, as the saints discuss how best to preserve the
integrity of their society:

PURECRAFT: O brother *Busy*! Your helpe heere to edifie, and raise vs vp in
    a scruple; my daughter *Win-the-fight* is visited with a naturall disease of
    women; call'd, A longing to eate Pigge.
JOHN: I Sir, a *Bartholomew*-pigge: and in the *Fayre*.
PURECRAFT: And I would be satisfied from you, Religiously-wise, whether
    a widdow of the sanctified assembly, or a widdowes daughter, may
    commit the act, without offence to the weaker sisters.
BUSY: Verily, for the disease of longing, it is a disease, a carnall disease, or
    appetite, incident to women: and as it is carnall, and incident, it is

naturall, very naturall: Now Pigge, it is a meat, and a meat that is nourishing, and may be long'd for, and so consequently eaten; it may be eaten; very exceeding well eaten: but in the *Fayre*, and as a *Bartholomew*-pig, it cannot be eaten, for the very calling it a *Bartholomew*-pigge, and to eat it so, is a spice of *Idolatry*. . .

. . .

PURECRAFT: Good Brother *Zeale-of-the-land*, thinke to make it as lawfull as you can.

. . .

BUSY: Surely, it may be otherwise, but it is subiect, to construction, subiect, and hath a face of offence, with the weake, a great face, a foule face, but that face may haue a vaile put ouer it, and be shaddowed, as it were, it may be eaten, and in the *Fayre*, I take it, in a Booth, the tents of the wicked: the place is not much, but very much, we may be religious in midst of the prophane, so it be eaten with a reformed mouth, with *sobriety*, and humblenesse; not gorg'd in with gluttony, or greedinesse; there's the feare: for, should she goe there, as taking pride in the place, or delight in the vncleane dressing, to feed the vanity of the eye, or the lust of the palat, it were not fit, it were abominable, and not good.

JOHN: . . . we'll seeke out the homeliest Booth i' the *Fayre*, that's certaine, rather then faile, wee'll eate it o' the ground.

PURECRAFT: I, and I'll goe with you my selfe, *Win-the-fight*, and my brother, *Zeale-of-the-land*, shall goe with vs too, for our better consolation.

. . .

BUSY: In the way of comfort to the weake, I will goe, and eat. I will eate exceedingly, and prophesie; there may be a good vse made of it, too, now I thinke on't: by the publike eating of Swines flesh, to professe our hate, and loathing of *Iudaisme*, whereof the brethren stand taxed. I will therefore eate, yea, I will eate exceedingly.   (1.6.39–97)

Purecraft's concern about the impact of pig-eating on the morals of the weaker sisters thus develops (through extensive equivocal wrangling on Busy's part) into a call for a show of unity and an ecstatic demonstration of religious fervor. Rather than allowing the encroachment of pig to pollute their society, the little band of brethren will fearlessly – and excessively – eat pig as an affirmation of group identity.

In his separatist ways, Busy "affects the violence of *Singularity* in all he do's" (1.3.139). But this singular character now heads directly into the plurality of the fair. Busy's resolution to "be religious in midst of the prophane," to maintain an isolated godly community in the tents of the wicked, requires absurd measures. His strategy mirrors Purecraft's advice to Win: marching before his followers like a flamboyant tourguide, Busy directs them to seal off their bodily margins so that they cannot be penetrated by the world around them. "So, walke on in the middle way, fore-right, turne neyther to the right hand, nor to the left: let not your eyes be drawne aside with vanity, nor your eare with noyses," he barks (3.2.30–32). The puritan society is accosted by the cries of hawkers and the sounds of the fair, and Busy calls out to fortify his followers:

Look not toward them, harken not: the place is *Smithfield*, or the field of the Smiths, the Groue of Hobbi-horses and trinkets, the wares are the wares of diuels. And the whole *Fayre* is the shop of *Satan!* They are hooks, and baites, very baites, that are hung out on euery side, to catch you, and to hold you as it were, by the gills; and by the nostrills, as the Fisher doth: therefore, you must not looke, nor turne toward them. (3.2.39–48)

Busy's sense of vulnerability to the fair's social evils grows almost to the point of paranoia. Having already instructed his group not to look at the fair, Busy now advises, "The Heathen man could stop his eares with wax, against the harlot o' the sea: Doe you the like, with your fingers, against the bells of the Beast" (3.2.46–48). As a compensatory measure against the carnival ambiance of the fair, Busy seeks to enact the impermeability of the classical form. The impracticality of this method of social interaction is quickly pointed out by Littlewit, who complains, "Good mother, how shall we finde a pigge, if we doe not looke about for't? will it run off o' the spit, into our mouths, thinke you? As in *Lubberland*? And cry, *we, we*?" (3.2.75–77). Busy's response is to track down a pig tent by smell, finally pronouncing in a magnanimous gesture of self-sacrifice, "Enter the Tents of the vncleane, for once, and satisfie your wiues frailty. Let your fraile wife be satisfied: your zealous mother, and my suffering selfe, will also be satisfied" (3.2.84–87).

Busy does not suffer for long. His advice for remaining religious in the midst of the profane – his dictate that the Bartholomew pig must only "be eaten with a reformed mouth, with *sobriety*, and humbleness; not gorg'd in with gluttony" – is almost instantly forgotten in the face of porcine pleasures. The greeting of the host suggests that the puritans' reputation precedes them: "good guests, I say, right hypocrites, good gluttons. In, and set a couple o' pigs o' the board, and a halfe a dozen of the biggest bottles afore 'hem, . . . I doe not loue to heare Innocents abus'd: Fine ambling hypocrites! And a stone-puritane, with a sorrel head, and beard, good-mouth'd glut-tons: two to a pigge, away" (3.2.116–22). Knockem again commands, "feare the ale out o' the bottles, into the bellies of the brethren, and the sisters, drinke to the cause" (129–31). The puritan bellies thus expand. Busy proclaims that "bottle-ale is a drinke of Sathan's, a diet-drinke of Sathan's, deuised to puffe vs vp, and make vs swell in this latter age of vanity" (3.6.30–33). Busy's own swelling is not simply the result of a perverse Satanic "diet-drinke," however. Knockem's initial offering of "two to a pigge" is a gesture of lavish abundance; Busy downs five times that much, consuming two and a half pigs on his own, and hopes that there is more (3.6.50, 41). In addition, he "has drunke a pailefull" (51). Whereas he earlier refused to so much as look at the fair, keeping his body closed to its influence, now even his eyes become organs of devouring consumption, as "he eates with his eyes, as well as his teeth" (51).

Through this superfluous eating, Busy is seemingly brought into the fair. Busy's behavior resembles that of his direct contemporary, the separatist Button-Maker of Amsterdame in Overbury's *A Wife*. This character has not only left England in search of religious isolation, but hesitates to mingle with his new Dutch neighbors. And yet, "if there bee a great feast in the Towne, though most of the wicked (as he cals them) be there, hee wil be sure to be a guest, and to out-eat sixe of the fattest *Burgers*" (sig. K2ᵛ). The Button-Maker's gastronomic desires overwhelm his attempt at spiritual segregation. Not only does he join in the feast, but as his participation is cast in the superlative ("*out*-eating" even the "fattest" diners), he becomes its apotheosis. Surrounded by Burgers, the would-be separatist is transformed into a bellygod: "[he] doth *sacrifice* to his own belly" (sig. K2ᵛ).

Zeal-of-the-Land Busy, too, becomes a bellygod. Or, more accurately, once he is in the fair Busy is unveiled as the bellygod he always has been. At the very beginning of the play, Busy's entrance is delayed by his need to "purify" himself of the evidence of his eating (1.6.38); Littlewit announces that Busy will arrive "as soone as he has cleans'd his beard. I found him, fast by the teeth, i' the cold Turkey-pye, i' the cupboard, with a great white loafe on his left hand, and a glasse of *Malmesey* on the right" (1.6.33–36). In this image of gastronomic excess, with a turkey pie hanging out of his mouth, Busy already resembles the Epicure of Ormerod's *Pictvre*. Win-the-fight complains, "we haue such a tedious life with him for his dyet, and his clothes too, he breaks his buttons, and cracks seames at euery saying he sobs out" (1.2.71–73). Busy's bursting seams are evidence of a bellygod barely contained; the moralizing, Lenten figure lives on the verge of exploding into a bloated Carnival.

Joseph Loewenstein writes, "Jonsonian gourmandise catches the physiology of hoarding at a profoundly ambivalent moment, a moment at which Rabelaisian gusto is on the verge of collapsing into an antisocial, indeed repulsive, miserliness of the body. Volpone fascinates us as he pursues his seduction by gastronomy precisely because of the way his Epicurean imaginings teeter between Rabelaisian gusto and Puritanical retentions."[27] This ambivalent position of the figure who is at once indulgent and retentive is made more striking when that character is not only "puritanical," but is indeed a puritan. The early modern image of the puritan was one of competing stereotypes: while accusations of antinomianism spurred legends of unbounded gastronomic and libidinous desires, the stricter reformers' moral prohibitions against weekend festivities conferred upon them a reputation as killjoys. In satiric representations, the puritan body can be either open or closed, grotesque or classical. In the figure of the puritan bellygod, it becomes both at once.

For Busy, this paradoxical form reflects his separatist impulses and conflicted social identity. From the very opening of the play, the puritans' place in the larger community is ambiguous. The play opens with a "Prologve to the Kings Maiesty":

> Your *Maiesty* is welcome to a *Fayre*;
> Such place, such men, such language & such ware,
> You must expect: with these, the zealous noyse
> Of your lands *Faction*, scandaliz'd at toyes,
> As Babies, Hobby-horses, Puppet-playes,
> And such like rage, whereof the petulant wayes
> Your selfe haue knowne, and haue bin vext with long.
> These for your sport, without perticular wrong,
> Or iust complaint of any priuate man,
> (Who of himselfe, or shall thinke well or can)
> The Maker doth present: and hopes, to night
> To giue you for a *Fayring*, true delight.

The puritans are thus distinguished from the main body of festive celebrants; they are added — "with these" — as a supplement to the established social corpus. In their objection to the wares of the fair, the puritans are further excluded from economic circulation, since they themselves are "scandalized" or expulsed from the community.

Jonson further isolates the zealous by disallowing the voice of any "priuate man" ("private" being a word frequently employed, with negative implications, in anti-separatist pamphlets). In Bakhtin's model of carnival, there is no place for the "private, egoistic" man at the fair[28] – but then there is no place for him to go, either, since there is no external space beyond the fair's all-engrossing social sphere. Busy cannot remain isolated in the midst of the fair, communal nexus that it is; neither can he be expelled. If "with these" attempts expulsion, "these for your sport" necessitates inclusion. Unlike the separatists in Amsterdam, these English puritans are a faction that is "Of your lands," belonging to the kingdom – a sense of belonging that is reciprocated in Zeal-of-the-Land's own name.

Busy's relationship to the greater community, then, is fraught with contradictory and vacillating impulses. He himself has a conflicted history with the fair, having shifted from a position of inclusion to an attempt at self-exclusion. As we learn early in the play, Busy was formerly a baker, and thus played a central role in the communal alimentary economy. He gave up his trade "out of a scruple hee tooke, that (in spic'd conscience) those Cakes hee made, were seru'd to *Bridales, May-poles, Morrisses,* and such prophane feasts and meetings" (1.3.121–24). Once a creator of carnival feasts, Busy now attempts to overthrow the fair ("fitter may it be called a foule, then a *Faire,*" in his view [3.6.88]). Having drunk a pailful, Busy is soon intoxicated by more than his own zeal, and he proceeds to stagger through the fair railing against "toyes, as Babies, Hobby-horses, Puppet-playes," attacking a basket of gingerbread which he condemns as "an Idolatrous Groue of Images" (3.6.98). His attempt at destroying the fair, however, only leads to his incorporation within it. Busy's destructive outburst lands him in the stocks, where the issues of religious separatism assume graphic form. "I am glad to be thus separated from the *heathen* of the land, and put apart in the stocks, for the holy cause," Busy proclaims. "[I am] one that reioyceth in his affliction, and sitteth here to prophesie the destruction of *Fayres* and *May-games, Wakes,* and *Whitson-ales,* and doth sigh and groane for the reformation, of these abuses" (4.6.85–86; 89–92).

In the end, a free but depleted Busy finds himself confuting with puppets. The once-overflowing, superfluous bellygod now needs to cry, "assist me zeale, fill me, fill me, that is, make me full" (5.5.45–46). The diminutive stature of his forensic opponents renders such an appeal pathetic, as his observers note. Busy's zeal, in any event, fails him. When Busy's "old stale argument against the players" is easily overcome by a lack of puppet genitalia, he admits,

BUSY: I am confuted, the *Cause* hath failed me.
PUPPET: *Then be conuerted, be conuerted.*
LANTHERN: Be conuerted, I pray you, and let the Play goe on!
BUSY: Let it goe on. For I am changed, and will become a beholder with
　　　 you.
　　　　　　　　　　　　　　　　　　　　　　　　　　　　　(5.5.113–17)

Busy's acquiescence enables the puppets' play to go on, but it marks the beginning of the end of *Bartholomew Fair*. As a desiccated bellygod, seemingly re-incorporated into the communal body of the fair, Busy ceases to be a cause of faction, but he also vanishes as a source of sport, and the play draws to its close.

While Busy is momentarily silenced, the nature of nonconformist speech proves irrepressible. At the end of *The Alchemist*, we witness another spectacular conversion: Sir Epicure Mammon, having lost his hope of endless wealth, runs off to become a millenarian preacher. In his final line of the play, Mammon declares, "I will go mount a turnip-cart and preach the end o' the world, within these two months" (5.5.81–82). After Mammon's effusive and exuberant discourses on his material, sexual, and gastronomic fantasies, this statement is initially stunning. The line could simply be read as a sarcastic or embittered joke – but within the larger context of the play, Mammon's announcement that he will assume the role of a tub preacher is perfectly fitting. As Robert M. Schuler has noted, Mammon "is the fun-house mirror's image of the Anabaptists," and his speech patterns exemplify those of the stage puritan.[29] The image of Epicure Mammon preaching from the back of a turnip cart serves as a visual emblem for seventeenth-century depictions of radical puritan speech. Throughout pamphlets and plays, the physical excesses of the bellygod were directly allied with discursive excess, with modes of speech that exceeded the conventional bounds of preaching and prayer. As Mammon's turnip cart illustrates, this speech was peripatetic and marginal, and yet an integral part of a greater social economy. As such, the discursive effusiveness of the puritan bellygod becomes impossible to contain.

In seventeenth-century sermons and pamphlets, the nature of religious language is given material form through alimentary images. A sermon on 1 Timothy, for example, opens by categorizing the

Scripture into three parts (preface, doctrine, and epilogue) and asserts, "Here's meat, and sauce, and a stomach. We have in the doctrine spirituall food, the bread of life, the Manna which came down from heaven, Christs merits, sinners redemption. Here's meat which should need no sauce were not our stomachs vitiated, and squeamish of what is most nutritive."[30] Scripture, either in its pure form or as prepared in a sermon, is to be eaten. John Geree, in his nostalgic *The Character of an old English Pvritane, or Non-Conformist* (1646), describes a puritan as "a man of good spirituall appetite, [one who] could not be contented with one meale a day. An afternoone Sermon did relish as wel to him as one in the morning" (2). (Geree goes on to claim that "The Lords Supper hee accounted part of his soules foode: to which he laboured to keep an appetite" [3].[31])

In satiric representations, this association of food and religious discourse becomes fodder for endless mockery. The "good spirituall appetite" Geree describes is frequently transformed into insatiable spiritual gluttony, and gastronomic overindulgence produces zealous speech. For Overbury's Puritane in *A Wife*, "Where the meate is best, there hee confutes most, for his arguing is but the efficacy of his eating: good bits hee holds breedes good positions, and the Pope he best concludes against, in Plum-broth" (sig. FI[r]). The form of the food and the form of the prophesying frequently mirror each other. An account of mechanic preachers claims that they "spoyle Bibles, while they thumbe over the leaves with their greasie fingers, and sit by the fire-side scumming their porridge-pot, while their zeale seethes over in applications and interpretations of Scriptures"; as the Bible is basted, the scum of the porridge pot and the zealous pontificating simultaneously overflow.[32] In another account, the form of the prayer itself displays this greasy and protracted excess: "In prayer they say, Lard, Lard, Lard, Lard, / Lard; Lard, a hundred times."[33]

Even as they are mocked for their prolific eating, fictional puritans are also ridiculed for their extended prayers. Alimentary and discursive expansion converge in Taylor's *The Brownists Conventicle: Or an assemble of Brownists, Separatists, and Non-Conformists* (1641), where the prayer and the food become virtually inseparable. Here, in a boiled down version, is the minister's prayer:

The Grace before Dinner

Corroborate these thy good gifts unto our use, I beseech thee good Father, and make us thankful for all these thy bountifull blessings upon this boord, to nourish our corrupt bodies. These are boyl'd Chickens (I take it) let this dish of Chickens put us in mind of our Saviour, who would have gathered *Hierusalem* together as an Hen gathereth her chickens, but she would not: but let us praise God for these chickens, which are set before us, being six in number. Let this leg of Mutton call us to remembrance, that King *David* was once a Shepherd, and so was *Christ* the son of *David*, that good Shepherd . . . These Rabbets recollect us to think (having worne fur upon their backs) of the two wicked Elders, that lay in wait to betray the chastity of *Susanna*: but I feare I have too much over-shot my selfe in alleaging any example out of the profane Apocrypha. What see I there? a Potato pye, and a Sallad of Sparagus, these are stirring meats, and provocations to procreation . . . And as for these thy good blessings that are from the land, so likewise make us thankfull for this thy bounty sent us from the sea, and first for this Sole of Sturgeon, and let it so far edifie in us, as to thinke how great that Whales head was, which swallowed the Prophet *Ionas*, . . . And though these Lobsters seeme to be in red coats like Cardinals; having clawes like Usurers, and more hornes than the Beast of Rome, which is the Whore of Babylon; yet having taken off their Papisticall copes and cases, let us freely feed upon what is within; for God regardeth not the outside, but the inside of man. I conclude with the fruit, which may it by thy grace so fructifie in our hearts, that these Pippins may put us in mind of the Apple of the forbidden Tree, . . . Thus as briefly as I can, I have gone thorow every dish on the boord, for every sundry dish ought to have a severall blessing. And now let us fall too, and feed exceedingly, that after our full repast, wee may the better prophesie. (4–5)

While the minister attempts to present the meal as symbolic and commemorative – as the chickens "put us in mind of our Saviour" at Jerusalem, and the mutton "call[s] us to remembrance" of David and Christ as shepherds – the sheer quantity of food transforms it into a carnivalesque feast. As they devour these various dishes with their assigned symbolic import, the nonconformist diners assume the role not of the (silenced) "Prophet *Ionas*," but that of his all-consuming blubbery leviathan. The nonconformists threaten to swallow all: New Testament, Old Testament, Apocrypha, Catholicism, Genesis.

But this promise of consumption is temporally deferred by the copiousness of the prayer itself. In its length, the prayer presents a parodic variation on "dilation." This rhetorical tradition, the subject of extensive early modern discussion, required the preacher to expand his discourse through a process of "partition," or "the multiplication of . . . rhetorical dividing walls," as Patricia Parker summarizes the practice.[34] The point of dilation, however, is to return to a "point." As Parker observes, this rhetorical strategy brought its own anxieties: "not only how to expand a discourse . . .

but also how to control that expansion, to keep dilation from getting out of bounds, [is] a concern repeated in the countless Renaissance rhetorical handbooks which both teach their pupils how to amplify and repeatedly warn them against the intimately related vice of 'Excesse' . . . Dilation, then, is always something to be kept within the horizon of ending, mastery, and control" (13–14).

Representations of puritan prayer and speech, however, frequently appear to evade both mastery and control. Significantly, such moments of verbal excess are linked to moments of eating. In *Bartholomew Fair*, Quarlous envisions a puritan meal in which the grace expands so far beyond its limits that the food itself seems endlessly deferred: "Dost thou euer thinke to bring thine eares or stomack, to the patience of a drie *grace*, as long as thy Tablecloth? and droan'd out . . . till all the meat o' thy board has forgot, it was that day i' the Kitchin?" (1.3.87–91). But the puritans do not often forget to eat. In a more common pattern of verbal excess, the puritan speech dilates so that it even exceeds the body of the speaker, and the discourse is summarily forced to a "point" when the mouth is stopped by food or drink. Zeal-of-the-Land Busy, as described by Littlewit, is

a Suitor that puts in heere at meale-tyde, to praise the painefull brethren, or pray that the sweet singer may be restor'd; Sayes a grace as long as his breath lasts him! Some time the spirit is so strong with him, it gets quite out of him, and then my mother, or *Win*, are faine to fetch it againe with Malmesey, or *Aqua cælestis*. (1.2.65)

In a similar vision, the "she precise Hypocrite" from John Earle's *Microcosmographie* (1628; "A shee-Puritan" in the manuscript), is a character who

overflows so with the Bible, that she spills it upon every occasion, and will not Cudgel her Maids without Scripture. It is a question whether she is more troubled with the Devil or the Devil with her: she is always challenging and daring him, and her weapons are Spells no less potent than different; as being the sage Sentences of some of her own Sectaries. Nothing angers her so much, as that Women cannot Preach, and in this point only thinks the Brownist erroneous: but what she cannot at the Church, she does at the Table, where she prattles more than any against sense, and Antichrist, till a Capon's wing silence her.[35]

Incapable of holding the Scripture which sloshes around within her, the she-Puritan becomes not only a weaker but a "leaky vessel,"[36] her verbal incontinence seemingly controlled only by eating.

In all of these examples, from the "Grace before Dinner" to the she-Puritan's discursive excess, puritan speech prolongs the moment of consumption, dilates to postpone the moment of completion. *Bartholomew Fair* follows a similar structure. The play overflows with increasingly uncontrollable discursive difference, from Wasp's profanities to Whit's speech defect to Zeal's zealous preaching, only coming to a close with Justice Adam Overdoo's universal invitation to supper. The Justice's invitation – "I inuite you home, with mee to my house, to supper" (5.6.110) – with its excess of first-person pronouns and reiteration of domestic boundaries, appears to bring the chaos of the fair into an ordered space governed by a now more moderate Adam. The "enormities" of the fair that Justice Overdoo so adamantly pursued have seemingly been tamed, and the dilation of the play is brought to a point.[37] Parker writes that "the play's *copia* is controlled, at last, and it ends with an address to the judgment and authority of the king, ruler and patriarch at once."[38] Not only is Adam Overdoo's status as Justice seemingly reaffirmed, but the Epilogue appears to assert the King's role as ultimate discursive arbiter, as he is asked to pass judgment on the language of the play.

But Adam's last supper, while promising an affirmation of communal identity and a return to linguistic, social, and religious orthodoxy, becomes corrupted as a point of closure, the control of *copia*. Wedged between Adam's invitation to supper and the Epilogue addressed to the king is the crucial final line of the play. Cokes accepts the Justice's invitation: "Yes, and bring the *Actors* along, wee'll ha' the rest o' the *Play* at home" (5.6.114–15). With this one small line, the play defies ending and regulation.[39] Rather than coming to a point, *Bartholomew Fair* continues to dilate beyond the walls of the theatre, slipping beyond the king's realm of judgment, as the "Actors" (the metatheatrical reference encompassing the puppet performers as well as the real-life players) will take their unruly verbal exuberance with them as they exit the stage. The greasy language of Smithfield is thus to be transported into Adam's domestic sphere.

Moreover, the final promise of a meal, however well circumscribed by authoritative and domestic bounds, potentially reactivates Busy's discourse and the Babel that accompanies it. While puritan speech is portrayed as ending with the insertion of food into the mouth of the speaker, this moment is repeatedly demonstrated as temporary discursive suspension, not its closure; in the examples cited above, although the dilation of puritan discourse comes to a food-induced "point," the speakers quickly resume their prophesying. Continuing his description of a puritan meal, Quarlous describes "the noise made, in a question of *Predestination*, by the good labourers and painefull eaters, assembled together, put to them by the Matron, your Spouse; who moderates with a cup of wine, euer and anone, and a Sentence out of *Knoxe* between" (1.3.91–96). Ecstatic, uncontrolled speech becomes a product of eating.[40] The minister of *The Brownists Conventicle* exhorts, "And now let us fall too, and feed exceedingly, that after our full repast, wee may the better prophesie" – and, as the pamphlet continues, they do just that. Similarly, Busy exclaims "I will eate exceedingly, and prophesie" – and he does. Closing with yet another festive, albeit more subdued, communal meal, *Bartholomew Fair* seems to re-animate this discursive cycle.

The fantasy of a return to uniformity and order presented at the end of *Bartholomew Fair* is therefore preempted not only by the continuation of the "*Play*," but by the very impossibility of incorporating Busy and his puritan cohort. While Busy ceases his opposition to the puppets' play, his integration into the carnival community is not so easily achieved, and his paradoxical identity is not so simply resolved. It is significant that despite the cries for Busy to "convert," he only claims to be "changed" into a "beholder" with the audience of the play, a metatheatrical moment which also integrates him with the theatre audience itself. Although Busy is assimilated into the crowd, he has given no signs of religious "conversion" or heartfelt conformity.

The difficulties of incorporating religious nonconformists into the communal framework were frequently cast in discursive terms. Overbury begins his description of "A Puritane" with a warning: "A Puritane is a diseas'd peece of *Apocripha*, bind him to the Bible and hee corrupts the whole text" (sig. E8ʳ). Overbury's analogy to apocrypha typifies Busy's semi-separatist desires to be at once part of the greater community and separate from it. The example of apocrypha (a charged topic in seventeenth-century England) also demonstrates the problems posed by incorporating a social paradox. To include the puritan is to infect the socio-ecclesiastical body: but to exclude him is to demonstrate the arbitrary, constructed nature of the ecclesiastical corpus. After the 1604 conference at Hampton Court, which put an end to many hopes for further church reform,

King James rejected the apocryphal books of the Bible and commissioned a standard form of the Scripture; in a parallel gesture, James and his bishops deprived ministers who refused to conform to a new set of canons. James sought to create an ecclesiastical body that was uniform and unified. But in forcibly binding his ministers to a central text – or by shutting them out of it altogether – James created a public relations disaster. Although the actual number of deprived ministers was relatively small,[41] their silencing was a source of significant discontent amongst the godly. These "silenced saints" are invoked, for example, by the puritan characters in *Bartholomew Fair* (3.5.199) and *The Alchemist* (3.1.36–38). Such allusions infuse both plays with a sense of the King's discursive control even while displaying the futility of this control, since the silencing of the saints becomes itself a source of further discussion and disputation.

Early modern commentators, like Overbury, frequently perceive separatists as "diseas'd." Pamphlets call for amputations and other forms of surgical removal to excise the separatists from the ecclesiastical body. But this language of excision even further destabilized the communal categories that separatists and the milder semi-separatists were perceived to undermine. If church and state comprised one coterminous body, how could an individual be hacked out of the body of Christ without doing injury to the body of state? The idea of excision or amputation also implied that there was an "outside," a conceptual zone into which such offending elements could be removed. This, too, threatened the orthodox premise that, by birth, every individual was a member of both nation and national church. The only mode of elimination which did not structurally compromise categorical boundaries was outright execution. Hovering behind *Bartholomew Fair* are the ghosts of the violent religious repressions of the previous century. The overt setting of the play, Smithfield, geographically superimposes the fair on one site of the executions so graphically recounted in John Foxe's *Actes and Monumentes*; Cokes, in his usual obnoxious way, even makes jokes about the Marian martyrs (4.2.71–73). The very title of the play, *Bartholomew Fair*, also invokes the infamous horrors of the Saint Bartholomew's Day massacre (1572), in which thousands of Huguenots were butchered in the streets of Paris. As he is being beaten by Wasp, Adam Overdoo, in a panicked frenzy, alludes to the massacre and fears that he is the victim of another (2.6.146–51). Overdoo's cries of "Murther, murther, murther" (2.6.154), however, are comically out of place in the extremity of their alarm. In the Jacobean fair, as in the pacific Jacobean state, it is pigs, not Protestants, that get roasted.

These pigs themselves seem to suggest an alternative solution for controlling the irritant of religious nonconformity, for the puritans could be swallowed whole into the fair. In the absence of a conceptual "outside," the separatists could be contained through becoming decidedly "inside." According to the fair's carnival (and carnivorous) logic, sharing in the communal feast unites the festive body; individuals are united through alimentary circulation. While Busy attempts to defy this circulation, Win-the-fight, despite her name, is ingested into the fair. At the very beginning of the play, her husband launches into ecstatic encomiums on her "dressing," which also inspires fruity blazons from Winwife, who praises her "*Straw-berry*-breath, *Chery*-lips, *Apricot*-cheekes, and a soft velvet head, like a *Melicotton*" (1.2.15–16). Littlewit proclaims Win a "dainty" to be shared, and even Dame Purecraft becomes a "fruict" to be "taste[d]" (20–21). Later, as Win is converted into a prostitute, she is again described in terms of food: "fowle," "Plouer" and "Quaile" in Ursula's cant (4.5.14–17). Before the puritan eaters can consume the fair, the fair – like Jonah's whale – encompasses some of the puritans.

Seventeenth-century religious literature is peppered with meta-phoric images of consumption as a means of containing religious opposition. At times, the nonconformists themselves are portrayed as the eaters; a tract responding to the presbyterian authors collec-tively writings under the pseudonym "Smectymnuus" (a name which itself signals the combination of many bodies into one), is entitled *A Fresh Bit of Mutton, for those Fleshy minded Cannibals that cannot endure Pottadge* (1642). Elsewhere, however, it is the nonconformists and separatists who are themselves eaten. A mid-century royalist tract translates such images into strikingly cannibalistic terms. The author describes a feast consisting of

> Two fat Presbyters sides, collerd in Lawne,
> In Jesuites urin souc'd, shall be thy Brawne.
> . . .
> An Ollio we must have, a dish of State,
> (A Spanish dish) ne'r heard of till of late.
> The Nymphaes of six vvanton sisters vvombes,
> In their own liquor stew'd vvith Stygean plummes.
> Tvvelve Round-heads inchpinnes of the largest size,

Minc'd vvith the marrovv of a Letchers thighs.
Two dozen of pious preaching Sisters tongues,
As many Woodcocks heads, two Foxes lungs.
Who eats this Ollio, he shall quickly find
A strange encrease of braine, and length of wind.
Twelve Independents Gammons shall be set
Upon the board, well smoak'd, and black as jet.
. . .

Six Anabaptists hearts with Garlick stuck:
Two Jesuites braines, a sincere Brownists Pluck,
Stew'd in a Traitours skull with sublimate:
We vvith this Hogoost poyson many a State.
We for our Fruit will of those Apples have
Which *Eve* our Mother unto *Adam* gave.
Our Cheese must be rebellious too, and made
Among those States where you have learnt your trade.
Then wee'll conclude our Feast; and drink a Health
In Royall blood to our new Common-wealth.
Thus you may see what honour shall be done
To him the Devill styles his dearest sonne.[42]

This "new Common-wealth," sanctified by a toast of Royal blood, counters the factious effects of religious nonconformity through dismemberment and violent, albeit carnivalesque consumption. In this feast, the nonconformist body – lungs, womb, heart, brain, phallus, thighs, tongue – is reconstituted within the body of the eater.

The ingestion of the dissenters thus successfully contains them within the larger body of the Commonwealth; but this containment itself transforms the nature of the social corpus. In consuming the nonconformist, the Royalist experiences "a strange encrease of braine": the mind of the eater is literally changed. The incorporation of schism thus inevitably converts, or at the very least alters, the original body. In order to avoid this somatic corruption, Overbury suggests a solution to the ingestion of "The Hypocrite": "If the *Body* of the *company* into which he is taken, can make . . . .[no use] of him, let him not long offende the stomake of your company; your best way is to spue him out" (sig. G3^{r-v}). The title page of a later pamphlet, *The Welsh Physitian* (1646), promises a similar remedy, claiming that the author "will purge the stomack of [the] Church of all her Errours." Vomit, however, does not present a useful solution. Like amputation, such an image requires a religious reality outside of the bounds of the central church. The social body can thus neither safely contain nor purge the presence of schism.

Were the central church to expulse these sectarian "Errours," it would itself reproduce a dynamic associated with separatist congregations. One of the frequent accusations against the separatists was their willingness to quickly excommunicate their members. In Thomas White's *A Discoverie of Brownisme: or, A briefe declaration of some of the errors and abhominations daily practiced and increased among the English company of the seperation remayning for the present at Amsterdam in Holland* (1605), the Brownists are castigated for their condemnation of "the Dutch, for beccoming one body, with excommunicates, when as they excommunicate their owne members onely for hearing the word so much as preached amongst the Dutch or French" (19). The propensity to expel individuals from the community is attacked, while the ability to become "one body," even with the excommunicate, is implicitly praised. White's own text, however, itself demonstrates a conflicted response to the Brownists. The title of his tract seems to condemn the Brownists' geographical separation, and his emphatic identification of them as "English" implies where they truly belong. And yet, throughout the tract, the re-incorporation of a sect believing such *"errors and abhominations"* seems highly undesirable. The Brownists, then, present a seemingly irreconcilable contradiction, as White cannot place them in a clear categorical (or geographical) space. To exclude them from the corporate church is simply to duplicate the separatist practice of excommunication; to become one body, however, "will corrupt the whole text."

"Puritanes," a term which expanded to encompass the Brownists as well as the quasi-sectarianism of Busy's group of saints, could thus neither be wholly expelled nor wholly assimilated. While the Epilogue to *Bartholomew Fair* pays homage to the King as the ultimate judge and regulator of discursive control, the Prologue indicates the King's inability to eliminate discursive variance. While pointing to the "lands Faction" as an object of derision, the Prologue also reminds the king of the nonconformists' "petulant wayes / [which] Your selfe haue knowne, and haue bin vext with long" (6–7). Although a perpetual source of vexation, the factious puritans cannot be expelled; rather, the church body – despite the irritation of indigestion – must encompass them all. Despite his resistance to further reform at Hampton Court, and despite his concern with discursive orthodoxy, for much of his reign James endorsed relatively

tolerant religious policies, avoiding the burning of martyrs. The
church body thus dilated, accommodating orthodox conformists and
devout semi-separatists and suffering the presence of peaceable
sectarians. The ecclesiastical body assumed the form of the *Mater
misericordiae*, the medieval representation of the church as a woman
whose open cloak contains thousands of little Christians;[43] this
accommodation allowed the Jacobean state to maintain the political
order and harmony represented in a similar image, the oft-repro-
duced illustration from Thomas Hobbes's *Leviathan*, where the body
of the king contains (whale-like) his little subjects.[44] In order to avoid
the exclusionary tendencies of separatist religion, the central church
assumes the form of a bellygod, dilating to envelop its members.

The containment of the likes of Zeal-of-the-Land Busy and his
fellow turnip-cart preacher Epicure Mammon does not last,
however. While these two fictional constructs are obviously gross
caricatures of nonconformist preachers, they nonetheless reveal the
subversive potential of taking the Word out of the pulpit and away
from authoritative discursive control. In *The Pictvre of a Puritane*,
Ormerod warns that such independence will lead to religious
fragmentation: "If we suffer euery headie & brainles fellow so soone
as he hath conceiued any new thing in his minde, to publish it
abroad, gather disciples, and make a new sect: in short time we shall
haue so many sects & factions, that Christ which scarce with a great
paine and labour is brought to vnitie in euery church, should be
deuided againe into many parts."[45] Towards the end of his reign,
James too sensed corporate dissolution in the face of independent,
non-ordained lecturers, preachers who were either privately supported by a parish or who led an itinerant life (the subsequent career
of some of the "silenced saints").[46] In his 1622 Directions Concerning Preachers, James defined lecturers as "a new body severed
from the ancient clergy of England, as being neither parsons, vicars,
or curates."[47] Long encompassed within the body of the church,
these preachers were now "severed," even composing a "new body"
of their own. Beyond the corporate bounds of the church, they
achieve a seemingly unbounded discursive freedom.

The social and religious consequences of such separation can be
seen in another trip to the fair. In 1641, a pamphlet appeared entitled
Bartholomevv Faire. The pamphlet seems to take its inspiration from
Jonson's play, displaying a variety of "enormities." The constitution
of the body of the fair has changed, however. As opposed to the

small (if vocal) group of religious extremists in Jonson's theatrical representation, we now find a community openly teeming with religious diversity: "Hither resort people of all sorts, High and Low, Rich and Poore, from cities, townes, and countrys; of all sects, Papists, Atheists, Anabaptists, and Brownists" (1). Ormerod's prophesy has come true. The body of Christ is no longer whole, but through discursive variance has become "devided . . . into many parts." The body of Bartholomew Fair, like the body of *Bartholomew Fair*, has exploded beyond its hegemonic limits, as sectarianism overwhelms the pressures of uniformity, and pluralism bursts through the constraints of orthodoxy.

CHAPTER 3

Lewd conversations: the perversions of the Family of Love

The holy whore no fellow hath,
The Pruritane [*sic*] is shee,
That midst her praiers sends her eie,
The purest man to see.
The purer man, the better grace,
The clearest hue the cherefulst face.
Sprite moues her first to wish him wel,
And discipline decaied
Doth make her seeke so far from wood
To haue Gods word obaied.
Ile tel you plaine, the matter is fresh,
They gin in sprite but end in flesh.

Mar-Martine [pseud.], *I know not why a*
trueth in rime set out (1593), sig. A2ʳ

The Family of Love was renowned as the wildest of sects. Reputed to hold heretical doctrines and to freely gratify its libidinous appetites, the Family haunted the fledgling Elizabethan church. The minister John Knewstub, in *A Confutation of monstrous and horrible heresies, taught by H. N. and embraced of a number, who call themselues the Familie of Loue* (1579), warns that in the Family the specter of the "Puritan" so many feared had finally arrived:

A number in this lande, vppon a false alarme, haue beene in a vaine iealousie and feare of Puritanisme. Now the iustice of GOD hath payed vs. For that which was spoken before in slaunder, now may bee spoken in trueth: and that which was beleeued, when it was not, is scarce suspected when it is. For if you seeke after the Puritans, these they bee. Which although for their loosenesse of life, they are from the toppe to the toe nothing but blottes: yet bragge they of all perfection, euen vnto a verie deifying of themselues, what mischiefe therefore yee feare might come from the Puritans, that looke for assuredly at their handes. ("To the Reader," sig. **4ʳ)

74

Knewstub's use of "Puritan" opens up a significance of the word to which we are not readily attuned. "Puritan" here does not indicate a person seeking ecclesiastical or moral reform; rather, it denotes a person who believes in the doctrine of perfectionism, the belief that for the spiritually pure there can be no carnal sin.

This doctrine is succinctly expressed by W. C., a "godly learned man," who wrote one of the prefatory letters to Knewstub's tract. W. C. claims that the Familists are "indeed the true succession of those ancient *Catharists* & *Puritans,* who thought themselues not to sinne, but actually to bee possessed with absolute holinesse and purenesse" (sig. **8ᵛ). In subsequent generations, authors continued to equate the Family of Love with this doctrine of perfectionism. King James, for example, qualified his use of the word "Puritan" in the second edition of *Basilikon Doron*: "as to the name of Puritans, I am not ignorant that the style thereof doth properly belong only to that vile sect amongst the Anabaptists, called the Family of love, because they think themselves only pure, and in a manner, without sin."[1]

Throughout early modern literature, the Family of Love is heralded as the worst of even the most dastardly sects; in a religious discourse given to hyperbole, the descriptions of the Family are often the most hyperbolic. William Wilkinson, in *A Confutation of Certaine Articles Deliuered Vnto the Familye of Loue* (1579), describes the Family as "wily as Serpents," with "lothsome spottes and ougly deformities"; they are "the most perstiferous, & deadly Heresie of all others, because there is not almost any one particular erroneous & Schismaticall phantasie, whereof the *Familie of Loue* hath not borrowed one braunche or other thereof" (sig. *iiiᵛ). The author of *A Discovery of the Abhominable Delusions of those, who call themselues the Family of Loue* (1622) proclaims, "They haue bene and are the greatest enemies of righteousnes that euer were, faining a God, and a Christ, according to their owne fleshly hearts: and haue more peruerted the straight way of the Lord, then euer did any" ("To the Reader"). Half a century later, in *Heresiography, or a description of the Hereticks & Sectaries sprang up in these latter times* (1647), Ephraim Pagitt unequivocally asserts: "This Sect of the *Family of Love* is one of the most erroneous and dangerous Sects that ever was."[2]

This emphatic insistence upon the superlative perils of Familism is initially surprising. The Family was a quiet, apolitical, conformist sect; unlike many other types of sectarians, the Family did not advocate ecclesiastical separation and did not have a history of political dissension.[3] In the sixteenth century the Family existed as a small and secretive community; in the seventeenth century the Family appears to have dissipated altogether. But in spite of its absence – or perhaps *because* of its absence – the Family of Love assumed a prominent cultural position. Indeed, in the seventeenth century, when the Family was almost entirely silent (if it existed at all), the sect became even more notorious. The Family was a frequent subject of anti-sectarian pamphlets, and was often included in catalogues of social undesirables, "such as fidlers, stage-players, beare and bull-baiters, gamesters, drunkards, vsurers, papists, *families of loue*, theeues, vagrant rogues, swearers, oppressors, coseners, Epicures and voluptuous liuers."[4] The Family was persistently maligned by playwrights and poets.[5]

The intense anxieties aroused by the Family of Love, I would suggest, stemmed largely from the perceived social and discursive implications of perfectionist doctrine. Perfectionism implied, to hostile observers, a radical interpretive individualism: while Scripture is not dispensed with as a book of law, it becomes subject to modes of reading that are personal and idiosyncratic, rather than communal and authoritative. Pagitt directly links perfectionism to a rejection of biblical authority: "In a word," Pagitt writes, "their Doctrine is perverse, blasphemous, and erroneous: it openeth a doore to all wickednesse, . . . not accounting of the Law of God, and making but a jest of the Gospel of Jesus Christ" (97). Such individualistic interpretation leads to a semantic crisis. The Familists' perfectionist doctrine was perceived as emerging from and enabling deviant discursive practices – "darke wordes & double speaches" according to Wilkinson (sig. C2r). More than any other radical sect, the Family was popularly associated with verbal perversions. The sect was represented as practicing equivocation, dissembling participation in the communal liturgy, and legitimating allegorical readings of Scripture.

Perfectionism, as Knewstub indicates, was also associated with other, more carnal forms of transgression and "loosenesse of life." William P. Holden notes that in early modern literature the anxieties raised by radical religion were distilled, isolated, and attached to a particular sect; "Familism" was indicative of sexual promiscuity.[6] Believing themselves to be free from sin, "euen vnto a verie deifying of themselues," the Familists, according to polemicists and satirists, licensed themselves to commit all manner of sexual sins: the Family was renowned for endorsing "free love," practicing group sex, and sanctioning incest.[7] This reputation pervades pamphlet literature and is a recurring feature of the stage Familist; in Middleton's *A Mad World, My Masters* (published 1608, written 1604–1606) a whore is identified as a Familist (1.2.67–68), and in Marston's *The Dutch Courtesan* (published 1605, written 1603–1604) the "Family of Love" is used as code for a brothel (1.1.139–40).[8]

However scurrilous, scandalous, or sexy these accounts of Familist behavior may be, such representations are not an end unto themselves. Reports of unconstrained Familist sexuality demonstrate not only the threat of antinomian chaos, but also the consequences of linguistic anarchy: the Familists' salacious reputation is consistently, directly correlated to their aberrant discursive practices. Pagitt's accusations of discursive transgression immediately lead to an intimation of sexual folly. Perfectionist doctrine "openeth a doore to all wickednesse, . . . not accounting of the Law of God, and making but a jest of the Gospel of Jesus Christ, leaving no manner of sinne uncommitted" (97). An arbitrary semantic code legitimated a subjective moral code as well. Sexual trespass is both a sign and a function of discursive iniquity.

Throughout anti-Familist texts, then, sexual and discursive corruption converge. This intersection is marked in descriptions of Familist "conversation." As Juliet Fleming has observed, in the early modern period "conversation" signified both "the exchange of words and ideas, and the act of sex."[9] Knewstub and Pagitt deploy this term in ways that exploit the simultaneity of these meanings. Knewstub writes: "Touching conuersation, howe may wee imagine that there is any soundnesse, when the doctrine and vitall partes be thus infected. For do we not read in the scriptures, that most shameful corruptio[n] of life hath alwaies followed as a due & deserued punishment, the corruption of doctrine" (sig. *4ᵛ). The sexual misdeeds insinuated in "shamefull corruptions of life" are a direct consequence of doctrinal aberrations. Pagitt makes the same claim, borrowing from Knewstub's text as he enumerates the Familist sins:[10]

4. *Their lewd Conversations.*

Of this holy Family we read, that most shamefull corruptions of life hath always followed corruption of doctrine, as *Rom*. I. 24. *God gaue them up to their owne hearts lusts, to uncleannesse, to defile their owne bodies between themselves, which turned the truth of God into a lye.*

> They are like *Priscillianus* the Heretique, of whom *H. N.* [the founder of Familism] borrowed not only that villanous wresting of the Word by allegories, as also the monstrous opinion that perjury and lying was lawfull, and to be done with a good conscience to conceale Religion.
>
> *Priscillianus* . . . was put to death at *Treversa* a City of *Germany*, confessing at his death what shamefull villanies he had committed with the women of his Sect. (99)

The biblical citation from Romans at once confirms the connection between the Familists' bodily and textual defilement, and affirms Pagitt's (and Knewstub's) own moral and discursive righteousness. The historical example of Priscillianus provides further testimony of the Familists' mutually constitutive verbal and sexual transgressions;[11] Priscillianus's mode of reading Scripture allegorically and his endorsement of lying and dissembling are implicitly connected to his shameful sexual villanies.

The Familists' alleged sexual misconduct thus not only emanates from discursive deviance, but represents it; the sexual body gives physical, visible form to the abstract, intangible sign. Throughout early modern pamphlets and sermons, accusations of sexual transgression give shape to the semantic destabilization associated with radical perfectionism. In this chapter, I will explore the various accusations of Familist discursive variance, from the clandestine circulation of Familist tracts to equivocation and allegorical readings of Scripture; I will then examine how these perceived discursive "sins" were translated into charges of sexual licentiousness. Finally, I will consider how Thomas Middleton's *The Family of Love* dramatizes the intertwined sexual and semantic consequences of perfectionist doctrine.

The Family of Love originated in the Netherlands in the mid-sixteenth century. The Family's self-proclaimed "father," Hendrik Niclaes, wrote a series of tracts in which he described his mystical union with the divine, declaring that his followers could also achieve spiritual perfection and become "godded with God."[12] In the 1570s, Christopher Vitells (described in hostile accounts as a lowly joiner) translated Niclaes's tracts into English, smuggled them across the Channel, and secretly disseminated them in England. As Christopher Marsh has recently demonstrated, in the sixteenth century the English Family of Love, though small in numbers, formed a cohesive and often close-knit community that ranged from the artisan classes to the court of Elizabeth herself.[13] The Family was hardly a group of dramatic martyrs, flamboyant evangelicals, or ecstatic prophets; Niclaes's tracts were carefully concealed, and members of the Family were exceptionally reticent about their beliefs (factors which, as Marsh points out, vex the historian's attempt to discover details about Familist identities and practices). The Family's public silence was momentarily broken in 1604 with the publication of *A Supplication of the Family of Love*, a text which defends Niclaes's teachings and pleads for toleration.[14] This vocal defense of the Family, however, appears to have been its swan song, as the group all but vanished in the seventeenth century.[15] But while traces of actual Familists faded during this period, the Family of Love continued to thrive and even grow as a conceptual category invoked by preachers, pamphleteers, and dramatists.

Given the sect's virtual invisibility, the Family of Love, as it existed within the wider cultural imagination, was a phenomenon created by an expanding print culture. Benedict Anderson has discussed how modern ideas of nationalism emerged, in part, through a community "imagining" itself into being by virtue of a shared print culture;[16] in early modern responses to the Family of Love, we find a dynamic that is at once related and quite the reverse – individuals imagined not themselves, but invisible others forming a communal network through the subterranean circulation of texts. In the 1570s, when Niclaes's tracts first appeared in England, pocket-sized books were still a rare commodity; the very concept of a clandestine, tract-reading religious group was a novelty, a source of fascination and fear. The sheer quantity of H. N.'s texts, eighteen of which entered England from 1573 to 1575, alarmed many (although "his disciples much bragge[d] of the multitude of *H. N.* his bookes"[17]). An imperceptible textual underground seemed to be infiltrating the parishes of the English Church. Elizabeth ordered these books burned, and pamphleteers helpfully suggested that the Familists could avoid "molestation, imprisonment, or persecution" if they would simply "leaue, burne, or deface these bookes of *H. N.*"[18]

Sixteenth-century anxieties over the Family are disproportionate to the group's actual disruptive potential. The group had minimal evangelical ambitions and no political aspirations; the Family was a small community which got on relatively peacefully with its neighbors. The tracts of H. N., though written in a difficult mystical style, did not appear blatantly heretical. (On the Continent, in fact,

Niclaes's writings had quickly attracted a high-profile intellectual readership.[19]) The hype over the Family of Love, then, seems to emerge largely from the incomprehension and suspicion aroused by a private group of bookworms. The Family's *Svpplication*, addressed to a new king who styled himself as a scholar, optimistically suggests that James (who had earlier smeared the Familist name in *Basilikon Doron*) would probably enjoy reading Niclaes's work. In response, the *Supplication* was reproduced (with extensive editorial rebuttal) in *A Svpplication of the Family of Loue . . . Examined, and found to be derogatory* (1606); the author scoffs at the Family for wanting to "only studie, read at their meetings, [and] delight in" the books of Hendrik Niclaes (64).

Unique among radical religious sects in early modern England, the Family was associated with a strong central author, and was governed by a set of printed texts which dictated the group's hierarchy and doctrine. The title of *Proverbia HN. The Prouerbes of HN. Which he in the Dayes of his Olde-age; hath set-fourth as Similitudes and mysticall Sayinges* (Cologne, 1575?) indicates the degree to which such tracts were positioned almost as sacred texts. Niclaes's own self-descriptions, rife with first-person pronouns, likewise indicate the extent to which he considered himself a prophetic, mystical leader: "[God] raised-vpp Mee HN, the Least among the holyons of God . . . from the Death, and made mee aliue, through Christ, as also annointed mee with his godlie Beeing, manned himself with Mee, and godded Mee with him to a liuing Tabernacle or howse for his Dwelling."[20] Given the centrality of H. N.'s tracts to the Family's structure and beliefs, the group placed a high premium on literacy; the ability to read was a condition for advancing to the more spiritually perfect status of "elder."[21] Another of Niclaes's texts, *All the letters of the A.B.C. in ryme* (Cologne, 1575), a sort of primer for those entering the sect, contains an illustration of a teacher instructing a roomful of boys how to read; this woodcut was also incorporated into the text of Niclaes's *Exhortatio I* (Figure 5). Initiation into the Family was therefore presented as initiation into the world of print; similarly, advancement through the ranks of the Family's spiritual hierarchy was regulated by gradual access to H. N.'s more mystical tracts.[22]

The image of the Familist schoolroom becomes self-reflexive if we consider that the text the boys are reading could be the *A.B.C.* itself. This reciprocity of reader and text becomes a recurring feature of

A ſhozte Inſtruction of an Howſhold-father, in the Cōmunialtie of the Loue of Jeſu Chziſt.

☧ Yee beloued Childzen and thou Famelie of Loue / reſpect well this good Doctrine and Exhoztation of HN / and take the Inſtructions of theſame, effectuallie to heart: and vnderſtande, what is requyred of you therwith-all.

Not that yee ſhoulde take vnto you alone the [a] Knowledge of thoſe-ſame / ether exerciſe you onlie in the Knowledge therof. but to take-heede rightlie vnto the Requiringe of thoſe-ſame / and [b] to ſhew-fourth Obedience therin .

2.   Foz to receaue onlie the Knowledge of the godlie Teſti-monies / and not to obey oz accompliſh thoſeſame and their Re-quiringe : and ſo to knowe and to ſpeake anything, againſt the Obedience / is verelie [c] the Seede of the olde Serpent : and that is the falſe [d] Light which ſeduceth and eſtraungeth the Man from God and his Trueth / and wozketh by hym much Conten-tion and Diſcozde .

3.   And the Diſobedience is [e] the Seede of the Woman / wherthzough ſo much Falſhod is com into the Wozlde : and

a Jaco.1.d.

b Mat.7.12.e.
Joan.15.b.

c Geneſ.3.

d Eſa.5.b.59.b

e Gene.3.

X 2   which

Figure 5 Illustration from Hendrik Niclaes's *Exhortatio I* (Cologne, 1574), sig. A2[r]

Familist representations. Members of the Family are depicted as entering into a textual body. In 1580, Leonard Romsey "confessed" his membership in the Family and described their means of recruitment: his master perceiving that he was a religious man, Romsey was sworn to secrecy and given a tract by H. N., with the assignment to not only read it but to "shewe him my jugement of it in writinge with myne owne hand and my name subscribed there vnto." Entrance into the Family is thus signified by a textual exchange. Members literally sub-scribed to the Family, and are literally inscribed into Familist text, their names "conueied to H. N. and written in his book which he calethe the booke of lyffe."[23] Not only are Familists registered in H. N.'s book, but H. N.'s texts seem to enter the bodies of the Familists themselves. Within anti-Familist pamphlets, the members of the sect are depicted as so dependent upon the word of H. N. that they almost bear his imprint, becoming the pages upon which he impresses his doctrine. Knewstub comments on the gullibility of Niclaes's followers, observing that "there is no wickednesse so grosse, the print whereof our waxie and pliable nature to all euill, is not meete to receyue" (sig. **4[r]). The inky nature of the Familist body is further reflected in his claim that "they are from the toppe to the toe nothing but blottes" (*ibid.*, sig. **4[r]). According to Thomas Rogers in *The Displaying of an horrible secte of grosse and wicked Heretiques, naming themselues the Familie of Loue* (1578), H. N.'s spurious doctrines are "deeply impressed in [the] minds" of his followers.[24] (Interestingly, under the 1581 parliamentary act against the Family, a second conviction of being a Familist would merit the punishment of being branded with the initials "H. N."[25] – a punishment which literalized accusations of Familist inscription.)

In hostile accounts of the Family, dependence on (and love for) Hendrik Niclaes's books leads to nefarious discursive practices. Familists arouse suspicion by refusing to share their books (or even to discuss H. N.'s doctrine) with those who are not members of their sect. Rogers writes of his frustration in gaining access to Niclaes's work:

Many Bookes are abroade, which I haue not seene, and many I haue seene, which I could not haue the vse of to reade. For except one will be pliant to their doctrine, and shewe good will thereto, he shall hardly get any of their bookes, no, nor they will not conferre, nor talke of any pointes of their doctrine with any, except it be to such as they find inclined & (as they tearme it) willingly minded thereto. (sig. A4[r])

In tantalizing fashion, these books at once reveal and conceal the presence of the sect.

Even worse than the Familists' careful guarding of their books is an insidious tendency to lie for the sake of preserving their secrecy. When questioned, it was allegedly Familist practice to deny all knowledge of the sect, and to refute Niclaes's teachings. Rogers paints a vivid picture of the Family as dissembling individuals:

> [Christopher Vittel, a ioyner] hath by his trudging about the countrie, infected sundrie simple men with this poysoned doctrine, & snared their minds so corruptly therein, that it is harde to plucke out of their heades those vaine toyes of *H. N.* which *Vittel* hath so deeply impressed in their minds, [that] although they denie publikely before the worlde, yea & set their handes against the same doctrine, yet they returne againe to their olde opinions, as is well seene by many that I could name. For it is a *Maxima* in the *Familie* to denie before men all their doctrine, so that they keepe the same secrete in their hearts: which is impious and vngodly.[26]

For their enemies, the Family's blithe willingness to embrace outward conformity while keeping their true religion "secrete in their hearts" was a source of sputtering outrage. Unable to simply "plucke" the offending doctrine out of the Familists' heads, W. C. recommends discovering it by making "a separation betweene thought and thought, betweene practise and practise, betweene secret & open paths of errour and contempt, betwene ioynts and marrow, betwene soule and spirit, that all the outgoings & escapes and dennes wherein these heresies either lye in waite and worke against the trueth, or hide themselues from discouery, may be discouered."[27] Accounts of Familist dissembling emphasize a body divided. In Rogers's description, the semantic cleft between internal thought and external testimony is illustrated in the hand which subscribes against the beliefs in the heart; in W. C.'s solution, the quest for the truth involves an endless process of probing these divisions.

The Family of Love thus seemed to embody verbal hypocrisy: outward conformity masked an interior adherence to the doctrine of Hendrik Niclaes. This perceived distinction between external appearance and internal belief was a product of the Familists' Nicodemist policies. In order to preserve the Family's secrecy, its members were seemingly encouraged to participate in the rituals of local worship while privately adhering to the teachings of H. N. Since the Family considered itself a transcendent, mystical community, the various forms of earthly religion were of little import, and did not merit protest.[28] This Nicodemist practice of outward doctrinal conformity was a common source of anti-Familist invective. We read in *A Svpplication . . . Examined*: "For howsoeuer they showe themelues obedient, and externally conformable by repairing vnto our Churches, frequenting of Sermons, vsing the Sacramentes, and the like: yet in their hearts and minde . . . they condemne them all" (15). Through this division of heart and mind, the Familists were perceived as destabilizing local community; parishioners gathering for worship – the collective affirmation of their group identity – could never be entirely certain of the sincerity of their neighbors, despite the communal recitation of the liturgy. Moreover, through such outward dissembling the Family appeared to undermine the sanctity of the Bible itself. The *Svpplication . . . Examined* continues, "the bodies of [Niclaes's] *Familistes* may be in our Churches, and at Seruice, Sermons, and Sacrame[n]ts, but their harts doe loath whatsoeuer they doe either see, or heare, though it be neuer so firmely grounded & apparantly deriued fro[m] Gods written word" (17). This secret dissent, masked by outward verbal and ritual compliance, eroded the sanctity of the Word – here specifically designated in its "written," material form.

The Familists' irreverence towards language became even more pronounced during interrogation. In addition to faking their liturgical participation, the Familists, according to their enemies, also held "the monstrous opinion that perjury and lying was lawfull, and to be done with a good conscience to conceale Religion."[29] The Familists' reputation for "pragmatic perjury," lying in order to preserve the secrecy of the sect, persisted for almost a century; indeed, this tendency rivaled, or even surpassed, the Family's identification with sexual promiscuity.[30] In his sixteenth-century "confession," Romsey admits "The disciples of H. N. make no conscience of lyinge and dissemblinge to all them that be not of their religion" (191); Pagitt would write that the Familists "dissent from the doctrine of the Church of *England*, opposing in every syllable, and yet being notorious hypocrites, if they be never so little questioned, wil make shew by outward seeming of conformity, as if they did highly approve the doctrine of our Church" (100). Accusations of Familist dissembling not only concerned outright lying; the Family of Love, virtually alone among English sects, was associated with equivocation and mental reservation.[31] Familists were alleged to have developed a private and idiosyncratic semantic code; assigning common words a secret, alternative signification, the Familists could be truthful to themselves while misleading others. In her analysis of Familist discursive practices, Janet E. Halley concludes that, "Because Familists implicitly show the relation between words and their meanings to be arbitrary, they suggest that *all* language may be conventional: they subvert not only the specific meanings attached to words by those in authority, but also their opponent's power to control language and meaning in the first place."[32]

Alarmed early modern commentators were also attuned to these subversive implications of Familist discursive practice. Here, in one mid-seventeenth-century tract, an author explains how sectarian error is spread:

First, They use sophisticall arguments, *argumenta tortuosa*, knotty and crooked questions, by which they puzzle and insnare the simple . . . This hath been [the sectarians'] constant indeavour, with pretences of words, and sophistry of arguments, to colour and paint their horrid opinions. This is that which *Cyril* calls . . . multivarious impostures, . . . the inventions of many-times-pleated senses, equivocations, amphibologies, the strength and garrisons of hereticks, unto which they retreat, being pursued . . .

Secondly, They use new and strange expressions, expressions not to be understood but by their own disciples. These the Apostle . . . calls . . . new language; and against these arms *Timothy*, commanding him to *keep the form of sound words which hee had heard of him:* This hath been of especiall use to hereticks in the primitive Church, and of later times; . . . That by their indistinct and confused expressions they eluded truth, and ensnared their unwary auditors by the ambiguity of their phrases . . . They so temper their words, pervert their order, mingle ambiguities, that in the same sentence they utter the truth and errour; their followers understand one thing, and strangers another.[33]

While this tract focuses on heresy more generally, the Family of Love was repeatedly targeted as the source of sectarian semantic distortions. At the end of *The Displaying of an horrible secte*, Rogers appends a confession from an erstwhile Familist, who discloses, "They haue certaine sleightes amongest them, to answere any questions that shall be demaunded of them, with deceiuing the demaundant: as for example: if one of them be demaunded howe he beleeueth in the Trinitie, he will answere: I am to learne of you, & so prouoketh the demandant to shew his opinion therein: which done, he will say then: I do beleeue so: by the which wordes he meaneth, that he beleeueth the demaundant saith as he thinketh: but not that he thinketh so" (sig. κ3^r). With this wily answer, a seeming affirmation of agreement is deflected back upon the inquisitor himself, as questions of doctrinal interpretation become enmeshed in a response which itself necessitates and defies interpretation.

This sinister verbal ambiguity seemed to underlie the very fabric of the Family, as perceived by its opponents. Hendrik Niclaes's eccentric writings, which shaped the Family's constitution and practice, were attacked as deliberately ambiguous and obscurely allegorical.[34] Knewstub complains that "not submitting them selues to the simplicitie of the word, [the Familists] haue desired to be fed with curious questions, matters of witte and subtile speculations" (sig. *3^r). Niclaes's mystical prose style "seemeth to be as a riddle, or darke speeche, and therefore more intricate to be followed"; Niclaes is accused of "wrongfull alledgyng, subuertyng, and misconstruyng his meanyng."[35] It is bad enough that Niclaes's own texts require (and deflect) allegorical interpretation – even worse, he endorses an allegorical reading of Scripture, undermining the very basis of Truth itself. The Familists, argues Rogers, "take not the creation of man at the first to be historicall, (according to the letter,) but meere allegoricall . . . applying still the allegorie they destroye the trueth of the historie" (sig. F4^r). Reading "according to the letter," the words in the Bible bear a direct and unquestionable relationship to historical event – it is this correlation that constitutes "trueth." Allegory, by contrast, destroys this truth by introducing a split between signified and signifier.

Allegorical biblical reading not only devalues the collective understanding of the past, but opens the floodgates for interpretative individualism. Anti-Familist authors repeatedly emphasize that the ultimate danger of allegorical reading was that it located meaning in a solipsistic, self-defining semantic universe. "[L]eauing the title of Christia[n]s . . . and coyning a new [title] of their owne braine,"[36] the Family of Love abandoned a traditional communal identity, turning inward and devising their own self-definition. W. C. condemns "the dark and deceauing words, the new phrases, and blasphemous allegoryes wherwith the Family of Loue, fill their bookes, which speaches . . . chaung[e] with euery change of person in that family."[37] Within this internalized configuration of meaning, God ceases to have control over the Word as it becomes subject to isolated human imaginations: "What a miserable case is this to see the holie Scriptures thus drawen from the true sense, into Allegories, whiche may be taken many wayes, euen as the vaine imagination of man can deuise," writes Rogers (sig. F4ᵛ). Another author intensifies this idea of "vaine imaginations": "Let all iudge if these wretches, abolish not the Scriptures, to set vp their owne deuillish inuentions."[38] Fiction, as implied here by "inuentions," supersedes the truth of the Word; the individual Familist, through his or her own random allegorical readings, supplants God as the author of the text. Wild allegorical readings render all truth arbitrary, malleable, and human: "And indeed they make od interpretations of Gods word, turning light into darkenesse; truth into falsehood; histories into allegories; and sound religion into fancies of men."[39]

This discursive distortion was perceived as both a product and a cause of the doctrine of perfectionism. In *The Description and Confutation of Mysticall Antichrist, the Familists* (1646), Benjamin Bourne describes how the Familists deceive "by cunning, sophistries, seeming Angelicall doctrines, such as can deliver their mindes so, that every expression shall be a mystery, a strange paradox, unheard of maximes, wordes that are neither according to the scriptures, nor according to the termes of Schooles, or those words which in our own language are commonly spoken amongst us" (sigs. A2ᵛ–A3ʳ). Here, perfectionism ("seeming Angelicall doctrines") becomes the tool for creating a corrupted language. But perfectionist doctrine was also considered not so much the tool, as the consequence of verbal distortions. Knewstub describes how "partly by [Niclaes's] dark speaking, & partly by his allegorical expositio[n], he hath hatched a monster of perfectio[n]" (sig. *7ʳ). Perfectionism and discursive corruption were thus perceived as mutually generating and mutually reinforcing. The interplay of these beliefs and practices led to a Familist conviction of the purity of their own "conversation," according to their critics. Knewstub describes how the Family of Love, perceiving themselves as "goddified," now believe that "as for their conuersation, [Niclaes] telleth them whatsoeuer their doinges be, they are no longer now to be said or accompted to haue any sinne in them" (36). In the minds of horrified contemporaries, the alleged sin-free "conversation" of this bookish sect was soon perceived as a license for sexual depravity. As we shall now see, the interrelated social and discursive implications of Familist perfectionism were quickly translated into allegations of sexual independence.

Linguistic free play appeared to legitimate free love. In *A Svpplication of the Family of Loue . . . Examined*, "the doctrine of dissimulation and temporizing [that] is so often dispersed, and rife in *H. N.* his wrightinges" (53) is linked, through a snide paraphrase of Niclaes's own text, with the claim that, "Not of a few, but of many *yea almost all, of the Familie of Loue*, . . . haue take[n] vnto the[m]selues the voluptuousnesse of the flesh, to be their *Freedome*, or *Felicitie*."[40] From the beginning, the Family of Love was tainted by accusations of sexual promiscuity. In part, this reputation developed out of the Family's associations with Anabaptism, long remembered for John of Leyden's polygamous escapades during his takeover of Muenster. When one ex-Familist "confessed" that the group encouraged its members to engage in extra-marital sexual relations, including compulsory adultery, the suspicions of many seemed to be confirmed.[41] Pamphleteers note the sect's alleged communism in having "all things common, not onely goods, & cattell, but wife and children," and claim that in the Family "a man may gaine salvation by shewing himselfe loving, especially to his neighbours wife."[42] The sect quickly became associated with sexual promiscuity; one critic notes that "literally scores of extended references, allusions, and winking circumlocutions reveal how their contemporaries jested with and jostled the Family name."[43] (It should be kept in mind that such accusations are not supported by historical evidence, and the idea that actual Familists spent their time wallowing in orgiastic passions seems unlikely; in the 1580s, many of the Familists Marsh discovers were "established householders and middle-aged parents" [*The Family of Love*, 52].)

In addition to its Anabaptist origins and alleged communist practices, the Family's libidinous reputation also emerged, I would argue, from their alleged discursive irregularities. The tenor of Niclaes's own tracts provided endless fodder for his opponents. His opaque, mystical prose frequently turns to somatic metaphors to describe spiritual states. In one of his more lucid passages, Niclaes describes the evils of using conventional religion to mask a lack of true faith and love of Christ:

after such a manner yee are towards the gratious word of the Lord, and his seruice of Loue, euen like vnto an whore, which after her hearts Good-thinking to a cloaking of her whoredome, chooseth an husband, & coupleth her selfe in marriage vnto him, for that she mought boast her as a married wife; & vnder such a couering and boasting that she hath a husband, committeth whoredome: Seeing that ye in like manner without Christ, and against Christ, although yee make great boast of him, committe whoredome, and deale nor walke not according to the doctrine or requiring of Christ.[44]

H. N. repeatedly uses whoredom to signify a lack of true inner belief. In Niclaes's vision of spiritual perfection, those who were "godded" would enter into another mystical realm, a paradise on earth; concerns of the flesh would be left behind.

In the hands of his enemies, however, these metaphors were perceived as self-incriminating statements about salacious living. The author of *A Svpplication . . . Examined* uses this quote as proof of the Family's iniquity, "seeing *H. N.* the oldest Father of that *Familie*, and priuie to all their actions and dealinges taketh them, I meane many, euen *Almost all of them*, to bee but an whorish company, making the voluptuousnesse of the flesh their freedome, or *summum bonum*" (13). Elsewhere, Niclaes's claim that the spiritually perfect are "like the Angels in Heauen" is interpreted as evidence that "*in their louely society*, they doe not vow, or binde themselues in the matrimony of men, nor yet suffer themselues to be bound therein."[45] H. N.'s tracts were designed to allow a spiritual development from the stage of the "young ones" to the "elders" who were over age thirty; as one grew in the sect, one learned more of the mysteries of "love." The language of these tracts provided another easy target: "It is obserued concerning *H. N.* that, for the propagating of his *Loue Seruice*, hee hath bookes of sundry natures . . . The latter sort containe the *Loue* secretes or priuie mysteries communicable only with such as are come vnto *the manly age, and haue Beards*" (*Svpplication . . . Examined*, 63). Throughout anti-Familist literature, the sect's mystical "*Loue* secretes or priuie mysteries" are given a decidedly sexual spin.

The Family protested such innuendoes and accusations, convinced that the group would be vindicated by their "obedience, peaceable, and honest liues, and conuersation."[46] Such, however, was not the case. The Familists' pious "conuersation" was itself viewed as a lure. Rogers hints darkly that the Family will "qualifie the bitter and poysoned doctrin of H. N. & Vittell, with such sweete pretences of a holy life and vpright conuersatio[n], which in deed are but mere visars & cloaks to shadow horrible blasphemie" (sigs. F5^v–F6^r). W. C. is more overt in the sexual direction of such "conuersation," as he envisions a scenario in which religious speech is used to draw prospective Familists into wanton pleasures:

> they seduce some goodly and zealous men & women of honest and godly *conuersation*, placing them at the porch of their Synagogue, to make a shewe of holinesse, and to stand there as baites and stalles to deceiue others: yet alas who can without blushing vtter the shame that is committed in the inwarde roomes, and as it were in the heart of that Synagogue of Satan.[47]

The evil enticements of the Familists' speech are here contrasted with Knewstub's own reticence; while the Familists employ language as a means of tempting innocent passers-by into depraved dens of iniquity, Knewstub maintains a modest language that prevents him from describing the salacious entertainment. This refusal to show us the "inwarde roomes" is a recurring feature of anti-Familist writing. The author of *A Discovery of the Abhominable Delusions of . . . the Family of Loue*, despite the revelatory promise of the title, proclaims, "Oh who would haue thought that so many abhominations had lurked in this wicked Family! though alas these bee not all that are knowne; and how many moe are vnknowne, men may imagine" (89). Upright anti-Familist authors thus deliberately remove their language from Familist scenes of desire – though we are invited to leave much to our imaginations.

Within seventeenth-century pamphlet literature, we witness Familist sexual depravity primarily through the eyes of naïve fictional characters who find themselves lured by Familist speech. In Henoch Clapham's pamphlet *Errovr on the Right Hand* (1608), for example, an inquisitive character named Flyer encounters a member of the Family of Love who (rather atypically) explains the Familists' perfectionist doctrine, stating that those truly united with God are free from vulgar carnal desires. Flyer then watches in dismay as the Familist proceeds to fondle the alewife.

FAM[ILIST]: Come, Tannikin; how dost thou Wench: let vs kisse; and tell me how thy pretty body doth? – – [*sic*]
FLYER: Why, how now sir; Are you a man that is Goddifyed, and hanges at a Wenches lippes so wantonly?
FAM[ILIST]: O sir, she is the seed of the *Louely-beeing*. We but *Loue*, we lust not, as you and others would, that be out of the *Louely-beeing*.
FLYER: Louely-beeing call you it: Keepe your *Loues* & your *Lusts* to your selfe: & God giue me to see mine owne home againe. There is money for the Beere, and adue leaud leacherous *Familist*.[48]

Thus Flyer flees from the Familist's "leaud" conversation. His disgust is fuelled as much by the Familist's manipulation of language as it is by the groping sexual display. "Lovely-beeing *call you it*": Flyer correlates the Familist's moral and verbal relativity. "Love," as it is translated in hostile pamphlet literature, functions as a euphemism for unrestricted libidinous appetites. "The Familists talke of love and being in love, and nothing but love; but their love turneth unto lust," remarks Pagitt.[49] The Family's perceived tendency to define words according to their own desires, and their continual exploitation of ambiguous definitions, seemed to distort even the meaning of "love." The Family of Love was thus quickly dubbed "The Family of Lust."[50]

Through their corruptions of "love," the sect was also perceived as undermining the concept of "family." Freed from normative linguistic and discursive codes, the Family allegedly re-organized the world around them in order to accommodate their narcissistic desires, becoming the "housholde of Selfeloue."[51] Knewstub writes that the Familists "thinke euerie thing lawfull (how filthie and howe disorderly soeuer) that their fantasticall spirite telleth them" (sig. **3ᵛ); personal desire, "fantasy," becomes the law. With meaning left to the discretion of the individual, even words like "mother," "father," "sister," and "brother" become arbitrary. Having destabilized not only these words but these relationships, the Family was perceived as legitimating incest. Within a community where the members define each other as "brother" and "sister," all sexual relations are figuratively incestuous.[52] But early modern critics of the Family of Love, almost from the beginning, claim that actual incest is also a feature of the sect. Hendrik Niclaes's own home is exposed as not only incestuous, but polygamous and abusive.[53] Robert Baillie writes in *Anabaptism, the True Fountaine of Independency, Brownisme, Antinomy, [and] Familisme* (1647):

divers of them not being content with the adulteries of Polygamy, have loosed the bonds of all matrimony, yea of all naturall relations; telling us . . . that among the Saints there ought to be no difference of husband and wife, Father and daughter, brother and sister, and that such differences were only for imperfect worldlings. (34)

Elsewhere, Baillie again contends, "These saints were exempted from all laws of Matrimony, of bloud and affinity: the difference of Father, Mother, Brother, Sister among them doth cease and vanish" (43).[54] The "differences" which structure and maintain the family are negated by Familist semantic variances, by their own brand of *différance.* Although continental labels for the sect (*Domus Amoris, Domus Charitatis, Haus der Liebe, Hüsgesinn der Lieften,* and *Famille de la Charité* [55]) indicate a strong sense of patriarchal household, and although Niclaes's writings re-construct his spiritual family along patriarchal lines, the "Family of Love" came to signify a travesty of patriarchal order.

Hostile representations of the Family emphasize this rejection of the father. In *A Description of the Sect called the Familie of Love* (1641), a chaste young maid, appropriately enough named Susanna Snow, develops a "great desire" to see the Family. Sneaking away from her father's house, the domestic boundaries of which are clearly demarcated, she meets up with the Family and joins them in an open pasture to hear the delivery of a bawdy sermon. This discourse is addressed to "saints" Ovid and Priapus and is based on a verse from Vergil's epigrams, *"Non stat bene mentula crassa"* – inviting the author of the pamphlet to comment, "Which to English I forbear, because it is obscene" (3). After the sermon, the preacher seduces the not-terribly-unwilling Miss Snow. The meeting of the Family thus seems to be a celebration of phallic dominance, from the figure of Priapus to the preacher's enjoyment of the "sisterhood." But the Latin epigram translates "a thick penis does not stand well" – thus despite the emphatic phallic presence, the sect has a decidedly flaccid basis. The law of the father is restored only when a contrite Susanna forsakes the Family and re-enters the walls of her father's house. The dominance of the father and the Bible is re-established when an orthodox Oxford divine reads passages of Scripture to her.

The Family of Love, driven by its perfectionist doctrine, thus appeared to be the antithesis of patriarchal and phallocentric order. Freed from normative semantic conventions, the Familists were perceived as freely gratifying their sexual desires at the expense of traditional social structures. Knewstub proclaims what he perceives as the proper way to control libidinous impulses: "when we haue our lust and longyng," Knewstub preaches, we should "be vnder the gouernment of the Gospel." [56] The unbounded Familist lust violates ideas of both government and the Gospell. Ultimately, the cultural anxieties surrounding the Family of Love reflect fears of a society based upon personal desire – the very name the "Family of Love" was probably a significant factor in positioning this sect as a favorite target of abuse. In addition to the errors of perfectionism, the Family – as a self-determined religious community – epitomized the perceived evils of voluntary religion. Arguing that religious community should be freely chosen according to personal and spiritual affinities, the Family threatened the very basis for a national church, membership in which was determined by virtue of one's birth, not one's desires.[57] The Family of Love, revolving around the interior, spiritual primacy of the enlightened individual, thus challenged not only the laws of semantics, but the government of men.

Thomas Middleton's *The Family of Love* explores these discursive and social ramifications of Familist doctrine.[58] While the Family of Love seems to present only one social subset in this play, the influence of the sect pervades the entire performance.[59] The sect's conceptual omnipresence is given an architectural manifestation in the form of the (stage) door, behind which the Family holds its nefarious gatherings. Much of the action of the play revolves around this door, and characters repeatedly call attention to it. The merchant Dryfat, for example, speaks of "the Hole in the Wall, where [the Familists] assemble together in the day-time" (5.3.1874–75).[60] We repeatedly meet the Familist Mistress Purge traveling to and from her sectarian meetings, and numerous characters try to gain access to the sect by passing through the door. This is no easy feat. The doorway is carefully guarded by a Familist watchman, and the numerous characters who try to follow Mistress Purge to a gathering of the Family of Love must disguise themselves or discover the precise password to gain entry. Even when Familist characters are not part of a scene, the door remains a visual tease about the possibilities which lie beyond it. The audience is placed in a position similar to that of Knewstub's reader, who is led to the "porch of [the Familists'] Synagogue," only to be left guessing (or imagining) "the shame that is committed in the inwarde roomes."

Throughout the play, various characters receive tantalizing hints about the nature of the Familists' meetings. In Act 4, a lecherous gallant feigns conversion to the sect so that he can gratify his lust with Mistress Purge. He finally asks the question that the play (and the audience?) has begged: "What are we bound unto during the time we remain in the Family?" Mistress Purge responds, "During the light of the candle you are to be very attentive; which being extinguished, how to behave yourselves I will deliver in private whisper" (4.1.1226–29). Much to the dismay of the eavesdropping husband Purge, who has begun to suspect that he is being cuckolded at the Family, the crucial, presumably juicy, details are inaudible. On the verge of discovery, a door is slammed; on the verge of revelation, description is lost. We do not hear a full account of the Family's gatherings until the end of the play, but until then (knowing that "they assemble together in the day-time" and learning that they meet by night as well) the stage door serves as a constant reminder of their continuous, hidden conventicles.

Within the play, the primary means of entering the sect – and entering the door which invites and excludes – is through the guidance of Mistress Purge. As discussed above, the historical Family of Love was structured to permit a gradual spiritual development; initiated "young ones" would gradually progress to the state of "elder," achieving an ever greater degree of spiritual perfection and ever more knowledge of the sect's "*Loue* secretes or priuie mysteries." Within the play, Mistress Purge is identified as an "illuminated elder," a term for those who are already "godded" and therefore sinless (as Rogers explains the term in *The Displaying of an horrible secte*[61]). She therefore repeatedly catechizes the members who desire to be "converted" to the sect. Mistress Purge gives "lessons" on doctrine, "instructions" on morality, and has a reputation for her "talent in edifying young men."[62]

Mistress Purge's "talents" appear to differ from those of the more grizzled schoolmaster depicted in the Familists' *A.B.C.*, however. Through a steady stream of sexual innuendo, Mistress Purge's catechizing becomes a form of seduction. On her way to a nocturnal meeting (a Familist practice again reported in Rogers's tract[63]), Mistress Purge encounters the merchant Dryfat. The two engage in religious discussion, and Mistress Purge attempts to explain the Familist emphasis on the spirit over the flesh – Hendrik Niclaes's idea that the spiritually enlightened have transcended the significance of the body.

DRYFAT: Whither away, Mistress Purge?
M. PURGE: To the Family, Master Dryfat, to our exercise.
DRYFAT: What, by night?
M. PURGE: O Lord, ay, sir, with the candles out too; we fructify best i' th' dark. The glance of the eye is a great matter; it leads us to other objects besides the right.
DRYFAT: Indeed I think we perform those functions best when we are not thrall to the fetters of the body.
M. PURGE: The fetters of the body? What call you them?

DRYFAT: The organs of the body, as some term them.

M. PURGE: Organs? Fie, fie, they have a most abominable squeaking sound in mine ears; they edify not a whit, I detest 'em. I hope my body has no organs.

DRYFAT: To speak more familiarly, Mistress Purge, they are the senses: the sight, hearing, smelling, taste and feeling.

M. PURGE: Ay, marry. Marry, said I? Lord, what a word's that in my mouth! You speak now, Master Dryfat, but yet let me tell you where you err too: this feeling I will prove to be neither organ nor fetter; it is a thing – a sense did you call it?

. . .

Why, then, a sense let it be – I say it is that we cannot be without: for, as I take it, it is a part belonging to understanding; understanding, you know, lifteth up the mind from earth; if the mind be lift up, you know, the body goes with it. Also it descends into the conscience, and there tickles us with our works and doings, so that we make singular use of feeling.

DRYFAT: And not of the rest?

M. PURGE: Not at that time; therefore we hold it not amiss to put out the candles, for the soul sees best i' th' dark.

DRYFAT: You come to me now, Mistress Purge.

M. PURGE: Nay, I will come to you else, Master Dryfat. These senses, as you term them, are of much efficacy in carnal mixtures; that is, when we crowd and thrust a man and woman together. (3.2.926–958)

The Familists' nocturnal meetings are ostensibly intended to create a spiritual, meditative environment, one in which the soul is not distracted by the body and the world. (It was this same division of the internal and the external which seemingly enabled the Familists' practice of verbal dissimulation.) In the course of this conversation, however, the notion of transcending corporeal constraints to achieve a greater spiritual satisfaction is transformed into a legitimization of carnal knowledge. Here, the Familist emphasis on spiritual "fructification" appears to follow the biblical dictate to be fruitful and multiply, and in spite of her rejection of "organs," Mistress Purge's speech becomes laden with sexual double entendre. Her equation of "a thing" (an early modern slang term for penis) with "sense" renders her entire description of spiritual enlightenment a description of sexual intercourse, culminating in Mistress Purge's "conscience" being "tickled." As the exchange continues, the tumescent implications of "under-standing" become even more explicit:

DRYFAT: I commend this zeal in you Mistress Purge; I desire much to be of your society.

M. PURGE: Do you indeed? blessing on your heart. Are you upright in your
    dealings?
DRYFAT: Yes, I do love to stand to any thing I do.   (3.2.963–67)

Mistress Purge's question about Dryfat's morality/potency appears
to express the prerequisites for joining the sect; while the two
meanings of "upright" might appear to contradict one another,
within the context of fictive Familist discourse the two become
mutually constitutive.

In *The Family of Love* such sexual punning is relentless, and is an
integral element of the Familist representation. As Joanne Altieri
comments, "Middleton works constantly and consistently
throughout the play in a double language. It seems at times that
every word can become a pun."[64] Altieri views such incessant
punning as part of Middleton's attempt to satirize "the confusion of
literal and figurative meanings fostered by sectarian rhetoric . . .
What interested Middleton was the metaphoric extensions in such
language as Niclaes's and the comic use that he could make of
his fleshly allegorizations by taking them literally – as he claims
Niclaes's followers selectively did" (48). Niclaes not only advocated
an allegorical reading of the Scripture, but seemed to demand an
allegorical reading of his own writing by virtue of his obscure,
elusive style, which, in the words of Julia G. Ebel, is "characterized
by an incomprehensible flow of nouns and adjectives, only rarely
linked by verbs."[65] The entire doctrine and literary corpus of
Familism, one could argue, is a move towards linguistic abstraction.
Middleton at once duplicates this process and reverses it. Through
incessantly pointing out double meanings, Middleton transforms
religious language back into somatic registers.[66]

Many of the puns in *The Family of Love*, like "conversation," exploit
the simultaneity of discursive and sexual activity. Reminded of
Wilkinson's description of how the "*vpright* seruice of the Familie is
ministred: whereunto all seruices and prophecies . . . do lead, as to the
right and very true perfection" (*A Confutation*, sig. B3ᵛ, my emphases),
we hear that Mistress Purge lies abed awaiting her lover Doctor
Glister, who comes to "minister" to her (1.3.261; 2.1.383). The
gallants Lipsalve and Gudgeon also use this expression; Lipsalve
jealously asks, "What, has she ministered to thee then?", to which
Gudgeon replies, "Faith, some lectuary or so" (2.3.452–53). The
discursive practices of reformist religion (the emphasis on the idea of

ministers and sermons) double as terms for coitus, as "lectuary"
becomes audibly indistinguishable from "lechery." Mistress Purge's
"iniquity at the Family of Love" (5.3.1871) is to be proven "with
notes out of her cotations" (1879–80). The practice of taking notes at
sermons is again given sexual significance through the phonic
allegiance of "cotations" and "coitus." Within the final trial scene,
even the language of legal certainty assumes a sexual register. When
he gives his testimony, Lipsalve is required to "Kiss the book" and
almost immediately recounts, "I think I kissed [Mistress Purge] at
the Family some three times" (5.3.1995, 1997–98); the act which
guarantees linguistic integrity is thus immediately elided into a sign
of sexual transgression. Finally, Dryfat (disguised as a Proctor)
proclaims that he has "spent some study in the mystical cases of
venery. I can describe how often a man may lie with another man's
wife before 'a come to the white sheet" (4.4.1543–45). In these few
lines, the discourses of law and sexuality become thoroughly
enmeshed through the puns on "case" (slang for vagina) and
"come"; the verbal and the sexual again converge through the
duality of "lie" and the blank page of the "white sheet."

Verbal ambiguity serves as both a description of sexual intercourse
and a condition for Familist sex. In his ongoing attempts to "woo"
Mistress Purge, Lipsalve claims that he can only enter the "Frater-
nity" if he "dissemble cunningly" (4.1.1204). It is through the verbal
machinations of such cunning linguists (the play seems to demand
the pun) that Familist adultery is sanctioned. At one point in the
play, Mistress Purge's apprentice is interrogated about the nature of
the sect:

M. GLISTER: And I prithee Club, what kind of creatures are these
    Familists? Thou art conversant with them.
CLUB: What are they? With reverence be it spoken, they are the most
    accomplished creatures under heaven; in them is all perfection.
M. GLISTER: As how, good Club?
CLUB: Omitting their outward graces, I'll show you only one instance,
    which includes all other: they love their neighbours better than
    themselves.
M. GLISTER: Not than themselves, Club.
CLUB: Yes, better than themselves, for they love them better than their
    husbands, and husband and wife are all one; therefore better than
    themselves.   (2.4.548–59)

The effect of such continual puns and verbal equivocation is the erosion of meaning, as Familist "perfection" becomes indicative of imperfect verbal and sexual systems.

Towards the end of the play we finally hear a description of the secretive Familist gatherings. Lipsalve, continually in pursuit of Mistress Purge, infiltrates the sect. At one of the Familist conventicles, he is on the verge of gratifying his appetite for Mistress Purge, when suddenly his desire is

> . . . counter-check'd
> By strange and unexpected accidents.
> For by disguise procuring full access,
> Nay, ready to have [seiz'd] th' expected prize,
> The candle out, steps 'twix my hopes and me
> Some pleasant groin, possess'd and full enjoy'd
> That sweet for which our vigilant eyes have watch'd.
>
> (4.4.1473–79)

Meeting in the dark, the Familist meetings are revealed as consisting of random, anonymous, haphazard couplings. Familist sexual activity, where sexual partners become endlessly replaceable, thus becomes a physical manifestation of a linguistic structure which ceases to have a determined order. Puns create a language in which signifiers are not only separated from their referent, but are endlessly and promiscuously re-aligned.

The Family's claims to perfectionism also enable a profound erasure of familial relations. Over the course of *The Family of Love*, radical Familist tenets seep into the lives of nearly all of the characters. The play interrogates the idea of "family" as it follows the interrelations of four familial groupings: the Doctor and Mistress Glister, and Glister's niece and ward, Maria; Maria, her lover Gerardine, and, by the end of the play, their unborn child; Purge the Apothecary, his wife Mistress Purge, and their apprentice Club; and the randy gallants Lipsalve and Gudgeon, who form their own homosocial couple. Through the circulation of rampant sexual energies the boundaries between these families are transgressed and eroded. The virtual collapse of patriarchal familial structures is due, in part, to the influence of the sexually independent Mistress Purge. This female Familist has, in fact, some sort of sexual relationship with nearly every male character in the play: she is Purge's wife, Glister's regular lover, possibly Dryfat's lover, and the gallants' object of desire. (The only characters who do not demonstrate a sexual desire for her are Gerardine, Club the apprentice and two minor servants.) Through Mistress Purge, most of the characters have direct contact with Familism: some are converted to the sect (Dryfat), are invited to convert (Gerardine), pretend to convert (Lipsalve, Gudgeon), infiltrate Familist meetings (Purge, Lipsalve, Gudgeon), have intimate knowledge of the Family via Mistress Purge (Club), or have intimate knowledge of Mistress Purge herself (Glister). Familist tenets are not isolated within the sect or incidental to the play, but a pervasive structural feature.

Familist notions are articulated, for instance, by the characters who seem to have the least to do with the Family of Love: Gerardine and Maria, the play's impassioned lovers. In their saccharine verse exchanges, these two profess the function of "love" as the defining force of social affinity. The lovers are separated by the monetary interests of Maria's ward and uncle, Doctor Glister. Maria vehemently argues against the validity of her confinement, claiming that she should be allowed to chose her own society: "why should mutual love, confirm'd by heaven, B'infring'd by men?" (3.1.7667–68). Throughout the play, Familist language and community are organized around desire, as *The Family of Love* performs a struggle between the competing claims of "love" and "law" as the basis for social order. The play opens with an attempt to define "love": the word appears thirty times in the first two short scenes. The play concludes with an interrogation of "law," which is used sixteen times in the final scene. Throughout the play, then, "love" and "law" wrestle for the supreme position in determining familial relations and structures. The final outcome is perhaps best expressed by Maria, who exclaims: "O silly men, which seek to keep in awe / Women's affections, which can know no law!" (1.1.55–56).

At the end of the play, Mistress Purge – and the tenets of the Family of Love – are actually put on trial. Purge has charged his wife with adultery, and the case is taken up by Gerardine and the Familist Dryfat, both in disguise and acting as a church court. Mistress Purge is called forward:

GERARDINE: Who is her accuser?
DRYFAT: Her own husband, upon the late discovery of a crew of narrow-[ruffed], strait-laced, yet loose-bodied dames, with a rout of omnium-gatherums, assembled by the title of the Family of Love; which, Master Doctor, if they be not punished and suppressed by our club law, each man's copyhold will become freehold, specialties will turn to generalities, and so from unity to parity, from parity to plurality, and from

plurality to universality; their wives, the only ornaments of their houses, and of all their wares, goods, and chattel[s], the chief moveables, will be made common.

PURGE: Most voluble and eloquent proctor!

GERARDINE: Byrlady, these enormities must and shall be redressed, otherwise I see their charter will be infringed, and their ancient staff of government the club (from whence we derive our law of castigation), this club, I say, they seeming nothing less than men by their fore-part, will be turned upon their own heads. Speak, Rebecca Purge: art thou one of this Family? hast thou ever known the body of any man there or elsewhere concupiscentically?

(5.3.1951–69)

In keeping with the pattern of the play, the abstract concept of the law is given a sexual, physical form through the idea of "club law."[67] The (female) Familists, through their claims of spiritual independence and sexual freedom, are credited with leveling the very structure of a patriarchal system. The violent phallic dominance implied by the reimposition of the "club" appears to be the means of restoring patriarchal social order. The "club" also promises to reassert a phallogocentric discursive order. In Dryfat's speech, the Family of Love is specifically identified with loquacious women, an association that Purge makes earlier when he grumbles, "for my part I like not this Family, nor indeed some kind of private lecturing that women use" (3.2.1006–08).[68]

But while the trial may begin as an overdue re-assertion of patriarchal hierarchy and control, it soon constitutes a mockery of "club law."[69] True to Familist form, Mistress Purge replies to the charge with a series of equivocal and dissembling answers. Her evasive strategy is effective, and she escapes punishment while also painting the Family as a chaste and charitable community. Her self-defense is so effective that in the end it is Purge (whom the audience knows to have a rightful suit) who is castigated as a jealous husband, his "evidence insufficient, and indeed too weak, to foil [his] wife's uprightness" (5.3.2135–36). Mistress Purge, not the club, proves "upright." The trial thus appears to legitimate not only Mistress Purge's slippery, ever-shifting language, but her random, promiscuous sexuality as well. Purge's emasculation is complete when the "court" advises him that, since Mistress Purge has become "a stranger in [his] land of Ham," he should "readvance [his] standard, give her new press-money" (5.3.2137–39). The means to earthly paradise, Purge's "land of Ham" (1 Chronicles 4:40, with a vivid sexual pun), is cast in terms of a return to military order and obedience. Purge complies with the advice, telling his wife, "so thou wilt promise me to come no more at the Family, I receive thee into the lists of my favour" (5.3.2146–48). But Mistress Purge's ambivalent response rejects her husband's offer of a truce, reasserting instead her right to love freely: "Truly husband, my love must be free still to God's creatures; yea nevertheless preserving you as the head of my body, I will do as the spirit shall enable me" (5.3.2149–51). In her final line, Mistress Purge reasserts her loyalty to the Family rather than to her husband.

The "trial," even as it represents the right of law, is in itself a mockery of legal and patriarchal privilege. The entire trial scene has been orchestrated by Gerardine in an attempt to trick Glister into giving consent for the marriage of his niece, the by-now-very-pregnant Maria. Gerardine and Dryfat have therefore disguised themselves in the roles of proctor and paritor in the church courts. The hostile call for the club law to suppress the Family is spoken by Dryfat, himself a Familist – thus the bitter castigation of the Family (as the audience realizes) is but a mocking travesty.[70] Even within the scene Gerardine makes a winking acknowledgement of Dryfat's Familism when he exclaims, "Leave your allegories, your metaphors and circumlocutions" (5.3.1939–40).[71] Both the authority of the church and the authority of the law are ridiculed and usurped. Patriarchal familial rights are also overturned when the feigned trial achieves its pur- pose, the marriage of Gerardine and Maria against the wishes of her legal guardian Doctor Glister. Rather than the reassertion of phallic, patriarchal dominance that takes place in the tale of Susanna Snow, the play thus concludes with an affirmation of families based on "love." The sexual freedom of Mistress Purge is vindicated and even sanctioned, and the coupling of Gerardine and Maria is determined according to their own personal wills and desires rather than the authority of the patriarch. As the court itself becomes an extended scene of dissembling, even the integrity of language and law is playfully undermined. It is difficult to read this final scene as anything but a stunning explosion of ecclesiastical, social, and discursive order – the consequences, it would seem, of the seeping influence of the Family of Love. In the final line of the play, Gerardine even appears to draw the audience into the all-encompassing sect: "Now join with me / For approbation of our Family" (5.3.2172–73). Rather than castigating the Family, the play ultimately celebrates it.

The Family of Love has been read as a mocking, even bitter, assault on the sect of the title. Literary critics seem to assume that a contemporary audience would have been morally outraged at the very thought of a secretive, literate, and possibly sexually innovative community. But the vitriolic and hyperbolic response the Family produced is perhaps not so much the expression of a universal condemnation as testament to a general tolerance of the Family. Texts such as those by Rogers, Knewstub, and Wilkinson, which emphatically warn of the insidious nature of this seemingly benign sect, claim that they sound the alarm because of the public's nonchalance – or even the public's attraction – towards Familist ideas. In fact, the public attitude to known Familists was surprisingly tolerant, as Christopher Marsh demonstrates; the rigorous opposition that appeared in print belies a degree of public acceptance of religious difference within the community.[72] Thus *The Family of Love*, which stages a victory for the subversive freedoms of Familism over the rigors of the law, may well have catered to an audience curious about and sympathetic to this form of radical religion. Indeed, the play itself, with its tolerant, albeit playfully mocking representation of the Family, may have been the cause for even further anti-Familist invective. In one narrative of events, *The Family of Love*, first performed between 1602 and 1604 by the Children of the Revels, attacked the sect by performing the practices Rogers and Wilkinson described; this negative depiction of the group inspired the actual Family to produce its *Supplication* in 1604. But in an alternative storyline, *The Family of Love* (revived by the King's Revels sometime in 1606 or 1607) – with its playful vindication of the Family – may have provoked the anti-Familist response *A Svpplication . . . Examined, and found to be derogatory* (1606). Given that the Family was virtually non-existent by this point, it is entirely possible that the new attack on the sect was inspired not by Familist activity but by the popularity of a play which condoned sectarian behavior.

But if *The Family of Love* concludes with a celebratory upheaval of patriarchal sexual and linguistic order, this disruption is not without cost. While Mistress Purge's libidinous lifestyle is exonerated and she leaves the play free to pursue the inclinations of her "spirit," this sexual liberty and its consequence, the reconfigured sectarian family, carry the potential of social and civil disruption. Underscoring *The Family of Love*, for example, are dark intimations of incest, the alleged

Familist practice which threatened socio-familial implosion. For Mistress Purge and her fellows, Familism implies sexual liberation, while for the Glisters sexual variance leads to the disintegration of domestic order; the discovery of her husband's alleged infidelity and seemingly incestuous relationship with his niece causes Mistress Glister, previously the keeper of meticulous household order, to cry in anguish, "Incest, fornication, abomination in my own house!" (4.3.1452–53). Seeking revenge, Mistress Glister resolves to engage in adultery with Gudgeon and Lipsalve. For these two gallants, however, the purgative influence of the Family has not only thwarted their attempts at sexual conquest, but has incapacitated them. In a remarkable moment of historical foreshadowing, the cavalier Gudgeon exclaims of the sectarian Mistress Purge, "I am sure she is ominous to me: she makes civil wars and insurrections in the state of my stomach" (2.3.448–49). Even while reveling in the possibilities of verbal ambiguity, and even while celebrating the idea of self-selected spiritual and sexual community, *The Family of Love* nonetheless hints at the potential social repercussions of such radical conversations.

CHAPTER 4

Dissecting sectarianism: swarms, forms, and Thomas Edwards's "Gangræna"

> We have the plague of *Egypt* upon us, frogs out of the bottom-lesse pit covering our land, comming into our Houses, Bedchambers, Beds, Churches; a man can hardly come into any place, but some croaking frog or other will be comming up on him.
>
> Thomas Edwards, *Gangræna*, 1646 (I: sig. RI^r)

Determined to illustrate the nature of Roman Catholic error, in 1580 George Gilpin translated a Dutch tract entitled *The Bee hiue of the Romishe Churche*. Although Gilpin admits that a treatise on ecclesiastical difference may "by reason of the manifoldnesse of the matter . . . be wearisome to reade" (3^v), he compensates for such "tediousnesse" by providing an extended animated comparison between the Catholic Church and the physical and hierarchical structure of a beehive. After describing the beehive's physical form and composition, the text proceeds to wax eloquent on "the qualitie and sundrie sortes of Bees" (352^v). We read of the bees with "redde scarlet wings" (353) who are closest to the king bee, down through the ranks to the bees who

haue nothing else to doe, but with an irksome buzzing by day and night doe swarme in their hiue. But they knowe their rule, howe and when they shall swarme, and are for that cause called *Regulares*, or by a Greeke worde *Canonici*. Some are appointed eache over his honicombe apart, which they call Parishes, by reason whereof they are called Parish Priests. The other are as Presidents in the conuocation house, and have eache about ten Bees under their iurisdiction, whereof they are called in Greeke *Decani*. (354^v)

This lengthy expostulation of the hive is graphically reinforced by an introductory woodcut depicting various bees engaged in nasty popish activities around a particularly grim-looking bee-pope. A variation on this woodcut, appearing at the end of the text, presents the hive from a more distanced perspective, at which point the "hive" is now clearly revealed as the pope's hat resting on a table.

The Bee hiue offers a fascinating commentary on the balance between order and disorder. While the bees are referred to as "swarming," this chaos is always contained within the regulations of the church. The swarming only takes place *within* the hive, for "they knowe their rule, howe and when they shall swarme"; the teeming mass is governed by social distinctions of the parish and the "iurisdiction" of the convocation house. This tension between images of chaos and organization is an inherent part of *The Bee hiue* from the start. John Stell's letter "To the Reader" informs us that "thou hast such a booke, as wil make thee priuie to all the practices of the Babylonicall beast, (Rome I meane) the denne of Dragons and diuels"; yet this "denne" is soon anatomized into "the Pope, the Colledge of Cardinals, Monasteries of Monkes, Fraternities of Friers, Nestes of Nonnes, and the rest of the Pharisaical Frie."

In the tumultuous decades of the mid-seventeenth century, the threat of religious division and dissension continued to be widely represented through images of insect life. But whereas texts such as *The Bee hiue* emphasize the ultimately regimented, social nature of the papist swarm (which is always acting under the auspices of the pope), the abundant pamphlet literature of the 1640s proclaims that the swarm has escaped from its containment; like the plagues of Egypt, swarms now seem to cover the land.[1] Anti-sectarian literature is infested with figurative accounts of teeming bees, frogs, locusts, serpents, eels, and maggots. Archbishop Laud, for example, employs the image of the swarm when commiserating with Sir William Boswell, then ambassador at The Hague, about the number of separatists spreading through England and The Netherlands. "I am sorry to heare," sympathizes Laud, "That such Swarmes of Waspes (for Bees they are not) are flowne over to those parts, & with such Clamors against Our Church-Affaires; for which (God be thanked) there's noe Cause. Nor hath the Church of England suffer'd of late any way so much, as by theire Base & Libellous both Tongues & Pennes. For which God forgive them."[2] Laud's pointed distinction between wasps and bees is an inversion of the classical image of the hive as the ideal model of political order, a motif that was perpetuated by the mid-seventeenth-century proliferation of scientific treatises on bee keeping.[3]

Significantly, Laud equates the swarm with noise ("Clamors") and verbal outpouring "by their Base and Libellous both Tongues & Pennes." The swarm functioned not only as a means of registering the perceived political anarchy of sectarianism, but also the unrestrained discursivity which created and accompanied the destruction of hierarchical order. In the decades prior to 1640, religious nonconformity was associated with divergent forms of religious speech, and the subversive implications of ecclesiastical separation seemed to be illustrated by the secretive circulation of tracts such as those by Hendrik Niclaes or Martin Marprelate.[4] In the 1640s, sectarianism became an issue of discursivity itself. Responding to social and economic turmoil, prophets prophesied, preachers sermonized, laymen and divines pamphleteered, wives petitioned, armies debated. The collapse of censorship and an eager readership propelled this verbal outpouring into print, as prophesies, sermons, petitions, and debates were recorded in material, commodified form. The statistics continue to astound: in 1640, twenty-two pamphlets were printed – in 1642, nearly 2,000.[5] Discussions over diverse socio-political and ecclesiastical perspectives often turned into an interrogation of the very media through which such debates were performed.

Conservative authors claimed that the sudden outburst of pamphleteering was perpetrated by radical sectarians. John Taylor repeatedly emphasizes the sectarians' dependence on print; or, as he puts it, "Inck-squittering Treacherous Pamphlets are the maine proppe and piller to uphold the soveraign unsavoury power of their Factious Conventicles."[6] To Taylor and others, this textual proliferation assumed the shape – or rather the shapelessness – of a swarm. In Taylor's pamphlet *A Swarme of Sectaries, and Schismatiqves* (1641), he writes that "These kind of Vermin swarm like Caterpillars" (7). An anonymous adversary (Henry Walker?) took offense at such comparisons, and replied with *An Answer to a Foolish Pamphlet Entitvled A swarme of Sectaries & Schismaticks* (1641);[7] Taylor himself fired back with *A Reply as true as Steele, to a Rusty, Rayling, Ridiculous, Lying Libell . . . called by the name of An Answer to a foolish Pamphlet Entituled, A Swarme of Sectaries and Schismatiques* (1641). Taylor appears to get the last word, comparing the sectarians to "Froggs and Toades [who] do breed from Putred slime" (*Reply*, 5). Taylor appears self-conscious, however, of his own role in this process of reproduction: the abundant pamphlets attacking arguments for congregational independence were themselves a large source of the textual outpouring.

The more religious conservatives attempted to contain the spread of religious division, the more they added to the uncontrollable discursive chaos.

This proliferation of published texts was accompanied by a profusion of radical speech. While pamphlets flew from the presses, extemporaneous prophesies flooded the air, as uneducated, mechanic "tub preachers" were reported to be delivering sermons throughout London. "What swarms are there of all sorts of illiterate mechanick Preachers, yea of Women and Boy Preachers!" exclaims Thomas Edwards.[8] Such radical activity was self-authorized by claims of "liberty of conscience," in which the individual spirit was granted primacy over the regulating strictures of social order. "Liberty of conscience" not only mandated a personal, interior freedom, but endorsed – even seemed to require – the vocal expression of one's spiritual beliefs. In the frenetic atmosphere of the 1640s, this spiritual individualism appeared to defy genre: the verbal outpourings of personal consciences created discursive as well as social anarchy. In this chapter, I will explore the discursive implications of liberty of conscience, and the ways in which the perceived linguistic disorder was represented by images of the swarm. I will then focus on the writings of Thomas Edwards, a presbyterian minister who set out to quell the sectarian chaos through an elaborate project of cataloguing and classifying the noise of the sectarian din. In his voluminous *Gangræna* (1646), Edwards self-consciously attempts to impose a taxonomic system on discursive dissonance as a means of re-establishing ecclesiastical and social harmony.

In the mid-seventeenth century, "liberty of conscience" became a buzz-word among radical authors. The idea indicated the primacy of the enlightened individual over worldly hierarchies and dictates.[9] A focus on the individual Christian believer had been an important facet of Protestantism from the sixteenth century onward; Geoffrey Nuttall notes how various intellectual strands "combined to direct men's attention, for the first time in their lives and with some suddenness, to the nature of religion in the Bible, and more especially in the New Testament, as something individually experienced, a living, personal relationship, open to Everyman, between God and his soul." In the radical theology of the 1640s, these elements develop into "pure and acknowledged individualism."[10] Many (or even most) of those authors writing for "liberty of

conscience" were primarily concerned with religious toleration and
the right of a Christian to choose his or her own congregation. But
those vehemently arguing for a strong central church hierarchy
perceived "liberty of conscience" as a cry for a radical individualism,
an anarchical substitute for ecclesiastical order.

The notion of an all-powerful individual conscience has obvious
subversive implications. For radical authors, "conscience" was the
interior voice of the divine, and they defend the rights of "every
naturall man . . . in whose *Conscience* God hath his *throne*, ruling him
by the light of *nature* to a Civill outward good and end."[11] Claims to
"liberty of conscience" positioned God and not the king as the
Christian's supreme "Civill" authority. But for opponents of such
spiritual liberty, the reliance upon an internal, invisible, and subjective conscience as the basis for civil order was obviously problematic. In *Of Conscience* (Oxford, 1645) Henry Hammond emphasizes
that, due to its abstract and self-referential nature, "conscience"
defies a universal definition; Hammond writes that the "specious
venerable name of *Conscience* . . . is now by some Christians . . .
worshipt in so many corporeous shapes, that there is at length scarce
any thing so vile (Phansie, humour, passion, prepossession, the
meanest worldly interest of the ambitious or covetous designer . . .)
but hath the favour or luck to be mistaken for *Conscience*" (1). Given
this arbitrary and inscrutable nature of conscience, it cannot be
controlled or disciplined by the authorities. Fearful pamphleteers
warn of the scores of sects "which could wish every Sectary might
have liberty to use their owne consciences and opinions, as if there
were no Rule of consciences."[12]

With no common "Rule of conscience," no universal creed of
morality, there can be no Ruler of conscience, no overriding figure
invested with social authority. "Independency" seemed to designate
an extreme form of political egocentrism; one author describes the
tub preacher as one who "hath neither reference, nor Dependency
with any other authority, but of his own body."[13] Even the idea of
universal "truth" itself becomes individualized and relative; another
author contends that when "truth is made the object of every
contentious fancy, and so becomes opinion, needes must there
proceed much tumult, much division, and much distraction to the
great disgrace and scandal of the true Protestant Religion."[14] Some
radical authors seemed to justify these conservative fears, as they
gleefully reveled in what they saw as the dawning of a new age of

spiritual autonomy and the dissolution of hierarchies. In *The Peasants Price of Spirituall Liberty* (1642), Nathaniel Homes declares that, "The partition wall is downe: all are subjects to Christs Kingdome; all brethren; no longer slaves, so much as *civilly*. And *Ecclesiastically*; all needlesse Ceremonies, superstitions and humane inventions put downe" (15). With victory for liberated consciences, the kingdom of God, in Homes's view, had at last replaced a worldly order of hierarchical separation.

Others arguing for "liberty of conscience," however, see not the elimination of "partitions," but their erection based on natural spiritual affinities and affections; a system of voluntary, self-organized congregations is perceived as the path to social harmony. In *Liberty of Conscience* (1643), Henry Robinson notes the value of religious toleration: "all degrees of people having once tasted the sweetnesse" of religious liberty, the enlightened man will "by that means become a sure establisher of the generall peace of the Kingdome, and dispose every one more willingly to submit to higher powers . . . when he apprehends himself certain to enjoy the Liberty of his Conscience."[15] In a gesture which reverses the prevalent anti-sectarian arguments, Robinson maintains that it is enforced ecclesiastical unity which leads to social turmoil, and religious separation which provides structure:

I crave leave to aske, if it be not a far greater confusion both before God and man, and of more dangerous consequence to the State, and their owne soules, for a thousand men and women of ten severall religions or opinions to assemble together every Sunday in a Parish Church for feare of imprisonment, fines, banishment and worse, or else that the same thousand men and women being permitted freely, may meet in a peaceable manner at ten severall places according to their respective differing opinions and religion.[16]

Left to follow their own consciences and opinions, Robinson argues, men and women will naturally arrange themselves into logical ecclesiastical divisions; forced together by the thousands, they will become an intermingled chaos. In this view, division leads to order, while unity creates confusion and disorder.[17]

Discussions over liberty of conscience thus frequently became discussions about the relationship of the individual to society, as radical claims of spiritual independence conflicted with older notions of communality. A word which encapsulates this conflict is "opinion"; the term at once applies to the thoughts of an individual mind, and to the collective mindset. "Opinion" is often used interchangeably or synonymously with "sect" and "religion." Robinson employs phrases such as "of ten severall religions or opinions"; another pamphleteer writes of "Sects, Schismes, and opinions."[18] John Milton and Thomas Edwards both use the phrase "other sects and opinions."[19] But "opinion" can also indicate the beliefs not of a community, but of one private individual: "There is such giddinesse in the profession of Religion, that every one almost is led by his own opinion, and most men in matters of judgement are divided one against another," writes John Taylor.[20] Henry Parker, in *A Discourse Concerning Puritans* (1641), perceived the compression of the community into the autonomous Christian: "There are almost as many Religions as Opinions, and as many Opinions as Men" (6). "Opinion" thus signifies religion, sect, and conscience; it is at once indicative of a communal phenomenon and an individual impulse. In its ambivalence, "opinion" resembles the paradoxical meaning of the word "individual"; as Peter Stallybrass has demonstrated, during the seventeenth century, "individual" signified both indivisible and discrete.[21] "Opinion," like "individual," is thus symptomatic of social relations and categories in flux, of the transforming relationship of the one to the many.

In their dependence on the ambivalence of "opinion," sectarians themselves seemed to become, as William Prynne proclaims, "Anarchicall Paradoxes."[22] This paradoxical nature of sectarianism is graphically illustrated in the image of the swarm: a tightly interwoven conglomerate of self-referential beings. The swarm registers the confluence of inseparability and divisibility. On the one hand, sects were perceived as exclusive, private gatherings of fellow worshippers whose intimacy often translated into physical terms; yet on the other hand, sectarian modes of prayer and preaching and the emphasis on liberty of conscience were perceived as creating an independent, self-enclosed individual, the one-person church. In anti-sectarian pamphlets, this tension between community and individuality is often explored through the dynamics of the tavern. With the resurgence of Marprelate-like tracts in the 1640s, anti-sectarian authors frequently portrayed alehouse scenarios. One pamphleteer laments that

So in these later times, through an unconfined liberty of expounding, and over publike and unseasonable reasoning and disputing upon that subject; every one presuming of his own Talent either of wit or grace; the sacred

Text is so abused and mangled with variety of Opinions that it is become the common subject of discourse, as well in tavernes and upon Alehouse benches, as in private houses and out walkings. No marvaile then that there are now well-nigh as many Sects and different opinions sprung as there be professors.[23]

Positioning religious debates in the context of an alehouse, site of carnival and communitas, accentuates the seeming absurdity of claims to religious autonomy, as the scene is simultaneously one of social union and spiritual disunion. The final clause of this passage – "as many Sects and different opinions sprung as there be professors" – epitomizes the paradox of "opinion," as the word hinges the collective and the independent.

As this passage also demonstrates, sectarianism was legitimated and produced by interpretive violence performed upon the "sacred Text." Pamphleteers routinely attack the sectarians for "set[ting] up the conscience above the Scriptures, making every mans conscience, even the polluted defiled seared consciences the rule of faith and holinesse, before the pure and unerring Word of God."[24] As the Bible becomes the "common discourse," it ceases to function as a basis for shared religion. For conservative authors, a common body of text was that which ensured a communal body of Christ. The integrity of the church was challenged by the interpretive freedoms afforded by "liberty of conscience"; it was even further eroded when in 1645 the Book of Common Prayer, that which affirmed and ordered liturgical ritual, was abolished altogether.[25] In lieu of an established liturgy, the sectaries favored extemporaneous prayer. "The *Brownist* would have no *Common Prayer*, onely extemporary Prayer, by the motion of the Spirit," observes Taylor.[26] Praying extemporaneously, the sectarians no longer adhere to scripted discourse, are no longer actors according to a religious ritual sanctioned by national church authorities, but become spontaneous and spurious improvisers. Already mocked for their lack of learning and biblical ignorance, sectarians become associated with the outright rejection of ecclesiastical text. In Abraham Cowley's *The Civil War*, for example, the ragged character "Schisme" carries torn liturgies.[27]

The sectarians' preaching, like their prayer, also appeared to avoid any textual dependence. Decades of reformist energies had been dedicated to ensuring a more educated, biblically trained preaching clergy; the radical extemporaneous preaching and "prophesying" of the 1640s appeared to flout these efforts. The sectary, according to one conservative pamphleteer, "had rather heare a Cobler, or a Feltmaker preach, so hee doth it *extempore*, then heare a premeditated Sermon, pend, and preach'd by a Scholler who can distinguish, and unloke the secrets of the Scripture."[28] The scholarly methods of unpacking and analyzing text – premeditation, writing, speaking from a script – are replaced by the immediacy of spontaneous speech. Tub preachers, in particular, became notorious for their lack of biblical authority. Their sermons are portrayed as a travesty of the traditional form; rather than a meticulous parsing of the biblical text, the Scripture is supplied only as an impetus for the imagination. In *A Swarme of Sectaries, and Schismatiques*, Taylor describes a sermon given by a notorious tub preacher named Samuel How: "A worthy Brother gave the Text, and than / The Cobler (How) his preachment strait began / Extemp'ry without any meditation, / But only by the Spirits revelation" (9).[29] In a pamphlet known as *Tobies Dog*, after initially citing a passage of (apocryphal) Scripture, the preacher begins to pontificate upon the finer points of his own canine companion.[30] Some unlearned radical preachers do not even pay lip service to the Bible, as the "text" of the sermon becomes loosely and abstractly defined: "My Text you heare is *Love*, a very necessary Text in these contentious times" preaches a joiner, who claims that his profession makes him an expert on the subject.[31]

These sermons, we might imagine, were not subdued performances. Richard Carter describes sectarian preaching in *The Schismatick Stigmatized* (1641):

And in stead of Orthodoxe Divines, they set up all kinde of Mechanicks, as Shooe-makers, Coblers, Taylors, and Botchers: Glovers, who preach of nothing but *Mag-pies*, and Crows, Boxe-Makers, and Button-Makers, Coach-men, and Felt-makers, and Bottle-Ale-sellers, these predicant Mechanicks, and lawlesse lads do affect an odde kind of gesture in their Poopits [*sic*], vapouring and throwing heads, hands, and shoulders this way, and that way, puffing and blowing, grinning, and gerning, shewing their teeth, and snuffling thorow their noses: hereby they astonish and amaze the poor ignorant multitude, perswading them that he is a fellow that looketh into deeper matters, than the common sort: when indeed hee hath lately rub'd over some old moth-eaten Schismaticall Pamphlet: then he stampeth with his feet, and belaboureth the poore Cushion, and maketh the dust thereof flye about both his eares, beating the Pulpit with both his fists, in a passion of blinde zeale, able to drive his unlucky Auditors, out of their little wits, or seven senses. (sig. B1^{r-v})

Such was the image of the liberated conscience. Through his wild physical antics, and through his dismissal of any text but an "old moth-eaten Schismaticall Pamphlet" (food for the swarm), the preacher dramatizes his self-referential, unregulated spirit. His auditors are impressed at his seeming ability to "see" further into matters, but the preacher's spiritual solipsism is evidenced by his "blinde" zeal.

While the preacher in this account does not actually *speak*, he does produce, like "*Mag-pies* and Crows," abundant noise, stamping, "snuffling," puffing and blowing. "Liberty of conscience" not only led to the paradoxical social features of the swarm, but by enabling the random articulations of interior spirituality it also seemed to create an audible chaos. In their widespread and vocal outpourings of the inner spirit, the disunited voices swell into a cacophonous din. Carter writes that sectarians "allow not any set formes of Prayer, because set formes doe limit and bind the Spirit (forsooth) but these *Mag-pies* with their chattering and vaine babling, doe horribly limit the devotion of all understanding men."[32] The auditory nature of the sectarian swarm is indicated in the full title of Taylor's pamphlet: *A Swarme of Sectaries, and Schismatiqves: Wherein is discovered the strange preaching (or prating) of such as are by their trades Coblers, Tinkers, Pedlers, Weavers, Sowgelders, and Chymney-Sweepers.*

Translated into auditory terms, the unbounded expressions of liberated consciences become inescapable, filling the air and thus surrounding conformists and sectarians alike. In *An Antidote against The Contagious Air of Independency* (1644), D. P. P. writes of "these numerous swarmes of Sectaries, that infest the Aire of the Land with their erroneous and blasphemous opinions" (24). Another author writes of "those infinite number of *Pamphlets* and *Libells*, wherewith . . . the Citie and Countrey is pestered, and the ayre thereof infected and poysoned with the sulphurous breathings of their vanitie, prophanenesse and lyes."[33] Anti-sectarian pamphlets reverberate with the hum, buzz, and clamor of public prayer and preaching. Sectarians are continually the source of "hubbubs and strange tumults raised," of "strange hub-bub, and formerly unheard of hurly-burly."[34] Pamphleteers frequently provide a rich soundtrack for the graphic images of swarming locusts, frogs, bees, and snakes. Richard Carter describes a sectarian gathering: "Then I conceited, I heard the fore-named Rout and Rabble whispering, crooking, and hissing, like Toads, Snakes, Adders, and Serpents, bussing, and huffing like whole swarmes of Bees, Waspes, and Hornets, thus croking, hissing, buzzing, and huffing on both sides mine eares" (15). As opposed to the organized, synthesized voice of standardized liturgy, this leaderless confluence of individual voices leads to ecclesiastical cacophony. Liberty of conscience, by enabling and even mandating the open, independent expression of the spirit, was perceived by many as transforming society into a discursive Babel.[35]

Sectarians, according to a character in one pamphlet, "must not be allowed to pray *ex tempore*, no not to pray at all without a set Form and Order (Order say I)."[36] While most pamphleteers of the 1640s critique sectarian discourse through emphasizing the disruptive, seething qualities of the swarm, Thomas Edwards exploits this same image only to reorganize sectarian speech and "opinions" according to his own form and order. While others hear only a collective hissing which defies categorization, Edwards endeavors to separate and to distinguish the disparate voices of the din. In his *Discourse on Language*, Michel Foucault writes of "a profound logophobia," a fear "of everything that could possibly be violent, discontinuous, querulous, disordered even and perilous in . . . the incessant, disorderly buzzing of discourse." As a means of analyzing this fear, Foucault claims that we must "restore to discourse its character as an event."[37] The image of the swarm, as it was used in the seventeenth century, registers this logophobia, the anxieties produced by the liberation of consciences and voices. Edwards, however, transforms the swarm into an event which can be scrutinized through a process of meticulous recording.

The cacophony of the sectarian swarm was often depicted as the result of collapsed sectarian categories. In the 1640s, anti-sectarian authors repeatedly complain that the numerous varieties of sectaries – once distinct, separate entities – have collapsed into a formless mass. In texts such as *The Schismatick Stigmatized*, borders between discrete sectarian kinds are disregarded, as schismatics intermingle indiscriminately. A character named Tom reports on his visit to a sectarian gathering:

There will be more than a good many, well knowne to thee and to me: these by name, besides Master *Faction* and Master *Tickle*, there will be also sir *Iohn Lack-Latine, Nebula Newes-carrier, Marmaduke Murmurer, Cabillus Complainer, Ralph Rayler, Roger Reviler, Randall Repiner, Rodrick Reprocher, Rodulphus Reformer,* and *Rowland Renegado, Clement Corner-creeper, Edgar Etonist,*

Triston Trakite, Patrick Peevish, Anthony Antinomist, Quintillian Quarrell-picker,
Pheb. Phantasticus, Sim Separatist, Franck Familist, Bat Brownist, and *Hercules*
Hatefull. Not onely all those subtle Buzzards, but also a rout of our sweet
sistren: as *Agnes Anabaptist, Kate Catabaptist, Franck Footbaptist, Penelope Punck,*
Merald Make-bare, Ruth Rake-hell, Tabitha Tattle, Pru Prattle. (15)

The sectarians here are melded together regardless of social or
theological differences. Anti-sectarian authors frequently cast this
confusion of categories in terms of "mixture." One writer complains,
"Such a mixture, such a variation there is in Gods present dispensa-
tions."[38] Daniel Featley writes that sectarians "print not onely
Anabaptisme, from whence they take their name; but many other most
damnable doctrines, tending to carnall liberty, Familisme, and a
medley and *hodg-podge* of all Religions."[39] Mixtures, compounds,
hermaphrodites, medleys and hodge-podges: these "puritans" were
walking emblems of diversified, often illogical compositions. The
confluence of sectarian beliefs renders them unnamable, as differences between sects are often subtle and beliefs infiltrate one another.

For Thomas Edwards, this category confusion demands resolution. In Edwards's view, congregational independence and liberty of
conscience indicate a disregard for form which is reflected in the
convoluted nature of the sects themselves. Doctrines, teachings, and
practices become exchanged and randomly incorporated within a
single sect. Edwards hears a confusion of sectarian voices which
cannot be distinguished one from the other:

among all these sorts of sects and sectaries, there are hardly now to be
found in England . . . any sect thats simple and pure, and not mixt and
compounded, that is, any sect (among them all) which holds only the
opinions and principles of its own way, without enterfering and mingling
with the errours of other sects; as for example, where can a man finde a
Church of simple Anabaptists, or simple Antinomians, or simple pure
Independents, each of them keeping to thir own principles, as Anabaptists,
to Anabaptisme, Independents to Independency, and holding no other?
(*Gangræna* I: sig. D4ᵛ)

Such intermingling, according to Edwards, violates biblical dictates
for separation. In *The Casting Down of the last and strongest hold of Satan.*
Or, A Treatise Against Toleration and pretended Liberty of Conscience (1647),
Edwards argues against religious toleration by citing "those prohibitions of not letting cattell gender with a diverse kind, of not sowing
fields with mingled seed, of not wearing garments mingled of linnen
and wollen, of not sowing of Vineyards of diverse seeds, and of not

ploughing with an Oxe and an Asse together. *Levit. 19.19 Deut. 22.9, 10*" (sig. B2ʳ).

In the gargantuan, three-part *Gangræna: Or A Catalogue and Discovery of many of the Errours, Heresies, Blasphemies and pernicious Practices of the Sectaries of this time* (1646), Edwards sets out on a mission not only to demonstrate the political invalidity of sects, but also to accomplish what they apparently cannot do themselves, to disentangle their diverse intermingled doctrines. While much of *Gangræna* is devoted to anecdotal reporting of scurrilous and scandalous sectarian practices, it also endeavors to make sense and distinctions out of perceived non-sense and chaos; even as he reports disorder, Edwards tries to control the swarm through discovering its order. In the very first pages of his text, Edwards acknowledges the force he opposes: "I well understand that I put my hand into a Hornets nest, and shall raise up against me all the spirit of separation, schisme and errour thorowout the Kingdome, from the highest Seeker to the lowest Independent" (1: sig. B2ʳ).[40] (This prophecy soon came true. One self-identified Anabaptist, objecting to *Gangræna*, writes that Edwards "is so in love with *devouring words*, and hath suck'd so long at the Hornets hony-combe that he hath got a *blister* upon his false tongue, which is swolne so bigge that he cannot keepe it within the compasses of his mouth" – an image which at once hopes to silence even as it registers Edwards's prolific writing.[41])

As mixtures and hodge-podges, sects tend to deflect an easy taxonomy. Throughout anti-sectarian literature, authors correlate the sectarian resistance to labels (given their mixed and confused nature) with the formation of the swarm: one frustrated author laments, "It were a troublesome and tedious Busines for a generall Counsell . . . to give these whom I write to, correspondent *Epithetes, Names, Titles,* and *Tittle-tattles* that may be sutable to their Educations and continuall practise; for . . . like swarmes of Caterpillers . . . so these Locusts are crawl'd out of the bottomlesse Pit."[42] The intertwined nature of the sect frustrates attempts to tame and contain it; the conceptual confusion presented by sectarians is so great, argues John Taylor, that the swarm is virtually indivisible. Even as Taylor entitles his pamphlet *The Anatomy of the Separatists . . . wherein This seditious Sect is fairly dissected, and perspicuously discovered to the view of the World,* he notes the difficulty (if not impossibility) of systematically displaying and classifying sectarians: "A man may with more facility reckon up all the species and kinds of Nature, then describe all the Sects, Divisions and Opinions in Religion that are at this time amongst us" (1).[43] In *A Sectary Dissected, or, The Anatomie of an Independent Flie, still buzzing about City and Country* (1647), the process of anatomy fails to silence the sectarian pest; in *Hell broke loose: Or, A Catalogue of many of the spreading Errors, Heresies and Blasphemies of these Times* (1646), the catalogue seems ineffectual in the face of hell's prolific maw. In another tract, even Satan himself appears confused by the bewildering array of his followers: "Yet notwithstanding there were so many Sects, that *Pluto* himself knew not which to elect to himself, or be conformable unto. First, he began with the *Puritans* . . . then he proceeded on with the *Brownists* . . . Then thirdly, he caluminously appropinquated to the *Round-heads*, but they also were busied about Cheap-side Crosse, so that he consequently ennumerated all into his own Catalogue."[44] (Elsewhere, we read that Independents have "with thousand souls / Fill'd up the Catalogue of [Satan's] sulphury rowles."[45])

Such problems in terminology and distinctions would appear to be a long-standing facet of ecclesiastical history. "The Fathers generally mistake in confounding these names of Heresies and Schisme," writes one pamphleteer, with the animadversion, "they doe not mistake them, but commonly distinguish them, or it is no great matter if they doe, they are so neerly linked together, that they are seldome seperated."[46] Even "Fathers," those determining categories and labels, cannot precisely distinguish between neighboring sectarian concepts. Many authors, self-consciously following Augustine, develop lists of the diverse kinds of sectarians. In his sermon *The White Wolf* (1627), Stephen Denison lists all eighty-eight sects reported by Augustine (9–10), while the title page of *A Discovery of 29. Sects here in London* (1641) prominently enumerates these sectarian varieties.[47] Ephraim Pagitt begins his *Heresiography* (1645) with a list of all sects:

Anabaptists, Brownists, Semi-separatists, Independents, Familists, Adamites, Antinomians, Arminians, Socinians, Antitrinitarians, Millenaries, Hetheringtonians, Anti-sabbatarians, Traskites, Jesuites, Muncerians, Apostolikes, Separatists, Catharists, Enthusiasts, Liberi, Hutites, Augustinians, Bewkeldians, Melchiorites, Georgians, Menonists, Pueris Similes, Servetians, Libertines, Denkians, Semper orantes, Deo-relicti, Monasterienses, Plunged Anabaptists, Barrowists, Wilkinsonians, Johnsonians, Ainsworthians, Robinsonians, Lemarists, Castalian Familists, Grindletonians, Familists of the mountains, Of the valleyes.

The list would appear to diffuse the swarm, to fulfill a project of taming through naming. The enumeration of sects into a catalogue seems to be one way of keeping (or making) them discrete; classification aims to eliminate confusion – or, quite literally, con-fusion.[48] Through listing the sects, authors thus appear to order the swarm and bring it back under control. But often the force of the list is not its logical declination but its overwhelming abundance. Such lists do not divide one from another, designating their differences, but inadvertently become further manifestations of the conglomerate swarm. In their lengthy compounds, these lists even serve as graphic representations of the swarm.

In his own catalogue Thomas Edwards seeks to go beyond mere naming and listing; he searches for the "superstructures" (I: sig. DI[r]) of the sect. Edwards acknowledges the sectarian resistance to labels, noting that "one and the same society of persons in our times, [is] both Anabaptisticall, Antinomian, Manifestarian, Libertine, Socinian, Millenary, Independent, Enthusiasticall," and inquiring, "among the Independents (who are of all the rest accounted best) where can any man shew me an Independent Church strictly so cal'd, or a man of them hardly, who symbolizes not with the other sects" (I: sig. D4[v]). But if actual sectarians defy doctrinal purity and strict labels, Edwards himself will impose categories and distinctions. Even as Edwards amasses information on sectarian confusion, he dissects the swarm into its constituent parts:

I put a wide difference between a simple pure Independent, yea a simple Anabaptist . . . and between an Arian, Antitrinitarian, Antiscripturist, Perfectist; Again, I put a difference between erroneous persons, that erre out of ignorance, weaknesse, and are seduced, . . . and are peaceably keeping their opinions also to themselves, and such persons as are wilfull seducers, the heads and leaders of faction, who make it their worke to disturbe the peace of the Church, and to subvert souls. (I: sig. DI[r])

In placing differences between these sects, in ordering them into categorical distinctions, Edwards reasserts the authority of the church and state that has been undermined, or "subverted" to use Edwards's term, by the leveling effects of sectarianism. Through a process of close, microscopic investigation, Edwards can restore structure to the swarm.

To modern readers, Edwards's system and process of classification has not exactly been transparent. Scholars write of Edwards's "very abandonment of the decencies of controversy" and describe his tone as one of "horror and fury."[49] J. C. Davis disparages the historical usefulness of *Gangræna*:

[Edwards's] views can never be accepted as anything but a biased perception of his own society. For him the vital aspect of that society was the swarming mass of plebeian heresy, blasphemy, irreligion, profanity, and licentiousness which he saw threatening to engulf all godliness and sobriety . . . Independency had long been Edwards's main target and, despite the sectarian proliferation taking place in its pages, remained the central object of attack in *Gangraena*.

By contrast, he praises the order of Christopher Hill:

The breathtaking quality of *The World Turned Upside Down* rested not only on the habitual mastery of Hill's scholarship, the quality of his insights, the verve and moving compassion of his writing but, above all, on the architectonic brilliance of the overall design of the work. What had hitherto appeared as a more or less promiscuously seething mass of heterodoxies took on pattern and social meaning in the groundplan of the book.[50]

The "master" Hill (whose own strong leftist political leanings are frequently insinuated in "the verve and moving compassion" of his writing) is thus credited (perhaps ironically) with organizing the sectarian swarm, while the "biased," plebeian-hating Edwards produces "teeming pages" (128) which not only register, but reproduce the sectarian phenomenon ("proliferation taking place in its pages"). To the modern or even postmodern eye, Hill's scholarship may appear a bastion of order and structure, while Edwards's catalogue may seem to resemble the rabble, and the Babel, he records. But positioned within its own historical literary context (in which Robert Burton's *Anatomy of Melancholy* was perceived as a model of systematic knowledge) and especially against the vast quantity of scurrilous, libelous anti-sectarian pamphlets, *Gangræna* emerges as an almost scientific attempt at documenting sectarianism.

Most (even all) of the sectarian catalogues which appear before *Gangræna* provide general definitions or cull together historical information from previous authors. Edwards, however, assumes the role of the natural scientist, taking his project into the field and collecting documentation of actual sectarian practice.[51] In his introduction, Edwards clearly articulates his scholarly methods of analysis and his system for ordering his material. At the beginning of his text, Edwards sets forth his methodology in very clear terms:

I here give the Reader a Synopsis of sectarisme, and have drawn as it were into one table, and do present at one view the errours and strange opinions scattered up and down, and vented in many books, manuscripts, Sermons, conferences, & c. and have disposed them under certain heads, and put them into their proper places, in a methodicall way for memories sake, that the Reader may the more easily finde them. The Reader cannot imagin I found them thus methodized and laid together, but confused and divided, lying far asunder, one or two in one book, some in another; others in this manuscript, other in that; this errour vented at such a private meeting, that errour in such a Sermon, this opinion at such a conference: For many of these opinions, the very same opinions and errours are maintained and held over and over in severall books and manuscripts, so that to have given them the Reader as I found them, would have been to have brought the Reader into a wildernesse, and to have presented to publike view a rude and undigested Chaos, with a heap of Tautologies, all which are carefully declined in this following discourse, by joyning in one things divided and scattered. (I: sig. C2^v)

In his attention to organization and arrangement, Edwards transforms the "rude and undigested Chaos" into something quantifiable, something that can be arranged into categories, lists, tables, put in the "proper places." In organizing the sectarian voices into "one table" and a form which can be "carefully declined," Edwards creates a grammar for the language of Babel; he decodes the linguistic confusion resulting from "liberty of prophesying" and returns sectarian speech to familiar discursive norms. By thus relegating the unstructured buzz of the swarm into a definable, controllable, and learnable form of speech, Edwards attempts to remove its sting.

Edwards's aim to "[join] in one things divided and scattered" serves, in fact, a dual function: he at once attempts to check the discursive confusion of sectarianism, and also to moderate the textual swarm created by the anti-sectarian writers themselves. Edwards notes with dismay that the increase of verbal opposition to the sects propels them even further: "And truly when I thinke of things by my selfe, and behold to what a height Errours, Heresies, & c. are come, and withall reflect upon the great things God hath done for you, the many powerfull Sermons you have had preached before you about the Nationall Covenant, and against the Sects, the many Petitions representing the evil and danger of these things, and yet how little is done, our evils of this kinde rising higher and higher, in the increase of false doctrines, and a greater multiplication of schismes every day then other; I tremble for fear" (I: sig. a3^r). The profusion of sermons and petitions only seems to propagate error, confusing and overwhelming the unseduced parishioners who, properly educated, could reject false sectarian tenets. These unfallen yet vulnerable individuals are Edwards's intended audience. In *Gangræna*, Edwards creates "a manuall that might be for every ones reading," a convenient reference guide in which the "Reader may the more easily finde" the various sectarian errors, and the refutation thereof (I: sigs. C4^v and C2^v).

Admitting that the extent of sectarian error is too great to be exhaustively documented, Edwards fears his "book be too voluminous, having already exceeded that proportion which I at first intended when I began it" (sig. i4^v). But while he cannot envelop schism within his text, he can categorize it. Edwards imposes a system of classification which separates out various sects, which isolates and enumerates their differences. Edwards divides the swarm and reinserts it into an organizing matrix. He depicts this process in bibliographical terms:

I premise this for the Christian Reader to remember, and for preventing mistakes in this worke, that though I set down and joyn together all the following opinions in one Catalogue, because they all agree in *uno tertio* in that common notion of errour, . . . in forsaking the communion of the Reformed Churches: yet I am far from thinking them all alike. A scholar that makes a Catalogue of Books, writes down *Decimo sextos* as well as *Folios* in it, because they be all Books, and yet puts a great deal of difference between the one and the other. (I: sigs. C4^v–DI^r)

Like his contemporary George Thomason, Edwards assumes the role of literary collector. Edwards's portrayal of this process is intriguing: his scholar organizes books not by their subject, author, period, or even place of printing, but simply by their size. In turning to the image of the book, Edwards enters into the same realm of textual proliferation and discursive freedom that was widely perceived as producing the swarm. But as opposed to the enthusiastic, unbounded sectarian discourse, or even the sputtering opposition presented by other conservatives, at this important moment when Edwards articulates his methodology he presents himself as a dispassionate observer.

Edwards's hypothetical scholar arranges texts according to their material conditions, not according to an engagement with their contents. Edwards, too, appears to be simply ordering the sectarians according to their "errors." The multi-headed sectarian hydra (another pervasive figure used for representing proliferation) is

seemingly tamed and made rational, as the "heads" to which
Edwards constantly refers are not those of an uncontrollable beast,
but rather titles signifying a highly systematic organization based
upon "difference." With the precision of a meticulous collector
arranging his data and specimens, Edwards determines that "the
Errours, Heresies, Blasphemies in this Catalogue particularized,
may be referred to sixteen heads or sorts of sectaries, as namely, 1.
Independents. 2. Brownists. 3. Chiliasts, or Millenaries. 4. Antinomians. 5. Anabaptists. 6. Manisectarians or Arminians. 7. Libertines.
8. Familists. 9. Enthusiasts. 10. Seekers and Waiters. 11. Perfectists.
12. Socians. 13. Arrians. 14. Antitrinitarians. 15. Antiscripturists. 16.
Scepticks and Questionists, who question every thing in matters of
Religion . . . saving the doctrine of pretended liberty of conscience
for all, and liberty of Prophesying" (sig. D4^r). In proceeding with this
division and categorization, Edwards effects the breakup of the
swarm; identifying not so much different sects as diverse forms of
error, assigning the sects particulars and autonomous "heads,"
Edwards translates the swarm into discrete components.

John Taylor's declaration that "A man may with more facility
reckon up all the species and kinds of Nature, then describe all the
Sects" is thus refuted by Edwards's claim that "in one or other of
these sixteen formes, may all the Errours and Blasphemies reckoned
up in the following Catalogue be well placed, and unto one of those
heads easily reduced" (I: sig. D4^r). "Species" and "kinds," of course,
were the seventeenth-century terms for what we now call genre. The
English Revolution, as Nigel Smith has demonstrated, was played
out, often very self-consciously, through literary generic forms.[52] But
while much of the "clamor" of the period was created through
genres which competed, subsumed, and inverted one another, the
swarm seems to represent that which defied genre. For Edwards, this
confusion arises largely from the inextricable intertwining of different forms of conscience and different forms of speech. Edwards
describes the sectarian body as a monstrous "hodge-podge" of
different sectarian body parts, and as one who "holds many wicked
opinions, being an Hermaphrodite and a compound of an Arminian,
Socinian, Libertine, Anabaptist, & c." (II: sig. E4^r). To this monstrosity Edwards attributes a cause which, "in one word . . . is
liberty of conscience, and liberty of preaching" (I: sig. E1^r). The
intermingled body, like the swarm, is thus a consequence of intermingled modes of discourse, speech which lacks categorization.

Detangling the forms of "error," Edwards restores a comprehensible sectarian body and identifiable kinds of sectarian speech.

Edwards is not unique in his enumeration of sects; but Edwards's text is distinctive in its repeated emphasis on its own literary and material form. Throughout, *Gangræna* is self-conscious and self-advertising of its form as a "Catalogue." Edwards's account of the scholar arranging his books initially seems to erase the importance of genre, giving precedence to size. But while modern literary critics may find themselves squinting in an attempt to see the titles on the spines of the scholar's books, what Edwards is here emphasizing are not the individual tomes, but the scholar's "Catalogue" itself. Unlike earlier authors, who largely employ "catalogue" simply in their titles, Edwards exploits the potential of this form to create – in a term he uses often – a "superstructure" for the discursive divisions. The genre of the catalogue subsumes all others. Through the form of the catalogue, Edwards thus imposes a genre on Babel: he positions the inherent discursive confusion of the swarm as a natural part of a larger discursive form.

Edwards's catalogue thus appears to reverse the turmoil created by "liberty of conscience" and its ensuing prolific speech. Rather than liberating sectarian voices, through recording conversations and reporting sermons Edwards attempts to encompass them within his own text – a text whose generic form allows it to dilate infinitely, like the swarm itself. Edwards admits from the start that, given the nature of proliferation, he can never produce an exhaustive survey, that the swarm will continue to require new analysis. But he can organize the diversity of sectarian "opinions," transforming that which is paradoxical and resistant to genre into that which conforms to logic and literary division. In the process, Edwards's prolific archive created the most extensive record of reported sectarian behavior and, ironically, created a venue for sectarian discourse. Provided their own genre, the sectarians are given, however unwittingly or begrudgingly, their own voice.

CHAPTER 5

The descent of dissent: monstrous genealogies and Milton's antiprelatical tracts

Here there is a kind of question, let us still call it historical, whose *conception, formation, gestation*, and *labor* we are only catching a glimpse of today. I employ these words, I admit, with a glance toward the operations of childbearing – but also with a glance toward those who, in a society from which I do not exclude myself, turn their eyes away when faced by the as yet unnamable which is proclaiming itself and which can do so, as is necessary whenever a birth is in the offing, only under the species of the nonspecies, in the formless, mute, infant, and terrifying form of monstrosity.

Jacques Derrida[1]

There's no question but there are many monsters conceived by some in this Intermisticall season, which are not yet brought forth, and others that are brought forth, yet like to bastard or misshapen children, are concealed from the publike view, made known only to a very few, being the hidden works of darknesse, the time not being yet to come to publishe them openly, waiting only for the midwife and nursing mother of a Toleration, to bring them forth and nourish them.

Thomas Edwards[2]

"First, concerning the common errors, we are to note, that as the wild beasts in *Africa* meeting at the rivers to drinke, engender one with another, and beget strange monsters; . . . so diverse kinds of heretiks and schismatiks meeting together at unlawfull conventicles, and having conference one with the other, have mingled their opinions, and brought forth *mungrell* heresies" (30). Thus Daniel Featley explains the origins of sectarian error in *The Dippers dipt. Or, The Anabaptists Dvck'd and Plvng'd Over Head and Eares* (1645). Here, the discursive exchange of radical sectarianism is translated into intercourse of a more carnal nature, as sectarians "meeting together," like the wild beasts "meeting at the rivers," (re)produce conceptual hybrids, monstrous distortions of thought. Featley's account of sectarian reproduction and mongrel progeny illustrates a typical feature of mid-century anti-sectarian pamphlets: repeatedly, authors attack and ridicule sectarians by pointing towards their problematic genealogies. The pamphleteers' emphasis on sectarian procreation is a manifestation of the discourse of heredity which pervades religious polemical literature more generally. Throughout the 1640s, authors of diverse political perspectives turn towards genealogies, "pedigrees," and images of grotesque offspring to validate their preferred form of ecclesiastical government or to scandalize the forms of others.

This concern with establishing the source of sectarian error taps into contemporary political debates over the basis of authority in church and state. During the years of revolution, royalists increasingly justify monarchy through formulating and endorsing a patriarchal philosophy of government; the notion of the monarch as *pater familias* becomes transformed from vague rhetoric into a systematic political theory in texts such as Robert Filmer's *Patriarcha*.[3] At the other political extreme, the Levellers, with their "Agreement of the People," locate political authority not in the traditions of the father, but in the immediate body of the populace. Such debates over the foundation of the state were intrinsically intertwined with discussions over the ideal form of ecclesiastical government. Those endorsing episcopacy sought to maintain a hierarchical ecclesiastical system with power located primarily in the bishops; presbyterians endeavored to instate a system with a more lateral base of authority, with many presbyters (ministers) overseeing a national network of congregations and a more active laity; and Independents largely endorsed a congregational system, with little overarching national control. Religious radicals maintained that the immediacy of individual conscience and the doctrine of Christian liberty (whereby the elect were freed from the laws of the Old Testament through the grace of God) eliminated the need for any authoritative ecclesiastical system (although some conceded that a national church was needed for the regulation and education of the unregenerate).

In order to validate the rights of bishops, authors provided lengthy genealogies and sought evidence out of patristic writing to demonstrate the continuity of prelatical primacy. Presbyterians countered these claims by pointing towards fallacies in the prelates' textual arguments, and marshaled evidence of their own to demonstrate that the bishops' corrupt line of descent had usurped the presbyters' true inheritance. This same hereditary argument was also applied to religious radicals (though in more scurrilous fashion) as conservative and moderate pamphleteers created a wild array of sectarian genealogies. Some of these texts traced sectarian descent back to the sectaries of the early church, while others identified Satan as the great heretical father, the *"sperma diaboli."*[4] But the vast majority of these "genealogies" deliberately fail in their etiological purpose; the invalidity of the sectarians is demonstrated through a family tree that is contorted through incest, bastardy, and incalculable proliferation.

At issue in these ecclesiastical debates and elaborate "pedigrees" is the authority of precedence. To what degree can history be used to validate or vilify the basis of an ecclesiastical system? To what degree can separation from Church Fathers, and political fathers, be justified? Political and ecclesiastical debates alike thus turned on issues of history and tradition. With the exclusion of bishops and king from Parliament in the 1640s, many saw an opportunity for creating and implementing a new ecclesiastical, political, and even social order. For others, radical innovation was obviously threatening to the familiar – and familial – order of things. In a period of rapid and revolutionary change, some authors cling to a historical past in order to argue for the preservation of episcopacy (and monarchy); more problematically, others also turn towards historical precedent to justify significant ecclesiastical and cultural innovation. Religious radicals, portrayed as the products of monstrous unions or as creatures lacking identifiable origins, realized the ultimate conservative nightmare: sectarianism implied a society which exists *sui generis*, one which does not emanate or depend upon the history of fathers.

Into the midst of this forensic fray stepped a novice pamphleteer named John Milton. Coming to the aid of the presbyterian divines who wrote under the collective pseudonym Smectymnuus, Milton originally gathered biblical and patristic evidence to justify a presbyterian system. As part of his attack on the bishops' position, Milton utilizes the verbal arsenal of the rabid anti-sectarian pamphleteers, describing the bishops in terms more likely to be found in popular broadsides than in compendious theological tomes. Employing such images, Milton also engages with issues of history and heredity; he not only refutes the bishops' perspective on history, but questions the feasibility of human historiography. In his efforts to discredit the bishops' own arguments, Milton repeatedly points towards the constructed, subjective, and ambiguous nature of text. This textual instability eliminates the bishops' claims to the mitre, and undercuts their stance as the interpretive authorities of patristic and holy writ. In refuting historical precedent as a basis for authority, Milton not only turns the anti-sectarian rhetoric against the bishops, but argues, like the sects themselves, for an ecclesiastical culture grounded upon the interpretive position of each individual conscience and each godly reader. In the course of his five antiprelatical pamphlets, Milton turns away from historical argument and the presbyterian cause, increasingly basing church government upon an educated and individualistic readership.

As episcopacy increasingly came under attack during the late 1630s and 1640s, numerous authors, including the bishops themselves, jumped to its defense. A repeated strategy in episcopal tracts is to demonstrate the novelty of presbyterianism as compared to the weighty and venerable history of the bishops' descent. Joseph Hall's *Episcopacie by Divine Right* (1640) is typical of prelatical rhetoric. In the epistle dedicatory, Hall provides a "short, but faithfull relation of the first ground, and originall of this unhappy division in the Church," claiming that

when *Petrus Balma*, the last Bishop of *Geneva* was by his mutining Citizens frighted, and driven out of his place, and that Church was now left headlesse: *Farrell*, and *Viret*, two zealous Preachers there, devised, and set up a new Platforme of Church-Government never before heard of in the Christian World; Themselves would supply the Bishop; and certaine Burgesses of the City should supply his assistant Clergie; and both these together would make up the body of an Ecclesiasticall Senate, or Consistory. This strange bird thus hatched by *Farell*, and *Viret*, was afterwards brooded by two more famous successours; and all this within the compasse of our present age.

This "new Platforme . . . never before heard of" has nothing to sustain it but "the meanest Plebeian Presbyter" (10), since it lacks a divine or historical source. This "strange bird," the motley "body" of church government, is of abnormal and indeterminate origins, being hatched, not born, of two usurping pseudo-bishops. While Hall later begrudgingly admits that presbyters may have a "pedigree deducible from an Apostolicall recommendation," he immediately continues, "In the meane time every (not ungracious) sonne of this spirituall Mother will learne to kisse the footsteps of the universall

Church of Christ, as knowing the deare and infallible respects betwixt him and this blessed Spouse of his" (49). The abnormal, adoptive family with two surrogate fathers is thus placed in contrast to the foundational marriage union of Christ and the church – and the Christian is once again safely positioned as the dutiful son.

Hall provides overwhelmingly detailed evidence of the bishops' hereditary rights in the form of lengthy "pedegrees" (which he associates with monarchical lineage as well).[5] He repeatedly emphasizes that his own arguments are "drawne from Antiquity, Continuance, Perpetuall Succession in and from Apostolike Churches, unanimous consent, universall practice of the Church, immediate practice of all the Churches succeeding the Apostles" (37) – as opposed to those of the "Schismatick[s] . . . some giddy corner-creeping upstarts, which come dropping in, some sixteene hundred years after" (60–61). "For the love of God, deare brethren," he implores, "marke the spirit of these men, and if you can think it a reasonable suggestion to believe that all ancient histories are false, all the holy and learned Fathers of the Church ignorant, and erroneous; and that none ever saw, or spake the truth . . . untill now that these men sprung up, follow them, and relie upon their absolute and unerring authority" (60–61). The contrast of "learned Fathers" and men "sprung up" again casts the argument for history in genealogical terms: bishops have a determinable, certifiable point of origin which the schismatics do not. Authority, for Hall, is locatable in the past. The biblical epigraph for another episcopal tract, *Certain Briefe Treatises* (Oxford, 1641), summarizes Hall's argument: "Enquire, I pray thee, of the former age; and prepare thy selfe to the search of their Fathers: For we are but of yesterday, and know nothing" (Job 8: 8, 9).[6]

Attempting to discredit radical Protestant sects, many mid-seventeenth-century authors take up this quest for the sectarian fathers. Ephraim Pagitt, in his *Heresiography: or, a Description of the Hereticks and Sectaries sprang up in these latter times* (1647), attempts to locate the "originalls" of diverse schismatics. George Cranmer's tract *Concerning the Nevv Chvrch Discipline* (1642) searches for the "foundations" of mid-seventeenth-century sectarianism in sixteenth-century reform, and finds, "Here come the *Brownists* in the first ranke, their lineall descendants, who have seised upon a number of strange opinions, whereof although their Ancestors the reformers were never actually possessed, yet by right and interest from them derived, the *Brownists* and *Barrowists* hath taken possession of them" (9). Robert Baillie was continually interested in tracing sectarian lineage; in *Anabaptism, the Trve Fovntaine of Independency, Brownisme, Antinomy, Familisme* (1647), he establishes the genealogical link between continental Anabaptism and contemporary sectarianism, hoping that the sects will "deny all affinity, all consanguinity with such monstrous Hereticks" (47).[7] In *A Dissvasive from the Errours of the Time* (1645), Baillie writes of Independents: "Concerning their Original; the Separatists were their Fathers. This is demonstrable, not onely by the Consanguinity of their Tenents, the one having borrowed all their chief Doctrines and Practices from the other, but also by deduction of their Pedigree in this clear line" (53–54).[8]

In writing such "Pedegrees," pamphleteers follow a century-old tradition of enumerating heretical sects and locating – or rather, attempting to locate – sectarian roots. An early example of such texts is the anonymous *The originall and sprynge of all sectes & orders by whome, wha[n] or were they beganne* (1537). Like a modern guidebook for bird-watchers, *The originall* facilitates sectarian identification by offering extensive detail of the clothing, hairstyles, and habits of no less than 110 species of sectarians, those "under the byshop of Rome," those "of Christendom," and those of the "iews and Hebrews." John Barthlet provides a similar document with *The Pedegrewe of Heretiques. Wherein is truely and plainely set out, the first roote of Heretiques begon in the Church, since the time and passage of the Gospell, together with an example of the offspring of the same* (1566). In encyclopedic fashion, Barthlet displays 105 varieties of colorful sectarians, including "Metamorphistes," "Mice Feeders," and "Hallowers" (who are said to baptize their children by belching upon them).

But despite the promise of their titles, these texts never do reveal "the originall and sprynge" or the "first roote of Heretiques"; while the sectarian offspring proliferate wildly, a definitive source is never immediately apparent. Rather than unraveling complex lines of familial descent, these texts merely reveal that the sectarian source cannot be located: the sectarian genealogy, more often than not, is a quest for origins which are, from the beginning, absent. Employing the form of a genealogy or pedigree, authors insinuate that they will outline familial and hereditary history; the failure of these texts to fulfill the promise of their genealogical project, their failure to comply with the reader's horizon of expectations, succeeds in demonstrating a contorted and inconclusive sectarian family tree. In such texts, then, the impossible genealogy becomes part of an argumentative strategy which ingeniously masks its own intent.

Seventeenth-century tracts mimic this strategy. In *A Survey of the Spiritvall Antichrist* (1648), for example, the presbyterian minister Samuel Rutherford charts a sectarian genealogy which, at first glance, appears to be historically specific. He writes in a chapter entitled "The Discent of Antinomians and Familists," that

> Though out of doubt, *Antinomians* have given signification of the first dawning of that Heresie, in *Paul* the *Apostles* time . . .
> Yet their Originall seems to be from the old *Katharoi*, called *Puritans*, who rose about the year 1115.1118. . . . or we may say they came from these called *Ætiani* from *Ætius* or *Eunomius* the Disciples of *Ætius*, who taught that sin and perseverance in sin could hurt the salvation of none . . .
> If we come a little lower, about the year, 1525. arose the *Libertines*, which are a kind of men that come near to the *Antinomians* and *Familists*, and all of them favour strongly of the *Manicheans*, *Valentinians*, and *Cerdonites* . . . The first man of the *Libertines* was an unlearned rude fellow, *Coppinus* a Flanders man; after him arose one *Quintus* a Taylor in *Piccardie*, a drunken proud man and to him was joyned one *Bertrandus*, who dyed soone, and one *Claudius persevalus*: . . . a Priest, who still said *Masse*. (sig. B1^{r-v})

This passage provides a prime example of genealogical equivocation. While the Antinomians would appear to trace their beginnings to the time of Paul (i.e., to the time when the foundations of the church and its doctrine were being laid), Rutherford refutes this claim by positing an alternative supposition about their "Originall" from the "old Katharoi" in the twelfth century; "or we may say" that they came from the fourth-century Aetius; "if" we look further, we discover their affinities with second- and third-century gnostics. The continual use of subjunctive and conditional phrasings, the historical flip-flopping and continual reconsideration of possibilities undercuts the apparent historical specificity. The "discent" of the Antinomians is no more clear at the end of the passage than at the beginning, although we are provided with numerous possibilities. The end result of this genealogy is the discovery of a multiplicity of potential parents, but no direct patrilinear origins; in an attempt to stabilize and define sectarian history, Rutherford calls attention to its ambiguous and indeterminate nature.

In the anti-sectarian pamphlets of the 1640s, the obsession with sectarian pedigrees is thus largely a preoccupation with elusive origins. Sectarian inauthenticity is frequently registered through accusations of "bastardy."[9] Hall writes of sectarian origins, "who was the father of this child, I profess I know not" (*Episcopacie*, 242), just as earlier in the century Thomas Overbury wrote of "A Puritane," "Truly whose childe he is, is yet unknown; For willingly his faith allowes no Father: onely thus far his pedigree is found, Bragger."[10] Descriptions of alleged sectarian practice illustrate the difficulties of determining fatherhood. In *A Nest of Serpents* (1641) we learn that the leader of a sect of Adamites

allowed promiscuous copulation any man with any woman, whom he best liked, yet it must be done by his assent; if any had any motions to lust, hee might take any woman, by the hand and come to Mr. *Pickard* and say, I desire this woman then *Pickards* word was, goe, increase, and multiply; they . . . called their congregations the faithfull, and true children of God, and all such children who were begotten in that promiscuous way they termed freeborne, and heires of paradise, with many other absurd and ridiculous positions. (4)[11]

In such pamphlet literature, the biblical dictate to "be fruitful and multiply" assumes the status of a sectarian rallying cry. "Promiscuous copulation" effaces not only paternity but patriarchal authority. As "freeborne" becomes a euphemism for "bastard," the revolutionary claims of mid-century figures such as the Leveller "Free Born John" Lilburne are shown to be lacking historical legitimacy.

When parents *can* be identified, the pedigree again becomes a display of lineal impurity. In *The Dippers dipt*, Featley deciphers the sectarian "mongrels" as he describes how the Anabaptists have mated with Millenaries, Catharists, Donatists, Priscillianists, Adamites, Apostolici, Enthusiasts, Jesuites, Arminians, Brownists or Barrowists, and "Separati" (31–32). The listing of each union is followed by the phrase, "and their joynt issue is . . ." With such repeated and random couplings, sectarian familial relations become nearly meaningless and difficult to trace. The proliferation of sects obscures patrilineal descent; here, it is not an absence of parents, but the multiplicitous matings and spawning of one parent which again renders an ever-sprawling family tree virtually incapable of being written.

Conservative constructions of sectarian genealogies are thus most often intentionally nonlinear and unfounded. Whether through the subtle equivocation in a "pedigree" or the blatant depiction of promiscuous mingling, these texts point to origins in order to sweep them away. This dynamic is perhaps best illustrated through the recurring use of "roots" and "springs" – as seen, for example, in *The Unveiling of Antichrist. Or, Antichrist stript naked out of all his Scripture-Attyre . . . So that we may the more cleerly see the very bottome-root, from whence he sprang* (1646), by (the rather ironically named) James Pope. The stasis of "roots" is seemingly complemented, but is in fact contradicted, by the spontaneous generation implied in "sprang." The ambivalence of "spring" encapsulates the paradoxical quest for origins which cannot be found: as a noun, "spring" indicates a source, a fountain and etiological point, but as a verb, "to spring" often indicates an emergence from nothing, as Athena springs from Zeus's head, or soldiers spring up from a dragon's teeth. "Spring" indicates at once a quest for birth, and an absence of source; it is at once the origin of a family tree, and the defiance of such genealogies.

The antithesis to texts which call attention to ever-flowing and non-existent origins appears to be the graphic form of the family tree itself. Through charts which trace lines of descent, authors appear to isolate and stabilize sectarian relationships. Twentieth-century historians of early modern dissent continue to discuss these relationships in genealogical terms. Christopher Hill speaks of Protestant "pedigree[s]," and Michael Walzer writes, "However important they are to latter-day genealogists, the sects (even, the Levellers) are of very minor importance in seventeenth-century history."[12] (A claim with which I would clearly disagree.) Jerome Friedman entitles a chapter "The Civil War, Sectarianism and the Ranter Family Tree."[13] This familial and ancestral discourse inspires elaborate charts delineating sectarian descent; M. M. Knappen, Murray Tolmie, and Michael R. Watts all provide graphic sectarian family trees (see Figure 6).[14] Such charts attempt to position the sects within a known social framework and visually demonstrate their continuities. Often, these graphic representations impose order and trace patterns of descent for groups which had no clear-cut boundaries and no self-evident etiology. The erratic and spontaneous nature of sectarian practice is cast into a familial mold as a means of creating a sense of logical development; the often random diffusion and dissemination of loose sectarian tenets is thus arranged into a pattern of discrete doctrines with historical precedent. The isolated, distinct places in the formation of the chart belie the complex and fluid sectarian interrelationships.

Seventeenth-century social commentators were also driven to illustrate this pervasive genealogical discourse. In a mid-century

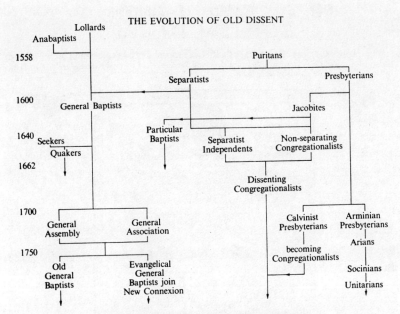

Figure 6 Graph from Michael R. Watts,
The Dissenters: From the Reformation to the French Revolution
(Oxford: Clarendon Press, 1978), 6.

broadside, *The True Emblem of Antichrist: Or, SCHISM Display'd* (1651), sectarian origins are explained through a chart surrounded by iconographic images of betailed devils and an accompanying text (Figure 7). (According to the catalogue of prints in the British Museum, this chart also appears in a broadside entitled *A Genealogie of Anti-Christ*.[15]) At the top of the tree sits Cromwell, "Chief Head of the *Fanaticks* and their *Vices*" who unites Anti-Christ and Pride in marriage, which results in the birth of numerous sects and evil forces: Hereticks, Blasphemers, Atheists, Arians, Socians, Deists, Schismaticks, Independents, Anabaptists, Tepidists, Muggletonians, Libertines, Puritans, Arminians, Quakers, Brownists, Enthusiasts, Impostures, Hypocrisie, Selfconceit and Vain-glory. From these come Presbytery, from whom emerge Ignorance and Persecution to produce Fanaticism, who marries Profaneness and produces seven daughters: Wrath, Strife, Sedition, Envy, Rebellion, Discord, and Civill-War. These daughters and their respective husbands (Hatred, Selfconceit [again], Presumption, Malice, Treason, Anarchy, and

Figure 7 Broadside, *The True Emblem of Antichrist: Or SCHISM Display'd* (1651)

Ruin) produce the final generation of Oppression, Contention, Tumults, Murders, Regicides, Confusion and Beggary. The form of the genealogy, rather than clarifying discrete sectarian identities (say, "Anabaptist"), enables the invalidation of the sects as they are indiscriminately intermingled with destructive abstract qualities (such as "Selfconceit").

Like the textual genealogies in the pamphlet literature, this chart appears, at first glance, to trace the origins and relations of sects and their by-products. The prominent image of Cromwell at the top of the chart seems to indicate a definitive origin of all the subsequent evils. Directly under Cromwell's head, the clasped hands – familiar from emblem books as the icon of conjugal union – appear to signify a foundational marriage; the lines emanating from these two figures signify the proper offspring. The tree opens at the bottom to indicate an ever-greater generation of grandchildren. But like the textual genealogies, this tree undermines its apparent intent of indicating schismatic lineage. The tree itself is obviously problematic in its lines of generation. "Antichrist" and "Pride," the two (supposedly) distinct entities being joined together, in fact both emanate from Cromwell, as does, in fact, the rest of the chart – the tree does not branch out so much as it folds upon itself. This implosion is also evident in the collision of many lines into one; the text informs us that *"Antichrist and cursed Pride*, these two / Were the begetters of a Factious Crew" (Hereticks, Quakers, Brownists, Hypocrites & co.), and that "from all these fore-nam'd does descend *Presbytery.*" Presbytery, then, is the result of a convergence of multiple siblings joined in an incestuous union.[16] Presbytery, alone, breeds Ignorance, and "from this false Zeal dire *Persecution* springs," only to lead to "Fanatacism being of a spurious *Birth,* / Like ill Weeds (as we say) spread o'er the Earth." Just as Presbytery has too many parents, so Persecution and Fanaticism have too few, apparently originating *sui generis*. The family tree thus becomes a graphic form which cannot graph sectarian familial relations since they are, in their irregularity, unwriteable; the sectarian genealogy at once proliferates and turns in upon itself. Through irregular processes of generation, the regenerate become the degenerate.

The origins of sectarian error are often presented as so grotesque that they defy even attempts at genealogical classification. Rutherford reports in gory detail the monstrous births of sectarians in New England,[17] and John Taylor's *The Devil Turn'd Round-head* (1642)

depicts a devil giving birth through his anus. Of particular interest in
the mid-seventeenth century were snake-like creatures who become
self-enclosed systems of generation. Hydras, both as a literary and a
graphic image, pervade anti-sectarian literature; always proliferating, yet always contained within its own bodily and historical
limits, the hydra presents a mode of reproduction which is at once
hyperphallic and lacking the control of a father. The maternal
counterpart to the hydra is the ever-spawning, ever-devouring, ever-
consumed serpent mother. John Eachard, in *THE AXE, Against SIN
and ERROR* (1646) attacks the sectarians, claiming:

[they] are no better then the *Pharisees*, which boasted they had *Abraham* to
their father, and yet being not in Christ, God was not their Father, but they
were the generation of Vipers before God, so are you . . . by generation as
abominable before God, as the generation of Vipers before men, a deadly
and poysonable generation, for the she-Viper in copulation, biteth off the
head of the sire, and kils him, and when she hath conceived, the young
Vipers gnaw out the bowels of their dam, and kill her, and therefore a most
cursed generation; so art thou so poysoned with sin, that thou wilt destroy
thy father that begat thee in the faith, and mother Church, as the
Anabaptists, and people of it by persecuting the children of God. (20–21)

The prolific spawn of the serpent mother entails self-destruction
even as it indicates self-reproduction; through its process of annihila-
tion, this creature not only eliminates the possibility of its own
genealogy, but destroys the hereditary chain of the church and
nation in which it exists. "As the Viper is not borne, but by eating
out a way to life: so neither is this new profession, but by the
destruction of the Commonwealth, our mother," contends one
pamphleteer.[18] Another writes that the state is threatened "not by
the incursions of foraign Nations, but by its own children, that have
(like yong Vipers) ripp'd up the womb of their Mother, to imbrue
their hands in their own blood."[19]

This image of the spawning, devouring serpent mother had been
used as an emblem of religious schism from at least the last decade of
the sixteenth century. The anti-Marprelate authors turn to this figure
as a means of expressing Martin Marprelate's ever-proliferating
pamphlets, and, of course, Edmund Spenser produced a memorable
version of this image in *The Faerie Queene*'s Errour, a creature whose
"vomit full of bookes and papers was" (I.i.20), and whose offspring
are "Deformed monsters, fowle, and blacke as inke" (I.i.22).[20] When
Milton wrote *Paradise Lost* over half a century later, he too authored

the monstrous serpent mother Sin, whose own genealogy develops from Errour as well as from the anti-sectarian pamphlets of the 1640s and 1650s. Sin's origins (sprung from the head of Satan, who then impregnates her with Death, who tears his way through Sin's entrails and promptly rapes her, impregnating her with hellish offspring that continually devour her) are as complex as any anti-sectarian genealogy could conceive. But Milton removes his serpent mother from her accustomed place as a signifier of religious schism, giving her the more general label of "Sin." Milton also removes Sin from the textual associations of Spenser's Errour.[21] While appropriating the image, Milton thus empties it of sectarian and discursive significance. In so doing, Milton followed a pattern he had earlier developed in the antiprelatical tracts, where he adopted the genealogical rhetoric of the anti-sectarian authors only to evacuate this discourse of its etiological authority.

In the early 1640s, the collective body of authors writing under the pseudonym Smectymnuus challenged the episcopate, arguing for the immediate erection of a presbyterian system. The basis of their argument was that presbyters and bishops were originally equals in the primitive church, but that a series of interpretative errors and greedy intents led to a deviation of evolutionary lines, as the prelates robbed their presbyter brothers of their birthright. The title page of *An Answer to a Book Entitvled, An Humble Remonstrance* (1641; a response to Hall), boldly summarizes the presbyterian case, as the text promises to contain "The PARITY of Bishops and Presbyters in Scripture Demonstrated. The occasion of their IMPARITIE in Antiquitie discovered. The DISPARITIE of the Ancient and our Moderne Bishops manifested. The ANTIQVITIE of Ruling Elders in the Church vindicated." The Smectymnuans' main argumentative weapon is Scripture. Responding to Bishop Hall's challenge for a *"Pedigree of this holy Calling,"* the Smectymnuans note "wee finde in Scripture (which by your owne Confession is *Originall Authoritie*) that Bishops and Presbyters were *originally* the same, though afterwards they came to be distinguished: and in processe of time, Episcopacy did swallow up all the *honour* and *power* of the *Presbytery"* (*Answer*, 21).

The Smectymnuans focus on the discrepancy between the church's historical foundations and its current deviation from those roots. "Whence then proceede these many *Additions* and *Alterations* . . . that have so changed the face and fabricke of the Liturgie, that

. . . if our fore-fathers should revive and see their daughters walking in *Cheapeside* with their fannes and farthingales, & c., they would wonder what kinde of creatures they were, and say Nature had forgot her selfe and brought forth a monster" (*Answer,* 5). The Smectymnuans look at history through the opposite end of the historical telescope; whereas their episcopal opponents trace back sectarian origins to a monstrous plurality of sources, the presbyterian authors return to a unified originary moment and look forward at the monstrosity episcopacy has engendered.

While Milton initially entered into these debates about church government in order to support his Smectymnuan friends, he quickly developed his own perspective on ecclesiastical genealogies. Rather than quarreling about lines of heredity, Milton largely rejects the legitimacy of "Antiquity" altogether. For Milton, it is not the sectarian presses (or the spewed and regurgitated tracts of Spenser's Errour) which create a proliferation of bastard texts; rather this discursive chaos is created by the bishops themselves. Milton attacks the prelatical tendency to call on evidence from the patristic writers, exclaiming, "they began after their owne lusts to heap to themselvs teachers, and as if the divine Scripture wanted a supplement, . . . they run to that indigested heap, and frie of Authors, which they call Antiquity. Whatsoever time, or the heedlesse hand of blind chance, hath drawne down from of old to this present, in her huge dragnet, whether Fish, or Sea-weed, Shells, or Shrubbs, unpickt, unchosen, those are the Fathers."[22] The Fathers no longer represent a foundational origin for patrilinear principles, but are themselves a random, indiscriminate "heap" – "the offalls, and sweepings of antiquity" (*PE*, 651). Far from functioning as a venerable, monumental bastion of truth, Milton's denigrated "antiquity" is but an artificial construct of prelatical compilations.

These discussions of prelatical fathers revolve, ultimately, around Canon formation. The creation of bishops from a "frie of Authors" is but a function of the misbegotten nature of patristic writing itself. Throughout the antiprelatical tracts, Milton points towards the problematic construction and transmission of patristic texts. Milton attests "that nothing hath been more attempted, nor with more subtility brought about, both anciently by other *Heretiks*, and modernly by Papists, then to falsifie the Editions of the Councels, of which wee have none but from our Adversaries hands, whence Canons, Acts, and whole spurious Councels are thrust upon us, and hard it would bee to prove in all, which are legitimat against the lawfull rejection of an urgent, and free disputer" (*PE*, 628–29). The legitimacy of ecclesiastical writ is itself represented as subject to human fallibility; in addition to deliberate "falsification," Milton points out the unreliability of writings based upon the memories of boys (*PE*, 640) and reminds us that even the Fathers "so easily miscarry" (*PE*, 634). Human conceit, too, influences the development of textual histories, since "it was the vanity of those next succeeding times not to content themselves with the simplicity of Scripture phrase, but must make a new Lexicon to name themselves by" (*PE*, 632).[23] In some instances, the textual justification for episcopacy comes from "a supposititious ofspring of some dozen Epistles, whereof five are rejected as spurious, containing in them Heresies and Trifles" (*PE*, 635). When the bishops do turn to biblical authority, they simply misread: some "have bin so rash to raise up such lofty Bishops and Bishopricks out of places in Scripture meerly misunderstood" (*PE*, 631).

Based upon apocryphal books – spurious, bastard texts – and human error, the entire episcopal system is revealed to fall outside of the patristic body the bishops claim as their father. Michael Lieb observes that "Milton's recourse to ecclesiastical history . . . performs the ironic function of revealing the unreliability of human testimony. Implicitly, Milton demonstrates that history based solely upon human testimony negates itself as a means of arriving at truth."[24] History itself, then, becomes a circuitous, self-generated and self-enclosed system. Milton repeatedly describes human historiography in genealogical terms ("legitimate," "elders," "miscarriage," "naming," "ofspring"). The bishops' historical genealogy, however, is a story of misbegotten, ill-conceived, abortive textuality. Their authoritative claims are undermined by the very texts which support them.

Like those self-generated and self-enclosed systems of reproduction, the hydra and the serpent mother, the bishops are depicted as creating a "frie of Authors" that will, in turn, self-authorize their own ecclesiastical power. Rather than a lineal model of descent and hereditary rights, the prelates depend upon a circular system of authority, the implications of which are dire. The bishops present "To our state a continuall *Hydra* of mischiefe, and molestation, the forge of discord and Rebellion: This is the Trophey of their Antiquity, the boasted Succession through so many Ages" (*OR*, 603).

The bishops also assume the role of the serpent mother, endlessly creating her self-enclosed brood; Milton accuses Lancelot Andrews of "enforcing himselfe with much ostentation of endless genealogies" (*RCG*, 774). Through such distorted genealogies, the bishops undermine their own claims to patriarchal power. In her analysis of Filmer's *Patriarcha*, Susan Wiseman notes that this "political theory operates not by the description of an ideal state but by tracing back a line of right to the past."[25] Patriarchal power is founded upon a diachronic progression rather than a synchronic moment; patriarchal authority is thus inherently archival, inherently authorial. But for Milton, the church Fathers essentially write themselves into being; as he points towards the ambiguous and abortive nature of patristic texts, Milton eliminates the basis of the bishops' linear descent.

Throughout Milton's antiprelatical tracts, it is the bishops that produce, like the serpentine Errour, religious schism and divisions. "Prelaty was not set up for prevention of Schisme, as is pretended, or if it were, . . . it performes not what it was first set up for, but quite the contrary," observes Milton (*RCG*, 779). He soon becomes more direct: "Still tell us that you prevent schisme, though schisme and combustion be the very issue of your bodies, your first born" (*RCG*, 793). Although Milton writes of "those wretched Fathers . . . [who] keep back their sordid sperm begotten in the lustinesse of their avarice" (*Animadversions*, 722), he primarily emphasizes their role as "the very wombe for a new subantichrist to breed in" (*RCG*, 783).The bishops, lounging self-satisfied in the filth that they create, breed dissension out of putrefaction.[26] In *Of Reformation*, Milton relates how, "The soure levin of humane Traditions mixt in one putrifi'd Masse with the poisonous dregs of hypocrisie in the hearts of *Prelates* that lye basking in the Sunny warmth of Wealth, and Promotion, is the Serpents Egge that will hatch an *Antichrist* wheresoever, and ingender the same Monster as big, or little as the Lump is which breeds him" (590). This serpent's egg, nestled in the hearts of the bishops, explodes in another tract, as it almost seems to devour its way through the bowels of the church. "So farre was [prelacy] from removing schisme, that if schisme parted the congregations before, now it rent and mangl'd, now it rag'd. Heresie begat heresie with a certain monstrous haste of pregnancy in her birth, at once borne and bringing forth" (*RCG*, 781). The rapid acceleration of reproduction seems to collapse historical progression, with heresies "at once borne and bringing forth"; the bishops' sacred Antiquity of the Fathers is thus exploded, as generation, and generations, become spontaneous and uncontrolled.

In contrast to the convoluted, distorted, and unfounded family governed by the bishops is the immediate relationship between God the Father and his followers in Christ. The antiprelatical tracts are not inherently anti-patriarchal; while they reject the bishops' father-hood, they glorify the believer's "filliall relation with God" (*RCG*, 842). Unlike the bishops' relationship with their church Fathers, which is mediated through a morass of tradition and textuality, the individual Christian has a relationship with the paternal God that is directly based on Scripture. Milton highlights the difference in these relationships by emphasizing the sheer material quantity of the bishops' arguments; "mistrusting to find the autority of their order in the immediat institution of Christ, or his Apostles by the cleer evidence of Scripture, they fly to the carnal supportment of tradition: when we appeal to the Bible, they to the unwieldy volumes of tradition" (*RCG*, 827). Episcopal authors often contrast the unified, bound tome of a writer such as Augustine with the scattered, floating antiprelatical pamphlets; the material forms of these texts reflect their ideological content, as the tradition of the Fathers appears in monumental volumes and the spawn of sectarian and independent authors appears in loose leaves of paper. Milton reverses this image, as, with an almost audible sigh, he describes the bursting volumes which clutter his desk and complicate a very simple truth. He laments that he must

leave a calme and plesing solitarynes fed with cherful and confident thoughts, to imbark in a troubl'd sea of noises and hoars disputes, put from beholding the bright countenance of truth in the quiet and still air of delightfull studies to come into the dim reflexion of hollow antiquities sold by the seeming bulk, and there be fain to club quotations with men whose learning and beleif lies in marginal stuffings, who when they have like good sumpters laid ye down their hors load of citations and fathers at your dore, with a rapsody of who and who were Bishops here or there, ye may take off their packsaddles, their days work is don, and episcopacy, as they think, stoutly vindicated. (*RCG*, 821–22)

The "bright countenance of truth" is posited in opposition to the "dim" textuality of overstuffed works of "antiquities." Through the "bulk" of such texts, the prelatical authors are not presented as learned scholars, but are reduced to manual laborers carting a "hors load of citations and fathers." The bishops are presented as justifying their claims by textual quantity, just as they seem to prove their point through the volume of their voices; the "hors load" of text finds a vocal analogue in their "hoars" disputes. Even here Milton continues to insinuate the unfounded basis for episcopal authority. The odd reference to "packsaddles" invokes bastardy; according to the *Oxford English Dictionary*, the etymological origin of "bastard" is from the French phrase for "pack-saddle child."[27]

Having established the illegitimate, human origin of patristic authority, Milton can position church government as a human form that is subject to human discretion:

Epyscopacy, as it is taken for an Order in the *Church* above a *Presbyter*, or as wee commonly name him, the Minister of a Congregation, is either of Divine constitution, or of humane. If onely humane, we have the same humane priviledge, that all men have ever had since *Adam*, being borne free, and in the Mistresse Iland of all the *British*, to retaine this *Episcopacy*, or to remove it, consulting with our owne occasions, and conveniences, and for the prevention of our owne dangers, and disquiets, in what best manner we can devise, without running at a losse, as wee must needs in those stale, and uselesse records of either uncertaine, or unsound antiquity. (*PE*, 624)

Ecclesiastical organization, liberated from the weight of human tradition, becomes a matter of one's "own . . . convenience." Slicing through centuries of patristic writ, Milton positions "us" (first-person plural pronouns appear six times in this short passage) in the role of Adam. In *The Reason of Church Government*, Milton had mocked the bishops' attempt to seek genealogical authority, claiming "that the Prelates have no sure foundation in the Gospell, their own guiltinesse doth manifest: they would not else run questing up as high as *Adam* to fetch their originall" (762). The bishops turn to Adam as the ultimate founding father, the beginning of a genealogical chain which determines and validates inherited authority. Milton, however, looks to Adam and sees not a debt to inheritance, but a justification for free ecclesiastical and moral choice. "When God gave [Adam] reason, he gave him freedom to choose, for reason is but choosing," he writes in *Areopagitica*.[28] Like Adam, Milton – and Milton's reader – is "borne free"; the epigraph to *Areopagitica*, a quotation from Euripides, claims "This is true Liberty when free born men / Having to advise the public may speak free." While the bishops are transformed into the children of packsaddles, Milton reverses the charges of bastardy against the presbyterians and sectarians; "free born" is no longer the prelates' euphemism for illegitimacy, but an affirmation of Christian and republican independence.

Liberated from the stale records of the past, the free-born man (as Milton would probably have gendered the individual) is accorded free speech. In *Areopagitica* Milton integrates sectarian tenets – freedom of choice, freedom of conscience, freedom of expression – into his social vision.[29] Whereas he attacks the bishops for their seemingly futile attempts to trace their genealogy, Milton devotes a significant stretch of *Areopagitica* to refuting censorship by providing its line of dissent, concluding:

And thus ye have the inventors and the original of book-licensing ripped up and drawn as lineally as any pedigree. We have it not, that can be heard of, from any ancient state, or polity, or church, nor by any statute left us by our ancestors elder or later; nor from the modern custom of any reformed city or church abroad; but from the most antichristian council and the most tyrannous inquisition that ever inquired.

Till then books were ever as freely admitted into the world as any other birth; the issue of the brain was no more stifled than the issue of the womb. (725)

In the antiprelatical tracts Milton seeks to "stop the mouths of his adversaries"; in *Areopagitica* he promotes a policy of (almost) uncensored free births. Proliferation is thus not only permitted, but celebrated. Throughout *Areopagitica*, negative images from the antisectarian pamphlets are transformed into a glorification of spawning ideas: "For books . . . contain a potency of life in them to be as active as that soul was whose progeny they are; nay, they do preserve as in a vial the purest efficacy and extraction of that living intellect that bred them. I know they are as lively and as vigorously productive as those fabulous dragon's teeth; and being sown up and down, may chance to spring up armed men" (720). Where antisectarian authors disparagingly discuss the "spring" of sectarianism, seeking its originary "fountain," Milton writes, "Truth is compared in scripture to a streaming fountain; if her waters flow not in perpetual progression, they sicken into a muddy pool of conformity and tradition" (739).

Milton's appropriation of the prelate's genealogical rhetoric is thus not concerned with finding (or negating) origins, but is rather an attempt to devalue the past as a basis for individual belief and opinion. Having disabled history, Milton enables the spontaneous generation of ideas; he creates a society which, free from the influence of fathers, can continually create and re-create its own identity. Stanley Fish writes, "Books are no more the subject of the *Areopagitica* than is free speech; both are subordinate to the process they make possible, the process of endless and proliferating inter-pretation whose goal is not the clarification of truth, but the making of us into members of her incorporate body."[30] The ecclesiastical and civic body is not the contained product of lineal descent, but a fluid, immediate, and timeless entity.

Free from history, the individual engenders himself and his world. "I conceav'd my selfe to be now not as mine own person, but as a member incorporate into that truth whereof I was perswaded, and whereof I had declar'd openly to be a partaker," Milton writes (*Apology*, 871). In conceiving himself, in bringing himself into being though his own mental processes, Milton claims an autonomy from genealogical chains and patrilinear histories. But he does not sever himself from social bonds. He becomes a member of the incorporate body of Truth by virtue of his internal persuasion, and by his own voluntary declaration. Conservative authors fear sectarian indepen-dence and mock the entangled branches of the sectarian family tree; Milton responds, "They fret and out of their own weakness are in agony, lest these divisions and subdivisions will undo us. The adversary again applauds and waits the hour. When they have branched themselves out, saith he, small enough into parties and partitions, then will be our time. Fool! he sees not the firm root, out of which we all grow, though into branches" (*Areopagitica*, 744). The very image of the family tree, emblem of hereditary right, is here employed to illustrate a community which is connected laterally, to each other and in the present, as opposed to being linked vertically, to a succession of past relations.

This invalidation of genealogical thinking is crucial for Milton's strategy for creating a republican readership.[31] But this was a lesson his readers perhaps already knew, or were learning. In 1640, even before Milton's antiprelatical tracts, between ten and twenty thou-sand people of London signed a document which called for the routing of bishops from Parliament and the elimination of epis-copacy. This text has long been known as the Root and Branch petition, but as Richard Strier notes, the petition is actually cast in plural terms of Roots and Branches; in the plurality of "roots," Strier argues that "even this seemingly vertical term is treated 'horizontally' – in terms, that is, of multiplicity rather than origination."[32] In appropriating the same vocabulary of heredity which was used to validate the bishops' authority, the citizens of London supplant the very basis of ecclesiastical hierarchy; the form of a petition itself, listing thousands of living individuals, overwrites the genre of the vertical pedigree into a horizontal record of the people.

For Milton, it is the people who, in their direct "fillial relation with God," can overthrow the bishops and their pseudo-patriarchal privilege. Rather than with tomes of patristic writ, the true Christian is armed only with his reason and the Word of God. Throughout the antiprelatical tracts, the corrupted volumes of prelatical exegesis are contrasted with the word of God, "who is the author of both purity and eloquence" (*Apology*, 902). God's authorship is here depicted not as originary and genealogical, so much as immediate and timeless. With this weapon, the individual can slay the error of prelacy and restore the Commonwealth and church to their proper popular grounding. Towards the end of *The Reason of Church Government* Milton seems to borrow another scenario from his own poetical predecessor, Edmund Spenser.[33] Milton exhorts the "knights" (that is, the members of Parliament) to play the role of Saint George in killing the prelatical monster:

And if our Princes and Knights will imitate the fame of that old champion, as by their order of Knighthood solemnly taken, the vow, . . . they should make it their Knightly adventure to pursue & vanquish this mighty sailewing'd monster that menaces to swallow up the Land, unlesse her bottomlesse gorge may be satisfi'd with the blood of the Kings daughter the Church; and may, as she was wont, fill her dark and infamous den with the bones of the Saints. Nor will any one have reason to this as too incredible or too tragical to be spok'n of Prelaty, if he consider well from what a masse of slime and mud, the sloathful, the covetous and ambitious hopes of Church-promotions and fat Bishopricks she is bred up and nuzzl'd in, like a great Python from her youth, to prove the general poyson both of doctrine and good discipline in the Land. For certainly such hopes and such principles of earth as these wherein she welters from a yong one, are the immediat generation both of a slavish and tyrannous life to follow, and a pestiferous contagion to the whole Kingdom, till like that fenborn serpent she be shot to death with the darts of the sun, the pure and powerful beams of Gods word. (857–58)

Although specifically addressed to the nation's peers, the possibility of overcoming this product of noisome breeding is available to all who are armed with Scripture. Through the pure word of God, the English can overcome the "immediate generation" of prelatical slavery and tyranny. While Errour is to be slain, the proliferation of ideas and texts is to be celebrated. The production of such texts, and the basis for ecclesiastical authority, is not validated by history and tradition, but by the valiant individual armed only with Scripture.

CHAPTER 6

Not so much as fig leaves: Adamites, naked Quakers, linguistic perfection and "Paradise Lost"

> If he lookes upon himselfe naked, he seeth the truth.
>
> *Mercurius Teutonicus*[1]

Abiezer Coppe, the fiery "Ranter" author, was said to have preached in the nude. In *Athenae Oxonienses* (1669), Anthony à Wood recalls the behavior of his fellow Mertonian: "'twas usual with him to preach stark-naked many blasphemies and unheard of villanies in the day-time, and in the night to be drunk and lye with a wench that had been also his hearer stark naked."[2] This claim, seemingly unsubstantiated by additional historical documentation, is less helpful as evidence of sectarian behavior than it is illustrative of mid-century modes of representing radical speech. From the 1640s through the early years of the Restoration, sectarian discursive activities were frequently associated with nakedness. As the elision of naked preaching and illicit sexual behavior here suggests, stripping at the altar became another sin to be added to the already substantial catalogue of sectarian transgressions.

But nakedness was emblematic of more than mere sins of the flesh. This idea of "going naked as a sign" – an expression used by the Quakers, several of whom publicly removed their clothing in the 1650s – was in itself an interrogation of the system of signs that compose language. Coppe himself explicitly associated nakedness and semiotics. Writing about those who "are at a distance from God, (in their own apprehensions) and are Strangers to a powerfull and glorious manifestation of their union with God," Coppe explains that "they cannot live without Shadows, Signs, Representations; It is death to them, to heare of living upon a pure & naked God, and upon, and in him alone, without the use of externalls." By contrast, those who "know their union *in* God" experience great "joy, and chear, being (now) a thousand fold more in the enjoyment of a naked

God *in them*, and of Christ *in them*, uncloathed of *flesh* and *forme*, then
it was when they saw and knew him otherwise, in and through
Signes, Vails, Glasses, Formes, Shaddows, & c."[3] Coppe looks
forward "to the comming of the *Day* of *God*" when "all *Forms*,
appearances, *Types*, *Signes*, *Shadows*, *Flesh*, do, and shall *melt away*
(with fervent heate) into *power*, reallity, *Truth*, *the thing signified*,
Substance, *Spirit*" (71).

Coppe's vibrant millennial vision demands a disintegration of
binary relationships, both linguistic and material. It is only through
the elimination of the distinction between "Signes" and "the thing
signified" that a pure and immediate union with the godhead can be
achieved. The apotheosis of this spiritual union, this moment
without binaries, is an intense realization of the self. In a passage
that reads as a combined paraphrase of God and Dr. Seuss, Coppe
expresses his mystical totality:

> I am what I am,
> and what I am
> *in I am*,
> that I am.
> So I am
> *in* the *Spirit*.[4]

Whether Coppe was actually naked when preaching such words, or
whether his speech alone became the figurative expression of a
"naked God *in* [*him*], . . . uncloathed of *flesh* and *forme*," the removal
of clothing functions as a powerful expression of that state in which
one achieves an entire, integrated relationship with Substance,
Spirit, and Truth.

While his forms of expression might be more emphatic than those
of his contemporaries, Coppe shares in a greater cultural quest for a
pure and "naked truth." Judy Kronenfeld has recently discussed the
significance of nakedness and clothing in sixteenth-century ecclesiastical discourse;[5] seventeenth-century literature continues to
abound with such references. Battles about religious nonconformity
were waged in pamphlets such as Herbert Croft's *The Naked Truth:
Or, The True State of the Primitive Church* (1675), which was rebutted by
Francis Turner's *Animadversions upon a Late Pamphlet entituled the Naked
Truth* (1676) and Philip Fell's *Lex Talionis: Or, The Author of the Naked
Truth Stript Naked* (1676).[6] The idiom of "the naked truth" pervaded
not only religious discourse, but the interconnected fields of linguistics, philosophy, and natural science.[7]

Nakedness provides a logical extension to – and the antithesis of – the textile rhetoric in which we clothe discussions of language. Discourse and clothing are conceptually intertwined in English thought and metaphor: a plot is woven, a story unfolds, a yarn is spun, arguments are tailored, lies unravel, clichés are worn and threats are veiled. Writing has style. "Text" itself emanates from the Latin "texere," to weave; the past participle form of "textus," according to the *Oxford English Dictionary*, signifies the "style, tissue of a literary work . . . , lit. that which is woven, web, texture." The very words we use to speak of language thus consistently reiterate that speech and writing are human constructions, fabricated in such a way that necessitates deceit, craft, and a division between "Signes" and "the thing signified." "The naked truth," on the other hand, signals a verbal purity that is untainted and unconcealed by human discursive systems. As such, although it is ever sought, the naked truth is that which can never entirely be articulated in a fallen, postlapsarian language.

To speak truth, an alternative, uncorrupted mode of language is required. While Abiezer Coppe looks for this language in the imminent millennium, many others peered deep into the origins of time. Throughout the sixteenth and seventeenth centuries, scholars, theologians, and scientists entered into an earnest project of recovering the pure language of Adam. Motivated by desires as diverse as communicating with native Americans, improving scientific efficiency, promoting religious evangelism, preparing for Christ's second coming and developing theories on linguistics, intellectuals from diverse social and political milieux took it upon themselves to recover, mimic, or reinvent Adam's speech. Linguists extensively analyzed the structures of ancient languages, searching for common etymological roots in an attempt to reconstruct the original Edenic language; Cabalists and Rosicrucians examined Hebrew letters to discover hidden divine truths; others turned to the tribal movements described in Genesis for clues about the migration of peoples and languages.[8] Traditionally, church fathers from Origen to Augustine had asserted, as a matter of fact, that the Adamic language was Hebrew, an idea that persisted into the seventeenth century. But humanist standards of linguistic scholarship, and Protestant suspicions of patristic writ, called such assumptions into question. New theories argued that Adam had spoken Dutch, or Chinese.[9]

Over the course of the sixteenth and seventeenth centuries, the scholarly emphasis shifted from recovering the exact language of Adam to creating a perfect or universal language which would at least duplicate the transparent nature of this primordial speech.[10] In seventeenth-century England, the concept of the *lingua adamica* pervaded – even dominated – intellectual pursuits. This fascination with the Edenic language was not simply a curiosity in the *Wunderkammer* of intellectual history, but a central and motivating cultural force. As Robert E. Stillman has argued, universal language schemes provided a space in which philosophers pondered, and manipulated, the vectors of political power.[11] And as M. M. Slaughter demonstrates, linguistic inquiries and scientific investigation were mutually constitutive, since a fundamental aim of natural science was the development of a perfect taxonomic organization of the world. Universal and philosophical languages sought a relationship between words and things which, like that of the Adamic language, was "precisely parallel or isomorphic."[12]

This quest for a perfect language, whether through the recovery of the actual *lingua adamica* or through the creation of a language that reproduced the transparency of Edenic speech, was primarily conducted by university-trained theologians or scientific intellectuals. But in the first half of the seventeenth century, and especially during the turbulent decades of the 1640s and 1650s, religious radicals undertook the daunting task of learning what they presumed to be the language of Adam. Zealous, illiterate individuals (guided by formally trained ministers) learned not only to read, but to read and speak Hebrew.[13] (As Nigel Smith points out, this phenomenon reminds us of the intellectual opportunities and excitement radical religion afforded those normally excluded from systems of formal education.[14]) These men and women were motivated in part by the pressing need to ready themselves for the return and conversion of the Jews, an event that would precipitate the second coming of Christ. But speaking Hebrew not only prepared one for the future; it also transported the speaker from the Babel of civil war into the linguistic and spiritual purity of a prelapsarian age. In his *Discourse on Orientall Tongues* (1648), Christian Raue wrote that Hebrew "makes us . . . to become *Adam* our selves."[15] Raue's ideas, in Smith's words, are clearly "the stuff of sectarian linguistic utopianism"; speaking Hebrew "holds the promise of attaining something like Edenic perfection."[16]

Through re-enacting the linguistic conditions of Eden, radical sectarians tried to assume a degree of agency over cosmic time, hastening the millennium or re-entering the prelapsarian moment. In their insistence upon speaking the Adamic language, one in which word–thing relationships were perfectly integral, religious radicals aimed to assert a degree of control over a fallen semiotic system. More conservative authors spoofed these sectarian endeavors by inventing a sect known as the Adamites. The Adamites, who flourished within pamphlet literature of the 1640s and 1650s, were represented as worshipping naked in order to re-create the innocence of Eden. In these literary representations, the Adamites' nakedness functioned as a means of ridiculing and repudiating the literalism through which radical sectarians attempted to achieve linguistic purity. In the early 1650s, "real-life" Quakers brought such behavior from the field of representation into that of praxis as they walked naked through villages and the streets of London; while this symbolic act held political and prophetic significance, like their fictional counterparts before them the Quakers' nakedness could also symbolize the desire to return to an Edenic spiritual and linguistic perfection. Within this culture animated by Adamites, naked Quakers, and serious scholarly efforts to speak the language of Adam, John Milton was contemplating and composing an epic poem in which the main characters converse, labor, and dine entirely naked. Milton's very choice of subject matter for *Paradise Lost*, far from depoliticizing the epic, immerses it in contemporary issues and modes of representation surrounding spiritual and linguistic perfectionism.

In 1641, just as the censors were losing their power, the London bookstalls suddenly featured accounts of a newly "discovered" religious sect, the Adamites.[17] Numerous pamphleteers report their alleged experiences at Adamite conventicles. These meetings are often ordinary enough, as men and women gather together for prayer and a sermon – except that the congregation is entirely nude. These pamphlets might have attracted interest by virtue of their colorful narratives alone;[18] but they probably aroused even greater curiosity through the graphic woodcuts illustrating their title pages. *The Adamites Sermon* (1641), for example, depicts a bucolic meadow scene in which naked men and women sit in a circle holding hands; the preacher, holding a book, stands behind a leafy branch that is wholly ineffectual as concealment, since his genitals (like those of the

The Adamites Sermon:

Containing their manner of Preaching, Expounding, and Prophe-

sying : As it was delivered in *Marie-bone* Park, by *Obadiah Couchman*, a grave Weaver, dwelling in *Southwark*, who with his compa- nie were taken and diſcovered by the Con- ſtable and other Officers of that plce ; by the meanes of a womans husband who dog- ged them thither.

And ſome part likewiſe by meanes of a Gentlewoman, a widow, which is a Miniſters daughter in the Citie of *London*, who was almoſt perſwaded to become one of their Societie, if her father hadnot diſſwaded her from it.

Alſo a Dialogue between an Adamite and a Browniſt, *concerning their Religion, &c.*

Printed for *Francis Coules*, in the Yeare 1641.

Figure 8 Title page of *The Adamites Sermon* (1641)

Figure 9 Title page of Thomas Bray's *A new Sect of Religion Descryed,*
called ADAMITES (1641)

Figure 10 Title page of John Taylor's *A Nest of Serpents Discovered. Or, A knot of old Heretiques revived, Called the ADAMITES* (1641)

other worshippers) are fully visible (Figure 8). In Thomas Bray's *A New Sect of Religion Descryed, called ADAMITES* (1641), the sect has now moved their meeting indoors. As opposed to the tranquillity of the previous scene, this Adamite preacher, inflamed by the sight of a naked female auditor, finds himself sexually aroused; another Adamite, wielding a long pole, attempts to subdue the preacher's erection, proclaiming, "Downe Proud Flesh Downe" (Figure 9). A cruder variation of this illustration appears on the title page of *A Nest of Serpents Discovered. Or, A knot of old Heretiques revived, Called the ADAMITES* (1641). Here the hapless man in the foreground also finds his tumescence being tamed, this time by a stick-wielding female Adamite who cries, "Downe lust" (Figure 10).[19]

These sensational pamphlet accounts of the Adamites' conventicles are, most likely, fictional constructs designed for an audience eager to consume prurient "information" about radical sects; there does not appear to be any historical evidence of such mid-century nudist activity.[20] Thomas Edwards, who meticulously catalogued known sectarian errors in his voluminous, three-part *Gangræna* (1646), only makes one tangential reference to an Adamite joke.[21] Perhaps because of this lack of historical evidence, the Adamites have been largely ignored, even by historians studying the radical "fringe" of the mid-century. As David Cressy notes, "Christopher Hill's classic *The World Turned Upside Down* gives them less than a complete sentence, while McGregor and Reay's collection on *Radical Religion in the English Revolution* makes no mention of the Adamites at all."[22] Yet as Cressy himself extensively demonstrates, the Adamites held a significant cultural position; if they didn't exist to join the New Model Army, they did thrive within the pages of innumerable textual sources and appear to have been the subject of widespread discussion.[23] The rapid proliferation of the Adamites within the pages of mid-seventeenth-century pamphlet literature indicates that they functioned as a potent imaginative cultural category. As I will argue here, the Adamites provided a conceptual vehicle for representing and interrogating radical ideas of linguistic perfection.

In the woodcut illustrations for the various Adamite pamphlets, the viewer is immediately struck by the sectarians' unabashed nakedness. The verbal descriptions of Adamite activities, however, emphasize not simply nudity, but the *process* of becoming naked. A character named Tom in Richard Carter's *The Schismatick Stigmatized* (1641) suggests a punishment for the Whore of Rome: "strip her

starke naked; make her a very *Adamite*" (13–14). (In a more con-
ciliatory tone, Tom goes on to speak of "that poore silly, simple,
sencelesse, sinlesse, shamelesse naked wretch, *Alice* the *Adamite* / As
bare as ones naile: / She shames not her taile" [15].) Accounts of
Adamite conventicles almost invariably begin with a detailed
moment of disrobing. *A Nest of Serpents Discovered*, for example, relates
the procedures of their (again, most likely fictional) meetings:

They had wont usually to meete in hot houses or stoves, or in such places
where they might have the conveniency of artificiall heate, to set their
naturall heat on fire: they put off their cloaths at their entrance and had
their officer to keepe them till they came out againe; the Seniors and the
chiefe had their seats uppermost, the rest sate all naked, mixt as they entred
men and women. (3)

The threshold to the conventicle is determined not only by the
physical doorway, but by the ritual of stripping; the symbolic
importance of the clothing is indicated by the "officer" who guards
it during the course of the service. Similarly, the report of Adamite
activity in Ephraim Pagitt's *Heresiography* (third edition, 1647) begins:
"These hereticks had their Conventicles in subterranean places,
called *Hypocausta*, because that under the place of their meetings a
Furnace of fire was kindled to warme the place of their Conventions;
for they uncloathed themselves when they entred into it, and stood
naked both men and women, according to the similitude of *Adam*,
and *Eve* before their fall. They call the place of their meeting
Paradise" (102). Entrance to the conventicle was marked and enacted
by this moment of unclothing.

As Pagitt's text testifies, Adamites were reputed to disrobe in order
to reconstruct an Edenic environment: they "called the place of their
meeting the true Paradise," claim pamphleteers.[24] According to *The
Brownists Conventicle* (1641), they gather together with "not so much as
fig-leave breeches upon them, thinking thereby to imitate our first
Parents in their innocency" (2), and *Bloudy Newes from the North, and
The Ranting Adamites Declaration* (1650) reports that Adamites have
"Not Fig-leaves, such as *Adam* wore long since, / When he had lost
his Robe of Innocence" (6). *The Humble Petition of the Brovvnists* (1641)
similarly claims that the "*Adamits* . . . thinke themselves as innocent
as *Adam* and *Eve* were in their nakednesse before the fall" (4).

This belief in the reconstruction of Paradise is given its fullest
expression in *The Adamites Sermon*. The fictional Adamite preacher
assures his congregation that naked, they are "like an innocent and

harmlesse Flock of sheep in this holy place, much like that Garden of Paradise wherein our first parents *Adam* and *Eve* were placed" (4). The preacher urges nakedness upon his congregation in keeping with the model established by the Edenic couple:

Let us (my holy Brethren, and more holy sisters) imitate their examples, for you know they were naked, which is to say (if we rightly expound it) they were naked or without Cloathes: therefore let us lay aside and set apart these unsanctified and wicked weeds, these ragges of ungodlinesse, and prophane Relicks of sin, that is to say our Cloathes; not only Gownes and Breeches, Peticoats and Doublets; but also our shirts and smocks. (4)[25]

Here again, the itemization of articles of clothing emphasizes the act of disrobing. As the character of the Adamite preacher explains further, nakedness does not simply mimic or imitate Adam and Eve's prelapsarian purity; instead, undressing becomes a process of literally stripping away sin. Expounding upon his text, *"And they were both naked"* (Genesis 2: 25), the Adamite preacher explains: "Beloved by these words understand a twofold nakedness; The first is a nakednesse, or being voyd . . . of garments to cover the body: whereunto a nakednesse of sin is incident, and appertaining to the naked of Garments; or to explaine it more fully, they that weare no cloathes, weare no coverings for sin" (4–5). Praising his nude congregation, the preacher reiterates his conviction of their perfection: "We therefore, my dearely affected, that are voyd of these superstitious coverings, . . . must needs be in the state of innocence, as he was, for we have not so much as fig-leaves upon us" (8). According to this line of reasoning, there is a direct causal link between removing one's clothing and donning a state of purity ("must needs be . . . for we have not"). The body is not merely a symbolic reflection of one's spiritual or moral condition, but actively functions as a means of determining and creating that condition. Adam was naked, Adam was sinless; the Adamites simply become naked in order to become sinless.

Claiming to be free from sin, these Adamite characters are used to ridicule the doctrine of perfectionism frequently associated with radical sectarians more generally. According to perfectionist doctrine, those who have achieved a state of inward spiritual elevation are incapable of committing sin; all actions are dictated by the pure Spirit. In early modern England, many construed such radical claims as a means of enabling and justifying a host of transgressive behaviors. Perfectionism was particularly associated, by wary contemporaries, with unbridled sexual activity. Not surprisingly, then, Adamite claims of perfection are sometimes portrayed as a mere cover for sexual licentiousness. *A Nest of Serpents* hints provocatively at random couplings, alleging that, "They are called Adamites pretending to ayme at [Adam's] purity in paradise; they hate marriages, they believe there should have beene none if hee had not sinned, and therfore they meet naked both men and women" (5). In *Religions Lotterie* (1642), Taylor is more explicit, defining "Adamites" as "a people which . . . would be meere Libertines and live as they list, following that place of Scripture, *Increase and multiply*, and in their society they are so overcome with the flesh that they cannot pray."[26] At the close of *The Adamites Sermon* the preacher recommends taking advantage of the bare state of affairs to "reioyce exceedingly, and expresse our joy in the lively act of Generation, and propagation of the godly, that may bee borne naked as we are at this present."[27] The Adamites' salacious reputation continued to the end of the century, as is indicated by the later translation of a French text, *The Adamite, or, The Loves of Father Rock and his intrigues with the nuns* (1683).

But in the 1640s these claims of sexual promiscuity are countered, and even overwhelmed, by an emphasis on the Adamites' *resistance* to sexual desire. While passing references to the Adamites take potshots at their sexual reputation, in more sustained narratives the Adamites' conventicles, consisting of naked men and women crowded into rooms or meeting in fields, only rarely degenerate (or perk up, depending on one's perspective) into uncontrolled orgies. Nakedness, rather than indicating unbridled libidinous sport, is insistently and directly linked to discursive activity. (It is significant that in all three of the illustrations reproduced here, naked Adamites are shown holding or reading books, presumably the Bible.) In *A Nest of Serpents* the Adamites "met as naked as they were when they came from their mothers womb, and thus they performed all their readings, prayers, lectures, exercises and whatever else they undertooke" (2–3).[28] Other authors contend that the Adamites "pray, heare, and celebrate communion naked according to the similitude of *Adam* before his fall," "will not heare the Word preached, nor have the Sacrament administred to them but naked," and "goe all naked whensoever the word is expounded."[29]

Nakedness, therefore, is not simply incidental to Adamite speech, a quirk of ritual or an extant circumstance into which speech happens to enter; rather, the Adamites' nakedness is a fundamental condition for their speech. This is illustrated in *The Adamites Sermon* when an Adamite invites a curious Brownist ("by trade a weaver") to attend one of their meetings. "So they both departed from that place where they held this conference, and went straight to *Mary-bone Park*, where were gathered at least one hundred men and women, and onely stayed for this *Adamite*; and so soone as he was come, they instantly stripped themselves naked to the bare skinne, both men and women: and then in the manner aforesaid, one of this holy Tribe ascends the Chaire, wherein he preached [his] Sermon" (4). We do not meet the Adamites wantonly luxuriating in their nakedness; their nudity is neither gratuitous nor sensual. The scores of Adamites gathered together, waiting in a field for a latecomer, begin to undress only when he arrives, and then the removal of clothing is quick and efficient. They strip so that the sermon might begin.

During the sermon, the Adamites often go to great lengths to quell tumescent impulses.[30] While the title page illustrations of *A Nest of Serpents* and *A new Sect of Religion Descryed* present intriguing depictions of nudity and sexual desire, the highly visible erect penises find themselves in the unfortunate position of being beaten down by sticks. *A new Sect of Religion Descryed* relates a similar practice:

Now it was an order among these naked fooles, that if the Plannet of *Venus* raigned in their lower parts, making them swell for pride, or rather for Lust, then should the *Clarke* with his long sticke strike down the presumpteous flesh.

This zealous brother which prophesied there, in the very midst of his Discourse was interrupted, and thus it hapned; A zealous sister which sate just opposite unto him, being somewhat weary of sitting, rose up, now this holy Brother being more lowly minded then was fitting for him, saw something which lay mumpping the upper lip like an old Rabbet, but sure it was a young Cony, which made his flesh to rise in such an unmeasurable manner, that the old *Clarke* was forced to use both hands to allay his courage, which put the Prophesier unto such paine, that the whole House could not hold him, but hee would kill the Clark. (6–7)

What is interesting about this incident is the emphasis on *discursus interruptus*. The transgression here is not so much the admission of lust as the disruption of speech. The clerk's reaction is not spontaneous, but part of a system designed to ensure that those who prophesy are not interrupted in their "Discourse"; significantly, the person assigned the task of controlling the prophetic flow is the clerk, a professional transcriber and maintainer of words. In their vigorous expulsion of desire from language – blatantly represented through the corrective actions needed to control the penis of the preacher – the Adamites present a parodic version of the quest for direct and uncorrupted speech. If postmodern theories of language (those emerging from both Derridean and Lacanian approaches) concern themselves with exploring the space between the signified and the signifier, early modern linguistic theories concerned themselves with eliminating (or at least controlling) this intermediary space.[31] Here the intervention of desire into the preacher's sermon is graphically controlled, as the relationship of desire to language is blatantly literalized.

The naked Adamites, I would therefore suggest, represent not so much the carnal pitfalls of perfectionist doctrine, but rather mock sectarian desires for discursive purity. In many of the pamphlets about Adamites, nakedness is associated with linguistic perfectionism. As one Adamite explains:

For my selfe, I am the Sonne of *Adam*, who begot me in his innocencie; I follow his steps before he fell: that is, I am an *Adamite*. And though at this present you see me cloathed in garments, which in verity and truth ought not to be worne but by the wicked, yet know, that when we expound, we lay aside those superstitious weeds and coverings of our bodies: and as my father Adam was naked, whilst he was in Paradise, so doe we prophesie naked; that is to say, free from sin, as our Father was whilst he was naked. (*Adamites Sermon*, 3)

The phrase "free from sin" links the moment of prophesy to the spiritual state of the prelapsarian Adam; for the duration of the Adamite's "expounding," speech and body are equally pure. The "lay[ing] aside" of the "coverings" of the body creates this purity, and symbolically represents the elimination of a division between internal and external significance. In a crude and literal form, these fictional Adamites – merely through undressing – attempt to abolish the binary structures inherent to postlapsarian language. By imitating Adam's nakedness, the Adamites assume Adamic speech.

Through this dumbfoundingly simple rationale, these representational Adamites claim to achieve the linguistic purity later given articulation by Abiezer Coppe.[32] The vision of Coppe preaching naked graphically illustrates his message that "all *Forms*, appearances, *Types, Signes, Shadows, Flesh*, do, and shall *melt away . . .* [into] *Truth, the thing signified*." So too the Adamites, in their naked splendor, are mockingly portrayed as claiming the purity of a truth which is

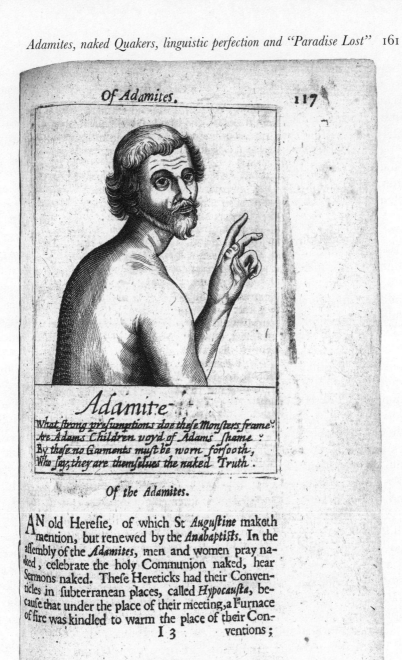

Figure 11 Illustration from Ephraim Pagitt's
Heresiography (1661), 117

beyond language. As the poetic conclusion to the *Bloudy Newse* summarizes this Adamite perspective: "All must be barely naked, 'cause they say / Truth itself naked goes, and so should they" (6). In 1661 Ephraim Pagitt's *Heresiography* was expanded to include an illustration of an Adamite (Figure 11), the caption of which similarly epitomizes the sect's reputation for naked discursivity: "By these no Garments must be worn, forsooth, / Who say, they are themselues the naked Truth" (117). The Adamites do not merely seek the "naked truth": they claim to embody it.

The preacher of *The Adamites Sermon*, earnestly speaking *sans* fig leaf, asserts the origins of his text: "No question but the Prophet *Genesis* himselfe was naked when hee writ these words" (4). This extravagant vision of naked composition not only reiterates the link between nudity and a pure discourse, but serves as a farcical rendition of the quest for Edenic speech. In the absurd reference to "the Prophet Genesis" (a title that at once looks back to the inception of time and forward to millennial promise), the Adamite preacher ascribes ancient scripture to a specific scene of primordial writing. The radical sectarians had long been ridiculed for this presumed literal, material understanding of the quest for the *lingua adamica*. In Ben Jonson's *The Alchemist*, for example, Epicure Mammon (who, as I discussed in chapter 2, has numerous connections with religious extremism and leaves the stage declaring he will become a millennial tub preacher) proudly proclaims that he is in possession of "a treatise penn'd by Adam . . . in *high-Dutch* . . . Which proues it was the primitiue tongue" (2.1.83–86). (The dialogue continues: Surly: "What paper?" Mammon: "On cedar board." Surly: "O that, indeed (they say) / Will last 'gainst worms" [86–88].) In the mid-seventeenth century, scholarly attempts to recover Adam's exact speech were largely re-channeled into an effort to create a universal language, one which would nonetheless recapture the isomorphic nature of the Edenic word–thing relationship. The search for the "primitive tongue" of Adam, meanwhile, became increasingly associated with radical religious sectarianism and mysticism.

This latter trend is exemplified in the work of John Webster, a protean character who over the course of his life was a curate, master of a grammar school, army chaplain, medical practitioner, and author of devotional tracts. In *Academiarum Examen; or the Examination of Academies. Wherein is discussed and examined the Matter,*

Method, and Customes of Academick and Scholastick Learning, and the insufficiency thereof discovered and laid open (1654), Webster criticizes the universities for the scant attention they have paid to the project of recovering the primitive, mystical language of Eden. Webster, a "fanatick Reformer" in the words of his opponent, was deeply involved with the intellectual and spiritual ambitions of mid-century sectarians.[33] Unlike many of his contemporaries, however, Webster argues against Hebrew – or any other known language – as the Edenic tongue. "For Languages change and alter, as fashions and garments," he writes. "And that it which in itself is dubious and uncertain, should be the means of manifesting the indubitable truth to others, seems not very probable or perswasive" (6–7). Instead of analyzing known human languages, Webster puts forth his own theory of linguistic creation. He argues that when God created the world he impressed upon it indelible mysterious "signatures." Adam was able to perceive and understand these signatures, and to give spoken names that corresponded to them: "for this was the *Paradisical* language of the outflown word which *Adam* understood while he was unfaln in *Eden*, and lost after . . . For this *Angelical* and *Paradisical* language speaks and breaths forth those central mysteries that lay hid in the heavenly *magick*, which was in that ineffable word that was with God, and lay wrapped up in the bosome of the eternal essence, wherein were hidden and involved in the way of a wonderful and inscrutable mystery, all the treasury of those *ideal*-signatures" (27).

As a consequence of the Fall, Webster claims, human beings lost access to these ideal signatures. While "Many do superficially and by way of *Analogy* . . . acknowledge the Macrocosm to be the great unsealed book of God, and every creature as a Capital letter or character, and all put together make up that one word or sentence of his immense wisdome, glory and power," this reading is but partial and inadequate at best, and woefully inaccurate at worst:

but alas! who spells them aright, or conjoyns them so together that they may perfectly read all that is therein contained? Alas! we all study; and read too much upon the dead paper idolls of creaturely-invented letters, but do not, nor cannot read the legible characters that are onely written and impressed by the finger of the Almighty; . . . but alas! who truely reads it and experiences it to be so? And yet indeed they ever remain legible and indelible letters speaking and sounding forth his glory, wisdome and power, and all the mysteries of their own secret and internal vertues and qualities, and are not as mute statues, but as living and speaking pictures, not as dead letters, but as preaching *Symbols*. And the not understanding and right reading of these starry characters, therein to behold the light of *Abyssal* glory and immortality, is the condemnation of all the sons of lost *Adam*. (28)

Webster perceives the entire universe around him as composed of God's language. The world becomes the written text of God, the paper upon which the divine has "impressed" his meaning; this text is not only visual, but becomes audible as well, "sounding forth his glory." But Webster, like the rest of Adam's sons, is cosmically illiterate, and uncomprehending of the sounds that he hears. If only the universities would decode these mystical signatures, Webster rather unhelpfully suggests, mankind might once again understand and fully join in creation, beholding the "*Abyssal* glory."

Webster's notion of signatures draws considerably from the ideas of Jacob Boehme, a mystical writer whose work achieved tremendous popularity in mid-seventeenth-century England. (All of Boehme's prolific writings were translated into English between 1644 and 1662, and his writings influenced diverse modes of sectarian thought.[34]) But whereas Webster expresses profound frustration at his inability to "read" the divine signatures, Boehme tells of his own mystical experience in 1600 when these divine signatures suddenly became transparent to him.[35] Like Adam, in this moment Boehme saw the world with brilliant clarity. Boehme compares his moment of transparency with the process of Adam naming the animals: God brings the animals to Adam "that he should look upon them, and give to every one their Name, according to their Essence and vertue; as the Spirit of every one was figured in them. And *Adam* knew all what every Creature was, and he gave every one their Name according to the quality . . . of their Spirit. As God can see into the heart of all things, so could *Adam* also doe, in which his perfection may very well be observed."[36] Adam's naming of the animals is not the invention of language, but merely his own expression of the intrinsic divine creative signatures, which he is able to read perfectly.

Quakerism finds its genesis in a similar moment of linguistic transparency. Like Boehme (and like Adam), George Fox, the first father of the Society of Friends, relates that he achieved a moment of lucid cosmic comprehension. Towards the beginning of his journal, a spiritual autobiography, Fox describes his conversion:

Now was I come up in the spirit, through the flaming sword, into the paradise of God. All things were new, and all the creation gave another smell unto me than before, beyond what words can utter. I knew nothing but pureness, innocency, and righteousness, being renewed up into the image of God by Christ Jesus; so that I was come up to the state of Adam, which he was in before he fell. The creation was open to me; and it was showed me, how all things had their names given to them, according to their nature and virtue . . . I was immediately taken up in spirit, to see into another and more steadfast state than Adam's in innocency, even into a state in Christ Jesus, that should never fall. And the Lord showed me, that such as were faithful to him, in the power and light of Christ, should come up into that state in which Adam was before he fell; in which the admirable works of the creation, and the virtues thereof may be known, through the openings of that divine word of wisdom and power by which they were made.[37]

The apotheosis of Fox's mystic revelation is an ecstatic vision of prelapsarian linguistic perfectionism; Fox does not learn the *lingua adamica* so much as he is able to comprehend its origins, to perceive a perfect, harmonic word–thing relationship, "beyond what words can utter." The achievement of Edenic language, for Fox, is not a human process of becoming multilingual, as many of the scholars searching for the grammatical structures of Adam's speech had seemed to imply. Rather, as Fox later explains, "human learning doth not help in the ways and things of God, as it is in itself, but as the spirit doth open through all things, and beyond all things, and comprehends all languages, and sees before languages were."[38] Comprehension of Adam's speech achieves a mystical understanding of the Word before it was language.

While Fox's perception of divine language has been linked to Boehme's work,[39] the relationship of Fox and Webster – or, more broadly speaking, the intersection of perfect language movements and Quakerism – has remained largely unexplored. But throughout Fox's voluminous writings, we find numerous articulations of a linguistic theory which closely resembles Webster's ideas of divine "signatures."[40] Unlike Webster, however, Fox does not turn to the universities for a programmatic attempt to discover the mystical imprint; rather, for Fox the Word can only be read through a profound reliance upon one's own interior manifestation of the spirit. Fox writes: "And the light within, which cometh from Christ the word, is not against the word, nor scriptures, which are the words, but it owns them, and with them hath unity; and no one sees the word but with the light within."[41] Since God has imprinted his signatures upon all creation, each human being also carries his or her own "signature"; the only way to become literate in the creative workings of the divine is to acknowledge one's own inner light. As with Coppe's vision of the disintegration of the division between signifiers and signifieds, here too mystical understanding involves a dissolution of the binary of internal and external: the light is not "against" the Word and words, but "with them hath unity." Christ, Scripture, Word, Creation, and Christian are one and integral.

A word which recurs throughout Fox's writings is "immediate" – he writes, for example, of "the immediate revelation of the scriptures . . . by the spirit that gave them forth" (II: 258). "Immediate" assumes a temporal significance, as revelation becomes a present reality, not a postponed, future prophesy. But the word also insists upon its meaning as "not mediated." In contrast to those who live by the spirit are the "minister[s] of the letter" who only know God by a "mediate revelation" (III: 258). In Fox's writings, this concept of "mediation" is registered through references to clothes. Fox (who was the son of a weaver, and who was known for his own eccentric leather outfits[42]) frequently turns to images of clothing when describing various relationships to language, especially when highlighting a fission between the internal and the external. The ministers of the letter are repeatedly clothed: "And as for thy lies, and all thy slanders, and revilings, they will be thy own clothing"; "As for the rest of thy stuff in thy book, it will be thy own garment"; "you are blindfolded who lead people from the spirit within, . . . and have the sheep's clothing. Human learning is from the earth, from the ground, and that cannot distinguish the naked truth."[43] Clothing metaphors, in Fox, are almost always negative and repeatedly associated with discursive forms – the worldly speech and writing that conceal rather than reveal divine mysteries.

By contrast, the sartorial habits of actual Quakers demonstrated, in a highly public and visible way, their own sense of linguistic purity. The Quakers endeavored to speak in a self-proclaimed "pure language."[44] The most notorious feature of this Quaker speech was an insistence on using the informal pronouns of "thee" and "thou" – a usage justified in Richard Farnworth's *The Pure Language of the Spirit of Truth* (1655). The Quakers' plain speech found a material parallel in their plain style of dress.[45] Hugh Ormsby-Lennon writes that Fox "suggested how their plain language could find a physical embodiment, its semiological correlate, not merely in the rejection of hat honour (intimately related as that was to an insistence upon *thee* and *thou*) but also in the elimination of ornament and frippery from garments" ("From Shibboleth to Apocalypse," 80). The Quakers thus publicly demonstrated their sense of personal difference through language and clothing.[46]

If plain dress was a correlate of plain speech, nakedness became a manifestation of pure Adamic language. In the late 1650s and 1660s, scores of Quakers were reported going naked – walking naked in market squares, strolling naked through city streets, speaking naked in American churches, and running naked through the Yorkshire Dales. Kenneth L. Carroll provides an extensive catalogue of such naked Quaker behavior.[47] The explanations for such practice are numerous: some went naked as a prophetic gesture, imitating the actions of the prophet Isaiah (20: 3–4); some protested worldly vanity; others exploited the thresholds of shame.[48] Nakedness could signify the Friends' own suffering and the spiritual poverty and depravity of the world around them. The degree to which nakedness became overburdened with symbolic import is exemplified in a contemporary account of William Peares (a Quaker who in 1654 was imprisoned for going naked and consequently died in jail) which reads, "It was the naked that suffered for the naked truth, a figure of your nakedness."[49]

The Quaker practice of "going naked as a sign" was thus generally portrayed and perceived as reflecting the spiritual nakedness of a fallen world – but at times it was also interpreted as a sign of the Quakers' own Adamic perfection. George Fox, in his early writings, espoused a perfectionist doctrine. Braithwaite writes: "It is clear that [Fox] regarded himself as kept through the power and light of Christ in a state of perfection like that of Adam in paradise" (*The Beginnings of Quakerism*, 39). Hostile critics overtly attacked the Quakers' nakedness as a manifestation of perfectionism. Francis Higginson, in *A Briefe Relation of the Irreligion of the Northern Quakers* (1653), explains: "To go naked, is with some of them accounted a decency becoming their imagined state of innocency better then apparrel; the ablest of their way plead for this obscenitie" (29–30). (Equating nakedness with "obscenitie," Higginson again inflects this perfectionist practice with linguistic significance.) Higginson's example suggests that some Quakers did indeed intend their nakedness to be seen as proof of an Adamic state: "Two others of their

societie, a Man, and a Woman, that called themselves *Adam* and *Eve*,
. . . discover[ed] their nakednesse to the eye of every beholder"
(30).[50] In a similar instance, the spirited tailor-turned-Quaker James
Milner and his wife Elizabeth repeatedly called themselves Adam
and Eve.[51]

Portraying themselves as the first parents, these Quaker couples –
like the fictional Adamites before them – re-enacted the sartorial
conditions of Eden as a demonstration of their innocence. The
perfection being portrayed was probably linguistic as well as spiritual. While I have not encountered any reports of Quakers explicitly
describing their nakedness as a sign of linguistic perfection, as
Ormsby-Lennon demonstrates early Quakers of the 1650s frequently
perceived themselves to be speaking in the pure language of Adam:

From the Johannine logos Friends derived their experience of being in the
world and their strategies for representing it as "plain" and "pure"
language. During the Last Days – which Quakers, in common with other
radical sectaries, perceived in their own era – the "pure language"
constituted both *alpha* and *omega*, both the original from which all creation
had sprung and the millennial glory that shone out from the Friends'
vergeistigen Chiliasmus . . . In this fullness of time, God would, Zephaniah had
prophesied, "turn to the people a pure language, that they may all call
upon the name of the LORD to serve him with one consent" (3: 9) . . .
Quaker shibboleths thus represented the outward manifestation of an inner
state in which the second coming had already occurred, spiritually not
carnally, and in which the fallen world had arrived at its predestined end,
the restoration within (and not without) of all things. ("From Shibboleth to
Apocalypse," 85–86)

These early radical Quakers, believing themselves to have already
arrived at an interior millennial state, thus considered themselves
not only to be speaking a pure language, but to have actually *become*
a pure language. As such, they embodied the linguistic clarity of
Adam as well as the millennial linguistic unity described by Coppe.
In 1661 Isaac Penington explained that the Quaker use of pure
language revealed (as Ormsby-Lennon phrases it) "their inner
attainment both of Adam's 'state of innocency' and of a chiliastic
'state of true redemption'."[52]

It is unlikely that many Quakers self-consciously modeled their
activities on the Adamites, those often ludicrous creations of conservative pamphleteers. But to the casual seventeenth-century observer, the sight of an actual naked Quaker walking down the street
held a visual continuity with the fictional naked Adamite featured on

the title pages of numerous pamphlets. While the radical Quakers may have been situating themselves largely within a biblical and millennial context, their more orthodox contemporaries may have been perceiving them within the already prevalent symbolic and discursive world of the Adamites. Reports of the Quakers' behavior, for example, resonate with earlier accounts of the Adamites. In Pagitt's *Heresiography* (1647), the Adamites burn all of their clothes, even down to their hair ribbons, and "rushed into the street starke naked, . . . running and crying horribly throughout the Town, *Woe, woe, woe, the divine vengeance, the divine vengeance*" (103); in Higginson's *Briefe Relation*, the Quakers burn their "good cloaths," and one "ran like a madde man naked, all but his shirt, through *Kendall* crying, *Repent, Repent, wo, wo, come out of Sodome, Remember Lots wife*, with other such stuff" (29, 30). Not only the Quakers' actions, but their beliefs are described in ways which again rehearse the familiar perfectionist assumptions of the Adamites' nudity. Jonathan Clapham's *A Full Discovery and Confutation of the wicked and damnable Doctrines of the Quakers* (1656), for instance, specifically links the Quakers' claim that they are "perfectly free from the being of sin" with "such actions as tend directly to lead men to such filthinesse, as going naked, & c." (52). Both the Adamites and the Quakers are represented as believing in their own linguistic perfection, perceiving themselves as speaking the naked truth of Adam.

From the beginning of the 1640s to the years preceding the Restoration, nakedness thus pervaded the discursive and material fields of English culture. As a figure of speech, "the naked truth" served as a constant invocation of theological, scientific, and popular quests for a form of perfect language. As graphic figures appearing on pamphlets, or as actual figures walking through geographic spaces, naked Adamites and Quakers represented a literalization of this spiritual and linguistic perfection, a means of bringing the comprehension of Adam into the fallen world of civil wars and social traumas. Nakedness signaled a primal purity, and human attempts to re-enter the peace of Eden.

The year 1640 finds John Milton lodging with a tailor and seeking topics suitable for a heroic poetic undertaking. The epic he had begun about King Arthur had borne no fruit, and so the poet, now turning two and thirty, began methodically compiling lists of subjects from which to choose his inspiration. The Trinity Manuscript contains seven pages of his notes sketching out various possibilities: an epic on King Alfred, a pastoral poem based on passages of Scripture, diverse dramas drawn from Old Testament stories, trage- dies from early British history, and stories about Scotland. He seems at this point to have favored a play on "Paradise Lost," and begins to draft the *dramatis personae*. Twice he lists the characters, and crosses them out; between the two attempts his mind wanders in other directions, contemplating "other Tragedies, Adam in Banishment, The flood, Abram in Egypt." He tries to draw up the plot of the play, but turns the page and makes a fresh start, resolutely penning "The Deluge"; next he writes "Sodom," and "Dinah" with a list of characters. He then methodically lists all of the topics he can think of from the Old Testament, sketches the plot for a play on Abram, then one on John the Baptist, thinks more about Sodom, looks for ideas in the New Testament, and finally goes back to his original idea for a play about Adam.[53] These notes are a testament to Milton's process of false starts and writerly frustrations. The difficul- ties in committing to his preferred topic of Adam, William Riley Parker suggests, may have been due in part to the performative limitations of his preferred subject. In a second sketch of the drama "Paradise Lost," the Fall takes place off stage, and only then do we first see Adam. As Parker parenthetically explains, "Prelapsarian nudity inhibited the playwright" (*Milton*, 192).

It was during this same period, however, that prelapsarian nudity was being represented in bookstalls via accounts of the infamously uninhibited Adamites. The Adamites make their first public appear- ance, in print at least, during the summer of 1641. Their fame spread quickly; Cressy cites their cameo appearances in such disparate sources as pamphlets about news-sheet hawkers and dramas like Richard Brome's *A Joviall Crew* (first performed 1641), in which a character is off to London "to see . . . the Adamites run naked before the ladies."[54] Milton was not far behind, running to join the Adamite fray. In *The Reason of Church Government*, which he wrote in December of 1641,[55] Milton lashes out at those who tar reformers with derogatory sectarian labels. He begins by noting that those who "were call'd Lollards and Hussites, so now by you be term'd Puritans, and Brownists"; he goes on to hope "that the people of England will not suffer themselves to be juggl'd thus out of their faith and religion by a mist of names cast before their eyes, but will search wisely by the Scriptures, and look quite through this fraudulent aspersion of a disgracefull name into the things themselves: knowing that the Primitive Christians in their times were accounted such as are now call'd Familists and Adamites, or worse."[56] In a rhetorical gesture sure to shock many of his contemporaries, Milton associates a scandalous sect of nudists with the very founders of Christianity. While his argument is not an overt defense of the Adamites, the logic at work subtly validates them: just as closed-minded, foolish men taunted the original true Christians, so too those attacking the Adamites could unwittingly be assailing true spirituality. Sharing in his culture's fascination with the implications of such a sect, Milton exhibits a profoundly ambivalent attitude towards the Adamites, at once repulsed and attracted to the idea of this radical religion.

The genesis of *Paradise Lost* is thus co-incidental with the emergence of the Adamite phenomenon. While I do not mean to suggest that this epic poem was specifically and deliberately created in the Adamites' image, I would point out that Milton, while contemplating the prospect of a literary work centered on the naked Adam and Eve, was enmeshed in an exploding and explosive literary culture in which the Adamites were a prime topic of conversation, a target for scorn and the butt of many jokes.[57] The construction of *Paradise Lost* was, in fact, temporally framed by cultural moments in which nakedness was a focus of debate: while the arrival of the Adamite pamphlets in 1641 coincided with the crystallization of the idea for the poem, the wave of Quakers "going naked as a sign" in 1659–62 took place during the poem's composition in 1658–63.

During this twenty-year span, Milton – like his contemporaries – found himself engaged with a kaleidoscopic set of religious, political, scientific and linguistic concerns which revolved around the perfect speech of the naked Adam. Like many of the Quakers, Milton appears to have been reading the popular works of Jacob Boehme, who was preoccupied with the nature of Adam's language and his own mystical experience of that language.[58] As a friend of those involved in the formation of the Royal Society, Milton was conversant with men at the heart of the quest for a philosophical or universal language; his admiration for Samuel Hartlib, the author of an unpublished treatise on universal writing entitled *Ephemerides*,[59] was proclaimed in the full title of his treatise *Of Education: To Master Samuel Hartlib.* More tangentially, Milton was intellectually fascinated by the concept of religious sectarianism, and was an active linguist concerned with language pedagogy.

At first glance, however, Milton seems deliberately to refrain from speculations on the Adamic tongue. *De Doctrina Christiana*, Milton's treatise on his religious beliefs and perhaps the most likely place for an excursus on the question of the primordial language, is notably reticent about the subject. *Paradise Lost*, a poem which relates extensive Edenic dialogues, also does not appear overtly to engage with questions of the *lingua adamica*. Given the centrality of debates about the primordial tongue, some of Milton's contemporaries may well have expected the Edenic conversations in *Paradise Lost* to function as something of a laboratory for reconstructing Adam's speech; these dialogues, however, are noteworthy for their apparent lack of engagement with the prevalent theories of Adamic language. D. C. Allen argued that the Edenic nature of speech is implicit to *Paradise Lost*: "There is no doubt that like most of his coevals [Milton] believed that Hebrew was the original mother tongue, and the modern reader sometimes forgets that all of the conversations in the three great poems are couched in that language."[60] But the reader of *Paradise Lost* does not simply "forget" that Adam and Eve are supposed to be speaking in Hebrew; rather, there is never any indication, either directly or through patterns in these characters' speech, that they are conversing in this language. While incorporating wordplay and patterns that depend upon a knowledge of Greek or Latin, Milton seems assiduously to avoid including Hebraisms in his epic poem, despite his mastery of that language, and despite the assumption of many of his readers that Hebrew was the Edenic tongue.[61] Rather than infusing the discourse of Adam and Eve with Hebraic constructions, Milton thus appears self-consciously to thwart the expectations of his contemporary readers.

Various critics have tried to redeem Milton from this apparent lack of engagement with one of the foremost intellectual pursuits of his time. Christopher Ricks, for example, suggests that Milton likes to use words according to their original etymologies in order to "re-create something of the pre-lapsarian state of language."[62] John Leonard positions *Paradise Lost* within the context of treatises on seventeenth-century universal languages, and argues that "Although Milton is unable to impart to Adam and Eve a sustained congruency between 'the word and the thing', he does create an eloquence which suspends time and penetrates outward appearances."[63] But eloquence, however penetrating, is not the same as prelapsarian linguistic purity – in fact, as the character of Satan demonstrates, eloquence can even be the antithesis of purity. Leonard's study focuses on the implications and processes of naming in *Paradise Lost*; at the time Milton wrote his poem, the biblical moment when Adam names the animals had been at the very heart of fierce religio-linguistic debates for over a century. Milton, however, gives this seminal (or in any event, nominal) action a stunningly brief three lines: "I nam'd them, as they pass'd, and understood / Thir Nature, with such knowledge God endu'd / My sudden apprehension" (8: 352–54).[64] As Leonard himself points out, later in the poem even God "dismiss[es] the naming of the animals as a comparatively unimportant affair."[65]

Thus while Milton's intellectual contemporaries, from Hobbes to Newton, were involved in the quest for the perfect language, and while numerous sectarians were taking it upon themselves to speak the presumed primordial language of Hebrew, Milton appears to distance himself from these linguistic projects. In *Surprised by Sin*, Stanley Fish positions the poem within a constellation of texts discussing a perfect language (including Bacon's *Novum Organum*, Plato's *Cratylus*, Webster's *Academiarum Examen*, Hobbes's *Leviathan*, Wilkins's *An Essay Towards a Real Character and a Philosophical Language*, and Sprat's *History of the Royal Society*) and argues that Milton deliberately controverts the dominant seventeenth-century belief in the possibility of recovering or inventing such a language. "By using language to point up the distortion that results whenever fallen man attempts to make sense of the world around him," Fish writes, "Milton passes judgment on the scientific and linguistic optimism of his own century."[66] Rather than engaging with the language schemes concocted by his peers, Milton seeks

to instill [humility] in his readers by exploding the promise of a terrestrial Paradise which they may have accepted in the name of a secular faith. Every time a reader is unable to limit his response to the literal signification of a word descriptive of Paradise or its inhabitants, he is in effect attesting to the speciousness of a programme that offers salvation in the guise of linguistic reform. If ambiguity and metaphor are the enemies because they are the basis of all distortion, then the enemies live within him, for it is beyond his power to withhold the metaphorical or ambiguous reading. Milton need not believe wholeheartedly in the ideal language in order to take advantage of his reader's belief in it. As long as the reader identifies Edenic perfection with a word–thing vocabulary, he must admit his distance from that perfection whenever he reads into the word more than is literally there, more than the thing. (*Surprised by Sin*, 128)

As an example of this process, Fish discusses the introduction of Eve and her "wanton ringlets." The sensuousness of the scene seduces the reader into lustful thought; "he" must then correct himself by realizing that "wanton," in prelapsarian terms, merely indicates "unrestrained," without negative moral valence. "In short, the reader will declare Eve innocent of a sensuality whose only existence is in his mind; but it is a conscious effort, made necessary ultimately by his inability to delimit the connotations of a prelapsarian vocabulary" (102).

Fish continues, "Adam and Eve are not troubled by their nakedness, but we are" (129). I would like here to historicize this "we," to consider the ways in which Milton's contemporaries would have responded to such images of nakedness. Fish's argument that Milton is challenging assumptions about human capabilities for achieving a perfect language – with the poet repeatedly demonstrating the fallen nature of the reader's own semiotic process – certainly rings true. Within the poem, however, this dialectic is itself positioned in relationship to a pervasive discourse of nakedness. A seventeenth-century reader might be "troubled" by Adam and Eve's nakedness, but not in the same way as the twenty-first century "we" might be – or at least, the earlier reader might associate nakedness with vexed representational issues in addition to the "sins" of the eroticized reading Fish traces. *Paradise Lost*, as Barbara Lewalski has demonstrated, is informed by a complex interweaving of discursive genres, as the reader is "invited to identify certain patterns . . . as subtexts for portions of Milton's poem, and then to attend to the completion or transformation of those allusive patterns as the poem proceeds."[67] Dilating this model to include graphic images of nakedness as well as the topos of "the naked truth," we discover another representational mode through which Milton engages with the quest for perfect language. To a reading audience familiar with the legacy of the Adamites and the naked Quakers, nakedness could indicate the enactment of pure linguistic conditions. Milton, however, repeatedly invokes the image of nakedness only to frustrate its symbolic significance.

Before the Fall, the poem frequently draws our attention to the naked bodies of Adam and (especially) Eve. In Book 5, for example, Raphael and Adam arrive at the first couple's bower and are greeted by their naked hostess:

> . . . So to the Silvan Lodge
> They came, that like *Pomona's* Arbor smil'd
> With flow'rets deck't and fragrant smells; but *Eve*
> Undeckt, save with herself more lovely fair
> Than Wood-Nymph, or the fairest Goddess feign'd
> Of three that in Mount *Ida* naked strove,
> Stood to entertain her guest from Heav'n; no veil
> Shee needed, Virtue-proof, no thought infirme
> Alter'd her cheek . . .
> . . .
> . . . Meanwhile at Table *Eve*
> Minister'd naked, and thir flowing cups
> With pleasant liquors crown'd: O innocence
> Deserving Paradise! if ever, then,
> Then had the Sons of God excuse to have been
> Enamour'd at that sight; but in those hearts
> Love unlibidinous reign'd . . .   (5: 377–85, 443–49)

This moment gratifies expectations of a symbolic system in which nakedness signifies pure speech. Eve herself seems to represent the precepts of a perfect language, as the word–thing relationship (here rendered into the word–body relationship) is direct and unmitigated; Eve needs no veil because her outward appearance and inward idea are one and the same, both innocent. As opposed to Belial, who speaks with "words cloth'd in reason's garb" (2: 226), Eve embodies the naked truth. The discursive purity of this moment is further enhanced by the emphasis on the absence of desire, as the "unlibidinous" environment is precisely that which the Adamites so aggressively pursued in their attempts to achieve linguistic perfection.

But any smug satisfaction the reader might experience at identifying nakedness as an indication of pure speech would be shortlived. This scene is virtually the only one in which we can "see" the purely naked Eve. Throughout the rest of the account of prelapsarian Eden, the naked bodies of Adam and Eve disappear from view – even when they appear to stand blatantly before us. The first vision of Adam and Eve is from Satan's perspective, as we find ourselves peering through the bushes with him, discovering:

> Two of far nobler shape erect and tall,
> Godlike erect, with native Honor clad
> In naked Majesty seem'd Lords of all,
> And worthy seem'd, for in thir looks Divine
> The image of thir glorious Maker shone . . .   (4: 288–292)

Exposed to a pervasive iconographic tradition, and having even a tangential familiarity with the book of Genesis, "we" (both the early and postmodern readers) expect the first parents to be naked. And so they are – barely. It is in fact difficult to focus on the naked bodies of the couple. Before we read of their "naked Majesty," they are presented "with native Honor clad"; in their looks we see only the image of God. "Looks" itself is deceiving, and confuses our perspective as a viewer; "looks" could signify their outer bodily appearance, or their own gaze. The repeated "seem'd" has Spenserian overtones, suggesting a doubtful relationship between our perception and reality. (One is tempted to detect a pun on "seamed," another contradiction to the emphasis on the uncloathed.) As a word, the little lower-cased adjective of "naked" is subsumed by the authoritative nouns that surround it, "Honor," "Majesty," "Lords," "Maker," and even the capitalized adjective of "Divine." "Naked" itself does not even directly describe Adam and Eve, but serves to modify "Majesty," which dominates the scansion of the line.

As the reader's gaze falls upon more specific bodily detail, nakedness seems to be immediately before us. But here again, a vision of nakedness proves to be an illusion or is veiled by the larger environment. The oft-invoked lines, "half her swelling Breast / Naked met his under the flowing Gold / Of her loose tresses hid" (4: 495–97), seem to provide an explicit vision of Eve's breast; but all we can really "see" is the hair that hides the breast beneath it. The only body part which receives substantial description is, in fact, the couple's hair; while critics have discussed the implications of Eve's "wanton ringlets" at great length, we should note that Adam's coiffure is given nearly equal attention, as his "Hyacinthine Locks / Round from his parted forelock manly hung / Clust'ring" (4: 301–03) (lines which similarly invite an eroticized reading). This botanical description of Adam's hair, like the account of Eve's "golden tresses" that "wav'd / As the Vine curls her tendrils" (4: 305–07) integrate the couple with their natural surroundings. As Satan watches Eve labor, her nakedness again becomes invisible: "Beyond his hope, *Eve* separate he spies, / Veil'd in a Cloud of Fragrance, where she stood, / Half spi'd, so thick the Roses bushing round / About her glow'd" (9:422–27). Not only is Eve "veil'd" by fragrance, but she almost appears to be wearing the roses. As flowers are transformed into a form of clothing, the signification of "naked" becomes confused, as the naked body is nonetheless shrouded.

Again, when Adam and Eve retire for the night, "eas'd the putting off / These troublesome disguises which wee wear" (4: 739–40), the narrator relates how "These lull'd by Nightingales imbracing slept, / And on thir naked limbs the flow'ry roof / Showrd Roses" (4: 771–73).

Even the most emphatic descriptions of nakedness obscure the human form. "Nor those mysterious parts were then conceal'd" (4: 312), the narrator asserts – although in lieu of description, he quickly enters into a discursus which functions as a figurative fig leaf, concealing any possible description of the mysterious parts which were not concealed:

> Then was not guilty shame: dishonest shame
> Of Nature's works, honor dishonorable,
> Sin-bred, how have ye troubl'd all mankind
> With shows instead, meer shows of seeming pure,
> And banisht from man's life his happiest life,
> Simplicity and spotless innocence.   (4: 313–18)

This postlapsarian guilty shame not only prohibits the narrator's descriptive license, but, even more profoundly, precludes the possibility of the reader's comprehension of a world before shame. Instead of purity, the postlapsarian reader can only know "meer shows of seeming pure"; the compounding of descriptive qualifiers ("meer," "shows," "seeming") displays the fallen conception of "pure" as ever incomplete and fraudulent. That purity has become inaccessible is naturally a function of postlapsarian concupiscence. But perhaps even more fundamentally, Edenic purity is irrecoverable for a postlapsarian mental world which is conceptually organized into an elaborate and inescapable system of binary relations. "Then" – this distinction of temporal difference is invoked twice – purity was the condition of being integral and entire. Now, after the Fall, significance has become bifurcated: purity finds its opposition in "shows," and "honor" is only possible with the introduction of "dishonor."

The seventeenth-century reader of *Paradise Lost*, immersed in a discursive culture which addressed linguistic concerns in a sartorial vocabulary, might well seek a referential matrix structured, in part, through the oppositional terms of naked and clothed. The potency of this binary emanates from the stark, graphic distinction between the two, as well as their mutual interdependence; unlike many other paired antithetical terms (say, black and white), "naked" and "clothed" only signify through invoking the other. *Paradise Lost* is fundamentally a narrative about the emergence of this postlapsarian bifurcated system (as good only assumes significance in relationship to evil) and the ways in which the postlapsarian reader must negotiate these interrelated oppositions. As Lewalski states, "*Paradise Lost* is preeminently a poem about knowing and choosing" ("*Paradise Lost*" 3). But *Paradise Lost* is also an expression of the unknowable mysteries of creation – the same mysteries which Milton's contemporaries were so intently attempting to penetrate. The inaccessibility of the pure *lingua adamica* is reiterated not only through a vocabulary that continuously deconstructs as a function of the postlapsarian human state, as Fish argues, but also through a descriptive visual field that disallows an easy elision of nakedness with linguistic purity. Nakedness in Milton's prelapsarian Eden is "troubling" because it refuses to yield to a postlapsarian binary system of signification in which nakedness and clothing are allied with conditions or qualities of human language.

The reader expecting nakedness to signify the purity of Eden might be startled to discover that Paradise is a place strikingly devoid of nudity. This pure environment is, in fact, primarily constructed through incessant descriptions of cloth and clothing. In the beginning, the earth is naked, but God quickly sees that it requires cover:

> . . . the bare Earth, till then
> Desert and bare, unsightly, unadorn'd,
> Brought forth the tender Grass, whose verdure clad
> Her Universal Face with pleasant green,
> Then Herbs of every leaf, that sudden flow'r'd
> Op'ning thir various colors, and made gay
> Her bosom smelling sweet.   (7: 313–19)

The process of creation in *Paradise Lost* is an extended description of adorning the earth and its inhabitants in wondrous array, so that "Earth in her rich attire / Consummate lovely smil'd" (7: 501–02). Flowers cover the earth's surface with an elaborate tapestry: "underfoot the Violet, / Crocus, and Hyacinth with rich inlay / Broider'd the ground" (4: 700–702). Adam and Eve, in their morning orison, instruct the mists to rise "Till the Sun paint your fleecy skirts with Gold, / In honor to the World's great Author rise, / . . . to deck with Clouds th' uncolord sky" (5: 187–89). Within this sky the colors of the rainbow "serve they as a flow'ry verge to bind / The fluid skirts of that same wat'ry Cloud" (11: 881–82). The earth is adorned with "thick-wov'n Arborets and Flow'rs / Imborder'd on each Bank, the hand of *Eve*" (9: 437–38). In the sea the fish "Show to the Sun thir wav'd coats dropt with Gold," and lobsters search for food "in jointed Armor" (7: 406, 409). In treetops the birds "spred thir painted wings," while the swan forms a mantle with her wings, and the peacock struts as his "gay Train / Adorns him, color'd with the Florid hue / Of Rainbows and Starry Eyes" (7: 434, 439, 444–46). Even the tiniest of insects "wav'd thir limber fans / For wings, and smallest Lineaments exact / In all the Liveries deckt of Summer's pride / With spots of Gold and Purple, azure and green" (7: 476–79).

Heavenly beings are likewise gorgeously attired. In contrast to Coppe's vision of a "naked God," in *Paradise Lost* we find a deity who is not merely concealed but dressed in "utmost skirts / Of glory" (11: 332–33). The angels in particular are described through their figurative clothing. Raphael arrives in Eden "Veil'd with his gorgeous wings" (5: 250):

> . . . six wings he wore, to shade
> His lineaments Divine; the pair that clad
> Each shoulder broad, came mantling o'er his breast
> With regal Ornament; the middle pair
> Girt like a Starry Zone his waist, and round
> Skirted his loins and thighs with downy Gold
> And colors dipt in Heav'n; the third his feet
> Shaddow'd from either heel with feather'd mail
> Sky-tinctur'd grain. Like *Maia's* son he stood,
> And shook his Plumes, that Heav'nly fragrance filld
> The circuit wide.   (5: 277–87)

One critic, commenting on this passage, observes that "Raphael is really not *wearing* anything";[68] yet through the various and extensive descriptions of the wings "he wore" (which "clad," "mantled," "girt," and "skirted" his body) and their qualities (with "Ornament" and "feather'd mail"), the reader certainly has a visual impression of elaborate clothing. This pattern is repeated when Satan, not to be outdone, assumes a fabulous getup to disguise himself as an angel: "Under a Coronet his flowing hair / In curls on either cheek play'd, wings he wore / Of many a color'd plume sprinkl'd with Gold" (3: 640–642).[69]

In Eden, then, everything is naked and everything is clothed. (Or, conversely, in Eden nothing is naked and nothing is clothed.) Attempts to construct a symbolic system of meaning around this binary – so central to discussions of linguistic perfection – prove futile. The forms of "clothing" the earth and its species wear are a manifestation of their nakedness; clothing is not indicative of a divided sign, of a split between internal and external, but is an integrated element of the essence of creation. It is only after the Fall that the reader encounters extended and blatant representations of nakedness in *Paradise Lost*. The couple is suddenly "despoil'd / Of all [their] good, sham'd, naked, miserable" (9: 1138–39). They set about to gather leaves which,

> And with what skill they had, together sew'd,
> To gird thir waist, vain Covering as if to hide
> Thir guilt and dreaded shame; O how unlike
> To that first naked Glory   (9: 1112–15)

In the book of Genesis, Adam's shame about his nakedness reveals his sin to God; Milton of course follows this biblical tale. But postlapsarian nakedness looms disproportionately large in Milton's poem. In Genesis, Adam's naming of the animals takes two verses; Adam and Eve's realization of their nakedness and their construction of fig-leaf clothing takes only one.[70] In *Paradise Lost*, Adam's naming of the animals takes place in three lines; Adam's realization of his nakedness and his sewing of the fig-leaf clothing takes a full forty-six (9:1074–120). In Genesis, God's clothing of Adam takes one short verse; in *Paradise Lost*, Christ's clothing of Adam takes fourteen lines (10: 209–23).[71]

Thus while prelapsarian nakedness becomes invisible, postlapsarian nakedness – emblematic of human misery, insufficiency, exile and guilt – is the topic of extensive, reiterated discussion. This wretched, postlapsarian nakedness only emerges with the creation of dichotomous systems. Whereas in Eden the absence of binary structures rendered the division between naked and clothed fallacious ("that first naked Glory"), after the Fall nakedness assumes negative implications. Nakedness is now visible,

> . . . since our Eyes
> Op'n'd we find indeed, and find we know
> Both Good and Evil, Good lost, and Evil got,
> Bad Fruit of Knowledge, if this be to know,
> Which leaves us naked thus, of Honor void,
> Of Innocence, of Faith, of Purity,

> Our wonted Ornaments now soil'd and stain'd,
> And in our Faces evident the signs
> Of foul concupiscence . . .   (9: 1070–78)

Knowledge results from division, not only of good from evil, but from inward and outward human conditions. Adam and Eve become themselves divided "signes," as their faces attempt, however unsuccessfully, to mask their interior lust. The Fall is thus a split, a process of bifurcation. Nakedness, in the postlapsarian world, is no longer an expression of purity and integration, but a material sign of alienation.

Woven into the very fabric of *Paradise Lost*, then, are the conditions for the inaccessibility of paradise. While Milton entertains the concept of a pure world exemplified by its nakedness, such a world – and even the very concept of prelapsarian nakedness – remain unachievable through human means. Milton not only reminds his readers of their fallen state, but he creates an Eden which is removed from us by time and by its fundamental structural matrix, a unitary system that cannot be expressed through a binary linguistic structure.

The desire for the "naked truth" spurred many of Milton's contemporaries to seriously contemplate, and even to endeavor, a means of re-entering an Edenic state. While the fictional Adamites were created to mock radical attempts to become Adam, and while Webster's call for the universities to embark on a systematic program of uncovering the divinely imprinted "signatures" was rejected by scholars, Milton seriously contemplated the possibilities and difficulties of accessing Eden. Through employing the idea of nakedness, a dominant conceptual paradigm of the seventeenth century, Milton frustrates the reader's desire to use this postlapsarian binary for understanding the prelapsarian world, and thereby exposes the reader's imperfection. But if Milton rejects the radical hopes for re-entering the past Eden, his poem ends with an affirmation of the Quaker emphasis on the light within. For Adam, leaving Paradise and his immediate relationship with Creation is a process of learning to recognize the godhead within. This realization is not, as was the case for Coppe, a process of stripping away bifurcated, external systems of representation. Rather, like Fox and Boehme, Adam momentarily "attain[s] the summe of wisdome," an awesome realization of the wholeness of God. Knowing this, Adam is no longer "loath / To leave this Paradise, but shalt possess / A paradise within [him], happier far" (12: 585–87).

Epilogue: the fortunes of Hudibras

The many tragedies of civil war returned as farce with Samuel Butler's *Hudibras*. This mock-epic poem presents, in an overtly Cervantean fashion, the adventures of the over-zealous Presbyterian knight Hudibras and his philosophizing Independent sidekick Ralpho. The first part of the poem went on sale at the end of 1662; a year later, *Hudibras* had appeared in no less than five licensed and four pirated editions. During this time Butler also published the second part of the poem, but not before he had been beaten to it by an anonymous author who had produced his own sequel, a text which itself quickly went into four editions.[1] This spurious sequel was incorporated into the ever-dilating textual corpus of *Hudibras*, which expanded into three Books printed over the course of fifteen years. *Hudibras* quickly became, and long remained, one of the most popular and widely read texts of the seventeenth century, spawning "continuations" well into the eighteenth.[2]

As a capacious, expansive text, *Hudibras* thus appeared to encompass the anti-sectarian rhetoric that had pervaded pre-Restoration literature. Whereas attacks on religious sectarianism had previously been located in a flurry of separate pamphlets, *Hudibras* now provided a centralized poetic narrative which seemingly contained this discourse. Whereas earlier authors had written of religious sectarianism in terms of anatomy and dissection, Butler represents religious division through the corpulent and central figure of Hudibras. The text is virtually overflowing with the familiar accusations against sectarians, and the poem finds its own physical manifestation in Hudibras's bulging form. He becomes the puritan bellygod *par excellence*:

> Our knight did bear no less a Pack
> Of his own Buttocks on his back,
> . . .

> To poize this equally, he bore
> A *Paunch* of the same bulk before,
> Which still he had a speciall care
> To keep well cramm'd with thrifty fare,
> As White-pot, Butter-milk and Curds,
> Such as a Countrey house affords.   (1.1.289–90; 293–98)[3]

In addition to his own flesh, Hudibras's hose, "the Cup-board where he kept his meat . . . were lin'd with many a piece / Of Ammunition-Bread and Cheese, / And fat Black-puddings" (1.1.302, 311–13). As the poem progresses, images of food continually pour forth from the knight, as even his holsters contain "the surplus of such meat / As in his hose he could not get" (1.1.391–92). This body overflows, and overflows again, as the text, in its own terms, "dilates" (1.1.300) upon Hudibras's body.

As a bellygod, Hudibras continues the tradition of the grotesque puritan dramatized by Falstaff. Hudibras's cornucopian form situates him once again in the familiar setting of carnival, so frequently employed in depicting religious sectarianism. Indeed, much of *Hudibras* is overtly cast in terms of the Rabelaisian carnivalesque.[4] But while his earlier literary brethren were ridiculed for their participation *within* a carnival community, Hudibras is now firmly positioned *in opposition* to that community. In pre-Restoration pamphlet literature, it is the various sectarian characters who revel in the fields and feast in alehouses; even Zeal-of-the-Land Busy finds himself a participant in the fair. In *Hudibras*, the Presbyterian knight and his squire are pitted against the carnival revelers in a pitched mock-epic battle. The first Book revolves around the conflict between Hudibras and a carnival gathering enjoying a bear-baiting. Hudibras arrives on the scene, and preaches to the crowd on the danger such an event poses to the process of Reformation:

> For if *Bear-baiting* we allow,
> What good can *Reformation* doe?
> The bloud and treasure that's laid out,
> Is thrown away, and goes for nought.
> Are these the fruits o'th' *Protestation*,
> The Prototype of *Reformation*,
> . . .
> Did they for this draw down the Rabble,
> And make all *Cries* about the Town
> Joyn throats to cry the *Bishops* down?
> . . .

> When *Tinkers* bawl'd aloud, to settle
> *Church-Discipline*, for patching *Kettle*.
> No *Sow-gelder* did blow his horn
> To geld a Cat, but cry'd *Reform*.
> The *Oyster-women* lock'd their fish up,
> And trudg'd away, to cry *No Bishop*.
> . . .
> Instead of *Kitchin-stuff*, some cry
> A *Gospel-preaching-Ministry*:
> And some for *Old Suits, Coats, or Cloak,*
> No *Surplices*, nor *Service-book*.
> A strange harmonious inclination
> Of all degrees to *Reformation*.
> And is this all? is this the end
> To which these *carr'ings on* did tend?[5]

The knight's historical account of the mid-century social upheaval and religious protest describes a crowd very like the one he faces. The carnival mingling that Hudibras recalls, however, seeks the overturning of episcopal hierarchy; the carnival crowd now assembled seeks only the sport of bear-baiting. While the two activities could be said to have similar structural dynamics, the group that Hudibras addresses is seemingly free of ecclesiastical ambitions. The mock-hero's ideals are clearly out of place and out of date.

Hudibras is thus the tale of a bellygod who is expulsed by the carnival crowd. Throughout, the narrative contains a dual sense of expansion and bankruptcy, or of monumentality and decomposition (to borrow Alok Yadov's description ["Fractured Meanings," 530]). In Book 3, for example, the image of the prolific swarm returns in ways that look familiar:

> So ere the Storm of war broke out
> Religion spawn'd a various Rout,
> Of Petulent Capricious Sects,
> The Maggots of Corrupted Texts,
> That first Run all Religion down
> And after every swarm its own.   (3.2.7–12)

The sectarian swarm is again a product of textual proliferation (and *is* textual proliferation), but here it becomes self-annihilating. *Hudibras*, even as it revolves around the figure of a bellygod, and even as it overflows with descriptions of sectarianism, tells of decline and exhaustion. "The good old Cause now was grown Deform'd and Poor, / And fit to be turn'd out of Door" (3.2.103, 109–10). Hudibras, too, withers away. "I who was once as great as *Cæsar*, / Am now reduc'd to *Nebuchadnezar*," he tells his would be lover (*An Heroical Epistle of Hudibras to his Lady*, ll. 1–2). While Hudibras does not physically diminish, as Falstaff does over the course of *Henry IV*, Part 2, Hudibras does share in Falstaff's fortunes: just as the Lollard martyr finds himself emptied of religious significance and portrayed as a hapless lover in *The Merry Wives of Windsor*, so too Hudibras ends as a diminished Presbyterian pursuing an unrequited love.

As Hudibras dwindles (even as *Hudibras* expands), so too the complexities of religious dissent collapse into one category. Throughout the seventeenth century, and especially in the years of civil war, those advocating a presbyterian system of ecclesiastical governance were often as alarmed and as vocally opposed to religious sectarianism as were their episcopal neighbors. (Thomas Edwards is a case in point.) But in *Hudibras*, Presbyterians are blended together with the very sectarians they despised:

> Poor *Presbyter* was now Reduc'd
> Secluded, and Cashier'd, and Chews'd,
> Turn'd out, and Excommunicate,
> From all Affairs of Church and State.
> Reform'd t'a Reformado Saint,
> And glad to turn Itinierant.
> To strowl and teach from Town to Town,
> And those he had taught up, Teach down,
> And make those uses serve agen,
> Against the New-inlightned Men.
> As fit, as when at first, they were
> Reveal'd against the *Cavalier*.
> Damn *Anabaptist*, and *Fanatick*,
> As *Pat* as *Popish*, and *Prelatick*,
> And with as little variation,
> To serve for any Sect i'th' Nation.   (3.2.87–102)

While *Hudibras* begins with the comic partnership of the antithetical Presbyterian and Independent, by the end of the poem the distinction has nearly vanished. By merging together Presbyterians and Anabaptists, Butler recasts the multi-headed conflict of the civil wars into a polarized comparison: all those opposed to episcopacy are grouped together as dissenters. The saga begins to be told in terms which lend themselves to a labeling of "Puritans" and "Anglicans."

Thus even as *Hudibras* epitomizes the seventeenth-century tradition of depicting religious sectarianism in terms of the grotesque, the poem also marks the reversal of this representational mode. Earlier authors emphasized the fractured and scattered nature of religious dissent. *Hudibras*, both through its poetic form and its content, appears to present this conflict in a central character. This ever-dilating poem implies, paradoxically, a world of conflict that fundamentally assumes a dichotomous structure. Once this dichotomy takes shape, and once a character like Hudibras is positioned in opposition to the carnival crowd, the modern conception of "puritanical" begins to emerge. This formation is indicated by another text Butler probably composed while revising the 1674 edition of *Hudibras*: he entitled this text a "Satyr on the Licentious Age of Charles the 2d., Contrasted with the Puritanical One that Preceded It."[6] "Puritanical" becomes an antonym for "Licentious," and the Puritan is positioned as a marker for a repressive past. As the earlier alliance of puritans and license is reversed, the modern figure of the Puritan steps forth.

Notes

INTRODUCTION: DEFORMING REFORMATION

1 Numerous scholars have studied the role of Protestantism in forging a nationalistic consciousness; see, for example, Richard Helgerson, *Forms of Nationhood: The Elizabethan Writing of England* (University of Chicago Press, 1992), 258–61; Liah Greenfeld, *Nationalism: Five Roads to Modernity* (Cambridge, Mass.: Harvard University Press, 1992), 43, 51–66; Claire McEachern, *The Poetics of English Nationhood, 1590–1612* (Cambridge University Press, 1996), esp. 63–89; David Scott Kastan, "'The noyse of the new Bible': Reform and Reaction in Henrician England," in Claire McEachern and Debora Shuger, eds., *Religion and Culture in Renaissance England* (Cambridge University Press, 1997), 47–68.

2 *Gangræna: Or A Catalogue and Discovery of many of the Errours, Heresies, Blasphemies, and pernicious Practices of the Sectaries of this time* (1646; facsimile reprint, The Rota. Ilkley, UK: The Scolar Press, Ltd., 1977), I: sig. A4ʳ.

3 This play on "reformation"/"deformation" appears throughout seventeenth-century tracts. Richard Watson writes in *A Sermon Touching Schisme* (1642) of "some few Reformed Divines, such, it may be, as were rather Deformers, Authors of Schisme" (13); similarly, James Cranford writes in *Plain English: Or, The Sectaries Anatomized* (1646): "What, will such a Reformation (or rather deformation) content you now?" (3). Variations on this word play appear in the titles of *Conformities Deformity* (1646) and *The Scotch Presbyterian Weather-cock Pearch'd upon our English Steeple . . . or, Presbyterian Government in Scotland, and may consequently be in England with the Churches Deformation to the tune of Tom of Bedlam* (1647).

4 Many readers might find it useful to have a brief definition of terms. "Episcopal" refers to a form of ecclesiastical government in which authority resided primarily in a handful of bishops (and ultimately in the monarch). "Presbyterian" is a structure of church government in which authority is more diffuse: an individual congregation is headed by a Presbyter, groups of congregations are monitored by a classical assembly or classis, the various classes are brought together in a provincial synod, and at the top of the structure is a national synod. "Congregational" here signifies a congregation which is self-governing

(later termed "Independents"). Since the central church was the presumed status quo, it was not given a label; "Anglican" is a nineteenth-century invention with its own specific (and, for the early modern period, anachronistic) connotations.

A word might be in order about my use of capitalization. I have capitalized the names of specific religious groups in which one might claim to be a member (or could be imagined to be a member), such as "Anabaptist," "Protestant," or "Family of Love." I have not capitalized words which indicated a desired form of church government, such as "presbyterian" (it was only very late in the interregnum that the notion of a specific Presbyterian party emerged). As I will discuss below, within the contemporary usage of the time "puritan" most often was an ambiguous label that did not signify a specific group of people; I have kept the lower-case "p" as an indication of this general usage, and as a reminder that, as I discuss below, I am retaining the use of "puritan" as an entirely representational category.

5 See, for example, Thomas Edwards, *The Casting Down of the last and strongest hold of Satan* (1647), sig. BI^v; *The Presentment of a Schismaticke* (1642), 22; Christopher Lawne, *Brovvnisme tvrned the In-side out-ward* (1613), sig. A3^r. For a recent analysis of the ways in which this orthodox emphasis on ecclesiastical unity was played out within early modern culture, see Debora Kuller Shuger, *Habits of Thought in the English Renaissance: Religion, Politics, and the Dominant Culture* (Berkeley: University of California Press, 1990).

6 *The Arraignment of the Present Schism of New Separation in Old England* (1646), 2.

7 John Taylor, *A Cluster of Coxcombes* (1642), sig. A3^v; *Certaine Modest Observations and Considerations of the true Protestants of the Church of England* (1641), 2.

8 *The Pictvre of a Puritane*, 35, 1, 20, 8. Similarly, John Sprint, in *Propositions, Tending to prooue the Necessarie vse of the Christian Sabbaoth* (1607), defines a "puritan" as "a schismaticall, priuate, and præpared spirit to any headlesse error or brain-sicke hæresie" (7).

9 *A Puritane set forth In his Lively Colours: or, K. James his description of a Puritan* (1642), 2–3. As this passage indicates, in 1642 the question of definition for the term "puritan" was already "old" – and yet, it was still a question that was unresolved. Turning to King James as an authority appears to give the term a valid historical tradition, but the fact that James himself needed to define "puritan" indicates the word's ambiguous and evasive significance even from the moment it gained currency around the turn of the seventeenth century.

10 Cited in Lawrence A. Sasek, *Images of English Puritanism: A Collection of Contemporary Sources 1589–1646* (Baton Rouge and London: Louisiana State University Press, 1989), 287.

11 *The Master-piece of Round-heads* (1643), sigs. AI^v–A2^r.

12 "The Theatre Constructs Puritanism," in David L. Smith, Richard Strier, and David Bevington, eds., *The Theatrical City: Culture, Theatre and Politics in London, 1576–1649* (Cambridge University Press, 1995), 164.

13 Numerous scholars have provided substantial surveys of historical and historiographical uses of the term "puritan." Sasek, in *Images of English Puritanism*, provides an extremely useful overview of the term, summarizing contemporary historiographical uses as well as providing a brief summary of the term's sixteenth- and seventeenth-century meanings (1–27). John Morgan, in *Godly Learning: Puritan Attitudes towards Reason, Learning, and Education, 1560–1640* (Cambridge University Press, 1986), includes an entire chapter devoted to "The Problem of Definition" (9–22), which provides an excellent summary of recent historians' concepts of "puritanism." Christopher Hill notes the elasticity of the term and its contemporary application to religious separatists in *Society and Puritanism in Pre-Revolutionary England* (London: Secker and Warburg, 1964, 1–15). Patrick Collinson offers important considerations in "A Comment: Concerning the Name Puritan," *Journal of Ecclesiastical History* 31 (1980): 483–88; Collinson writes, "No laboratory-bench taxonomy of religious types and tendencies in pre-revolutionary England will serve if it sticks labels on isolated and inert specimens and fails to appreciate that the very terms themselves are evidence of an unstable and dynamic situation" (488). See also Collinson, *The Elizabethan Puritan Movement* (Oxford: Clarendon Press, 1990, first published 1967), 26–28. Peter Lake argues that contemporaries assigned the label of "puritan" based more upon a degree of zeal than on theological differences; see "Puritan Identities," *Journal of Ecclesiastical History* 35 (1984), 112–23. Another useful analysis of the historiographical function of the term is provided by Michael G. Finlayson, *Historians, Puritanism, and the English Revolution: The Religious Factor in English Politics before and after the Interregnum* (University of Toronto Press, 1983), 47–49, 57–76. The working definition that David Underdown uses in *Revel, Riot and Rebellion: Popular Politics and Culture in England 1603–1660* (Oxford University Press, 1985) is also valuable (41).

Annabel Patterson offers provocative speculation on the term in "The Very Name of the Game: Theories of Order and Disorder," in Thomas Healy and Jonathan Sawday, eds., *Literature and the English Civil War* (Cambridge University Press, 1990), 21–37. In *The Imaginary Puritan: Literature, Intellectual Labor, and the Origins of Personal Life* (Berkeley: University of California Press, 1992), Nancy Armstrong and Leonard Tennenhouse use the term to signify an abstract quality: "The phrase 'Imaginary Puritan' refers to a logical, ontological, and historical gap shared by historicisms old and new . . . To the gap and the continuity concealing it we have assigned the name 'puritan,' because the word invokes the generic intellectual ancestor that British and American scholars identify as the source of the power that makes individuals into subjects and vice versa. The puritan in question is 'imaginary' because the term does not come from or refer to anybody in particular. As far as we know, it never did. It came along and endowed an ensemble of cultural practices with a purely discursive body that made them vividly – indeed powerfully – graspable as an originary moment . . . Such an image does not arise from events but gives them meaning, places them in relation to us, and, in a word, makes them real" (8–9). While this notion is intriguing, the concept of the "imaginary puritan" is set forth as a unifying rubric for the diverse chapters in the book, and the authors do not really elaborate further on this abstract taxonomy.

In using "puritan" to signify religious separatism and sectarianism, I am following the descriptions reiterated throughout the sixteenth- and seventeenth-century pamphlets I have studied (see the Bibliography). In addition to the numerous derogatory uses of the term, even in its rare positive usage the word still signaled religious separatism. A significant instance of self-identification with "puritanism" is William Bradshawe, whose *English Puritanisme* (Amsterdam, 1605) was repeatedly published in the seventeenth century. Bradshaw's definition of "puritanism" as extreme congregationalism, in which each separate congregation would be self-sufficient (though political loyalties would continue to be owed to the state), is a lucid justification for what most of his contemporaries would deem "schism." When not applied specifically to religious separatism, "puritan" signaled nonconformist practices.

14 Cited in Sasek, *Images of English Puritanism*, 287.

15 Christopher Hill's comment that "puritan" presents an "admirable refuge from clarity of thought" (*Society and Puritanism*, 1) exemplifies this tension. As a historian, Hill requires a term with more classificatory precision; constructing a meaning of the term from early modern texts, however, seeks a pointed definition from a culture which repeatedly employed "puritan" to indicate a breakdown in clarity of thought.

16 J. D., *A Judgement or a Definition of the Visible and Invisible Church* (1641), 1.

17 Richard Byfield, *Temple-defilers defiled, Wherein a true Visible Church of Christ is Described. The Evils and pernicious Errours, especially appertaining to Schisme, Anabaptisme and Libertinisme, that infest our Church, are discovered* (1645), 3.

18 *A Protestants Account of his Orthodox Holding in Matters of Religion* (1642), 6. See also T. T., *A Myrror for Martinists, And all other Schismatiques, which in these dangerous daies do breake the godlie vnitie, and disturbe the Christian peace of the Church* (1590), 4.

19 *Rvles to Get Children by with Handsome Faces* (1642), sigs. AI^v–A2^r.

20 *Gangræna*, sigs. D4^v–EI^r.

21 John Taylor, *Rebels Anathematized, and Anatomized* (Oxford, 1645); James Cranford, *Plain English: Or, The Sectaries Anatomized* (1646); *The Sovndheads Description of the Rovndhead. Or, The Rovndhead Exactly Anatomized in his Integralls and Excrementalls* (1642). In addition to proclaimed anatomies,

we also find numerous texts such as *The Hunting of the Fox, or the Sectaries Dissected* (1648) which emphasize the idea of dissection. A tract written against Martin Marprelate, *Martins months minde, that is, A Certaine report, and true description of the Death, and Funeralls, of olde Martin Marre-prelate* (1589), describes his post-mortem: "His Heart, great, yet hollow; (as before manie gessed) especiallie to the peace of the Church, and quiet of the State. His Lungs, huge and made to prate. His Spleen large, that made him so gamesome. His Gall, wonderfullie ouerflowen with choller, that made him so testifie, & waiward withall. His Stomacke, full of grosse and stale humours, that procured him that same *Caninum appetitum*, that he had, an vnquenchable desire, to devoure all. His Entrailes full of filth, notwithstanding he had vttered so much before (marie of late daies indeed, as you heard, he voided nothing). I passe ouer the rest, whereof there was not one good part, but all disordered (as hee shewed himselfe aliue) and cleane rotten. I had forgotten his Tongue, which was wonderfullie swolne in his mouth; I thinke by reason of his blasphemie. But when they came to open the Head, (a straunge case) they found no crumme of braine within it" (sig. G2^v). For a discussion of the symbolic import of such representations, see Jonathan Sawday, *The Body Emblazoned: Dissection and the Human Body in Renaissance Culture* (London and New York: Routledge, 1995). For the impact of anatomies on literary form, see John G. Norman, *Literature after Dissection in Early Modern England* (forthcoming).

22 *Rabelais and his World*, trans. Hélène Iswolsky (Cambridge, Mass.: MIT Press, 1968; Bloomington: Indiana University Press, 1984), 26.

23 Spinola, *Rvles to Get Children By With Handsome Faces*, sigs. A4$^{r–v}$.

24 *The Rovting of the Ranters, Being a full Relation of their uncivil carriages, and blasphemous words and actions at their mad meetings, their several kind of musick, dances, and ryotings* (1650), 2.

25 It is interesting to note that in a society with restricted rights to assembly, religious reformers often had to disguise their meetings by gathering in places traditionally designated as sites of carnival – Elizabethan presbyterians convened in the anonymity of the throngs at Bartholomew Fair, while others disguised their conventicles as wedding celebrations; see Collinson, *Elizabethan Puritan Movement*, 250, 275, 320; Michael R. Watts, *The Dissenters: From the Reformation to the French Revolution* (Oxford: Clarendon Press, 1978), 19.

26 *Rovting of the Ranters*, 2.

27 John Taylor's *A Swarme of Sectaries and Schismatiques* (1641) portrays a group of nonconformists meeting in an alehouse; *A Brown Dozen of Drunkards* (1648) depicts a rabble of drinking, smoking, dancing, vomiting characters, many of whom are identified in the text as sectarians: "Drunken Wimble-tree" "staggers in his motions, like our old and new Enthusiasts, Familists, Anabablers" (sig. A3^r) and consorts

with "pot-professors" (sig. A3^v). "Drink-hard Helluoh" is compared to a "Gangrene" (invoking Edwards's text, note 2); "Drunken Barnabee" is a "Newter in Religion, halfe a Protestant, halfe a Papist" (sig. A4^v); "One drunken Tom Trouble-towne, or Troublesome" has associations with lay preaching, liberty of conscience, and sectarians such as Familists and Adamites (sig. B2^r); "Drunken Spermologus" is identified as a usurping lay preacher (sig. C3^r), as is "Drunken Phylautus" (sig. C3^r) and "Drunken Sip-Sobrine" (sig. C3^v).

28 It is important to remember that Malvolio's identity as a "puritan" is highly problematic. The primary basis for this identification, Maria's qualified statement "sometimes he is a kind of puritan" (*Twelfth Night*, 2.3.139), is almost immediately disavowed with her exclamation that "The dev'l a puritan that he is, or any thing constantly but a time-pleaser, an affection'd ass" (147–8). William P. Holden examines the vast array of literary puritan types in *Anti-Puritan Satire 1572–1642* (New Haven: Yale University Press, 1954), esp. 40–43. Holden's discussion of Malvolio (esp. 123–26) outlines the complications and ambiguities of labeling Malvolio as "puritan"; the notes for these pages provide a summary of early critical debate over Malvolio's puritanical and non-puritanical tendencies. Holden himself writes, "Thus, in a number of situations, Malvolio has violated established conventions for the satiric portrayal of the precision. But it is not without reason that Malvolio has been called a Puritan . . . for in his character there is just enough of the precisian so that the audience thinks of him as something more complicated than merely melancholic" (125). The upshot of Holden's argument is that while Malvolio is certainly "puritanical" (in the current, modern sense of the word), he is not, properly speaking, a puritan; I would agree with this position. Similarly, Holden continues to discuss *Measure for Measure*'s Angelo, noting that "in the course of the play, Angelo is never called a Puritan, and in no particular sense is he a Puritan; he belongs to no sect, he makes no pretense of a particular religious doctrine, and he has few of the conversational tags which labeled the stage Puritan for the audience" (127).

29 Gerald R. Cragg, *Freedom and Authority: A Study of English Thought in the Early Seventeenth Century* (Philadelphia: The Westminster Press, 1975), 219. While references to the violent uprisings of the earlier Lollards or continental Anabaptists occasionally hover in the background of anti-sectarian literature (the escapades of the Muenster Anabaptists becoming an increasingly popular topic during the rapid sectarian proliferation of the 1640s), for the overwhelming majority of authors sectarian violence did not seem to be a central concern.

30 Michael Walzer, *The Revolution of the Saints: A Study in the Origins of Radical Politics* (Cambridge, Mass.: Harvard University Press, 1965), viii.

1 THE PURITAN IN THE ALEHOUSE: FALSTAFF AND THE DRAMA
OF MARTIN MARPRELATE

1 John Bale, *Brefe Chronycle, concernynge the Examinacyon and death of the blessed martyr of Christ syr Johan Oldecastell the lorde Cobham* (Antwerp, 1544), fol. 4^v. All subsequent references are to this edition. Bale expands upon William Tyndale's account of Oldcastle, *The examinacion of master William Thorpe preste accused of heresye. The examinacion of Syr J. Oldcastell* (Antwerp, 1530).

2 Bale, *Brefe Chronycle*, fols. 9^r, 13^r, 49^r.

3 *Ibid.*, fols. 52^r, 53^r.

4 See Margaret Aston, *Lollards and Reformers: Images and Literacy in Late Medieval Religion* (London: The Hambledon Press, 1984), 237.

5 The most thorough catalogue of sixteenth-century references to Oldcastle can be found in Alice-Lyle Scoufos, *Shakespeare's Typological Satire: A Study of the Falstaff–Oldcastle Problem* (Athens, Ohio: Ohio University Press, 1979). See also Annabel Patterson, "Sir John Oldcastle as Symbol of Reformation Historiography," in Donna B. Hamilton and Richard Strier, eds., *Religion, Literature, and Politics in Post-Reformation England, 1540–1688* (Cambridge University Press, 1996), 6–26.

6 John Stowe's *Annales of England* (1592) describes Oldcastle as a "strong . . . [and] meetely good man of war, . . . a most perverse enimie to the state of the church at that time" (Scoufos, *Shakespeare's Typological Satire*, 65). This depiction of Oldcastle returns to the fifteenth-century tradition of portraying Oldcastle as an enemy to church and state; this image had predominated until Tyndale's pamphlet (see note 1). Responding to Tyndale, Sir Thomas More, in Scoufos's words, "cites the burning of Oldcastle as an English example of the wise use of fire to control destructive forces" (*ibid.*, 56; see 56–67).

7 For a detailed analysis of the historiographical conflict in fifteenth- and sixteenth-century accounts of Oldcastle, see Annabel Patterson, *Reading Holinshed's "Chronicles"* (Chicago and London: The University of Chicago Press, 1994), 130–53.

8 Scoufos provides extensive evidence that Shakespeare's contemporaries, as well as his eighteenth-century readers, recognized Falstaff as an alias for Oldcastle; see especially chapter 2 of *Shakespeare's Typological Satire*. See also Gary Taylor, "The Fortunes of Oldcastle," *Shakespeare Survey* 38 (1985): 85–100, esp. 91.

9 Taylor lists Thomas Middleton (1604), Nathan Field (*c.* 1611), the anonymous author of *Wandering-Jew, Telling Fortunes to Englishmen* (*c.* 1628), George Daniel (1647), Thomas Randolph (1651), and Thomas Fuller (1655, 1662) as those noting the original identity of "Oldcastle" ("Fortunes," 85–86); for evidence of court performances of *1 Henry IV* under the name of "Oldcastle," see Taylor, "Fortunes," 90–91.

10 Falstaff also has associations with Sir John Fastolfe, who is called "Falstaff" in *1 Henry VI* and who was considered a religious figure.

H. Mutschmann and K. Wentersdorf write: "The fact that the name chosen by Shakespeare as a substitute for Oldcastle, namely Falstaff, was that of another highly esteemed Protestant aroused the anger of the Puritans still more . . . The historical Sir John Fastolfe (1378?–1459) was one of the leaders of the English forces fighting in France during the reign of King Henry VI. He allegedly behaved 'with much cowardice' on one occasion, and in *1 Henry VI* (iii.2; iv.1), Shakespeare shows Fastolfe deserting the hero Talbot on the field of battle. The Puritans rejected this as a historical error if not a slander, because they regarded him as a Lollard sympathizer"; *Shakespeare and Catholicism* (New York: Sheed and Ward, 1952), 348.

11 Epilogue, ll. 31–32. This and all subsequent references to the Henriad are taken from the Arden edition, edited by A. R. Humphreys (London: Methuen and Co., 1966; London: Routledge, 1991).

12 Critics have almost universally claimed that the name-change was the direct result of protests by William Brooke, Lord Cobham; see Robert J. Fehrenbach, "When Lord Cobham and Edmund Tilney 'were at odds': Oldcastle, Falstaff, and the Date of *1 Henry VI*," *Shakespeare Studies* 18 (1986): 87–101. Thomas Pendleton provides what seems to me a more logical explanation for the switch, noting that Shakespeare, a man of seemingly conservative religious inclinations, "must have been surprised to find that his proto-Puritan figure of fun was for much of his audience a proto-Protestant martyr . . . The change from 'Oldcastle' to 'Falstaff' seems to have been motivated not just by Sir William Brooke's displeasure, but as much – and in the greatest likelihood, much more – by the displeasure of a significant part of Shakespeare's audience at his treatment of a hero of their religion"; " 'This is not the man': On Calling Falstaff Falstaff," *Analytical and Enumerative Bibliography* 4 (1990): 68–69. The Epilogue to *2 Henry VI* thus becomes more comprehensible: "a public apology implies that at least a considerable part of the public had been offended" (68). Late sixteenth- and seventeenth-century reformers frequently claimed an ideological hereditary connection with the Lollards, and Wyclif's name pervades pamphlet literature. Stephen Brachlow cites several examples of prominent reformers who claimed a genealogy from the Lollards in *The Communion of Saints: Radical Puritan and Separatist Ecclesiology* (Oxford University Press, 1988); among these were Walter Travers (81), William Ames (91), Robert Parker (91), and Foxe (90). See also Anthony Milton, "The Church of England, Rome, and the True Church: The Demise of a Jacobean Consensus," in Kenneth Fincham, ed., *The Early Stuart Church 1603–1642* (London: MacMillan Press, Ltd., 1993), esp. 191–92.

13 *A Critical Edition of* "I Sir John Oldcastle," ed. Jonathan Rittenhouse, *The Renaissance Imagination*, ed. Stephen Orgel, vol. 9 (New York: Garland Publishing, Inc., 1984), 104. Robert Wilson and Richard Hathaway also collaborated with Munday and Drayton.

14 Gary Taylor, Stanley Wells, John Jowett, and William Montgomery, *William Shakespeare: The Complete Works* (Oxford: Clarendon Press, 1986), 509.

15 In "The Fortunes of Oldcastle," Taylor defends his decision to reinstate "Oldcastle" as the name of Hal's companion. Taylor argues that "in the mouth of a fictional character called Falstaff, the words lose their historicity and ambiguity. To some extent, this is what happens to the whole character. The name 'Falstaff' fictionalizes, depoliticizes, secularizes, and in the process trivializes the play's most memorable character. It robs the play of that tension created by the distance between two available interpretations of one of its central figures" (95). While I appreciate the impulse to rescue Shakespeare from the evils of sixteenth-century court politics, I must disagree with Taylor's editorial decision. To annihilate the effects of Shakespeare's contemporary censors is to rewrite history in a disturbingly Orwellian fashion, and to deny the text's sociopolitical setting. In addition, if, as Taylor effectively argues, Elizabethan and Jacobean audiences were highly aware of Falstaff's "real" identity as Oldcastle, then part of the pleasure of this theatrical experience would have been the knowledge that one could "read" the clandestine identity hidden behind the name, much like the intrigue of a *roman à clef*. Since "Falstaff" is the name which was presented to the vast majority of viewers, changing his name would be the equivalent of demystifying allegory; *The Faerie Queene*, for example, would not be nearly as titillating if the veil of allegorical names were stripped, and Una, Britomart, and the Faerie Queene herself merely became "Queen Elizabeth." In short, rather than depoliticizing the play or robbing it of tension, the presence of the name "Falstaff" *combined with* the knowledge of the character's "true" identity heightens awareness of the political circumstances of the play. If "Oldcastle" were to become the predominant title for this character a hundred years from now, as Gary Taylor desires, the history of repression experienced by the Elizabethan stage (and indeed by the arts in general) could easily be overlooked; calling attention to the name "Oldcastle" while retaining the enforced name-change "Falstaff," on the other hand, highlights this repressive control.

The decision of the Oxford editors has spawned numerous responses; see Jonathan Goldberg, "The Commodity of Names: 'Falstaff' and 'Oldcastle' in *1 Henry IV,*" in *Reconfiguring the Renaissance: Essays in Critical Materialism*, ed. Jonathan Crewe (Cranbury, N.J.: Associated University Press, 1992), 76–88. David Scott Kastan, "'Killed With Hard Opinions': Oldcastle, Falstaff, and the Reformed Text of *1 Henry IV,*" in Thomas L. Berger and Laurie E. McGuire, eds., *Textual Formations and Reformations* (Newark: University of Delaware Press, 1998), 14. Pendleton notes the flaws in the assumption that only the name was changed, without corresponding changes in the text ("'This is not the man',"

59–71); David Bevington, who first disagreed with Taylor and Wells's decision, keeps the name of "Falstaff" in the single volume *1 Henry IV* that he edited for *The Oxford Shakespeare* (Oxford: Clarendon Press, 1987). For a pointed summation of this editorial "battle" (Bevington's term), see the review by John W. Velz in *Shakespeare Quarterly* 43 (1992): 107–09. In a different vein, Harry Berger Jr. explores how the ideological debates over Falstaff's true name cloud (in his view) the performative relationship of character and actor; see "The Prince's Dog: Falstaff and the perils of Speech-Prefixity," *Shakespeare Quarterly* 49 (1998): 40–73.

16 Fehrenbach, "When Lord Cobham," 92. Fehrenbach agrees with S. Schoenbaum, *Shakespeare's Lives* (Oxford: Clarendon Press, 1970), 144, that the name was simply a mistake.

17 These include Mark Dominik in *A Shakespeare Anomaly: Shakespeare's Hand in 'Sir John Oldcastle'* (Beaverton, Oregon: Alioth Press, 1991), 5. See also E. A. J. Honigmann, "Sir John Oldcastle: Shakespeare's Martyr," in *"Fanned and Winnowed Opinions": Shakespeare Essays Presented to Harold Jenkins*, ed. John W. Mahon and Thomas A. Pendleton (London: Methuen, 1987), 118–32. Scoufos repeatedly attributes Shakespeare's transformation of the historical Oldcastle to a desire to satirize the Cobham family, see *Shakespeare's Typological Satire*, esp. 107. After William's death in March 1597, we find Master Ford assuming the alias of "Brook" in *The Merry Wives of Windsor*, seemingly an allusion to the new Lord Cobham, Henry Brooke (and here again protests caused the name to be changed to "Broom"). The reference was apparently included for the entertainment of Sir George Carey, patron of the Chamberlain's Men and Henry Brooke's unsuccessful rival for government positions. The Carey–Brooke friction continued to provide satiric fodder for playwrights; Nashe's *Lenten Stuffe*, the lost *Isle of Dogs*, and Jonson's *Every Man in his Humour* all take jabs at the Brooke family. See Charles Nicholl, *A Cup of News: The Life of Thomas Nashe* (London: Routledge & Kegan Paul, 1984), 249–55.

18 See Scoufos, *Shakespeare's Typological Satire*, 35–36.

19 Harold Bloom, *Ruin the Sacred Truths: Poetry and Belief from the Bible to the Present* (Cambridge, Mass.: Harvard University Press, 1987), 86. Taylor states that Shakespeare's "decision to conflate the historical Oldcastle with the theatrical Vice" (J. Dover Wilson's reading) was a radical innovation ("Fortunes," 96).

20 The phrase is Nicholl's, *A Cup of News*, 64.

21 For a concise history of the Marprelate printings, as well as the related activities of Udall, Penry, Waldegrave, and Throkmorton, see Patrick Collinson, *The Elizabethan Puritan Movement* (Oxford: Clarendon Press, 1990, first published 1967), 391–96.

22 William Pierce, *An Historical Introduction to the Marprelate Tracts* (London: Archibald Constable, 1908), 152.

23 The authorship of the Marprelate tracts has been the subject of a centuries-old debate. Contemporaries tended to identify Penry as the principal author (see Nashe, *An Almond for a Parrat*, [1589] sig. E2ᵛ). One of the most convincing cases for authorship is made by Leland H. Carlson, *Martin Marprelate, Gentleman: Master Job Throkmorton Laid Open in his Colors* (San Marino, Calif.: The Huntington Library, 1981), while Donald J. McGinn argues exhaustively for Penry in *John Penry and the Marprelate Controversy* (New Brunswick: Rutgers University Press, 1966). J. Dover Wilson also advanced his own theory of authorship, suggesting that Martin was Sir Roger Williams; see *Martin Marprelate and Shakespeare's Fluellen: A New Theory of the Authorship of the Marprelate Tracts* (London: Alexander Moring Limited, 1912). As scholars become more attuned to the collaborative nature of early modern production, however, this search for a lone penman seems increasingly unrealistic.

24 This and all references to the Marprelate tracts come from The Scolar Press facsimile reprint (Menston, England, 1970). I will be following the tracts' original pagination; here, *The Epistle*, 1.

25 *The Collected Essays of Christopher Hill*, Volume One: *Writing and Revolution in 17th Century England* (Amherst: The University of Massachusetts Press, 1985), 76.

26 The promised *Epitome* of John Bridges's "right worshipful volume written against the Puritans" (end of November 1588) was followed in turn by the broadside *Minerall and metaphysicall schoolpoints* (mid-March 1589), *Hay any worke for Cooper* (March 1589), Martin Junior's *Theses Martinianae* (22 July 1589), and Martin Senior's *The iust censure and reproofe* (29 July 1589).

27 *Marre Mar-Martin: or Marre-Martins medling, in a manner misliked* (1590), sig. A3ʳ.

28 Hill, *Writing and Revolution*, 75.

29 *Ibid.*, 77.

30 *A sermon preached at Pauls Cross on 9 February 1588* (1588).

31 William Pierce, ed., *The Marprelate Tracts 1588, 1589* (London: James Clarke & Co., 1911), 200.

32 *Ibid.*, 357n. Martin Senior has Archbishop Whitgift give orders to search London for Martinist pamphlets: "'We will take order also that the Court may be watched, who disperse, or reade these libells there. And in faith I thinke they do my Lord of Essex greate wrong, that say he fauours Martin'" (*The iust censure and reproofe of Martin Iunior*, sig. A4ʳ).

33 *The iust censure and reproofe of Martin Iunior*, sig. A4ᵛ.

34 Lyly, *Pappe with an hatchet* (1589), sig. B2ᵛ.

35 Nicholl, *A Cup of News*, 74–75. Bacon takes on the role of peacemaker in *Advertisement touching the Controversies of the Church of England* (late 1589), and Richard Harvey takes on the persona of "Plaine Percevall the Peace-maker" in *Plaine Percevall* (late 1589). Gabriel Harvey's *Advertisement for Papp-hatchett and Martin Marprelate* (November 1589) is in part a

response to personal attacks from Lyly. Richard Harvey's "abuse of the anti-Martinists in *Plaine Percevall,* and of Nashe in *The Lamb of God* [1590], was the spark which ignited the Nashe–Harvey quarrel" (Nicholl, *A Cup of News,* 75). C. L. Barber discusses the ways in which those entering the Marprelate fray styled themselves as joining Martin's "Maygame" in *Shakespeare's Festive Comedy* (Princeton, N.J.: Princeton University Press, 1959), 55.

36 Neil Rhodes, *Elizabethan Grotesque* (London: Routledge & Kegan Paul, 1980), 4. Rhodes discusses Shakespeare's debt to the "Nasheian grotesque" in *1 and 2 Henry IV* (5). Nicholl writes, "Of all the anti-Martinists it was Nashe who took most readily to Martin's polemic 'vein,' caught its effervescence and bite, revelled in its ranging freedom" (*A Cup of News,* 76). The "Nasheian grotesque" was thus indirectly inherited from Marprelate himself.

37 *Hay,* 23; *Epistle,* 37; *Hay,* 33; *Hay,* 45.

38 *Martins months minde,* title page.

39 In *A Nevv Letter of Notable Contents* (1593), Gabriell Harvey attacks Nashe for his following of "Rabelays" (sig. B2^v). Nashe's anti-Martinist tract *An Almond for a Parrat* is found in *The Works of Thomas Nashe,* ed. Ronald B. McKerrow, 5 vols. (Oxford: Basil Blackwell, 1958); here, III: 374 and 341. Other anti-Martinist tracts possibly by Nashe, such as *A Countercuffe given to Martin Junior* (1589), *The Return of Pasquill* (1589), and *The First Part of Pasquills Apologie* (1590), are in Volume I. McKerrow lists *The Almond* under "Doubtful Works," but Nicholl describes this text as "the one anti-Martinist pamphlet accepted as entirely his," while establishing a collaborative relationship with Robert Greene for the authorship of the Pasquill tracts – with Nashe as the "news-hound" and Greene as the author (*A Cup of News,* 71–73, esp. 72). Textual references in parentheses all refer to the McKerrow edition.

40 Mikhail Bakhtin, *Rabelais and His World,* trans. Hélène Iswolsky (Cambridge, Mass.: MIT Press, 1968; Bloomington: Indiana University Press, 1984), 26.

41 *Almond,* in *The Works of Thomas Nashe,* III: 355.

42 Sig. E1^r. In a similar moment, Lyly writes: "There is small difference between Swallowes & Martins, either in shape or nature, saue onely, that the Martins, haue a more beetle head, they both breed in Churches, and hauing fledgde their young ones, leaue nothing behind them but durt. Vnworthie to come into the Church porch, or to be nourished vnder anie good mans Eues, that gnawe the bowels, in which they were bred, and defile the place, in which they were ingendered" (sigs. C1^v–C2^r).

43 Mary Grace Muse Adkins argues that *A Knack to Know a Knave* is a surviving anti-Martinist play, but while this play probably emanates from the Marprelate controversy, it is both too late (1592) and too formally constructed to be one of the grotesque anti-puritan interludes

referred to in the tracts themselves ("The Genesis of Dramatic Satire Against the Puritans, as Illustrated in *A Knack to Know a Knave*," *Review of English Studies* 22 [1946]: 81–95, esp. 81–85).

44 According to *Pappe with an hatchet*, Marprelate was mocked at St. Paul's by the choir children; at the Theatre, a playhouse near Finsbury; and at Thomas a Waterings in Southwark (Pierce, *Historical Introduction*, 222). For other references to the staging of Martinism, see *A Whip for an Ape* (1589), 3; *A Myrror for Martinists* (1590), 24; Harvey, *Plaine Percevall the Peace-Maker* (1589), 8; Lyly, *Pappe with an hatchet*, sig. E2^v. For other theatrical references, see Marphoreus, *Martins months minde* (1589), sigs. D2^r, D3^r.

45 Nicholl, *A Cup of News*, 68.

46 Rhodes notes that a particularly violent anti-Martinist play "was probably acted by Paul's Boys in 1589 and the company closed as a result. The public theatres were also engaged in anti-Marprelate satire, but they managed to escape official sanctions" (*Elizabethan Grotesque*, 66–67).

47 *The Works of Thomas Nashe*, I: 59.

48 Lyly writes in *Pappe with an hatchet*: "He shall not bee brought in as whilom he was, and yet verie well, with a cocks combe, an apes face, a wolfs bellie, cats clawes, & c . . . A stage plaier, though he bee but a cobler by occupation, yet his chance may bee to play the Kings part. Martin, of what calling so euer he be, can play nothing but the knaues part . . . Would it not bee a fine Tragedie, when *Mardocheus* shall play a Bishoppe in a Play, and Martin *Hamman*, and that he that seekes to pull downe those that are set in authoritie aboue him, should be hoysted vpon a tree aboue all others" (32). In this theatrical fantasy, Martin's jesting depictions of social inversion are graphically realized through the image of his hanging body.

49 Michel Foucault, *Discipline and Punish: The Birth of the Prison*, trans. Alan Sheridan (New York: Vintage Books, 1979), 49.

50 *Martins months minde*, sig. E3^v.

51 Nicholl, *A Cup of News*, 68.

52 *The Drama of Dissent: The Radical Poetics of Nonconformity, 1380–1590* (Chapel Hill and London: The University of North Carolina Press, 1986), 183–84.

53 *'Betwixt Jest and Earnest': Marprelate, Milton, Marvell, Swift, and the Decorum of Religious Ridicule* (University of Toronto Press, 1979), 51.

54 *Mar-Martine, I know not why a trueth in rime set out* (1589), sig. A4^v.

55 *Martins months minde*, sig. D1^v.

56 In *Margins and Marginality: The Printed Page in Early Modern England* (Charlottesville and London: University Press of Virginia, 1993), Evelyn Tribble writes that Lyly "goes to some pains to avoid a potential collapse of satirizer and satirized," and that Bacon, urging the suppres-

sion of the anti-Martinists, also "recognizes the tendency of the satirist and satirized to collapse" (118, 121).

57 *Margins and Marginality,* 117.

58 Nicholl, *A Cup of News,* 68. The letter is quoted in full in the notes to *Pappe with an hatchet,* Puritan Discipline Tracts (London: John Petheram, 1844), 48.

59 *Ibid.,* 49.

60 See, for example, *The Arraignment of Mr. Persecution . . . by Youngue MARTIN MAR-PRIEST, Son to old MARTIN the Metropolitane* (1645), *The Nativity of Sir John Presbyter* (1645), *The Character of a Puritan; and his Gallimaufrey of the Antichristian Clergie: prepared with D. Bridges Sawce for the present time to feed on. By the worthy Gentleman, D. Martin Mar-Prelate* (1643); *Divine Observations upon the London-Ministers Letter against Toleration, by . . . Martin Mar-Priest, Sonne, and Heire to Old Martin the Metrapolitane* (1646); Richard Overton [Martin Mar-Priest, pseud.], *The Arraignment of Mr. Persecution* (1645); Martin Claw-Clergey [pseud.], *A Sadre Decretall, or Hue and Cry. From his superlative Holinesse, Sir Symon Synod, for the Apprehension of Reverend Young Martin Mar-Priest* (1645); Martin the Metropolitan [pseud.], *Hay any worke for Cooper; or, A Brief Pistle directed by way of an Hublication* [*sic*] *to the Reverence Byshops* (1642); and *Tom Nash his Ghost. Written by Thomas Nash his Ghost, with Pap with a Hatchet, a little revived since the 30. Yeare of the late Qu. Elizabeths Reigne, when Martin Mar-prelate was as mad as any of his Tub-men are now* (1642). Nigel Smith discusses the Civil War resurgence of the Marprelate tradition in *Literature and Revolution in England 1640–1660* (New Haven and London: Yale University Press, 1994), 297–304. See also Hill, *Writing and Revolution,* 78–80.

61 See Anne Hudson, *The Premature Reformation: Wycliffite Texts and Lollard History* (Oxford: Clarendon Press, 1988), 510–12; 200. For Lollard literacy and dependence on text, see chapters 4 and 5.

62 Aston, *Lollards and Reformers,* 220–21, 231.

63 Tribble writes, "In particular, the author of the Marprelate pamphlets parodies the conventions of the page, seemingly subverting them – as well as the normal codes governing discourse – in order to draw attention to the need for the reform of church government" (*Margins and Marginality,* 102).

64 *Ibid.,* 109.

65 Udall was also sentenced to death, but received a reprieve, in large part through the efforts of Sir Walter Ralegh, related by marriage to Job Throkmorton; Udall later died in prison.

66 See Nicholl's discussion of the "Tale of the Beare and the Foxe" from *Pierce Penilesse,* which he convincingly reads as anti-puritan allegory, with pervasive references to the suppressed Marprelate controversy (*A Cup of News,* 112–15).

67 The date of the first performance was probably around 1586; it was licensed in 1594, printed in 1598 (with the title page referring to a

performance by the Queen's Players) and again in 1617 (with the title page referring to a performance by the King's Majesty's Servants). See Seymour M. Pitcher, *The Case for Shakespeare's Authorship of "The Famous Victories"* (London: Alvin Redman, 1962), 166–82. Pitcher's book contains many interesting observations about the playtext, but I do not find his argument for Shakespeare's authorship convincing.

68 *Reading Holinshed's "Chronicles,"* 152. The examples from Bale and Walsingham are also noted in *ibid.*, 137 and 151, respectively.

69 The greeting is from the anti-Martinist Cutbert Curryknave in *An Almond for a Parrat* (*The Works of Thomas Nashe*, III: 344), a text which is dedicated to Will Kemp, "vice-gerent [*sic*] to the Ghost of Dicke Tarlton."

70 "Sir John Oldcastle," 19, 23. Richard Helgerson also interconnects Oldcastle, Falstaff, and Martin Marprelate in *Forms of Nationhood: The Elizabethan Writing of England* (University of Chicago Press, 1992), 250–51. Neil Rhodes, too, positions *Henry IV* in the context of the Marprelate tracts and discusses the influence of Nashe on Shakespeare's earlier writing, but does not claim the same direct connection for Falstaff, perhaps because he seems unaware of Falstaff's Lollard origins (*Elizabethan Grotesque*, 89–99).

71 *Brefe Chronycle*, fol. 26^{r-v}.

72 See *The Works of Thomas Nashe*, I: 59 and 92. The success of *A Whip for an Ape* is suggested by the fact that it was quickly reprinted with a new title, *Rythmes against Martin Marre-Prelate* (1589?).

73 Similarly, Falstaff's references to Maid Marian (*1HIV* 3.3.112–13) are reminiscent of Martin's fate on stage, and although the Falstaff of *The Merry Wives of Windsor* is emptied of his religious associations, his cross-dressing (and even his repeated beatings) also duplicate the tenor of the anti-Martinist performances.

74 Nicholl writes: "Will Kemp may also have contributed his famous comic talents: a later Martinist tract mentions a 'Kemp' among the 'haggling and profane' detractors of Martin, and Nashe dedicated his own effort, *An Almond for a Parrat*, to Kemp. Both Lanham and Kemp were old members of Leicester's troupe, which had dispersed on the death of its patron in 1588 and joined ranks with Lord Strange's Men. The latter company was specifically mentioned by Lord Mayor Hart in November 1589, when the authorities were moving to suppress the unseemly plays they had originally encouraged. It seems probable that Strange's Men, including Kemp and Lanham, were responsible for some of these gruesome travesties of Martin" (*A Cup of News*, 68). Martin Holmes persuasively argues for Kemp's role as Falstaff in *Shakespeare and His Players* (New York: Charles Scribner's Sons, 1972), 47–50, and J. Dover Wilson writes: "We know very little about the casting of Shakespeare's plays, but William Kempe was the comic man of the Lord Chamberlain's men, one of the principal sharers, and very popular with the London public; so that it seems natural to assume that

the character of Falstaff was written for and, theatrically speaking, created by him. The Quarto of Part II even has a stage-direction, 'Enter Will' early in the Doll scene (2.4) which is paralleled by 'Enter Will Kemp' in the Second Quarto of *Romeo and Juliet* and is best explained, I think, as a Falstaff entry for the same player"; *The Fortunes of Falstaff* (Cambridge University Press, 1944), 124. Earlier critics such as Thomas Whitfield Baldwin suggested that Thomas Pope had played the part, based on the assumption that this actor did "high comedy" parts, while Kemp took the "low"; see *The Organization and Personnel of the Shakespearean Company* (Princeton University Press, 1927), 231.

75 *The Fortunes of Falstaff*, 16, 33.

76 *Lectures and Essays*, vol. I (London: Macmillan and Co., Limited, 1905), 141–42.

77 Naseeb Shaheen, *Biblical References in Shakespeare's History Plays* (Newark: University of Delaware Press, 1989), 137.

78 Giorgio Melchiori, the editor of *The Second Part of King Henry IV* for The New Cambridge Shakespeare (Cambridge University Press, 1989), also notes that "Falstaff's hymn-singing is . . . possibly a survival of the caricature of the original Oldcastle, a Lollard, equated by the Elizabethans with the Puritans" (76n). For the role of musical psalms in godly forms of worship see Collinson, *The Elizabethan Puritan Movement*, 359.

79 Mutschmann and Wentersdorf, *Shakespeare and Catholicism*, 347; see 345–49 for a discussion of Falstaff's status as a puritan. S. L. Bethell also discusses Falstaff's "Puritan" dialogue, "The Comic Elements in Shakespeare's Histories," *Anglia* 71 (1952), 94 and 98–99.

80 Christopher Baker, "The Christian Context of Falstaff's 'Finer End,' " *Explorations in Renaissance Culture* 12 (1986): 76; Goldberg, "The Commodity of Names," 77; Honigmann, "Sir John Oldcastle," 127.

81 New Variorum Shakespeare, 36, 37, 38n.

82 Part 1, 15n. The notes to Humphreys's edition provide fascinating examples of the editorial tunnel vision which preempts consideration of Falstaff as a representation of a religious figure. One example of Humphreys's editorial inconsistencies is the definition given for the terms "not-pated" and "knotty-pated." In a moment of anger, Hal calls Falstaff "thou knotty-pated fool" (*1HIV* 2.4.222). The footnote for this line glosses "knotty-pated" as "block-headed." The term "not-pated," however, which the Prince hurls at the unfortunate Francis in a similar tirade (*1HIV* 2.4.69), is defined as a reference to short hair, common among the lower and middle classes, "and the Puritans got the nickname of roundheads because they for the most part belonged to these ranks" (Part 1, 59–60n). Similarly, in Part 2 "smooth-pates" is defined as "city (Puritan) tradesmen who, despising long locks of fashion, cropped their hair short; known later as Roundheads" (1.2.38, note). Why couldn't Hal also be using the term "knotty-headed" with such connotations when he speaks to Falstaff?

83 Part 1, 18n; Part 2, 55n.
84 Bethell, "The Comic Elements in Shakespeare's Histories," 99; Bloom, *Ruin the Sacred Truths*, 84; Hemingway, New Variorum, cited in Arden edition, Part 1, 15.
85 This easy division continues to reinscribe, reinforce, and reinstitutionalize itself in contemporary criticism. One example of its usage is the equation of "puritan" with "antitheatrical." In a fascinating footnote, Jonas Barish justifies his choice of the term "Puritan" to describe the anti-theatrical Stephen Gosson: "I use the convenient shorthand term 'Puritan' despite the fact that not all writers against the stage were Puritans. Gosson, for example, . . . 'was actually a vigorous opponent of Puritanism.'" *The Antitheatrical Prejudice* (Berkeley: University of California Press, 1981), 82n. Noting Christopher Hill's warning against the indeterminacy of the term "puritan," Barish states that he is using this term to indicate "a complex of attitudes best represented by those strictly designated as Puritans" (*ibid.*, 82n) – yet Gosson, whom Barish himself acknowledges is anything but "strictly designated as a Puritan," is soon firmly located in the puritan camp based on his anti-theatrical tract, *Plays Confuted in Five Actions* (1582), which was possibly commissioned "by the London authorities" (*ibid.*, 89–90). The conceptual incongruity of an author who is simultaneously writing against the stage and against puritans is awkward and uncomfortable; the knowledge of Gosson's anti-puritan writings deconstructs Barish's system of these categories. This information is therefore textually repressed, becoming (quite literally) marginalized, hidden outside the parameters of the main text. As an anti-theatrical author, Gosson is seen as allied with the reformers, and that is where he remains – whether he likes it or not. Patrick Collinson observes a similar history of stigmatizing Philip Stubbes: "Stubbes is normally referred to as a 'puritan', on the basis of his comprehensive diatribe called *The Anatomie of Abuses* (1583). But Stubbes devoted much of *The second part of the Anatomie of Abuses*, called *The Display of Corruptions* . . . to a trenchant denunciation of the principles of ecclesiastical puritanism"; "Elizabethan and Jacobean Puritanism as Forms of Popular Religious Culture," in Christopher Durston and Jacqueline Eales, eds., *The Culture of English Puritanism, 1560–1700* (Houndmills and London: Macmillan Press Ltd., 1996), 34.
86 See my introduction, note 28.
87 Percy Alfred Scholes, *The Puritans and Music in England and New England: A Contribution to the Cultural History of Two Nations* (Oxford: Clarendon Press, 1934), 113–16; cited in Collinson, *The Elizabethan Puritan Movement*, 370.
88 This coexistence of debauchery and purity, a typical element of the hypocritical puritan figure, is highlighted in Falstaff's identification with "Ephesians . . . of the old church" (*2HIV* 2.2.142). The "prime church of Ephesus," as Middleton's stage puritan Mistress Purge would later note, was often cited as a model for godly living, established

according to the directives set out by St. Paul; the pre-Pauline Ephesians, on the other hand, were used as an example of those leading a wanton, ungodly lifestyle. The footnote to this line in the New Arden edition explains as follows: "The allusion is perhaps to the unregenerate Ephesians, with the sensual faults St Paul warns them against (particularly indulgence in wine: *Ephes.*, v. 18) before they 'put off the old man' and put on the new . . . The Page hardly seems to allude (unless ironically, and the irony would be lost on the stage) to 'the prime church of the Ephesians', whose conditions St Paul laid down, and which was the Puritan court of appeal for purity of life" (57n). This gloss, with its blanket refusal to consider the possibility of puritan overtones ("the Page *hardly* seems to allude"), preempts the valid possibility of irony even as it provides an ironic reading of the (otherwise gratuitous) line. Far from being "lost on the stage," the irony of the phrase would have been glaringly obvious to an audience aware of both Falstaff's Lollard origins and his bacchanalian behavior on stage.

89 Cited in Peter Corbin and Douglas Sedge, *The Oldcastle Controversy* (Manchester and New York: Manchester University Press, 1991), 220. In an instance of historical irony, the Jacobean bearers of the Cobham title would once again become involved in plots to overthrow the king, but this time the schemes involved pro-Catholic sympathizers. Despite their father's loyal service and prestige during the reign of Elizabeth, two of William Brooke's sons would later become traitors. Henry Brooke, Lord Cobham, was implicated in the "Main Plot" to replace James with Arabella Stuart, and (together with Ralegh, whom Brooke accused of being a co-conspirator) was condemned to life imprisonment in the Tower. His younger brother George was less fortunate, as he was accused of involvement in the "Bye" plot and was decapitated in 1603. See the *Dictionary of National Biography*, s.v. "Brooke, Henry, 1619." We might even speculate that Falstaff's premature death in *Henry V* is an effort to avoid the awkwardness of the historical Oldcastle's alliance with these traitors.

90 The resonance of these exchanges could result from what some see as the direct influence of Thomas Nashe, alias (presumably) Curryknave and Pasquill. Rhodes observes: "In the absence of any considerable drama, bar that of Shakespeare, in the middle years of the decade the literary battle between Nashe and Harvey provided spectacular entertainment of a different kind. It was a re-run of the Marprelate controversy conducted at a more sophisticated level . . . In these circumstances it is highly improbable that Shakespeare was unaware of what Nashe was doing, and in writing *1 Henry IV* in the winter of 1596–7, with its rhapsodies of grotesque abuse and its splendid evocation of low life in the city, he seems to be deliberately following that lead. After all, his instincts as a writer of comedy before this time were thoroughly romantic; Falstaff, though not without prototypes, declares

a sharp switch of direction. One begins to wonder, thinking again of Nashe's hopes of 'writing for the stage' in autumn 1596, not whether, but how closely, he and Shakespeare were associated" (*Elizabethan Grotesque*, 92). In his edition of *The First Part of the History of Henry IV* (Cambridge University Press, 1946) J. Dover Wilson notes many parallels to Nashe, and suggests that Nashe was involved in *The Famous Victories of Henry the Fifth* (191–96). Critics have also noted resonances of Nashe and the Marprelate tracts in the Jack Cade scenes from *2 Henry VI*; see, for example, Rhodes, *Elizabethan Grotesque*, 93–5.

91 *Rabelais and His World*, 12.

92 "The Theatre Constructs Puritanism," in David L. Smith, Richard Strier, and David Bevington, eds., *The Theatrical City: Culture, Theatre and Politics in London, 1576–1649* (Cambridge University Press, 1995), 168. See also Collinson, "'Ecclesiastical Vitriol': Religious Satire in the 1590s and the Invention of Puritanism," in John Guy, ed., *The Reign of Elizabeth I: Court and Culture in the Last Decade* (Cambridge University Press, 1995); Collinson writes: "it was Martin and Anti-Martin who created the Stage Puritan" (154).

93 *The History of Great Britaine* (1611), cited in John Munro, ed., *The Shakespeare Allusion Book: A Collection of Allusions to Shakespeare from 1591–1701*, vol. I (London: Humphrey Milford for Oxford University Press, 1932), 637.

94 *The Meeting of Gallants at an Ordinarie: or, The Walkes in Powles* (London, 1604), sig. B4ᵛ (cited in Munro, *The Shakespeare Allusion Book*, 136). In *Amends for Ladies* (1618), Nathaniel Field writes, "Did you neuer see / The play where the fat Knight, hight *Old-castle*, / Did tell you truly what this honor was?" (sig. G1ʳ; cited in Munro, *ibid.*, 270).

95 *Lectures and Essays*, 126. Ainger's argument was indirectly disseminated through J. Dover Wilson, who uses Ainger's essay as his primary source in discussing Falstaff's Lollardy; *Fortunes of Falstaff*, 16.

96 *Lectures and Essays*, 127–29. Ainger goes on to quote the passage from *The Meeting of Gallants*, and cites a "pamphlet of a few years later" (no title or date given), where a character called Glutton says: "I'm a fat man. It has been a West-Indian voyage for me to come reeking hither. A kitchin-stuff wench might pick up a living for the fat which I lose by straddling . . . Sir John Oldcastle was my great-grandfather's father's uncle – I came of a huge kindred!" (*ibid.*, 130).

97 *Rythmes against Martin Marre-Prelate*, 7.

98 Valerie Traub, *Desire and Anxiety: Circulations of Sexuality in Shakespearean Drama* (London and New York: Routledge, 1992), 57–58. David Womersley has recently argued that "the fatness of Falstaff was the corollary, not of any Catholic sympathies on Shakespeare's part, but of the playwright's intention to unify political and spiritual authority in the person of Henry"; "Why is Falstaff Fat?" *The Review of English Studies* 47 (1996): 21. Despite the title, this essay is primarily concerned with Henry.

99 *See Martins months minde*, sigs. B2^v–B3^r.
100 *The Structural Transformation of the Public Sphere: An Inquiry into a Category of Bourgeois Society*, trans. Thomas Burger (Cambridge, Mass.: MIT Press, 1989). For an intriguing study of print and the public sphere in the 1590s, see Douglas Bruster, "The Structural Transformation of Print in Late Elizabethan England," in Arthur Marotti and Michael Bristol, eds., *Print and the Other Media in Early Modern England* (Columbus, Ohio: Ohio State University Press, forthcoming).
101 John Taylor, *Religions Enemies, With a Brief and Ingenious Relation, as by Anabaptists, Brownists, Papists, Familists, Atheists, and Foolists, sawcily presuming to tosse Religion in a Blanquet* (1641), 6.

2 EATING DISORDER: FEASTING, FASTING, AND THE PURITAN BELLYGOD AT *BARTHOLOMEW FAIR*

1 Cited in G. P. V. Akrigg, ed. and intro., *Letters of King James VI & I* (Berkeley: University of California Press, 1984), 280. My thanks to Elizabeth Spiller for bringing this reference to my attention.
2 John Bale, *Brefe Chronycle, concernynge the Examinacyon and death of the blessed martyr of Christ syr Johan Oldecastell the lorde Cobham* (Antwerp, 1544), fol. 3^r; Martin Marprelate, *The Epistle*, in *The Marprelate Tracts*, Scolar Press facsimile reprint (Menston, England, 1970), 35. A later example of the use of this term appears in the anonymous *A Pack of Pvritans* (n.p., 1641), in which the author discribes the bishops: "Yet tell mee what labour there is within the Realme that is so deere sold as their idlenesse is? Oh you belly-Gods, did not Christs Apostles take paines and labour about the ministration of the word . . . ?" (30).
3 *A Short and Plaine Discourse, Fully containing the whole doctrine of Euangelicall Fastes* (1609), sig. H2^r.
4 *The Complete Prose Works of John Milton*, ed. Don. M. Wolfe (New Haven: Yale University Press, 1953), I: 549, 576–77.
5 *An Almond for a Parrat* (1589), sig. F2^v.
6 Facsimile reprint of *A Wife* (1616), in James E. Savage, *The "Conceited Newes" of Sir Thomas Overbury and His Friends* (Gainesville, Florida: Scholars' Facsimiles and Reprints, 1968). I will be citing original pagination; here, sig. H^r.
7 Thomas Harding expressed just such fears: "Let any man of reason iudge, whether he that maketh his belly his God would not holde with that gospell which mainteineth only faith to iustifie, the keping of the commaundementes to be impossible, confession of sins not to be necessarie, stedfast trust in Christes passion to be the only sufficient waye to save al men, lyve they never so loosly and disorderly"; *A Confutation of a Booke intituled An Apologie of the Churche of England*, 301; cited in Horton Davies, *Worship and Theology in England: from Cranmer to Hooker 1534–1603*, 5 vols. (Princeton University Press, 1970), I: 30.

8 See B. R. White, *The English Separatist Tradition: From the Marian Martyrs to the Pilgrim Fathers* (Oxford University Press, 1971).

9 Murray Tolmie, *The Triumph of the Saints: The Separate Churches of London 1616–1649* (Cambridge University Press, 1977), 28–34. See also Patrick Collinson, *The Religion of Protestants: The Church in English Society 1559–1625* (Oxford: Clarendon Press, 1982), 276–78. It should be noted that "semi-separatism" appears as a term in seventeenth-century pamphlets; the concept is endemic to the period, not simply a later historical construction.

10 See Tolmie, *Triumph of the Saints*, 33–4.

11 The tendency to perceive puritans as a "paradox" reflects the widespread early modern fascination with this idea. For a discussion of "paradox" as a recurrent structure in lyric poetry, see Rosalie L. Colie, *Paradoxia Epidemica: The Renaissance Tradition of Paradox* (Princeton University Press, 1966); for the rhetoric of paradox in theatrical and religious discourses, see Bryan Crockett, *The Play of Paradox: Stage and Sermon in Renaissance England* (Philadelphia: University of Pennsylvania Press, 1995), esp. ch. 1.

12 This discussion of the fast draws upon Tom Webster, *Godly Clergy in Early Stuart England: The Caroline Puritan Movement c. 1620–1643* (Cambridge University Press, 1997), ch. 3.

13 Richard L. Greaves, *Society and Religion in Elizabethan England* (Minneapolis: University of Minnesota Press, 1981), 491.

14 *Ibid.*, 493, 496.

15 Similarly, in the play *The Family of Love* (1604), the merchant Dryfat hopes to be admitted to the highly selective sect of the title, and proclaims his worthiness as a sectarian by attesting, "I keep no holydays nor fasts, but eat most flesh o' Fridays of all days i' the week" (3.2.974–75); the gallant Lipsalve also claims that the Familists have converted him "From two very notorious crimes; the first was from eating fish on Fridays, and the second from speaking reverently of the clergy" (4.1.1214–16). Citations are from the Nottingham Drama Texts edition, ed. Simon Shepherd (Nottingham University Press, 1979).

16 *A New Wind-Mil, A New* (Oxford, 1643), 4.

17 John Taylor, *All the Workes of Iohn Taylor "The Water Poet" Collected Into One Volum*, 1630, facsimile reprint (London: The Scolar Press, 1973), 119.

18 Another example of the more ascetic puritan is found in Brome's *The City Wit* (1628), where a puritan character cries out, "O mother, cold sobriety and modest melancholy becomes the face . . . un-edifying gawdes are Prophane vanities. Mirth is the fat of fools, onely vertue is the nourishment of purity and unsinning sincerity" (V.363); cited in William P. Holden, *Anti-Puritan Satire 1572–1642* (New Haven: Yale University Press, 1954), 121.

19 *A Book of Masques* (Cambridge University Press, 1967, 1980), 260 (ll. 60–66). For my discussion of Falstaff as a puritan, see chapter 1.

20 John Taylor, *The Brownists Conventicle, or an assemble of Brownists, Separatists, and Non-Conformists* (1641), 4. For a discussion of John Taylor's pamphlets and the battle of Carnival and Lent, see Michael D. Bristol, *Carnival and Theater: Plebeian Culture and the Structure of Authority in Renaissance England* (New York and London: Routledge, 1985), esp. 74–79.

21 This egocentric bellygod finds a parallel in a phenomenon of the Jacobean court. Leah Marcus has examined the significance of the extravagant banquets of Lord Hay and Buckingham, who "were indeed making a god of the belly"; the classical body associated with the upper classes is transformed, through its own gluttony, into a monument of economic retention. Courtly conspicuous consumption was not the populist celebration of the communal body that Bakhtin envisions, but was instead a celebration of egocentrism, a display of personal wealth gratifying personal desires. Such banquets, even as they assume the form of carnival, were a celebration of exclusivity, rather than inclusivity. See Marcus, *The Politics of Mirth: Jonson, Herrick, Milton, Marvell, and the Defense of Old Holiday Pastimes* (University of Chicago Press, 1986), 123.

22 The contradictions inherent to this figure are exemplified in Rabelais's tale of Pantagruel's encounter with the Gastrolaters, or Belly-worshippers. On the one hand the Gastrolaters are always circulating in close-knit bands and are eating extensively – seemingly an environment of communal feasting. Despite this apparent closeness of the community, the Gastrolater society is one of isolation and egocentrism, as the focus for each member of the group is his own interior belly and bodily desires. Pantagruel compares them to the Cyclops Polyphemus, who, according to Euripides, was known to say, "I only sacrifice to myself – to the gods never – and to this belly of mine, the greatest of all the gods"; François Rabelais, *The Histories of Gargantua and Pantagruel*, trans. J. M. Cohen (Harmondsworth and New York: Penguin Books, 1955, 1977), 574.

23 In *Ben Jonson: A Life* (Cambridge, Mass.: Harvard University Press, 1989) David Riggs notes that "by his late forties, [Jonson] had grown exceedingly fat. He was apparently becoming corpulent, then, during the years when he traveled to France and wrote *Bartholomew Fair*" (206–07). But even as Jonson was growing obese, he was also being identified as a figure of order and restraint. Riggs notes that Shakespeare's Malvolio was probably constructed, in part, as an attack on Jonson (84–85). Bruce Thomas Boehrer explores this paradox in "Renaissance Overeating: The Sad Case of Ben Jonson," *Publications of the Modern Language Association* 105 (1989): 1071–82. He writes: "Jonson's drama and poetry alike castigate vicious excess . . . and critics of Jonson's verse regularly praise its 'clarity and restraint,' . . . virtues it ostensibly promotes both formally and thematically. The result is one of the remarkable spectacles of English literary history: a famous fat man

and legendary drunkard constructing a cult of personality around his own excessive girth while excoriating his contemporaries for eating and drinking too much" (*ibid.*, 1072).

24 All references to *The Alchemist* and *Bartholomew Fair* are from C. H. Hereford and Percy and Evelyn Simpson, eds., *Ben Jonson* (Oxford: Clarendon Press, 1938). The shortened form of "Friers" also allows the deep Catholic history to shine through.

25 *The Politics and Poetics of Transgression* (Ithaca: Cornell University Press, 1986), 58.

26 In *The Alchemist*, Dol also states, "not a puritane in black-*friers*, will trust [you] / So much, as for a feather!" (1.1.128–29).

27 "The Jonsonian Corpulence, or The Poet as Mouthpiece," *English Literary History* 53 (1986): 508–09.

28 Mikhail Bakhtin, *Rabelais and his World*, trans. Hélène Iswolsky (Cambridge, Mass.: MIT Press, 1968; Bloomington: Indiana University Press, 1984), 19.

29 "Jonson's Alchemists, Epicures, and Puritans," in *Medieval and Renaissance Drama in England: An Annual Gathering of Research, Criticism and Reviews* 2, ed. J. Leeds Barroll, III (New York: AMS Press, 1985), 172; see also 179–81. For an analysis of some of Mammon's biblical references, see Myrddin Jones, "Sir Epicure Mammon: A Study in 'Spiritual Fornication'," *Renaissance Quarterly* 22 (1969): 233–42.

30 Laurence Sarson, *An Analysis of 1 Timothy* (1650), sig. B1^r.

31 Similarly, John Archer writes, "They are said not to hunger, because there is a Fullnes, *Via*, not *Patriae*, such a *Fullnes*, as suites their present Condition; a *Comparative*, though not an absolute fullnes; Therefore the Saintes speake of a Fullnes *Psal. 36.8.9. They shall be aboundantly satisfied with the fatnes of thy house*, and *Psal. 63.5. My Soule shall be satisfied, as with marrow & fatnes*; Such a fullnes, & satisfieing, as they are capable of in this Life"; *Instructions about Right Beleeving: Severall Sermons Leading unto Christ, directing unto Faith, and incouraging thereto* (1645), 61.

32 *The dolefull Lamentation of Cheap-side Crosse* (1641), 2.

33 Richard Carter, *The Schismatick Stigmatized* (1641), 16.

34 *Literary Fat Ladies: Rhetoric, Gender, Property* (London and New York: Methuen, 1987), 13.

35 Lawrence A. Sasek, ed., *Images of English Puritanism: A Collection of Contemporary Sources 1589–1646* (Baton Rouge: Louisiana State University Press, 1989), 279, 280.

36 See chapter 1 of Gail Kern Paster, *The Body Embarrassed: Drama and the Disciplines of Shame in Early Modern England* (Ithaca: Cornell University Press, 1993).

37 Busy has not been alone as a source of social and linguistic excess, and the gradual dissipation of these other characters furthers a sense of closure. Ursula the pig-woman – "the fatnesse of the *Fayre*" (2.2.118), "the very *wombe*, and *bedde* of enormitie!" (2.2.106) – embodies the

verbal pluralism of the fair: "the language some where sauours of *Smithfield*, the Booth, and the Pig-broath" we are told in the Induction (150–51). Ursula is initially described in terms of verbal expansion – "her language growes greasier then her Pigs" (2.5.133–34); soon, however, she melts away, as her flesh and "her *similes* . . . wan[e] a pace" (2.5.140–41). By the end of the play, even that other figure of excess, Adam Overdoo, has waned in his attempt at repressive control. Overdoo is the antithesis to the principle of dilation, obsessively preoccupied with the regulation of food; he sets off to "measure the length of puddings, take the gage of blacke pots, and cannes, I, and custards with a sticke; and their circumference, with a thrid; weigh the loaues of bread on his middle-finger" (2.1.19–22). His discursive control is so rigorous that Trouble-All will not do or say anything without Overdoo's written permission in the form of a "warrant."

38 Parker, *Literary Fat Ladies*, 26. Parker describes the finale as "a slightly more chastened feast, neither the leanness of the Puritan nor the enormity of the Fair" (26), a description with which I would disagree. Interestingly, in her chapter Parker dilates the character of Busy, dividing him into two characters – himself and the "Schoolmaster." When he first sees Busy Quarlous asks, "What Schole-master's that . . . ?" (3.2.27). In Parker's account, this reference grows into another character who speaks Busy's lines (3.6.30–33) and who becomes included in a list of Ursula's "overbearing judges . . . by the School-master's bloated speech, filled with classic instances of *amplificatio*; by Rabbi Busy, whose repetitive rhetoric evokes the notorious dilation of the often seemingly endless Puritan sermon; and by Adam 'Overdoo' himself" (*ibid.*, 25).

39 I am indebted to Barbara Silverstein and her observations about the ending of the play in "Puppets, Puritans, and Power Plays in *Bartholomew Fair*," unpublished essay.

40 In the words of a mid-seventeenth-century ditty: "But Father *Thunder* that's a man of zeal, / Can eat a well-siz'd Pigge even at a meal: / He with his Thund'ring voice would *Babel* shake, / When yet himself doth but a Babel make"; *Newes from the King's Bath* (Bristol, 1645), 55.

41 White, *English Separatist Tradition*, 119.

42 *Britanicus his Blessing* (1646), 4–6.

43 Parker includes this figure in her discussion of *Literary Fat Ladies*, 9.

44 I am grateful to Maureen Quilligan for pointing out this comparison to me.

45 A marginal note attributes this quote to Zwingli.

46 Paul S. Seaver, *The Puritan Lectureships: The Politics of Religious Dissent 1560–1662* (Stanford University Press, 1970), records that the practice of hiring lecturers reaching its peak in 1630, when 90 per cent of London parishes hired them (125).

47 *Ibid.*, 72.

3 LEWD CONVERSATIONS: THE PERVERSIONS OF THE FAMILY OF LOVE

1 Cited in Lawrence A. Sasek, *Images of English Puritanism: A Collection of Contemporary Sources 1589–1646* (Baton Rouge and London: Louisiana State University Press, 1989), 219. Although specifying that "Of this special sect I principally mean, when I speak of Puritans," James immediately proceeds to use the word as a catch-all term for sectarianism, including Brownism. The focus on the Family of Love was added to appease presbyterians who had been offended by James's use of "Puritan" in an earlier edition.

2 *Heresiography* (1647), 92. This is the third edition; the first was published in 1645.

3 While the Familists themselves were pacifists, it should be noted that their critics sometimes traced the Family's roots back to the German Anabaptists, notorious for their violent takeover of the German city of Muenster.

4 John Sprint, *Propositions, Tending to prooue the Necessarie vse of the Christian Sabbaoth* (1607), 26, my emphasis.

5 For an extensive account of literary Familist references, see William C. Johnson, "The Family of Love in Stuart Literature: A Chronology of Name-crossed Lovers," *The Journal of Medieval and Renaissance Studies* 7 (1977): 95–112.

6 William P. Holden, *Anti-Puritan Satire 1572–1642* (New Haven: Yale University Press, 1954), 42. See also Margot Heinemann, *Puritanism and Theatre: Thomas Middleton and Opposition Drama Under the Early Stuarts* (Cambridge University Press, 1980), 78; Jean Dietz Moss, " 'Godded with God': Hendrik Niclaes and his Family of Love," *Transactions of the American Philosophical Society* 71 (8) (Philadelphia: The American Philosophical Society, 1981), 53–54. Literary critics almost invariably cite the Family's reputation for sexual promiscuity.

7 The representations of Familist sexual deviancy I have found are invariably concerned with heterosexual intercourse. Although sectarians in general are sometimes named in lists containing "sodomites," I have not found any examples of sectarians themselves bearing this label.

8 Thomas Middleton, *A Mad World, My Masters*, ed. Standish Henning (Lincoln, Nebr.: University of Nebraska Press, 1965); John Marston, *The Dutch Courtesan*, ed. M. L. Wine (Lincoln, Nebr.: University of Nebraska Press, 1965).

9 "The Ladies' Man and the Age of Elizabeth," in James Grantham Turner, ed., *Sexuality and Gender in Early Modern Europe: Institutions, Texts, Images* (Cambridge University Press, 1993), 160.

10 Compare with Knewstub, *A Confutation*, sigs. *4ᵛ–*5. Pagitt also borrows from John Rogers, *The Displaying of an horrible secte* (1578); compare Pagitt, *Heresiography*, 100, and Rogers, *Displaying*, sig. B6ʳ.

11 In his positioning of the scriptural citation "which turned the truth of God into a lye," Pagitt even seems to be allowing for the popular sexual/verbal pun on "lie" (as exemplified in Shakespeare's sonnet 138: "When my love swears that she is made of truth, / I do believe her though I know she lies" [1–2]).

12 A typical expression of Niclaes's sense of godification is found, for example, in his *Evangelium Regni. A Joyfull Message of the Kingdom, published by the holie Spirit of the Love of Iesus Christ* (Cologne, 1575?): "[God] raised-vpp Mee HN, the Least among the holyons of God (which laye altogether dead, and without Breath and Life, among the Dead) from the Death, and made mee aliue, through Christ, as also annointed mee with his godlie Beeing, manned himself with Mee, and godded Mee with him to a liuing Tabernacle or howse for his Dwelling, and to a Seate of his Christ, the Seede of *David*)" (sig. LI^{r-v}).

13 Marsh addresses questions of membership throughout his detailed book, *The Family of Love in English Society, 1550–1630* (Cambridge University Press, 1994), esp. 116–24, 151–61.

14 The Familists' *Svpplication* in fact only appears in a text responding to it, *A Svpplication of the Family of Loue . . . Examined, and found to be derogatory in an hie degree* (Cambridge, 1606); in this text, the Familists' various arguments and positions are interspersed with acrid editorial commentary. The title page emphasizes the original *Svpplication*, rather than the derogatory examination, and prominently displays one of the emblems familiar from the writings of the sect's founder, Hendrik Niclaes. See Marsh, *The Family of Love*, 201–05.

15 Interest in the sect was renewed during the 1640s, although the term "Familism" was used loosely and does not seem to have applied to any cohesive community (Marsh, *The Family of Love*, 237). Niclaes's tracts themselves were reprinted between 1648 and 1656; see Nigel Smith, *Perfection Proclaimed: Language and Literature in English Radical Religion 1640–1660* (Oxford: Clarendon Press, 1989), ch. 4. See Alistair Hamilton, *The Family of Love* (Cambridge: James Clarke & Co., 1981), 135–41, for references to Familism through the end of the seventeenth century.

16 Benedict Anderson, *Imagined Communities: Reflections on the Origin and Spread of Nationalism* (London and New York: Verso, 1983, 1991), esp. 46.

17 *Svpplication . . . Examined*, 29.

18 *Ibid.*, 65.

19 See Herman de la Fontaine Verwey, "The Family of Love" (*Quærendo* 6 [1976]), 219–71; Verwey describes Niclaes's supporters as "rich merchants, intellectuals and artists" (247). The Continental Familists' claims to secrecy are somewhat called into question by the material form of Niclaes's texts, one of which (*Spiegel der gerechtigheid*) was a 600-page folio in a special Gothic type with elaborate engravings (234); unlike the later English counterparts, which were small and easy to

smuggle, this text is not designed for concealment, but rather for display. The printer for Niclaes's writings was Plantin of Antwerp, who had "the most famous printing establishment of all" according to Lucien Febvre and Henri-Jean Martin, *The Coming of the Book: The Impact of Printing 1450–1800*, trans. David Gerard (London and New York: Verso, 1990, first published 1958), 125.

20 *Evangelium Regni*, sig. LI^{r–v}. The cultural centrality of Niclaes in accounts of the Family is illustrated by the title of another pamphlet almost a century later: *A Brief Discovery of the Blasphemous Doctrin of Familisme, First conceived and brought forth into the world by one HENRY NICOLAS of the Low Countries of Germany about an hundred years agoe* (1645).

21 Moss, " 'Godded with God'," 17, 19. While contemporaries occasionally accused the Familist priests of trying to keep the Familist children from school, in general it was the Family's claim to knowledge rather than to ignorance which raised alarm.

22 Marsh, *The Family of Love*, 87.

23 This confession is reproduced in Jean Dietz Moss, "Variations on a Theme: The Family of Love in Renaissance England," *Renaissance Quarterly* 31 (1978): 190–91; here 190. Knowledge of this Familist "Booke of lyffe" was apparently widespread; the author of the *Svpplication . . . Examined* suggests consulting this book in order to prove that the Familists are wealthy: "They say they are also poore, or the most of them: but if the booke of their names, called of them *The Booke of Life*, could be seene, it would then appeare, I doubt not, that both the number of them is great, and most of them very rich" (57).

24 Sig. B4^v, misnumbered sig. D4 in the text.

25 J. E. Neale, *Elizabeth I and Her Parliaments 1559–1581* (New York, 1958), 410–11; cited in Julia G. Ebel, "The Family of Love: Sources of Its History in England," *The Huntington Library Quarterly* 30 (1967): 339.

26 Sig. B4^v, misnumbered sig. D4 in the text.

27 Knewstub, *A Confutation*, sig. **8^r.

28 Niclaes's vision of a mystical community even transcended the borders of national and religious difference; see *A Discovery of the Abhominable Delusions* (1622), sig. C3^r. Such Nicodemist policies were a well-known feature of the Family; pamphleteers write that "*Familists . . .* [hold] it lawfull to yeeld themselues and present their bodyes at any worship wheresoever, yea if it be of the Papists or any other, though never so wicked, being commaunded by Princes and Magistrates"; Henry Ainsworth and Francis Johnson, *An Apologie or Defence of Svch Trve Christians as are commonly (but vnjustly) called Brownists* (1604), sig. D3^v.

29 Pagitt, *Heresiography*, 99, also cited above.

30 Hamilton writes, "If there was one feature more than any other which made Familism despicable in the eyes of its English enemies it was this avowed policy of simulation" (*The Family of Love*, 125). Similarly, Marsh notes that "the tendency to dissemble before magistrates is perhaps the

characteristic most commonly associated with the Family of Love" (*The Family of Love*, 93).

31 At the end of the sixteenth century, these practices were primarily associated with the Jesuits. Earlier in the century, however, strategies of equivocation and mental reservation had been practiced (although with some debate) by the Protestant reformers forced to recant; see Susan Wabuda, "Equivocation and Recantation During the English Reformation: The 'Subtle Shadows' of Dr Edward Crome," *Journal of Ecclesiastical History* 44 (1993): 224–42.

32 "Heresy, Orthodoxy, and the Politics of Religious Discourse: The Case of the English Family of Love," in Stephen Greenblatt, ed., *Representing the English Renaissance* (Berkeley and Los Angeles: University of California Press, 1988), 319.

33 James Cranford, *Hæreseo-Machia, or, The mischiefe which Heresies doe, and the means to prevent it* (1646), 18–19.

34 Analyzing Niclaes's style, Nigel Smith observes that "the peculiar lack of clear reference between the literal and the allegorical levels (in some cases to the extent that the literal is omitted) results in a fundamental ambiguity in Niclaes's thought, which he does not explicitly resolve for the reader" (*Perfection Proclaimed*, 149).

35 Rogers, *The Displaying of an horrible secte*, sig. C4^r; Wilkinson, *A Confutation*, sig. H1^r.

36 Knewstub, *A Confutation*, sig. **5^r.

37 *Ibid.*, sig. **7^r.

38 *A Discovery of the Abhominable Delusions*, sig. A7^r.

39 *Svpplication . . . Examined*, 25.

40 *Ibid.*, 12.

41 Marsh, *The Family of Love*, 66; Hamilton, *The Family of Love*, 117.

42 *The Divisions of the Church of England* (1642), sig. A2^v; *A Discovery of 29. Sects here in London* (1641), 4.

43 Johnson, "The Family of Love," 95.

44 Quoted in the *Svpplication . . . Examined*, 13.

45 *A Discovery of the Abhominable Delusions*, 88.

46 *Supplication . . . Examined*, 58.

47 *Confutation*, sig. **8^v (my emphasis).

48 54–55. This exchange bears a strong resemblance to that of Freewill and Malheureux in Marston's *The Dutch Courtesan* (1605), where Freewill pursues a prostitute named "Tanakin" (1.1.139–45). The play contains several references to the Family in a sexual context.

49 *Heresiography*, 99–100.

50 For other references to the "Family of Lust," see Moss, "The Family of Love and its English Critics," *Sixteenth Century Journal* 6 (1975): 33–52.

51 The full quote from which this is taken indicates the degree to which the sect's status as a "Family" was a target for hostile pamphleteers: "the verie name of the householde of loue, is their great glory: so it may

breed in vs an opinion of their harmlesnesse. For who can feare any euill from loue, which doth good to all, and hurteth none. Howbeit . . . it is the housholde of Selfeloue: and then what mischiefe is there, which wee may not make iust account of" (Knewstub, *Confutation*, sig. **5ʳ).

52 See Marc Shell, *The End of Kinship: "Measure for Measure," Incest, and the Ideal of Universal Siblinghood* (Stanford University Press, 1988; Baltimore: The Johns Hopkins University Press, 1995), esp. 9–10.

53 In *The Displaying of an horrible secte* (1578), Rogers claims that Niclaes "had in his house three women, which went all alike in their apparell: the one he affirmed to be his wife, the other his sister, the thirde his cousin . . . [who] confessed that *Henrie Nicholas* had abused her bodie" (sig. B6ʳ).

54 Incest was a recurring feature of anti-sectarian invective. "Many of the Independents and Sectaries of these times are guilty of many kinds of uncleannesses; First, of Incest" writes Thomas Edwards in *Gangræna* (1646), III: sig. Bb2ʳ. Edwards goes on to give accounts of "one who married the mother, and afterwards the daughter . . . another marrying his owne brothers wife," and tells also "that a great Sectary in *Kent* hath married his Neece" (III: sig. Bb2ʳ). Citation from the Rota facsimile edition (Ilkley: The Scolar Press, 1977).

55 Moss, "'Godded with God'," 5; see also Herman de la Fontaine Verwey, "The Family of Love," 228, 256, 261.

56 John Knewstub, *A Sermon Preached at Paules Crosse the Fryday before Easter* (1579), sig. B2ᵛ.

57 To alarmed contemporaries, such self-determined spiritual families "tend to the supplanting of true religion, and ouerthrowe of Gods house, which is the Church of God, for the erecting of a *newe Family*, whereof they take their name" (*Svpplication*, D2ʳ). Actual sixteenth-century Familists also appeared to value their chosen religious community over their biological families. Studying archival traces of actual Familist practice in England, Marsh observes that the group fashioned itself as "truly a 'family,' whose members were linked to one another by ties of 'love,' which – through the vocabulary used in letters, books, and probably speech – deliberately mirrored the blood-ties of more conventional families" (*The Family of Love*, 100). Examining the wills of known English Familists, Marsh observes that members of the sect seemed to take these "familial" arrangements seriously, often bequeathing possessions to fellow sectarians rather than biological relatives. "It seems that the spiritual kinship of the Family of Love outweighed the blood-kinship to which most testators would have given priority . . . This was a 'Family' indeed" (*ibid.*, 159).

58 The authorship of *The Family of Love* has been the topic of considerable debate. David J. Lake argues for a textual evolution as follows: "first version by Middleton (perhaps with minor aid from Dekker), 1602–03; revision and/or additions by Dekker, mid-1605; transfer to King's

Revels' company, 1606–07; revision by Barry, 1607"; *The Canon of Thomas Middleton's Plays: Internal Evidence for the Major Problems of Authorship* (Cambridge University Press, 1975), 102; see also 91–101. See also Richard Hindry Barker, *Thomas Middleton* (Westport, Conn.: Greenwood Press, 1974; New York: Columbia University Press, 1958), 159–61. It would seem that editors of the forthcoming Oxford edition of Middleton's complete works have decided to exclude *The Family of Love*, although I have not seen a justification for this decision. For the time being, I will consider Middleton and company as the author(s), although for the purposes of my argument questions of authorship are not germane.

59 Literary critics have long debated the degree to which *The Family of Love* is intended as a satire aimed specifically against the sect of the title. Richard Levin immediately begins his discussion of the play by dismissing "the older critics" who ("misled perhaps by the title") considered the play as a religious satire; *The Multiple Plot in English Renaissance Drama* (University of Chicago Press, 1971), 60; see also Levin's "The Family of Lust and *The Family of Love*," *Studies in English Literature 1500–1900* 6 (1966): 309–10, 313. Other critics claimed the play as general anti-puritan satire; see Bertil Johansson, *Religion and Superstition in the Plays of Ben Jonson and Thomas Middleton* (New York: Haskell House, 1966), 102, and John F. McElroy, "Middleton, Entertainer or Moralist? An Interpretation of *The Family of Love* and *Your Five Gallants*," *Modern Language Quarterly* 37 (1976): 38. One of the first critics to suggest that the play was specifically targeted at the Family was Clifford Davidson ("Middleton and the Family of Love," *English Miscellany* 20, ed. Mario Praz [Rome: The British Council, 1969], 81–92); Margot Heinemann focuses her (surprisingly brief, five-page [*Puritanism and Theatre*, 77–82]) discussion of *The Family of Love* on the sect's reputation for "free-love practices (which was probably all that most of the audience would know about them)" (78) – a claim with which I would disagree. More recently, Joanne Altieri (drawing upon Janet Halley's analysis of Familist rhetoric) has examined the play and the dynamics of Familist speech; "Pregnant Puns and Sectarian Rhetoric: Middleton's *Family of Love*," *Mosaic* 22 (4) (1989): 45–57. Oddly, even as Altieri astutely points out Middleton's exploitation of the Family's reputation for verbal ambiguity she prefaces her discussion with the claim that "A search for specific Familist doctrine misses the point because the various 'tenets' that can be attributed to the sect *are* basically ecumenical radical sectarian ideas" (48); I would maintain that within early modern culture diverse sects held strongly differentiated reputations, negating the idea of "ecumenical" sectarian ideas.

60 All citations to the text are from the Nottingham Drama Texts edition, ed. Simon Shepherd (Nottingham: Nottingham University Press, 1979).

This edition divides the play into acts and scenes while line numbers
are continuous.

61 Noted in Davidson, "Middleton and the Family of Love," 84.

62 See 3.2.988; 4.1.1219; 4.1.1216–17.

63 See *The Displaying of an horrible secte*, sig. 15^r.

64 Altieri, "Pregnant Puns," 49.

65 Ebel, "The Family of Love," 333.

66 Most blatantly, the abstract notion of spiritual perfectionism – and
indeed the idea of ecclesiastical purification more generally – are
translated not merely into the physical, but into the overtly scatological
through the very names of the central characters, the "Purges" and the
"Glisters," both early modern terms for an enema. Given the pervasive
use of the purge, it is not surprising to find the cleansing of the
ecclesiastical body described in such terms. John Robinson, in *A
Justification of Separation from the Church of England* (1610), excuses religious
separation by portraying the Church of England as a body suffering
from serious constipation: "And for true Churches not vsing aright the
power they have for reformation, they are like true bodyes which
through some obstructions, or stoppings for a time cannot voyd things
noxious, & hurtful til there be a remedy: but the Church without this
power is as a monstrous body wanting the faculties & instruments of
evacuation and expulsion of excrements, or other noysome things"
(sig. L2^r). Discussions over the Family of Love were particularly prone to
such images and metaphors. W. C. identifies the Family as "*Catharists* &
Puritans" ("catharsis" literally meaning a cleansing of the bowels)
(Knewstub, *Confutation*, sig. **8^v). The Familists' perfectionism, or belief
that they were free from sin, is portrayed in terms of somatic evacuation. An alternative use of this vocabulary is presented by John Rogers,
who views the Familists themselves as the vile matter which needs to be
expelled. He insists upon the need "to cleanse and purge the Church
from such errours & false doctrine, as through the malice of Sathan
daily creepeth in" (sig. A3^r). The very origins of the Family, according to
Rogers, grew out of an excremental ecclesiastical history. Rogers cites a
long catalogue of ancient sects "*whose nature vnlike to* Turdus Syluestris,
*by whose fyling on the oke or fruite trees, the Mistle groweth: so of the dounge of these
filthie sectes haue proceeded a newe* Mergus, *a cormorant fowle, the* Familie of
Loue, *an hereticall sect, that hath, to bring foorth a newe puritie in religion, supped
vp the moste part of former errours*" (sig. A8^v). For a discussion of *The Family of
Love* and the consumer dynamics of the purge, see Gail Kern Paster,
"Purgation as the Allure of Mastery: Early Modern Medicine and the
Technology of the Self," in Lena Cowen Orlin, ed., *Material London*
(University of Pennsylvania Press, forthcoming). For a more extended
discussion of the uses of "purging," see Arthur F. Marotti, "The
Purgations of Middleton's *The Family of Love*," *Papers on Language and
Literature* 7 (1971): 81–84.

67 "Club law," in this play, seems to signify patriarchal order in general. However, the term carries resonances of the more physical means to enforce phallic dominance. In the play entitled *Club Law* (performed at Cambridge between 1597 and 1600) " 'club-law' meant the use of the stick, not argument, to knock down one's opponent"; Swapan Chakravorty, *Society and Politics in the Plays of Thomas Middleton* (Oxford: Clarendon Press, 1996), 31. The implicit sexual violence implied by "club law" is expressed by the apprentice Club: " 'tis as easily learned as the felling of wood and getting of children; all is but laying on load the downright blow" (5.3.1809–11) – a description which Dryfat repeats (5.3.1836–37).

68 The feminization of the Family in this final trial scene reinforces a cultural association of women with the radical sects. In Samuel Rutherford's *A Survey of the Spirituall Antichrist* (1648) a chapter on Hendrik Niclaes claims that "he came over to *England* and spread his foule heresies, and seduced a number of Artificers, and silly women, and wrote an Epistle to two daughters of *Warwicke*, . . . and laboured to perswade the maids to a spirituall new birth" (55). Rutherford goes on to claim that in America Anne Hutchinson quoted from Hendrik Niclaes; his description of Hutchinson could apply to Mistress Purge as well: "She was hau[g]hty, bold, active in wit, eloquent, vaine, and selfe-conceited, would not stick to lye" (176). Certain aspects of the Family's organization and beliefs (as with many nonconformist groups) did allow certain freedoms that were prohibited in the Church of England. In the Family, for example, women were allowed to become priests of the first rank in Niclaes's hierarchy (Moss, "Variations," 192). This feminized portrayal of the Family is undermined, however, by the fact that the lines castigating the Family as "strait-laced, yet loose-bodied dames" are spoken by Dryfat, himself a Familist. In his discussion of the trial scene, Simon Shepherd claims that the hostilities towards women in radical religion would have fueled an audience's desire to see Mistress Purge subdued: "Not just the men on stage, but we in the audience are grinning, in expectation of seeing the female Puritan traditionally thwarted" (*Amazons and Warrior Women: Varieties of Feminism in Seventeenth-Century Drama* [Brighton: The Harvester Press, 1981], 61). I would argue, conversely, that the entire last scene becomes a triumphant celebration of the type of spiritual/sexual independence embodied in Mistress Purge.

69 The character who is most earnest and enthusiastic about the idea of using "club law" against Mistress Purge is her own apprentice, Club. Throughout the play, Club displays his resentment against his subordinate social position to Mistress Purge, and seems to seek retribution for what he perceives as the social inequities of the apprentice system. Through its ultimate rejection of "club law" the play also mocks Club's claims to spiritual and social equality.

70 Chakravorty contends that "*[The] Family of Love* ends by calling for [club law's] reimposition," citing the lines spoken by Dryfat and Gerardine (*Society and Politics*, 32); Chakravorty seems to ignore the fact that these lines are spoken by Dryfat, who at this point is a full member of the Family. Dryfat tries to convert Gerardine, telling him, "I hope to see you a Familist before I die" (4.2.1315–16).

71 Gerardine makes a similar allusion to the Family when he proclaims "yet because I see you punished and purged already, my advice is, that you learn the ABC of better manners" (5.3.2131–33) – very probably a reference to Hendrik Niclaes's *All the letters of the A.B.C. in ryme.*

72 Marsh writes: "although the early modern period is not renowned as one of religious tolerance, this study presents compelling evidence to suggest that most people were content to live peacefully alongside those who were known to hold religious beliefs that had been publicly attacked by Queen, Privy Council and Church. The available resources of actual, positive religious tolerance – not to be confused with apathy – were much more considerable than has often been recognised. There existed in common practice a capacity to countenance the presence within society of those who deviated from orthodoxy" (*The Family of Love*, 14); see also *ibid.*, 187–96.

4 DISSECTING SECTARIANISM: SWARMS, FORM, AND THOMAS EDWARDS'S *GANGRÆNA*

1 The image of the Egyptian plagues, which God sent to punish the Egyptians for the Hebrews' captivity, became a contested political metaphor in the 1640s. As Christopher Hill notes, Egypt was a favorite metaphor with religious radicals, and as late as 1675 Quakers were still describing themselves as Israelites among the Egyptians; *The English Bible and the Seventeenth-Century Revolution* (London: Penguin Books, 1994), 113. See also Michael A. Mullett, *Radical Religious Movements in Early Modern Europe* (London: George Allen and Unwin, 1980), 85. In the radical view, prelates or presbyters were the oppressors of their English congregations just as the pharaohs had been the oppressors of God's chosen people; the allusion recurs throughout tracts arguing for the abolition of episcopacy, and becomes a central metaphor justifying separation (Hill, *The English Bible*, 113–15). A typical example of this usage can be found in Obadiah Sedgwick, *Haman's Vanity, or, a Sermon displaying the birthlesse Issues of Church-destroying Adversaries* (1643): "When *Pharaoh* (that Egyptian adversary) from oppression, advanced to the destruction of the *Israelites*; then God looks down, pitties his people, delivers them with an out-stretched arme, and not only defeats but destroyes their adversaries" (11). Given the prominence of the Egyptian analogy in the writings of sectarians and separatists, who identified themselves with the oppressed Israelites, this use of the reference by

conservative and moderate authors is surprising; see John Taylor, *The Anatomy of the Separatists* (1642), 2; *Brownists Synagogue* (1641), sig. A2ʳ; Abraham Cowley, *The Civil War*, in *The Collected Works of Abraham Cowley*, eds. Thomas O. Calhoun, Laurence Heyworth, and Allan Pritchard (Newark: University of Delaware Press; London and Toronto: Associated University Press, 1989), II: 601.

2 Letter dated May 1638; British Library, Additional MS 6394, f. 291.

3 In a fascinating essay, Timothy Raylor discusses the reciprocal relationship of political-religious discourse and the development of natural scientific writing; see "Samuel Hartlib and the Commonwealth of Bees," in Michael Leslie and Timothy Raylor, eds., *Culture and Cultivation in Early Modern England: Writing and the Land* (Leicester and London: Leicester University Press, 1992), 91–129. For a summary of recent work discussing the political and religious uses of the hive metaphor, see Paul Hammond, "The Language of the Hive: Political Discourse in Seventeenth-Century England," *The Seventeenth Century* 9 (1994): 119–33.

4 See chapters 3 and 1, respectively.

5 Figures taken from Elizabeth Skerpan, *The Rhetoric of Politics in the English Revolution 1642–1660* (Columbia and London: University of Missouri Press, 1992), 9. The actual number in 1642 was 1,966.

6 *Crop-Eare Curried, or, Tom Nash His Ghost* (1644), 6.

7 The author to *An Answer* writes: "What is the Poet mad to lay the rod in pisse, that must lash his owne fat knavish buttocks; to describe the knave Puritan (as hee calls him) to bee so like his owne picture? Surely did not the *Printer* mistake, and put in *Puritan* instead of Poet?" (4).

8 *Gangræna: Or A Catalogue and Discovery of many of the Errours, Heresies, Blasphemies and pernicious Practices of the Sectaries of this time* (1646), I: aᵛ. All quotations from *Gangræna* will be taken from the Rota facsimile reprint (Ilkley: The Scolar Press, 1977).

9 Derek Hirst writes that "the zealous took to an extreme the twin Protestant teachings that the dispensation of grace in the New Testament superseded that of the law in the Old, and that the overthrow of the tyranny of the mediating priesthood had brought 'Christian liberty' to believers. Radicals had an alarming tendency to claim that spiritual illumination freed them from the bonds of moral law"; *Authority and Conflict: England, 1603–1658* (Cambridge, Mass.: Harvard University Press, 1986), 72.

10 Geoffrey F. Nuttall, *The Holy Spirit in Puritan Faith and Experience*, second edition (Chicago and London: University of Chicago Press, 1992; Oxford: Basil Blackwell, 1947), 4, 12.

11 *The Ancient Bounds, or Liberty of Conscience, Tenderly Stated, Modestly Asserted, and Mildly Vindicated* (1645), 1.

12 *Certain Modest Observations and Considerations of the true Protestants of the Church of England* (1641), 2.

13 D. P. P., *An Antidote against The Contagious Air of Independency* (1644), 8.

14 *The dolefull Lamentation of Cheap-side Crosse* (1641), 6.
15 In William Haller, ed., *Tracts on Liberty in the Puritan Revolution 1638–1647*, 3 vols. (New York: Columbia University Press, 1933), III: 121.
16 *Ibid.*, 133–34.
17 In *Vniformity Examined* (1646), Wil[liam] Dell reverses the traditional emphasis on unity: "me thinks external Uniformity is a monstrous thing" (sig. A4^v). Dell dispells the ideal of uniformity as the natural state: "In nature is no externall Uniformity extended to al the works of nature. For look into the world & see if there be not variety of formes; heavenly and earthly bodies having severall formes; and in the earth each bird, beast, tree, plant, creature, differs one from another in outward form. If the whole creation should appear in one form, or externall uniformity, what a monstrous thing would it be, nothing differing from the first chaos? but the variety of forms in the world is the beauty of the world. So that though there be a most admirable unity among all the creatures, yet there is nothing lesse then external Uniformity" (sigs. A4^v–B1^r).
18 *Certaine Modest Observations*, 4.
19 *Areopagitica*, in Merritt Y. Hughes, ed., *John Milton: Complete Poems and Major Prose* (Indianapolis: The Odyssey Press, 1957; 1980), 721; *Gangræna*, I: sig. N4^r.
20 *The Anatomy of the Separatists, alias, Brownists, the factious Brethren in these Times, wherein This seditious Sect is fairly dissected, and perspicuously discovered to the view of the World* (1642), 1.
21 "Shakespeare, the Individual, and the Text," in *Cultural Studies*, ed. Lawrence Grossberg *et al.* (New York and London: Routledge, 1992), esp. 594–95.
22 From the extended title of *Trvth Trivmphing Over Falshood, Antiquity Over Novelty* (1645).
23 *The Rovnd-Head Uncovered . . . With a distinction betwixt the Round-heads, and such as Papists call Puritans* (1642), 4.
24 Thomas Edwards, *The Casting Down of the last and strongest hold of Satan* (1647), sig. B3^r.
25 Peter King, "The Reasons for the Abolition of the Book of Common Prayer in 1645," *Journal of Ecclesiastical History* 21 (1970): 327–39.
26 *Religions Lotterie, or the Churches Amazement. Wherein is declared how many sorts of Religions there is crept into the very bowels of this Kingdome, striving to shake the whole foundation and to destroy both Church and Kingdom* (1642), sig. A4^r. Elsewhere, Brownists would have "the booke of Common-prayer no more used . . . and no prayers to be used but *extemporary* prayers, and that whosoever have received the guift [*sic*] of preaching, may freely preach"; John Taylor, *The Divisions of the Church of England crept in at XV several doores* (1642), sig. A3^v.
27 In *Collected Works of Abraham Cowley*, I: 119.
28 *A Discovery of 29. Sects here in London, all of which, except the first, are most Divelish and Damnable* (1641), 3. Thomas Edwards lists sectarian error

no. 127: "That men ought to preach and exercise their gifts without study and premeditation, and not to thinke of what they are to say till they speak, because it shall be given them in that hour, and the Spirit shall teach them" (*Gangræna*, I: sig. F3ᵛ).

29 Similarly, Abraham Cowley satirizes such a preacher in *The Puritans Lecture*: "For now he comes too't, / *As you shall finde it writ*, / Repeats his text, and takes his leave of it, / And strait to's Sermon in such furious wise / As made it what they call't, an exercise" (97–100).

30 In the Thomason Tracts collection, the printed title of Taylor's pamphlet, *A Seasonable Lecture* (1642), is supplemented by the hand-written "Tobie's Dog" on the title page, and this appears to be the name by which the pamphlet came to be known. In *The Modest Vindication of Henry Walker. In answer to certaine scandalous Pamphlets, forged and vented abroad in his name (withou[t]: his privity)* (1642), Walker responds to "Tobies Dog" by protesting his innocence in the authorship of such sermons, and also reaffirms his loyalty to the Church of England: "I was never yet a member of any separated congregation: I pray God so to heare my prayers, as I have been a faithfull member of the Church of *England*, established by the Lawes of the Land, and free from conventi-cling with Papists, Brownists, Anabaptists, or any factious Assemblies whatsoever" (6). In "Tobies Dog," Walker is portrayed as beginning his sermon, "*Omnium gatherum* attend to my Text, as you shall find it written in the fifth Chapter of the Booke of *Tobias*, and part of the sixteenth verse, so they went forth both and departed, and the dog of the young man went with them" (2–3). This apparently specific textual referent immediately becomes farcical as the preacher's dilation upon this verse becomes an exposition upon a dog:

Before I enter upon my Text, Beloved, it is correspondent, meet, necessario and convenient, that I do unveile, lay open, describe, discover, and manifest unto you, some reasons why, wherefore, upon what causes, grounds, or reasons, this Dog is mentioned in my Text.

This portion that I shall administer unto you at this time, I have divided into six parts; first, the time when this Dog lived; secondly, whose Dog hee was; thirdly, whither he went; fourthly, what fashion'd or kind of Dog hee was; fifthly, his demeanour and carriage; and lastly, his name: Of all these in order, as 3 houres short time, and your long patience will permit. (2–3)

31 *Love one another: A Tvb Lectvre, Preached at Watford in Hartfordshire at a Conventicle on the 25. of December . . . by John Alexander, a Joyner* (1642), sig. A3ʳ.

32 *The Schismatick Stigmatized* (1641), 6 (misprinted in text as "4").

33 *The Sovndheads Description of the Rovndhead* (1642), 2.

34 *The Brownists Conventicle: Or an assemble [sic] of Brownists, Separatists, and Non-Conformists* (1641), 5 (misprinted in text as "4"); Taylor, *Anatomy of the Separatists*, taken from the full title.

35 For a discussion of the various uses of "Babel" in mid-century political debates, see Sharon Achinstein, *Milton and the Revolutionary Reader*

(Princeton University Press, 1994, ch. 2); for an account of seventeenth-century attempts to reinstate linguistic order, see Robert Markley, *Fallen Languages: Crises of Representation in Newtonian England, 1660–1740* (Ithaca and London: Cornell University Press, 1993), ch. 2.

36 Owen Dogerell [pseud?], *A Brief Dialogue Between Zelotopit one of the Daughters of a Zealous Round-head, and Superstition a Holy Fryer* (1642?), sig. A2^r.

37 Foucault, trans. A. M. Sheridan Smith, *The Archeology of Knowledge and the Discourse on Language* (New York: Pantheon Books, 1972), 228–29.

38 Obadiah Sedgwick, *Haman's Vanity, or, a Sermon displaying the birthlesse Issues of Church-destroying Adversaries* (1643), sig. A3^r.

39 *The Dippers dipt. Or, The Anabaptists Dvck'd and Plvng'd Over Head and Eares, at a Disputation in Southwark* (1645), sig. B2^v.

40 Edwards continues, "but . . . I can comfort my self with that of *David,* Psal. 118.12. *They compassed me about like Bees, they are quenched as the fire of thorns, but in the Name of the Lord I will cut them off.*"

41 John Maddocks and Henry Pinnell, *Gangrænachrestum* (1646), 6.

42 *Tom NASH his Ghost . . . Written by Thomas Nash his Ghost, with Pap with a Hatchet, a little revived since the 30. Yeare of the late Qu. Elizabeths Reigne, when Martin Mar-Prelate was as mad as any of his Tub-men are now* (1642), 1.

43 Similarly, "It is easier to reckon up all the Species and kinds of nature, than to describe all the Sects, Divisions, and opinions in Religion, that is now in *London,*" laments the author of *The Doleful Lamentation of Cheapside Crosse* (1641), 3.

44 *The Devil Turn'd Round-Head: or, Plvto becomes a Brownist* (1642), sig. A2^v.

45 *Carmina Colloquia: or, A Demonaicall and Damnable Dialogue between the Devil and an Independent* (1649), 1.

46 *A Tract Concerning Schisme and Schismatiques. Wherein, Is briefly discovered the originall causes of all Schisme* (1642), 4.

47 The sects listed are "Protestants, Puritans, Papists, Brownists, Calvinists, Lutherans, Fam. of love, Mahometans, Adamites, Brightanists, Armenians, Sosinians, Thessalonians, Anabaptists, Separatists, Chaldeans, Electrians, Donatists, Persians, Antinomians, Assyrians, Macedonians, Heathens, Panonians, Saturnians, Junonians, Bacchanalians, Damassians, The Brotherhood" (title page).

48 Peter Stallybrass notes a related phenomenon in nineteenth-century literary representations of the lower classes, where "the heterogeneity that defied all boundaries produced a veritable hysteria of naming," and "the homogeneity of the bourgeois subject is . . . constituted through the spectacle of heterogeneity"; "Marx and Heterogeneity: Thinking the Lumpenproletariat," *Representations* 31 (1990): 72–73.

49 A. L. Morton, *The World of the Ranters: Religious Radicalism in the English Revolution* (London: Lawrence & Wishart, 1970), 21; Christopher Hill, *Milton and the English Revolution* (Harmondsworth: Penguin Books, 1977), 94.

50 *Fear, Myth and History: The Ranters and the historians* (Cambridge University Press, 1986), 126, 7. Davis discusses the ideology of Hill's work in greater detail, 130–33.

51 Professor Ann Hughes, in her forthcoming book *Presbyterians, Print Culture, and the English Revolution: A Study of Thomas Edward's "Gangraena,"* is exploring, among many other important aspects of the construction and impact of this text, Edwards's process of gathering and collating records of conversations, letters from others, official records, and his own observations. I am grateful to Professor Hughes for sharing a prospectus of this project with me.

52 *Literature and Revolution in England, 1640–1660* (New Haven: Yale University Press, 1994). Smith builds his argument (4) upon Mikhail Bakhtin's analysis of genre as a source of social transformations, as described in Bakhtin's "The Problem of Speech Genres," in *Speech Genres and Other Essays* (Austin: University of Texas Press, 1986).

5 THE DESCENT OF DISSENT: MONSTROUS GENEALOGIES AND MILTON'S ANTIPRELATICAL TRACTS

1 "Structure, Sign, and Play," in *Writing and Difference*, trans. Alan Bass (University of Chicago Press, 1978), 293.

2 *Gangræna: Or a Catalogue and Discovery of many of the Errours, Heresies, Blasphemies, and pernicious Practices of the Sectaries of this time* (1646), I: sig. C2^r; Rota facsimile edition (Ilkley: The Scolar Press, 1977).

3 See Susan Wiseman, "'Adam, the Father of all Flesh': Porno-Political Rhetoric and Political Theory In and After the English Civil War," in James Holstun, ed., *Pamphlet Wars: Prose in the English Revolution* (London: Frank Cass & Co. Ltd., 1992), 136.

4 "Of what made?" inquires one pamphleteer of sectarian origins. "[W]hy, as first his case or outside he is made of dust as your Round-head is, . . . but for his pitch or inside it is *semen incuba*, or *sperma diaboli* he is made of the seed or spaun of the Devill"; *An exact Description of a Roundhead, and a Long-Head Shag-Poll: Taken out of the purest Antiquities and Records* (1642), 6. See also *Grand Plvtoes Remonstrance, or, The Devill Horn-mad at Roundheads and Brownists* (1642), sig. A2^r.

5 As, for example, "you may please to see out of *Eusebius, Egesippus, Socrates, Hierom, Epiphanius*, others, as exact a pedegree of all the holy Bishops of the Primitive Church, succeeding each other in the foure Apostolicall Sees untill the time of the *Nicene* Councell, as our *Godwin* or *Mason* can give us of our Bishops of England; or a *Speed* or *Stow* of our English Kings. There you shall finde from *Iames* the Lords brother, who, (as *Ierom* himselfe expresly) sate as Bishop in the Church of *Ierusalem*, to *Macarius*, who sate in the *Nicene* Councell, 40. Bishops punctually named. From St. *Peter* who governed the Church of *Antioch*, and was succeeded by *Evodius*, (and he by *Ignatius*) twenty seven. In the See of

Rome, thirty seven. In the See of *Alexandria,* from *Marke* the Evangelist, twenty three; A Catalogue which cannot be questioned without too much injurious incredulity; nor denied without an unreasonable bold-nesse" (*Episcopacie,* sig. Gg3^{r-v}).

6 This tract, a collection of writings by famous divines, contains extensive genealogies of the bishops; in the section by Lancelot Andrewes, for example, we find the following explanation of "The forme of the Ecclesiastical government under Moses":

> The *Priesthood* was setled in the Tribe of *Levi* by God.
> *Levi* had three sons: *Cohath, Gershon,* and *Merari.* Of these, the line of
>   *Cohath* was preferred before the rest.
> From *him* descended four Families: *Amram, Izhar, Hebron,* and *Vzziel.*
> Of these the stock of *Amram* was made chiefe.
> He had two sons: *Aaron* and *Moses.*
> *Aaron* was by God appointed *High Priest.*
> So that there came to be four distinctions of *Levits*:
>   1. *Aaron,* as chiefe.
>   2. *Cohath.*
>   3. *Gershon.*
>   4. *Merari.*
> . . . Yea he[God] maketh not *Eleazar* and *Ithamar* to be absolute *equals*:
> But giveth *Eleazar* preeminence over *Ithamar;* and therefore termeth
> him *Nasi Nesiim, Princeps Principum* or *Prælatus Prælatorum.* (Num. 3.32.)
> And all these under *Aaron* the *High Priest.*
> So that,
>   1. *Aaron* was the *High Priest.*
>   2. Under him *Eleazar:* who, as hee had his peculiar charge to look unto,
>   so was he generally to rule both *Ithmars* jurisdiction and his owne.
>   3. Under him *Ithamar,* over two families.
>   4. Under him the three Prelats.
>   5. Under each of them, their severall *chiefe Fathers* . . .
>   6. Under these, the severall persons of their kindreds.   (sigs. B2^{r}–B3^{v})

7 More graphically, Baillie writes in *A Dissvuasive,* "the undeniable foot-steps of the Spirit of Errour and Schism walking among us, and bringing forth in great plenty the births of his darknesse, to the end that such a multitude of Satans Brats, appearing openly in the arms and bosoms of otherwise (I suppose) well-meaning people, the beholders may tremble, and with all carefulnesse avoid the deep decept of that Angel of Light; and the deceived themselves seeing with their eyes what they hugg and dandle, to carry in the face the cleer lineaments of a mishant [*sic*] Parent, for grief and shame that they have been so long Nursing-Fathers to Satans brood, may become the first to dash the brains of these cursed Brats against the stones; or if they needs must obstinately continue fond of that bastard Generation, they may enjoy what they love, themselves alone; all well-advised men standing aloofe from the danger of so misordered and irrationall affection" (6).

8 Similarly, Lewis Owen sets out to identify the Catholic "sects," as he

terms them, in *A Genealogie of all Popish Monks, Friers, and Jesuits. Shewing their first Founders, Beginnings, Proceedings, and present State* (1646). Owen clearly is conceptualizing Catholics as sectarians; in his account of the Benedictine monks, he writes, "All these seuerall Sects of *Monks* (who apply their minds to nothing else but to sloth, idlenesse, gluttony, idolatry, whordome, fornication, and like impietie) . . . bring in daily more new sects of *Monks* and *Friers*" (11).

9 See, for example, Hall, *Episcopacie*, 138. In his *Christian Advertisements and Counsels of Peace also disuasions from the Separatists Schism* (1608), Richard Bernard writes, "this vnthankfulnesse is also to the mother, this Church of England, that bare them [i.e., the separatists], which they desire to make whore, before Christ her husband so co[n]demne her . . . But are not these children worthie to be accounted bastards, that wil needs denie their father that begat them, and also gladly would haue all to take their mother for a whore that bare them, and would vnbowell her of all her deare children viperously? Oh vnkinde and vnnatural children, vnworthie to breathe in their fathers aire, or to inhabite neere the skirts of their mother!" (48–49).

10 Overbury, *A Wife* (1616; facsimile reprint, Gainesville, FL: Scholars' Facsimiles and Reprints, 1968), sig. E8^v.

11 A similar passage is found in John Reading, *The Ranters Ranting* (1650): "They affirm that all Women ought to be in common, and when they are assembled together (this is a known truth) they first entertaine one another, the men those of their own sex, and the Women their fellow females: with horrid oaths and execrations, then they fall to bowzing and drink deep healths (O cursed Caitiffes) to their Brother God, and their Brother Devill; then being well heated with Liquor, each brother takes his she Other upon his knee, and the word (spoken in derision of the sacred Wit) being given, viz. *Increase and Multiply*, they fall to their lascivious imbraces, with a joynt motion, & C." (5); cited in Nigel Smith, ed., *A Collection of Ranter Writings from the 17th Century* (London: Junction Books, 1983), 19.

12 Hill, *The World Turned Upside Down: Radical Ideas During the English Revolution* (London: Penguin Books, 1975), 33; Walzer, *The Revolution of the Saints: A Study in the Origins of Radical Politics* (Cambridge, Mass.: Harvard University Press, 1965), viii.

13 Friedman, *Blasphemy, Immorality, and Anarchy: The Ranters and the English Revolution* (Athens, Ohio: Ohio University Press, 1987), ch. 1. Patrick Collinson also uses the language of heredity in discussing the prelatical side of things: "On the subject of episcopacy there have been special motives in the Church of England for fixation on what might appear to be arid questions of title and pedigree"; *The Religion of Protestants: The Church in English Society 1559–1625* (Oxford: Clarendon Press, 1982), 1. Elsewhere he observes: "The genealogical approach so apparent in much of the historiography of early Dissent owes something to the

nature of the task, something to the way in which it has been tackled. If the story is told on a chronological plan, the historian is driven down a tunnel which shuts out any expansive views on either side"; "Towards a Broader Understanding of the Early Dissenting Tradition," in C. Robert Cole and Michael E. Moody, eds., *The Dissenting Tradition: Essays for Leland H. Carlson* (Athens, Ohio: Ohio University Press, 1975), 3.

14 Knappen, *Tudor Puritanism: A Chapter in the History of Idealism* (University of Chicago Press, 1939; Gloucester, Mass.: Peter Smith, 1963), 493; Tolmie, *The Triumph of the Saints: The Separate Churches of London 1616–1649* (Cambridge University Press, 1977), 20; Watts, *The Dissenters: From the Reformation to the French Revolution* (Oxford: Clarendon Press, 1978), 6.

15 Cited in *Catalogue of Prints and Drawings in the British Museum*, vol. I (London: Chiswick Press, 1870), 485.

16 For examples of sectarian incest, see chapter 3. Often these references are allegorical: "This conscience is a Sea-horse, according to *Plutarch*, kils the fire, that he may more easily couple with the dam; so these mad men, that they may with more freedome abuse the Commonwealth, which is the mother of us all, to their owne lusts, they strive to disenthrone, and put downe all Kings and Magistrates, who are the common fathers of the people"; *Mock-Majesty: or, The Seige of Munster* (1644), sig. A4^r.

17 In Samuel Rutherford's *Survey of the Spiritvall Antichrist* (1648), he describes a monstrous child born in Boston: "The child was a fearfull and rarely prodigious Monster: It had no head, but a face which stood so low on the brest, as the eares, most like an Apes eares, grew on the shoulders, the eyes and mouth stood farre out, the nose was hooking upward, the brest and back was full of sharpe prickles like a Thornback, the Navell and all the belly, with the distinction of the sex, were where the lower part of the back and hips should have been, and those back-parts were on the side the face stood, the armes and hands were as other childrens, but instead of toes, it had upon each foot three claws, with talons like a young foule, upon the back above the belly, it had two great holes like mouths, and in each of them stuck out a piece of flesh, it had no forehead, but in the place thereof above the eyes foure hornes, whereof two were above an inch long, hard and sharpe, the other two shorter. The Father and mother were the grossest and most active *Familists*, malicious opposers of the godly" (181).

18 *Mock-Majesty*, sig. A4^r.

19 D. P. P., *An Antidote against The Contagious Air of Independency* (1644), 3. The serpent mother can also be associated with male leaders. Butler's character "A Leader of a Faction" "gathers his Party as *Fanatics* do a Church . . . When he has led his Faction into any Inconvenience, they all run into his Mouth, as young Snakes do into the old ones"; Samuel Butler, *Characters*, ed. Charles W. Daves (Cleveland and London: The Press of Case Western Reserve University, 1970), 190.

20 Even before Spenser's Errour appeared on the scene, Martin's pamphleteering opponent Pasquill likens this disruptive religious dissenter to a
spawning monster. Martin has "the very poyson of Dragons and the
gall of Aspes," his followers "swell . . . with enuie like a nest of foule
Toades, till their bodies splyt, and pour out theyr bowels vppon the
earth," and, like "*Vipers,* to giue light and estimation vnto themselues,
they teare open the bowels of theyr owne Damme, and liue by the
death of her that bred them" (*Pasquills Returne,* 103, 93).

21 For an extended analysis of the relationship of Spenser's Errour and
Milton's Sin, see Maureen Quilligan, *Milton's Spenser: The Politics of
Reading* (Ithaca and London: Cornell University Press, 1983), ch. 2.

22 All citations to the antiprelatical tracts taken from *The Complete Prose
Works of John Milton,* vol. I, ed. Don M. Wolfe (New Haven: Yale
University Press, 1953). In the text, I will be using the abbreviations *PE*
for *Of Prelatical Episcopacy, RCG* for *The Reason of Church Government,* and
OR for *Of Reformation.* Here, *PE,* 626.

23 In *Episcopacie by Divine Right* (1640), Bishop Hall asserts (somewhat
defensively), "As for the syntaxe of words and sentences, who of us ever
said they were, or needed to be, fathered upon those great Legates of
the Sonne of God? Our Cause is no whit poorer, if we grant there were
some universall termes derived by Tradition to the following ages,
whereof the Original Authors are not knowne" (47).

24 "Milton's *Of Reformation* and the Dynamics of Controversy," in Michael
Lieb and John T. Shawcross, eds., *Achievements of the Left Hand: Essays on
the Prose of John Milton* (Amherst: University of Massachusetts Press,
1974), 58. Milton does not quibble with genealogies so much as he casts
history aside – even those whom his fellow presbyterians admire (Foxe's
martyrs, Constantine) must be swept away (58–59).

25 "'Adam, the Father of all Flesh'," 137. In her examination of pamphlets
from the 1650s, Wiseman argues irregular modes of reproduction
illustrate "the republican and Leveller refusal of the predominantly
patriarchal and hierarchical assumptions which supported kingship"
(*ibid.,* 143).

26 For an intriguing analysis of Milton's distrust of history in the antiprelatical tracts, see David Loewenstein, *Milton and the Drama of History:
Historical Vision, Iconoclasm, and the Literary Imagination* (Cambridge University Press, 1990), 13–20, esp. 16.

27 Thanks to Jonathan Grossman for bringing this etymology to my
attention.

28 John Milton, *Complete Poems and Major Prose,* ed. Merritt Y. Hughes
(Indianapolis: The Odyssey Press, 1957), 733.

29 For a discussion of *Areopagitica* as a defense of sectarianism, see Michael
Wilding, "Milton's *Areopagitica*: Liberty for the Sects," *Prose Studies* 9 (2)
(1986): 7–38.

30 "Driving from the Letter: Truth and Indeterminacy in Milton's

Areopagitica," in Mary Nyquist and Margaret W. Ferguson, eds., *Re-membering Milton: Essays on the texts and traditions* (New York and London: Methuen, 1988), 246.

31 In *Milton and the Revolutionary Reader* (Princeton University Press, 1994), Sharon Achinstein describes the ways in which Milton and his contemporaries construct and educate their audience as critical readers; see ch. 6, esp. 208–10.

32 "The Root and Branch Petition and the Grand Remonstrance: From Diagnosis to Operation," in David L. Smith, Richard Strier and David Bevington, eds., *The Theatrical City: Culture, Theatre and Politics in London, 1576–1649* (Cambridge University Press, 1995), 226. In footnote 9, Strier points out that "the singular form never appears in the document."

33 Raphael Falco discusses Milton's relationship to his poetical "family tree" in chapter 4 of *Conceived Presences: Literary Genealogy in Renaissance England* (Amherst: University of Massachusetts Press, 1994). Falco's account of Milton's attitude towards the literary past is strikingly similar to that Milton advocates to the patristic past in the anti-prelatical pamphlets. Falco writes that Milton "sets out to overturn literary genealogy, to supplant his precursors" (166) and that, "for Milton, descent relations are less important than divine election" (168).

6 NOT SO MUCH AS FIG LEAVES: ADAMITES, NAKED QUAKERS, LINGUISTIC PERFECTION AND *PARADISE LOST*

1 *Mercurius Teutonicus. Or a Christian Information concerning the Last Times. Being divers propheticall passages of the Fall of Babel, and the New Building in Zion. Gathered out of the Mysticall Writings of that famous Germane Author, Jacob Behmen* (1649), 43.

2 *Athenae Oxonienses,* II: 367; cited in A. L. Morton, *The World of the Ranters: Religious Radicalism in the English Revolution* (London: Lawrence & Wishart, 1970), 99.

3 *Some Sweet Sips, of some Spirituall Wine* (1649); in Nigel Smith, ed., *A Collection of Ranter Writings from the Seventeenth Century* (London: Junction Books, 1983), 49.

4 *Ibid.,* 50.

5 *King Lear and the Naked Truth: Rethinking the Language of Religion and Resistance* (Durham, NC and London: Duke University Press, 1998), chs. 1 and 2.

6 See Ethyn Williams Kirby, " 'The Naked Truth': A Plea for Church Unity," *Church History* 7 (1938): 45–61.

7 Russell Fraser conveniently cites numerous examples of this idiom in *The Language of Adam: On the Limits and Systems of Discourse* (New York: Columbia University Press, 1977) (although he does not discuss the implications of nakedness). In some of the examples he mentions, the

minister demands skillful preaching, since the "efficacy of the holy Spirit doth more clearly appear in a naked simplicity of words than in elegancy and neatness" (William Ames, *The Marrow of Sacred Divinity* [1642], 180–82) (32); the grammarian sought out the "truth itself, naked and delightful" (Sainte-Beuve, trans. T. S. Baynes, *Port-Royal Logic* [1685], preface) (20); the philosopher "retired to search into truth," when "he at once rejected all the impressions which he had before received from what he had heard and read, and wholly gave himself over to a reflection on the naked ideas of his own mind" (Thomas Sprat, *Notes Directed Against a Certain Program* [1647], 442–43) (10).

8 James Knowlson, *Universal Language Schemes in England and France 1600–1800* (Toronto and Buffalo: University of Toronto Press, 1975), 12–13.

9 "*S. Augustine* mouing this argument doth also determyne it, and saith, that the first language of the world was the *Hebrew*," wrote the recusant Richard Verstegan in *A Restitution of Decayed Intelligence* (1605; facsimile reprint London: The Scolar Press, 1976), 6–7. In a discussion with the cartographer Ortelius, Verstegan argues against the misguided people who believe Teutonic was "the first of all languages of the world, to wit, that which was spoke[n] by *Adam*" (190). The idea that a purified form of Dutch would be the preferred language for the Holy Spirit was promoted by the spiritualist and Anabaptist David Joris; see Gary K. Waite, "The Holy Spirit Speaks Dutch: David Joris and the Promotion of the Dutch Language, 1538–1545," *Church History* 61 (1992): 47–59. John Webb similarly scoffs at the "ridiculous" idea "that *Adam* spake *Dutch* in Paradice"; *An Historical Essay Endeavoring a Probability that the Language of the Empire of China is the Primitive Language* (1669), 42. But Webb also rejects Hebrew as the original language, since "the *Hebrews* have no surer foundation to erect their Language upon, than only a bare Tradition of their own" (42). Webb, oposing the writings of Saint Hierome, proposes his own rational candidate for "that Sacred Language, which even in the time of innocency was spoken between God and Man" (43). For a number of reasons, including "their infinite multitudes of People," Webb logically concludes that "it may with much probability be asserted, *That the Language of the Empire of CHINA, is, the PRIMITIVE Tongue, which was common to the whole World before the Flood*" (44).

10 See Umberto Eco, *The Search for the Perfect Language*, trans. James Fentress (Oxford: Blackwell Publishers Ltd., 1995), especially ch. 5.

11 *The New Philosophy and Universal Languages in Seventeenth-Century England: Bacon, Hobbes, and Wilkins* (Lewisburg: Bucknell University Press and London: Associated University Presses, 1995). Stillman writes that, "In the distinctive discourses of Bacon, Hobbes, and Wilkins, discussions about language created a kind of laboratory in which massive problems of authorizing artificially constructed systems of signs supplied both a

space and a technology for authorizing sovereign authorities to intervene against cultural crises" (14).

12 *Universal Languages and Scientific Taxonomy in the Seventeenth Century* (Cambridge University Press, 1982), 2. As Slaughter emphasizes, these coterminous scientific and linguistic aims were intrinsically interconnected with socio-religious goals: "Wherever we turn in the seventeenth century, we see evidence of a desire, need, will to establish the fundamental order of God's creation and of the 'world politick'. Religion and science could go hand in hand because science seemed to demonstrate so clearly the Creator's stable and providential plan for the well-being of man. Science could also suggest a model for a regulated and orderly church and polity, a model desperately needed after the ravages of the revolution and with the beginning of a market economy" (7).

13 See Nigel Smith, "The Uses of Hebrew in the English Revolution," in Peter Burke and Roy Porter, eds., *Language, Self, and Society: A Social History of Language* (Oxford: Polity Press, 1991), 52. Later in the century, this courageous autodidactic enterprise was facilitated by a growing market of language text-books. Edward Leigh, in *Critica Sacra, Philologicall and Theologicall Observations Upon All the Greek Words of the New Testament* (1646), urges that biblical translation "ought more and more to be perfected" by returning to the original languages. While this particular book promotes Greek, Leigh proclaims that "the Hebrew (I say) is the most ancient and maternall Language; for *Adam* used it, and all men before the flood, as is manifest from the Scripture, and Fathers" (*Epistle Dedicatory*).

14 See Smith, "Hebrew," 53.

15 18; cited in Smith, "Hebrew," 56.

16 Smith, "Hebrew," 56. Stillman notes a similar, if more institutional, desire being expressed in the universal and philosophical language schemes, which served "as a device for achieving an Adamic renewal of self and society" (40).

17 An actual sect known as the Adamites appears to have existed in early fifteenth-century Bohemia; see Norman Cohn, *The Pursuit of the Millennium: Revolutionary Millenarians and Mystical Anarchists of the Middle Ages*, second edition (New York: Oxford University Press, 1970), 219–21. English pamphleteers often refer to this sect; see *A Relation of severall Heresies* (1646), 14. Others claim that the sect is a reincarnation of previous heresies, such as the early Christian sects reported by Augustine, or the fifteenth-century Bohemian Adamites. For a survey of historic naked sects, see David Cressy, "The Adamites Exposed: Naked Radicals in the English Revolution," in *Travesties and Transgressions: Cultural Collisions in Tudor and Stuart England* (Oxford University Press, forthcoming 2000), 6–9. All page numbers refer to the draft of this chapter that David Cressy has very graciously shared with me.

18 The Adamites are often reported to engage in wacky behavior; in *A Nest of Serpents Discovered*, for example, they climb naked into trees and wait for bread to drop from heaven, fainting from hunger when none appears (5). In a later tract, *Bloudy Newse from the North* (1650), the Adamites decide to massacre their spouses (1).

19 This particular woodcut would be reused for two subsequent anti-sectarian tracts, indicating the popularity of nudity as an early modern marketing device. The title page is reproduced in *A Sermon Preached the last Fast Day* (1643) to represent a naked congregation of the more generic "zealous brethren" and "holy Sisters," and on the cover of *The Ranters Religion* (1650).

20 Cressy, "The Adamites Exposed," 26.

21 Professor Ann Hughes, currently working on an extensive study of *Gangræna* and its sources, only locates one reference to the Adamites in an indirect quotation: "some who come from the Army tell me, that the Sectaries in the Army do exceedingly raile against the City and Citizens, and call them the Sect of the *Adamites*" (III: D4ᵛ). I am grateful to Professor Hughes for this information.

22 Cressy, "The Adamites Exposed," 2.

23 In the 1650s, many of the attributes of the Adamites were shifted onto accounts of the Ranters; Cressy, "The Adamites Exposed," 19–20. The full title of *Bloudy Newse from the North*, for example, refers to "the Ranting Adamites" and tells of their resolution "to murther all those that will not turn *Ranters*."

24 *Nest of Serpents*, 3; *A Relation of severall Heresies* similarly claims that they "call the place of their meeting Paradise" (2).

25 Similarly, one of the faithful from *A new Sect of Religion Descryed, called Adamites* (1641) explains, "we weare but fig leaves, because our ancient Parents *Adam* & *Eve*, did cloath themselves in no other when they fled from the presence of God in the garden of *Paradice*" (4).

26 Sig. A2ᵛ. This definition is largely repeated in *The Divisions of the Church of England* (1642), sig. A2ᵛ. In another tract, *XXXIII Religions, Sects, Societies, and Factions, Of the Cavaliers now in Armes against the Parliament* (1644) (the title of which indicates the ubiquity and non-partisan fear of sectarianism), we learn that "*Adamites* have all things common, and hold it a paradice to live so, because their discipline allows both Sects to *Court* naked, in which they blush no more than *Adam* at his first Creation" (sig. A1ᵛ).

27 8. Claims of sexual misconduct are generally aimed specifically at the Bohemian Adamites. Pagitt's *Heresiography*, for example, segregates the Dutch and Bohemian kinds of Adamites. Whereas the former do not exhibit even a glint of sexual desire in their naked meetings, the latter "use promiscuous marriages" (104). The English Adamites are often presented as gentle if a bit goofy; the Bohemian Adamites, in Pagitt's account, massacre two hundred men in a village; the Adamite women

are all burnt at the stake for their errors, and in a distinctly un-martyr-like way "did undergoe their punishment with great alacrity, singing and laughing in the fire" (104).

28 And again, in the same tract: "they heare their lectures naked, pray naked, receive the sacrament naked, and their meeting they hold to be as pleasant as paradise" (5).

29 *A Relation of severall Heresies* (1646), 7; *The Brownists Conventicle* (1641), 2; *A new Sect of Religion Descryed, called Adamites* (1641), 4.

30 Explaining the tenets of the Familists, for example, one author writes "that it is expedient to manifest their whole hearts with all their counsells, minds, and will together, with their thoughts and doings; and exercises, bare and naked, and not to cover or hide any thing, before the children of *Love*"; *A Relation of severall Heresies*, 14.

31 Stillman writes about the seventeenth-century "efforts to free language from figuration." "Such efforts," he argues, "are comprehensible . . . only as part of the century's larger project to remedy the potentially dangerous insinuations of desire into language. By banishing desire from language (or, sometimes, by mastering desire in language) discourse gains objectivity and the new philosopher authority and power" (*The New Philosophy*, 36).

32 The Adamites' attempt to re-create the spiritual perfection of Eden by re-enacting its physical conditions precipitates the ideology of another (real-life) radical sect, the Diggers, who in the 1650s began cultivating common ground in an act that was as much symbolic as it was practical. In an analysis of Gerrard Winstanley's writing, John Rogers comments how "the gradual realization of a social utopia is figured throughout his work . . . as a return to the Edenic state of communality," and that "Winstanley's revolutionary agenda . . . involves the attempt to regain a lost paradise, to reunite in a startlingly literal and hermetic sense the body of the human animal to the land and vegetation that surrounds it"; *The Matter of Revolution: Science, Poetry, and Politics in the Age of Milton* (Ithaca and London: Cornell University Press, 1996), 43, 44.

33 Wilkins, *Vindiciae academiarum* (1654), 5. Slaughter notes that "Webster is a good example of the reformative zeal of the more radical Puritan sectaries as well as a good example of the sectarian sympathies with the more mystical of the scientific movements . . . During the wars, he was variously associated with the Levellers, Seekers, Familiasts [*sic*], Grindletonians and the New Model Army" (*Universal Languages*, 135). For the intertwined and often conflicting relationship of language reformers and religious reformers, see Robert Markley, *Fallen Languages: Crises of Representation in Newtonian England, 1660–1740* (Ithaca and London: Cornell University Press, 1993). On the one hand, Markley notes that "most proponents of real characters and universal languages invoke the theological argument that postlapsarian language conceals or corrupts the underlying order of nature to justify their appeal to the Adamic and

utopian vision of a lost origin – the dream of a common language – rediscovered" (70). But while these ideas were often promoted by radical sectarianism, Markley also notes that "the personification of noise" (Serres's concept of the "third man" in communication), the element "who, by continually disrupting exchanges of information, midwifes ongoing reformulations or more complex forms of order. For Dalgarno, Wilkins, Boyle, Sprat, Glanvill, Newton, and others involved in language reform and universal language schemes in seventeenth-century England, the third man assumes a number of specific names: Levelers, sectaries, Hobbists, atheists, Quakers, Ranters, Fifth Monarchists, materialists, dissenters, and other commonly invoked bogeymen who appear in the demonology of Restoration literary, historical, and political writing" (73).

34 See Nigel Smith, *Perfection Proclaimed: Language and Literature in English Radical Religion 1640–1660* (Oxford: Clarendon Press, 1989), ch. 5.

35 While scholars occasionally make implicit comparisons between Webster and Boehme (Slaughter, for example, links them parenthetically, *Universal Languages*, 136), I have not found any sustained discussion of Boehme's influence on Webster.

36 Jacob Behmen [Boehme], *The Second Booke. Concerning the Three Principles of the Divine Essence of the Eternall, Dark, Light, and Temporary World* (1648), 81.

37 *A Journal, or Historical Account of the Life, Travels, Sufferings, and Christian Experiences, and Labour of Love in the Work of the Ministry of that Ancient, Eminent, and Faithful Servant of Jesus Christ, George Fox* (Philadelphia: Marcus T. C. Gould and New York: Isaac T. Hopper, 1831), 84–85.

38 *The Works of George Fox* (Philadelphia: Marcus T. C. Gould and New York: Isaac T. Hopper, 1831), III: 389.

39 Richard Bauman, in *Let Your Words Be Few: Symbolism of Speaking and Silence among Seventeenth-Century Quakers* (Cambridge University Press, 1983), writes of Fox that "We have no clear evidence that Fox drew his ideas directly from Boehme; his own insistence on personal revelation and validation of spiritual truth predisposed him against any acknowledgement of a spiritual or intellectual debt to any authority. But several scholars have pointed out significant connections and correspondences between Quaker doctrine and the ideas of Boehme, hermetic philosophy, and other occult lines of religioscientific thought" (4); Bauman cites numerous scholars who have made this connection. See also Hugh Ormsby-Lennon, "From Shibboleth to Apocalypse: Quaker Speechways during the Puritan Revolution," in Burke and Porter, eds., *Language, Self, and Society*, 87.

40 Where Webster writes against those who "read too much upon the dead paper idols of creaturely-invented letters, but do not, nor cannot read the legible characters that are onely written and impressed by the finger of the Almighty" (*Academarium Examen* 28), Fox contends, "And

the letter itself is dead, as it is of paper and ink. And all ministers of letters and books written in paper and ink, and who speak from letters of paper and ink, and have not received from God what they preach, are ministers of the letter" (*Works*, III: 271). Fox even directly defends the idea of "natural languages" discovered in creation, an idea expressed by both Webster and Boehme. When one of the Quakers' critics writes that "to attain spiritual wisdom by depending upon miraculous revelation from heaven, is tempting the good spirit of God," Fox replies "no one knows the son but by revelation, nor the Father, nor the scripture; not a Hebrew, nor a Greek, nor a Latinist" and defends those "that think to find it out by natural languages . . . from the spirit of God which reveals the deep things of God" (*Works*, III: 393).

41 *Works*, III: 154. Elsewhere, Fox seems to attack those who sought to recover biblical language through the taxonomic methodologies of natural science: "If one get all the naturals upon the earth, and the scriptures in all the natural languages, and one supreme power of a nation tolerate all these languages to be the original, and they have the scriptures in all these languages, these are 'witty ones'; but these know not God nor Christ by all this, though they have all the scriptures, while they are from the spirit of God that gave forth scriptures" (*Works*, III: 255).

42 William C. Braithwaite, *The Beginnings of Quakerism*, second edition (Cambridge University Press, 1955), 66. Braithwaite explains that "He was dressed in leathern breeches and doublet, and a white hat, the leathern dress being chosen for its simplicity and durability" (66).

43 *Works*, III: 296, 156, 393.

44 Bauman writes that "The early Quakers themselves used speaking as a symbolic classifier, distinguishing themselves from all others as speakers of the 'pure' or the 'plain' language, thereby identifying themselves as the remnant of Israel singled out by the Lord as the people of the 'pure language,' as foretold by the prophet Zephaniah" (*Let Your Words Be Few*, 7); Bauman cites examples from George Fox, *Concerning Good-Morrow and Good-Even* (1657), 6–7, and John Payne, *A Discovery of the Priests* (1655), 17. For a reading of the practice of going naked as a sign as an ambiguous and faulty metaphor, see Bauman, *ibid.*, 88–94.

45 Early modern discussions of religious language were frequently cast in sartorial terms. Early seventeenth-century discussions of "the plain style," for example, frequently linked debates about how the minister should preach to what he should wear in the pulpit. In the first half of the seventeenth century, religious sectarians are generally known for their verbal flourishes. For Samuel Rutherford, such rhetorical extravagance was a blatant violation of a desired simplicity: "They have a sort of high & lofty speaking, but far from the Scripture-stile . . . now their eloquence is a combing, decking and busking of Christ, as the beauty and glory of the Gospel, which is, as if you would clothe the noonday-

sun with a gowne of cloath of gold, set with rubies and precious stones" (*A Survey of the Spiritual Antichrist* [1648], 313). This florid oratory, according to James Cranford in *Hæreseo-Machia, or, The Mischiefe which Heresies doe, and the means to prevent it* (1646), serves as cover for the sectarians' heretical thought. Rather than express their ideas "in plain English" (20), Cranford explains, "they parget [*sic*] over the nakednesse and deformity of their opinions, representing sometimes *them* as the wayes of God, sometimes *themselves* as the men of God; . . . As strumpets paint their faces, and adorne their bodies in greatest bravery, to hide the filthinesse of their practices, and insnare by their neatnesse: so hereticks shadow their destructive opinions with the beautifull veile of godlinesse, and their errours with the flowers of truth" (20–21). The Quaker plain speech (and dress) was thus as much a reaction against the pervasive representation of sectarianism as it was against mainstream society.

46 As Nigel Smith observes, "Since so much early Quaker protest depended upon bodily as well as verbal gesture, body and language were inextricably linked as the sites in which the workings of the inner light were known"; "Hidden Things Brought to Light: Enthusiasm and Quaker Discourse," in Thomas N. Corns and David Loewenstein, eds., *The Emergence of Quaker Writing: Dissenting Literature in Seventeenth-Century England* (London: Frank Cass, 1995), 57.

47 See "Early Quakers and 'Going Naked as a Sign'," *Quaker History* 67 (2) (1978): 69–87. See also Braithwaite, *The Beginnings of Quakerism*, 147–51. Carroll notes that there were two waves of such behavior, the first from 1652 to 1655, and a second beginning in 1659 to 1662 (with a peak of naked instances occurring in 1661) ("Early Quakers," 81–82). (The hiatus of 1655–59 is probably the result of Quaker retrenchment and restraint in the wake of the escapades of James Naylor, who shocked even those in favor of religious toleration with his 1656 arrival at Bristol, in which he re-enacted Jesus Christ's entrance into Jerusalem.) Carroll lists dozens of Quakers who went naked, a term which, in early modern parlance, could mean scantily clad as well as utterly unclothed. In 1653, an anonymous Quaker wearing only his shirt ran through Kendal, crying for the people to repent; his example was followed in that town by Thomas Castly, Elizabeth Levens, and Miles Newby, and one Edmund Adlington's wife (*ibid.*, 77). Numerous Quakers were reported to have braved the elements by running "stark naked" through the Yorkshire Dales. On separate occasions, William Simpson (*ibid.*, 78) and Elizabeth Fletcher (in contemporary reports "a very modest, grave young woman" [*ibid.*, 80]) went naked through Oxford, and Thomas Holme revealed himself and his message between 1653 and 1655 (*ibid.*, 79). In New England, Lydia Wardel attended church naked, while Deborah Wilson was whipped in Salem for her fleshy spiritual display (*ibid.*, 82). The Quaker that Pepys probably witnessed,

Solomon Eccles, made (so to speak) a habit of nakedness, repeatedly showing his "sign" from 1659 to 1669, and from London to Galway, sometimes accessorizing with a chafing-dish of fire and brimstone upon his head; Barry Reay, *The Quakers and the English Revolution* (London: Temple Smith, 1985), 36.

48 Some Quakers, such as William Simpson, went naked as a sign that "the day was neare att hand, even at the Dore, in which the Lord would stripp you naked & bare, both from the Rule & authority they were then under in this Nation, & also from that Covering of Religion with which they seemed to be covered"; cited in Carroll, "Early Quakers," 78. Leo Damrosch discusses the Quaker strategies of reversing shame in *The Sorrows of the Quaker Jesus: James Naylor and the Puritan Crackdown on the Free Spirit* (Cambridge, Mass.: Harvard University Press, 1996), 165. While George Fox did not advocate the practice, he did defend it, writing to the Quakers' enemies: "the scripture shows that the Lord made his prophet Isaiah to put off his clothes, and go naked among the Egyptians and Ethiopeans, for a sign to them, a figure of their nakedness: and if the Lord has made some as figures among you, or to go naked, as a figure of your nakedness, who are of the spiritual Egypt, . . . look upon your own shame that that may be covered" (*Works*, III: 137).

49 Document cited in Braithwaite, *The Beginnings of Quakerism*, 192n.

50 Carroll, "Early Quakers," 77, cites *The Querers and Quakers Cause at the Second Hearing* (1653), 35, as an additional source for this reference. The identification of Milner as a tailor is made in Braithwaite, *The Beginnings of Quakerism*, 147.

51 Carroll, "Early Quakers," 76. Carroll cites stories about the Milners from John Gilpin, *The Quakers Shaken, or a Warning Against Quakers* (1655), 19; Christopher Wade, *Quakery slain irrecoverably, by the principal Quakers themselves with a spiritual Sword of their own Forgery, whose names are here underwritten* (1657), 7–8.

52 Quoted in Ormsby-Lennon, "From Shibboleth to Apocalypse," 90. This strand of Quaker perfectionist thinking seems to have been overlooked or overwritten by earlier generations of historians who attempted to mold the events and writings of the 1650s into subsequent developments and beliefs. Winthrop S. Hudson, for example, wrote that "The practice of Quakers 'going naked as a sign' also has been confusing. Braithwaite say[s] that they did this 'to show that Cromwell, his Parliament and priests would be stripped of their power,' although Fox had said that it meant that they were 'not covered with truth.' One would suspect, owing to their emphasis on the Genesis story, that it might have something to do with Adam's nakedness in the Garden, but this seemingly would make it a sign of their own innocency"; "Gerrard Winstanley and the Early Quakers," *Church History* 12 (1943): 189. The question of perfectionism is a vexed

one even within Quaker writings. J. William Frost writes that "The ambiguity in perfectionist terminology was not eased by the varying usages among Friends. Fox often referred to Quakers as renewed to the first Adam and even at times saw them reaching unto the second Adam . . . Certainly the assertion that Friends were renewed to the second Adam because Christ was purer than Adam ran the legal risk of blasphemy . . . Later Quaker theologians toned down the definition of perfection"; "The Dry Bones of Quaker Theology," *Church History* 39 (1970): 517.

53 William Riley Parker, *Milton: A Biography* (Oxford: Clarendon Press, 1968), 191. My account of the Trinity Manuscript is indebted to Parker's description, pp. 190–91. For Milton lodging with a tailor, see 186.

54 Cressy, "The Adamites Exposed," 10, cites *The Downefall of Temporizing Poets, unlicenst Printers, upstart Booksellers, trotting Mercuries, and bawling Hawkers* (1641), 2, and *A Joviall Crew: or, The Merry Beggars. Presented in a Comedie, at the Cok-Pit in Drury-Lane, in the yeer 1641* (1652), Act 2, sc. 1, sig. D3^r.

55 Parker's dating, *Milton*, 212.

56 *The Complete Prose Works of John Milton*, vol. 1, ed. Don M. Wolfe (New Haven: Yale University Press, 1953), 788.

57 Bishop Henry King, in an example cited by David Cressy, joked in a sermon of 1662 that to put no clothes on an argument "were to establish the heresy of the Adamites in the pulpit, and to dogmatize nakedness"; Cressy, "The Adamites Exposed," 27, citing Mary Hobbs, ed., *The Sermons of Henry King (1592–1669), Bishop of Chichester* (Rutherford: Farleigh Dickinson University Press; Aldershot: Scolar Press, 1992), 258.

58 Smith, *Perfection Proclaimed*, 185; Smith cites M. L. Bailey, *Milton and Jakob Boehme: A Study of German Mysticism in Seventeenth-Century England* (New York, 1914). The parallels between Milton's *Paradise Lost* and Boehme's writing are extensive; see Boehme, trans. John Sparrow, *Mysterium Magnum, or An Exposition of the First Book of Moses called Genesis*, vol. 1 (London: John M. Watkins, 1924).

59 Knowlson, *Universal Language Schemes*, 270.

60 "Some Theories on the Growth and Origin of Language in Milton's Age," *Philological Quarterly* 28 (1949): 5. Given the extensive seventeenth-century refutations of Hebrew as the primordial language, this assumption is ill-founded; in Milton's extensive prose tracts, he never claims Hebrew (or any other language) as the Edenic speech. John Leonard writes that "Milton makes his greatest claim for Hebrew in *Tetrachordon*," where Milton labels it "the Metropolitan language." Leonard comments, "In the sense 'principal, chief' (*OED* 4), 'Metropolitan' asserts that Hebrew is the nearest we have to a natural language, but Milton does not say that Hebrew is identical with the language spoken by Adam and Eve in Paradise"; *Naming in Paradise: Milton and the Language of Adam and Eve* (Oxford: Clarendon Press, 1990), 15.

61 See Harold Fisch, "Hebraic Style and Motifs in *Paradise Lost*," in Ronald David Emma and John T. Shawcross, eds., *Language and Style in Milton: A Symposium in Honor of the Tercentenary of "Paradise Lost"* (New York: Frederick Ungar Publishing Co., 1967). Fisch primarily examines how Milton's subject matter and the content of the poem was influenced by Hebraic sources, and only briefly touches on ways in which the style could imitate the Hebrew. Fisch equates the *genus humile* with the Hebraic style, noting that, in contrast to the *genus grande*, "The *genus humile* . . . is a style of inquiry, of inward dialogue, of domestic realism; and it implies a nonepic universe, a universe which has less of traditional order, less ceremony, less artifice, more everyday simplicity and earnestness, the earnestness of simple people making simple choices. The presence of this Hebraic style, therefore, implies an unevenness in the heart of the poem, in its very basic conception; it implies an inner tension, an inner dialectic. More than that, it implies a threat to the epic world itself – its order and balance" (*ibid.*, 58). This idea is certainly intriguing, but Fisch only cites a few lines to back up his point (8: 494–99), and in re-reading much of the lines of Adam and Eve, I do not see this as a prominent, or even frequent, speech pattern. In *Milton's Language* (Oxford: Basil Blackwell, 1990), an extensive analysis of Milton's vocabulary, Thomas N. Corns discusses Milton's use of Greek and Latin, but (as far as I can see) makes no mention of Hebrew. John K. Hale writes in *Milton's Languages: The Impact of Multilingualism on Style* (Cambridge University Press, 1997), that "Hebra*isms*, of diction or syntax, are few" (123).

62 *Milton's Grand Style* (Oxford: Clarendon Press, 1963), 110.

63 Leonard, *Naming in Paradise*, 261.

64 This and all references to *Paradise Lost* are from Merriott Y. Hughes, ed., *John Milton: Complete Poems and Major Prose* (Indianapolis: The Odyssey Press, 1957).

65 Referring to Book 8.437–48. The speaker of the lines is God, although the subject of Leonard's sentence (32) which I have quoted is Milton.

66 *Surprised by Sin: The Reader in Paradise Lost*, second edition (Berkeley: University of California Press, 1967; London: MacMillan Press Ltd., 1997), 107.

67 *"Paradise Lost" and the Rhetoric of Literary Forms* (Princeton University Press, 1985), 20.

68 Dennis Danielson, "Milton, Bunyan, and the Clothing of Truth and Righteousness," in Margo Swiss and David A. Kent, eds., *Heirs of Fame: Milton and Writers of the English Renaissance* (Lewisburg: Bucknell University Press, 1995), 258. This is the only extended discussion of nakedness in Milton's writings that I know of.

69 While many of these examples of "clothing" remain in the realm of metaphoric garb, the angels also don battle gear which achieves a tangible materiality. Zophiel instructs them, "let each / His Adamantine

coat gird well, and each / Fit well his Helme, grip fast his orbed Shield" (6: 541–43). In Book 11, our attention is even drawn to the very fabric worn by the archangel. He approaches "Not in his shape Celestial, but as Man / Clad to meet Man; over his lucid Arme / A military Vest of purple flow'd / Livelier then *Melibœan*, or the grain / Of *Sarra*, worn by Kings and Heroes old / In time of Truce; *Iris* had dipt the woof" (11: 239–244).

70 Genesis 2: 19–20: "And out of the ground the Lord God formed every beast of the field, and every fowl of the air; and brought them unto Adam to see what he would call them: and whatsoever Adam called every living creature, that was the name thereof. And Adam gave names to all the cattle, and to the fowl of the air, and to every beast of the field; but for Adam there was not found an help meet for him." Genesis 3: 7: "And the eyes of them both were opened, and they knew that they were naked; and they sewed fig leaves together, and made themselves aprons."

71 Genesis 3: 21: "Unto Adam also and to his wife did the Lord God make coats of skins, and clothed them."

EPILOGUE: THE FORTUNES OF HUDIBRAS

1 George Wasserman, "That *Paultry Story*: The Spurious *Hudibras*: *The Second Part*," *Philological Quarterly* 71 (1992): 459.

2 This publication history is summarized by Alok Yadav in "Fractured Meanings: *Hudibras* and the Historicity of the Literary Text," *English Literary History* 62 (1995): 530–31.

3 This and all quotations are from Samuel Butler, *Hudibras*, ed. John Wilders (Oxford: Clarendon Press, 1967).

4 See George Wasserman, "Carnival in *Hudibras*," *English Literary History* 55 (1988): 79–97.

5 1.2. 517–22, 527–30, 535–40, 549–56.

6 Cited in George Wasserman, *Samuel "Hudibras" Butler*, updated edition (Boston: Twayne Publishers, 1989), 15.

Selected bibliography of pamphlets and sermons

The Adamite, or, The Loves of Father Rock and his intrigues with the nuns. 1683.

Adams, Mary. *The Ranters monster*. 1652.

Ainsworth, Henry. *Counterpoyson. Considerations touching the poynts in difference between the godly ministers and people of the Church of England, and the seduced brethren of the Separation*. 1642.

An epistle sent vnto two daughters of VVarwick. Amsterdam, 1608.

The old orthodox foundation of religion left for a patterne to a new reformation. 1653.

A Seasonable discourse, or, A censure upon a dialogue of the Anabaptists. 1644.

A trve confession of the faith, and hvmble acknowledgment of the aleageance, which wee Hir Maiesties subjects, falsely called Brownists, doo hould towards God. 1596.

Ainsworth, Henry and Francis Johnson. *An Apologie or Defence of Svch Trve Christians as are commonly (but vnjustly) called Brownists*. 1604. Facsimile reprint, Amsterdam and New York: Da Capo Press, Theatrvm Orbis Terrarvm, 1970.

An Alarum: To the last warning peece to London by way of Answer: Discovering the Danger of Sectaries suffered: and the necessity of Order, and Vniformity to bee Established. 1646.

Alison, Richard. *A plaine confvtation of a Treatise of Brownisme*. 1590. Facsimile reprint: Amsterdam and New York: Da Capo Press, Theatrvm Orbis Terrarvm, 1968.

Allen, Thomas. *A Brief Narration of the Truth of some Particulars in Mr. Thomas Edwards his Book called Gangræna*. 1646.

Almonds for Parrets . . . Composed, heretofore, by a well-knowne Moderne Author. 1647.

Ames, William. *Conscience with the Power and Cases Thereof*. 1639.

English Puritanisme. Containing the Maine Opinions of the rigidest sort of those that are called Puritans in the Realme of England. 1641.

The Ancient Bounds, or Liberty of Conscience, Tenderly Stated, Modestly Asserted, and Mildly Vindicated. 1645.

The Answer to the Rattle-heads concerning their fictionate Resolution of the Round-heads. 1641.

Antidotes against some infectious passages in a Tract concerning Schisme. 1642.

Antidoton: Or A Soveraigne Remedie Against Schisme and Heresie. 1600.

Antinomians and Familists Condemned by the Synod of the Elders in New England. 1644.

The Antiquity of Reformation: or, An Observation Proving the Great Turke a Triangle, and the rest of the world Round-Heads. 1647.

Anti-Toleration. 1646.

Archer, John. *Instructions about Right Beleeving: Several Sermons leading unto Christ, directing unto Faith, and incouraging thereto.* 1645.

The Arraignement of Svperstition. Or a Discourse betweene a Protestant, a Glasier, and a Separatist. 1641.

Aylmer, John. *A harborovve for faithfull and trevve subjects.* n.p., 1559.

B., I. *The Fortresse of Fathers, ernestlie defending the purity of religion.* n.p., 1566.

B., O. *A Dialogue or Discourse betwixt two old acquaintance of contrary Opinions.* 1647.

B., R. *Strange and Prodigious Religions, Customs, and Manners, of Sundry Nations.* 1683.

Baillie, Robert. *Anabaptism, the Trve Fovntaine of Independency, Brownisme, Antimony, [and] Familisme.* 1647.

A Dissvasive from the Errours of the Time. 1645.

Bakewell, Thomas. *An Answer or Confutation of Divers Errors Broached and Maintained by the Seven Churches of Anabaptists.* 1646.

A Iustification of two points now in controversie with the Anabaptists concerning Baptisme. 1646.

Bale, John. *Brefe Chronycle, concernynge the Examinacyon and death of the blessed martyr of Christ syr Johan Oldecastell the lorde Cobham.* Antwerp, 1544.

Bancroft, Richard. *Dangerous Positions and Proceedings, published and practiced within this Iland of Brytaine, vnder pretence of Reformation.* 1595.

A sermon preached at Pauls Cross on 9 February 1588. 1588.

A Svrvay of the Pretended Holy Discipline. Contayning the beginninges, successe, parts, proceedings, authority, and doctrine of it: with some of the manifold, and material repugnances, varieties and vncertaineties, in that behalfe. 1593. Facsimile reprint, Amsterdam: Theatrvm Orbis Terrarvm Ltd., 1972.

Barlow, William. *A dyaloge descrybyng the orygynall group of these Lutheran faccyons, and many of theyr abusys.* n.p., 1531.

Barthlet, John. *The Pedegrewe of Heretiques.* 1566.

Bartholomevv Faire. 1641.

Bastwick, John. *The Second Part of the Book call'd Independency not Gods Ordinance.* 1645.

The Storming of the Anabaptists Garrisons. 1647.

The utter routing of the whole army of all the Independents and Sectaries, or, Independency not Gods Ordinance. 1646.

Bell, Thomas. *The downefall of Poperie.* 1608.

Benbrigge, John. *Gods Fury, Englands Fire. Or, A Plaine Discovery of those Spirituall Incendiaries, which have set Church and State on Fire.* 1646.

Bentham, Joseph. *The Societie of the Saints.* 1638?

Bernard, Richard. *Christian Advertisements and Counsels of Peace also disuasions from the Separatists Schism.* 1608.

Christian See to thy Conscience, Or, A treatise of the nature, the kinds, and manifold differences of Conscience. 1631.

The fabulous foundation of the popedome . . . A chronological description. 1619.

Good christian, looke to thy creede: for the truth of religion, from all crooked by-paths. 1630.

Ioshvahs Resolution for the well ordering of his Household. 1629.

Looke beyond Luther: or an answer to that question . . . where this our religion was before Luther's time? 1623.

Plaine euidences: the church of England is apostolicall, the separation schismaticall. 1610.

Ruths Recompence: Or A Commentarie Vpon the Booke of Rvth. 1628.

Berwick, John. *An Antidote against Lay-Preaching, or The preachers plea.* 1642.

Blome, Richard. *The Fanatic History, or, An exact relation and account of the old Anabaptists and new Quakers.* 1660.

Bloody Newes from Dover. Being a True Relation of the great and bloudy Murder, committed by Mary Champions (an Anabaptist) who cut off her Childs head, being 7 weeks old, and held it to her husband to baptize. 1647.

Bodonius. *The fortresse of faith defended.* 1570.

Boehme, Jacob. *Mercurius Teutonicus. Or a Christian Information concerning the Last Times. Being divers propheticall passages of the Fall of Babel . . . Gathered out of the Mysticall Writings of that famous Germane Author, Jacob Behmen.* 1656.

Mysterium Magnum, or An Exposition of the First Book of Moses called Genesis, 1654.

The Second Booke. Concerning the Three Principles of the Divine Essence. 1648.

Bolton, Robert. *A Discourse About the State of True Happinesse.* 1611.

Bourne, Benjamin. *The Description and Confutation of Mysticall Antichrist, the Familists.* 1646.

Bourne, Immanuel. *The Anatomie of Conscience.* 1623.

Bownde, Nicholas. *The True Doctrine of the Sabbath.* 1606.

Bradshaw, William. *English Puritanisme.* Amsterdam, 1605.

Bramley, David. *A Preacher of the Gospel.* 1646.

Bray, Thomas [Samoth Yarb, pseud.]. *The anatomy of et caetera.* 1641.

A Brief Discovery of the Blasphemous Doctrin of Familisme, First conceived and brought forth into the world by one HENRY NICOLAS of the Low Countries of Germany about an hundred years agoe. 1645.

A Brief Remonstrance of the reasons and grounds of those people commonly called Anabaptists for their separation. 1645.

Brinsley, John. *The Arraignment of the Present Schism of New Separation in Old England.* 1646.

Church Reformation, Tenderly Handled in Fovre Sermons. 1643.

The Doctrine and Practice of Paedobaptisme, Asserted and Vindicated. 1645.

Bristow, Richard. *A Briefe Treatise of Divers Plaine and sure waies to finde out the* truth in this doubtfull and dangerous time of Heresie. Conteyning Svndrie worthy motives vnto the Catholike Faith, or Considerations to moue a man to beleeue the Catholikes, and not the Heretikes. Antwerp, 1599.

Ways to find truth in time of heresy. 1574.

Britanicus his Blessing. Cambridge, 1646.

Broad, Thomas. *Three Questions Answered.* 1621.

The Brothers of the Separation. Or A true Relation of a company of Brownists. 1641.

Buddle, George. *A Short and Plaine Discourse, Fully containing the whole doctrine of Euangelicall Fastes.* 1609.

Burgess, Anthony. *The difficulty of and the encouragements to a reformation.* 1643.

　The Reformation of the Church to be endeavoured more then that of the Commonwealth. 1645.

Burrough, Edward. *A Declaration to all the World of our Faith and what we believe who are called Quakers.* 1660.

Burton, Henry. *A Divine Tragedie Lately Acted, or A Collection of sundrie memorable examples of Gods judgments upon Sabbath-breakers, and other like Libertines, in their unlawfull Sports.* 1641.

　Grounds of Christian religion. 1631.

　Vindication of churches commonly called Independent. 1644.

Brown, David. *Two conferences between some of those that are called Separatists.* 1650.

The Brownists faith and beliefe opened. 1641.

The Brownist haeresies confvted. 1641.

Bugg, Francis. *The painted-harlot both stript and whipt, or, The second part of the Naked Truth.* 1683.

Bullinger, Heinrich, trans. J. Vernon. *An Holsome Antidotus or counter poysen against the pestylent heresye and secte of the Anabaptistes.* n.p., 1548.

Burroughes, Jer[emy]. *A Vindication of Mr. Burroughes, Against Mr. Edwards his foule Aspersions, in his spreading Gangræna, and his Angry Antiapologia.* 1646.

Byfield, Richard. *Temple-defilers defiled, Wherein a true Visible Church of Christ is Described. The Evils and pernicious Errours, especially appertaining to Schisme, Anabaptisme, and Libertinisme, that infest our Church, are Discovered.* 1645.

　Short treatise describing the true church of Christ, and the evills of schisme. 1653.

C., T. *The Schismaticke Sifted Through a Sive of the Largest size.* 1646.

Calfine, Giles [Thexylvenio, Drupheyra, pseud.]. *A Fresh Bit of Mutton, for those Fleshly minded Cannibals that cannot endure Pottadge.* 1642.

Canne, Abednego. *A New Wind-Mil, a New.* Oxford, 1643.

Carmina Colloquia: or, A Demonaicall and Damnable Dialogue between the Devil and an Independent. 1649.

Carpenter, Richard. *The Conscionable Christian, or the Indevour of Saint Paul.* 1623.

　The Anabaptist, washt and washt, and shrunk in the washing. 1653.

Carter, Richard. *The Schismatick Stigmatized.* 1641.

Caryl, Joseph. *The Present Duty and Endeavour of the Saints.* 1646.

Case, Thomas. *Deliverance-Obstruction: or, The Set-backs of Reformation.* 1646.

Certain Briefe Treatises. Oxford, 1641.

Certain Queres modestly propounded to such as affect the Congregational-way. 1646.

Certain considerable and most materiall Cases of Conscience. Oxford, 1645.

Certain Considerations shewing the imminent Danger of this City, together with the Remedies. 1644.

Certaine Modest Observations and Considerations of the true Protestants of the Church of England. 1641.

Cheshire, Thomas. *A True Copy of the Sermon which was preached at S. Pauls the tenth day of October Last.* 1641.

Cheynell, Fr[ancis]. *The Rise, Growth, and Danger of Socinianisme. Together with A plaine discovery of a desperate designe of corrupting the Protestant Religion.* 1643.

Chidley, Katherine. *The Ivstification of the Independent Chvrches of Christ.* 1641.

Clapham, Jonathan. *A Full Discovery and Confutation of the wicked and damnable Doctrines of the Quakers.* 1656.

Clapham, Henoch. *Antidoton or a Soveraigne Remedie against Schisme and Heresie.* 1600.

The Description of a true visible Christian. 1599.

Errovr on the Left Hand. Throvgh a Frozen Securitie. 1608.

Errovr on the Right Hand, through a preposterous Zeale. 1608.

Clarke, John. *Leaven, corrupting the Childrens Bread; or, Christs Caveat to beware of sectarians and their dangerous Doctrines in two Sermons.* 1646.

Cleaver, Robert and John Dod. *A plaine and familiar exposition of the Ninth and Tenth Chapters of the Proverbs of Solomon.* 1606.

Coachman, Robert. *The Cry of a Stone, or, A Treatise Shewing What is the Right Matter, Forme, and Government of the visible Church of Christ . . . Together with a just reproofe of the over-strained and excessive separation, contentions and divisions of such as commonly are called Brownists.* 1642.

Conformities Deformity. 1646.

Considerations Tending to the Happy Accomplishment of Englands Reformation in Church and State. 1647.

Cornucopia, or, Roome for a Ram-head. Wherein is described the dignity of the Ram-head above the Round-head, or Rattle-head. 1642.

Cotton, John. *The controversy concerning Liberty of Conscience in Matters of Religion.* 1646.

Cowley, Abraham. *The Collected Works of Abraham Cowley.* Eds. Thomas O. Calhoun, Laurence Heyworth, and Allan Pritchard. Newark: University of Delaware Press; London: Associated University Press, 1989.

Cowper, William. *The Anatomie of a Christian Man.* 1613.

Cranford, James. *Hæreseo-Machia, or, The mischiefe which Heresies doe, and the means to prevent it.* 1646.

Plain English: Or, the Sectaries Anatomized. 1646.

Truth triumphing over errour and heresie. 1646.

Cranmer, George. *Concerning the Nevv Chvrch Discipline.* 1642.

Croft, Herbert. *The Naked Truth: Or, The True State of the Primitive Church.* 1675.

A Curb for Sectaries and Bold Propheciers. 1641.

D., J. *A Iudgement or a Definition of the Visible and Invisible Chvrch.* 1641.

The Dangers of New Discipline, to the State and Church Discovered, Fit to be Considered by them who seeke (as they terme it) the Reformation of the Church of England. 1642.

D'Ewes, Simonds. *The Primitive Practice for Preserving Truth, or, An historicall narration, shewing what course the primitive church anciently, and the best reformed churches since have taken to suppresse heresie and schisme.* 1645.

A Declaration, Of a Strange and Wonderfull Monster. 1646.

Dell, Wil[liam]. *Vniformity Examined, Whether it may be found in the Gospel, Or, In the practices of the Churches of Christ.* 1646.

Denison, Stephen. *The White Wolfe.* 1627.

A Description of the sect called The Familie of Love. 1641.

A Dialogue between a Brownist and a Schismatick. 1643.

A Dialogve betwixt Rattle-Head and Rovnd-Head. 1641.

A Dialogue betwixt Three Travellers, as accidentally they did meet on the High-way: Crvey Cringe, a Papist, Accepted Weigh All, a Professour of the Church of England, and Factiovs Wrest-Writ, a Brownist. 1641.

Dillingham, Francis. *Christian Oeconomy. Or Housbold Government.* 1609.

A Discovery of 29. Sects here in London, all of which, except the first, are most Divelish and Damnable. 1641.

The Discovery of a swarm of seperatists. 1641.

Divine Observations upon the London-Ministers Letter against Toleration, by . . . Martin Mar-Priest, Sonne, and Heire to Old Martin the Metrapolitane. 1646.

Dogerell, Owen. *A Brief Dialogue Between Zelotopit one of the Daughters of a Zealous Round-head, and Superstition a Holy Fryer.* 1642.

The dolefull Lamentation of Cheap-side Crosse. 1641.

Downing, Galybute. *An Appeale to Every Impartiall, Iudicious, and Godly Reader: Whether the Presbyterie or Prelacie be the better Church-Government, according to the Word of God.* 1641.

Eachard, John. *The Axe, Against Sin and Error.* 1646.

Earle, John. *Microcosmography, or a Peece of the World Discovered in Essays and Characters.* 1628.

Edwards, Thomas. *The Casting Down of the last and strongest hold of Satan. Or, A Treatise Against Toleration and pretended Liberty of Conscience.* 1647.

    Gangræna: Or a Catalogue and Discovery of many of the Errours, Heresies, Blasphemies, and pernicious Practices of the Sectaries of this time. 1646. Facsimile reprint, The Rota. Ilkley, UK: The Scolar Press, Ltd., 1977.

Elidad [pseud.]. *A good and fruitfull exhortation unto the Family of Love.* 1574?

Episcopal Government instituted by Christ, and confirmed by cleere evidence of Scripture. 1641.

Etherington, John. *The Anabaptists ground-work for reformation.* 1644.

False Prophets Discovered. 1642.

Farmer, Ra[lph]. *The Great Mysteries of Godlinesse and Ungodlinesse . . . the other discovered from the writings and speakings of a generation of deceivers, called Quakers.* 1655.

Fawcet, Samuel. *A Seasonable Sermon for these Troublesome Times.* 1641.

Featley, Daniel. *The Dippers dipt. Or, The Anabaptists Dvck'd and Plvng'd Over Head and Eares.* 1645.

Fell, Philip. *Lex Talionis: Or, The Author of the Naked Truth Stript Naked.* 1676.

Fenner, Dudley. *A Counter-Poyson, modestly written for the time, to make aunswere to the obiections and reproches, wherewith the aunswerer to the Abstract, would disgrace the holy Discipline of Christ.* 1584?

The First and Large Petition of the Citie of London . . . for a Reformation in Church-government and also for the abolishment of Episcopacie. 1641.

Five Lookes Over the Professors of the English Bible. 1642.

The Fortresse of fathers, ernestlie defending the puritie of religion. n.p., 1566.

G., I. *Truths Victory Against Heresie.* 1645.

Gataker, Thomas. *Shadowes without Substance, or Pretended new Lights: together, with the Impieties and Blasphemies that lurk under them, further discovered and drawn forth into the Light.* 1646.

Geree, John. *The Character of an old English Pvritane, or Non-Conformist.* 1646.

Gifford, George. *A Plaine Declaration that our Brownists be full Donatists.* 1590. Facsimile reprint, Amsterdam and Norwood, N.J.: Walter J. Johnson, Inc., Theatrvm Orbis Terrarvm, Ltd., 1974.

Gilpin, George. *The Bee hiue of the Romishe Churche.* 1580.

Gilpin, John. *The Quakers Shaken.* 1653.

A Glimpse of Sions Glory, or, the Churches Beautie specified. 1641.

Goodwin, John. *Cretensis: or, A Briefe Answer to an ulcerous Treatise, lately published by Mr. Thomas Edwards intituled, Gangræna.* 1646.

Grand Plvtoes Remonstrance, or, The Devill Horn-mad at Roundheads and Brownists. 1642.

Gregory, Martin. *A treastise of schisme.* 1578.

Gwynneth, John. *The state in which hereticks lead their liues.* 1554.

H., I. *A Description of the Church of Christ.* 1610.

Hacket, William, Edmund Coppinger, and Henry Arthington. *Conspiracie for Pretended Reformation: viz. Presbyteriall Discipline.* 1592.

Hales, John. *A Tract Concerning Schism and Schismatiques. Wherein, Is briefly discovered the originall causes of all Schism.* 1642.

Hall, Joseph. *A Common Apologie of the Chvrch of England: Against the vniust Challenges of the ouer-iust Sect, Commonly called Brownists.* 1610.
Episcopacie by Divine Right. 1640.

Hallywell, Henry. *An Account of Familism.* 1673.

Hammond, Henry. *Of Conscience.* Oxford, 1645.

Harris, John. *The Antipodes, or Reformation with the Heeles Upward.* Oxford, 1647.

A True Relation of a Company of Brownists, Separatists, and Non-Conformists. 1641.

Hartlib, Samuel. *The Parliaments Reformation, or, a Worke for Presbyters, Elders, and Deacons, to Engage themselves, for the Education of all poore Children.* 1646.

Harvey, Gabriel. *Pierces supererogation.* 1593.

Harvey, Richard. *Plaine Percevall the Peace-Maker of England. Sweetly Indevoring with his blunt persuasions to botch up a Reconciliation between Mar-ton and Mar-tother.* 1589.

Hausted, Peter. *Ad populum, or, A lecture to the people, with a satyr against separatists.* 1678.

Hayne, Thomas, Melchior Adam, and Francis Quarles. *The Life and Death of Dr. Martin Luther.* 1641.

Hell broke loose: Or, A Catalogue of many of the spreading Errors, Heresies and Blasphemies of these Times. 1646.

Helwys, Thomas. *Obiections: Answered by way of Dialogue, where is proved . . . That no man ought to be persecuted for his religion.* 1615.

Hieron, Samuel. *Discoverie of hypocrisie.* 1607.

Higginson, Francis. *A Briefe Relation of the Irreligion of the Northern Quakers.* 1653.

Hodges, Thomas. *The Growth and Spreading of Hæresie.* 1647.

Hogarde, Miles. *The Displaying of the Protestants.* 1556.

Homes, Nathaniel. *The Peasants Price of Spirituall Liberty.* 1642.

Hooke, William. *New Englands Teares, for Old Englands Feares.* 1641.

Howell, James. *The Pre-eminence and Pedigree of Parlement.* 1644.

Howgill, Francis. *The popish inquisition newly erected in New-England, whereby their church is manifested to be a daughter of mysterie Babylon, which did drink the blood of the Saints.* 1659.

Hudson, Samuel. *The Essence and Unitie of the Church Catholike Visible.* 1645.

The Humble Petition of the Brovvnists. 1641.

The Hunting of the Fox, or the Sectaries Dissected. 1648.

Jacobson, O. *Romyshe Foxe.* n.p. 1543.

Jordan, Thomas. *A Medicine for the Times. Or, An Antidote against Faction.* 1641.

Knewstub, John. *A Confutation of monstrous and horrible heresies, taught by H. N. and embraced of a number, who call themselues the Familie of Loue.* 1579.

A Sermon Preached at Paules Crosse the Friday before Easter. n.p., 1579.

L., A. *Antimartinus.* 1589.

L., W. *The Bramble Berry: or, A Briefe discourse touching participating in mixt Assemblies at the Sacrament of the Lords Supper.* 1643.

Langbaine, Gerard. *Episcopall Inheritance.* Oxford, 1641.

Lanseters Lance, For Edwards'es [sic] Gangrene: or, A Ripping up, and laying open some rotten, purrified, corrupt, stinking Matter in Mr. Thomas Edwards his Gangren. 1646.

Lauder, William. *Ane Prettie mirrour or conference betwixt the faithful Protestant a[n]d the dissemblit false hypo[c]rite.* Edinburgh, 1570.

Laurence, Richard. *The Antichristian Presbyter: or, Antichrist transformed; assuming the New Shape of a Reformed Presbyter.* 1646.

Lawrence, R. *The Wolf Stript of his Sheeps Clothing or the Antichristian Clergy-man turn'd right side outwards.* 1647.

Lawne, Christopher. *Brovvnisme tvrned the In-side out-ward. Being a Parallel Betweene the Profession and Practise of the Brownists Religion.* 1613.

The Lay-Divine, or, The simple House-preaching Taylor; who whilest by his pretended Enthusiasms he would seem to divert his Brethren from the way to Hell. 1647.

Leigh, Edward. *Critica Sacra: Or, Philogicall and Theologicall Observations Upon All the Greek Words of the New Testament, in order Alphabeticall.* 1646.

A Long-Winded Lay Lecture. 1647.

Love, Christopher. *Englands Distemper, Having Division and Error, as its Cause.* 1645.

Loveday, Samuel. *An Answer to the Lamentation of Cheap-side Crosse. Together with the Reasons why so many doe desire the downfall of it, and all such Popish Reliques.* 1642.

Lyly, John. *Pappe with an hatchet. Alias, a figge for my God sonne.* 1589.

Mackock, John. *The Pictvre of Independency Lively (yet Lovingly) Delineated.* 1645.

Maddocks, John and Pinnell, Henry. *Gangrænachrestum, or A Plaister to alay the tumor, and prevent the spreading of a pernitious Vlcer, like to have growne upon, and putrified the good report of Jo. Maddocks and Henry Pinnell.* 1646.

Manton, Thomas. *Meate out of the Eater, or, Hopes of Vnity in . . . divided and distracted Times.* 1647.

Mar-Martine [pseud.]. *I know not why a trueth in rime set out.* 1593.

Marphoreus [pseud.]. *Martins months minde.* 1589.

Marprelate, Martin [pseud.]. *Oh read ouer D. John Bridges ["The Epitome."]* 1588. Menston: The Scolar Press facsimile reprint, 1970.

Certaine Minerall and Metaphysicall Schoolpoints. 1589. Menston: The Scolar Press facsimile reprint, 1970.

Hay any worke for Cooper. 1589. Menston: The Scolar Press facsimile reprint, 1970.

Theses Martinianæ. 1589. Menston: The Scolar Press facsimile reprint, 1970.

The iust censure and reproofe of Martin Iunior. 1589. Menston: The Scolar Press facsimile reprint, 1970.

The Protestatyon of Martin Marprelat. 1589. Menston: The Scolar Press facsimile reprint, 1970.

Mar-Prelate, Martin [pseud.]. *The Character of a Puritan; and His Gallimaufrey of the Antichristian Clergie; prepared with D. Bridges Sawce for the present time to feed on. By the worthy Gentleman, D. Martin Mar-Prelat, Doctor in all the Faculties.* 1643.

Martin Claw-Clergey [pseud.]. *A Sadre Decretall, or Hue and Cry. From his superlative Holinesse, Sir Symon Synod, for the Apprehension of Reverend Young Martin Mar-Priest.* 1645.

Martin the Metropolitan [pseud.]. *Hay any worke for Cooper: or, A Brief Pistle directed by way of an Hublication [sic] to the Reverend Byshops.* 1642.

Martins months minde, that is, A Certaine report, and true description of the Death, and Funeralls, of olde Martin Marre-prelate. 1589.

Marre Mar-Martine: or Marre-Martins medling, in a manner misliked. 1590?

Martin's Eccho. 1590?.

The Master-piece of Round-heads. 1643.

Mercurius Anti-mechanicus. Or the Simple Coblers Boy. With his Lap-full of Caveats (or Take heeds) Documents, Advertisements, and Præmonitions to all his honest-fellow-tradesmen-Preachers. 1648.

Mock-Majesty: or, The Seige of Munster. 1644.

Moore, Thomas. *A Discovery of Seducers, that Creep into Houses.* 1646.

Morley, George. *A modest advertisement concerning the present controversie about Church-government.* 1641.

Morton, Thomas. *The Presentment of a Schismaticke.* 1642.

Musgrave, John. *Good Covnsel in Bad Times . . . Being a discovery of an old way to root out Sects and heresies.* 1647.

N., M. *Independencie no Schisme. Or, an Answer to a Scandalous Book, entituled, The Schismatick sifted.* 1646.

Nalton, James. *Delay of Reformation Provoking Gods further Indignation.* 1646.

The Nativity of Sir John Presbyter. 1645.

A Nest of Serpents Discovered. Or, a Knot of old Heretiques revived, Called the Adamites. 1641?.

New Orders New, Agreed upon by a Parliament of Round-Heads. Confirmed by the Brethren of the New Separation Assembled at Round-heads-Hall. 1642.

New Preachers New. 1641.

Newcomen, Matthew. *The Dvty of such as would walke worthy of the Gospel: to Endeavour Union not Divisions nor Toleration.* 1646.

Newes from the King's Bath. Bristol, 1645.

Newes from New-England of a most strange and prodigious Birth. 1642.

Niclaes, Hendrik. *Dicta H.N. Documentall Sentences; eauen-as those-same were spoken-fourth by HN, and written-vp out of the Woordes of his Mouth.* Cologne? 1574?.

    Epistola XI. H.N. Correction and Exhoration out of heartie Loue to a plucking under the Obedience of the Loue and to Repentance for their Sinnes. Cologne? 1574 ?.

    Euangelium Regni. A Joyfull message of the Kingdom, published by the holie Spirit of the loue of Iesus Christ. Cologne ?, 1575?.

    Exhortatio I. The first Exhortation of H. N. to his Children, and to the Famelye of Loue. Cologne (?), 1574?.

    Proverbia HN. The Prouerbes of HN. Which he in the Dayes of his Olde-age; hath set-fourth as Similitudes and mysticall Sayinges. Cologne? 1575 ?.

No Post from Heaven, Nor yet from Hell: But a true Relation, and Animadversions, written, and sent as an Antidote to all, Unbelieving Brownists, Prophane Anabaptists, Schismaticall Monsters, and such like Incendiaries of the State. Oxford, 1643.

The Noble Pamphlet, or, A Pigs Hed and a Poppet-Play provided for the Rebels at Westminster, against this Bartholomew Faire. 1648.

The Old Protestant Letanie: Against all Sectaries, and their Defendants, Both Presbyterians, and Independents. 1647.

The originall and sprynge of all sectes & orders by whome, wha[n] or where they beganne. n.p., 1537.

Ormerod, Oliver. *The Pictvre of a Puritane.* 1605. Facsimile reprint. Amsterdam: Theatrvm Orbis Terrarvm, Ltd.; New Jersey: Walter J. Johnson, Inc., 1975.

The Picture of a Papist. 1606. Facsimile reprint. Amsterdam: Theatrvm Orbis Terrarvm, Ltd.; New Jersey: Walter J. Johnson, Inc., 1975.

Overton, Richard [Martin Mar-Priest, pseud.]. *The Arraignment of Mr. Persecution.* 1645.

Owen, David. *The Pvritans Impvritie: or the Anatomie of a Puritane or Separatist.* 1641.

Owen, Lewis. *A Genealogie of all Popish Monks, Friers, and Jesuits. Shewing their first Founders, Beginnings, Proceedings, and present State.* 1646.

P., D. P. *An Antidote against The Contagious Air of Independency.* 1644.

A Pack of old Puritans. 1650.

A Pack of Pvritans, Maintayning the Vnlavvfvlnesse, or Vnexpediencie or Both of Pluralities and Nonresidency: Unpreaching prelates and Ministers. 1641.

Page, William and John Hales. *Tracte concerning schisme and schismatiques.* Oxford, 1642.

Pagitt, Ephraim. *Heresiography: or, a description of the Hereticks and Sectaries sprang up in these latter times.* 1647.

Palmer, George. *Sectaries Vnmasked and Confvted.* 1647.

Panke, John. *The Fal of Babel.* Oxford, 1608.

Parker, Henry. *A Discourse Concerning Puritans.* 1641.

Persecutio Undecima. The Chvrches Eleventh Persecution. Or, A Briefe View of the Pvritan Persecution of the Protestant Clergy of the Church. 1648.

A Plea for Congregationall Government: Or, A defense of the Assemblies Petition, Against Mr. John Saltmarsh. 1646.

Pope, James. *The Unveiling of Antichrist. Or, Antichrist stript naked out of all his Scripture-Attyre . . . So that we may the more cleerly see the very bottome-root, from whence he sprang.* 1646.

The Presbyterians Letany. Set forth, and ordained to be used, for the more speedy supressing of the growth of Independency. 1647.

Price, John. *The Pulpit Incendiary.* 1648.

Prynne, William. *A Fresh Discovery of some Prodigious New-Wandering-Blasing-Stars, and Firebrands, Stiling themselves New-Lights, Firing our Church and State into New Combustions.* 1646.

Independency Examined, Vnmasked, Refuted. 1644.

Trvth Trivmphing Over Falshood, Antiquity over Novelty, or, The First Part of a just and seasonable Vindication of the undoubted Ecclesiastical Iurisdiction. 1645.

The Pulpit Incendiary Anatomized. 1648.

Purchas, Samuel. *Purchas his Pilgrim. Microcosmus, or the History of Man.* 1619.

A Puritane set forth In his Lively Colours: or K. James his Description of a puritan. 1642.

Pvritano-Iesvitismvs. The Puritan Tvrn'd Jesuite. 1643.

Rawlinson, John. *Fishermen Fishers of Men.* 1609.

A Reflex upon our Reformers. 1648.

The Reformed Malignants. Or, A Discourse Vpon the Present State of our Affaires. 1643.

A Relation of severall Heresies. 1646.

Religions Lotterie, or the Churches Amazement. Wherein is declared how many sorts of Religions there is crept into the very bowels of this Kingdome, striving to shake the whole foundations and to destroy both Church and Kingdom. 1642.

Religious Peace: or, A Plea for Liberty of Conscience. 1646.

Of Resisting the Lawfull Magistrate upon Colovr of Religion. 1643.

The Resolution of the Roundheads: Being a Zealous Declaration of the Grievances wherewith their little wits are consumed to destruction. 1642.

Reynoldes, Edward. *Israels Prayer in time of Trouble with Gods Gracious Ansvver thereunto.* 1645.

Richardson, Samuel. *Some brief Considerations on Doctor Featley his Book, intitled, The Dipper Dip't.* 1645.

Ricraft, Josiah. *A Looking Glasse for the Anabaptists and the rest of the Separatists.* 1645.

A Nosegay of Rank-smelling Flowers, such as grow in Mr. Iohn Goodwins Garden. Gathered upon occasion of his late lying Libell against M. Thomas Edwards. 1646.

Robinson, Henry. *Liberty of Conscience.* 1643.

Robinson, John. *Essayes; or Observations Divine and Morall.* 1638.

A Justification of Separation from the Church of England. 1610.

Rogers, John. *A treatise of love.* 1632.

Rogers, Thomas. *The Displaying of an horrible secte of grosse and wicked Heretiques, naming themselues the Familie of Loue.* n.p., 1578.

Rogers, Thomas. *The faith, doctrine, and religion professed and protected in the Realm of England.* 1621.

Rogers, Timothy. *The Roman-Catharist: Or, The Papist is a Pvritane.* 1621.

Rollenson, Francis. *Sermons preached before his Maiestie.* 1611.

Ross, Alexander. *Gods House, or The Hovse of Prayer vindicated from prophanenesse and sacriledge.* 1642.

The Rovnd-Head Uncovered . . . With a distinction betwixt the Round-heads, and such as Papists call Puritans. 1642.

The Rovting of the Ranters, Being a full Relation of their uncivil carriages, and blasphemous words and actions at their mad meetings, their several kind of musick, dances, and ryotings. 1650.

Rutherford, Samuel. *A Survey of the Spiritvall Antichrist opening the Secrets of Familisme and Antinomianisme in the Antichristian Doctrine of John Saltmarsh.* 1648.

Rythmes against Martin Marre-prelate. 1589?.

A Sad Warning to all Prophane Malignant Spirits, who Reproach True Protestants with the name of Round-Heads. 1642.

Saltmarsh, John. *Groanes for Liberty, Present From the Presbyterians (formerly Non-conforming) Brethren.* 1646.

  Perfume Against the Sulpherous Stinke of the Snuffe of the Light for Smoak. 1646.

  The Smoke in the Temple. Wherein is a Designe for Peace and Reconciliation of Believers of the several Opinions of these Times. 1646.

Sarson, Laurence. *An Analysis of 1 Timothy.* 1650.

Sclater, William. *The Remedie of Schisme, or, A means to settle the divisions of the times.* 1642.

The Scotch Presbyterian Weather-cock Pearch'd upon our English Steeple: or, An Historicall Narration of the variable Chances and Changes, or Presbyterian Government in Scotland, and may consequently be in England with the Churches Deformation to the tune of Tom of Bedlam. 1647.

A Sectary Dissected, or, The Anatomie of an Independent Flie, still buzzing about City and Country. 1647.

Sedgwick, Obadiah. *Haman's Vanity, or a Sermon displaying the birthlesse Issues of Church-destroying Adversaries.* 1643.

  The Natvre and Danger of Heresies, Opened in a Sermon Before the Honourable House of Commons. 1647.

Semper Idem: Or a Parallel betwixt the Ancient and Modern Phanatics. 1661.

A Sermon Preached the last Fast Day in Leaden-Hall Street, in the house of one Pamore, a Cheesmonger, by one of the zealous brethren. 1643.

Shepherd, Thomas. *New Englands Lamentation for Old Englands present errours, and divisions, and their feared future desolations if not timeley prevented. Occasioned by the increase of Anabaptists, Rigid Separatists, Antinomians, and Familists.* 1645.

Sheringham, Robert. *Two Sermons Preached in St. Maries Church in Cambridge.* 1645.

A Short Discourse, Tovching the Cause of the present unhappy Distractions, and Distempers in this Kingdome, and the ready Meanes to Compose, and Quiet them. 1642.

A Short History of the Anabaptists of High and Low Germany. 1642.

Sibbs, [Richard?]. *A Consolatory Letter to an afflicted Conscience.* 1641.

Simpson, William. *A Discovery of the Priests and Professors, And of their Nakedness and Shame, which is coming upon them.* 1660.

Sir Martin Mar-People, his Coller of Esses. 1590.

Smectymnuus [pseud.]. *An Answer to a Book Entitvled, An Humble Remonstrance, in which the originall of liturgy, episcopacy is discussed.* 1641.

Smith, George. *Englands Pressvres: or, The Peoples Complaint.* 1645.

Smith, Henry. *Gods Arrovve against Atheists.* n.p., 1593.

Smyth, John. *Paralleles, censures, observations.* Amsterdam ?, 1609.

  Churches of the separation. 1612.

Some, Robert. *A Godly Treatise containing and deciding certaine questions, mooued of late in London.* 1588. Facsimile reprint, Amsterdam: Theatrvm Orbis Terrarvm, Ltd., and Norwood, N.J.: Walter J. Johnson, Inc., 1974.

The Sovndheads Description of the Rovndhead. Or, The Rovndhead Exactly Anatomized in his Integralls and Excrementalls. 1642.

Sparke, Thomas. *A Brotherly Persuasion to Vnitie, and Vniformitie in Ivdjement.* 1607.

Spelman, Henry. *A Protestants Account of his Orthodox Holding in Matters of Religion.* 1642.

Spencer, Benjamin. *Chrysomeson, a golden meane: or, A middle way for Christians to walk by.* 1659.

Spinola, George. *Rvles to Get Children by with Handsome Faces: or, Precepts for the extemporary Sectaries which Preach, and Pray, and get Children without Book to consider and look on, before they leap.* 1642.

A Spirit Moving in the Women Preachers: or, Certaine Quæries, Vented and put forth unto this affronted, brazen-faced, strange, new Feminine Brood. 1646.

Sprigg, Joshua. *The Ancient Bounds, or Liberty of Conscience, Tenderly Stated, Modestly Asserted, and Mildly Vindicated.* 1645.

Sprint, John. *Propositions, Tending to prooue the Necessarie vse of the Christian Sabbaoth.* 1607.

Squarecaps turned into Rovnd-heads or the Bishops Vindication, and the Brownists Conviction. 1642.

Stone, Samuel. *A congregational church is a catholike visible church.* 1652.

A Svpplication of the Family of Loue . . . Examined, and found to be derogatory in an hie degree. Cambridge, 1606.

Syms, Christopher. *Great Britans Alarm discovering National Sinns.* 1647.

T., C. *A spirituall purgation of Luthers error.* 1555?.

T., T. *A Myrror for Martinists, and all other Schismatiques, which in these dangerous daies do breake the godlie vnitie, and disturbe the Christian peace of the Church.* 1590.

Taylor, Jeremy. *Discourse concerning prayer ex tempore or by pretense of the Spirit.* 1647.

A Discourse of the Liberty of Prophesying shewing the Unreasonablenes of prescribing to other mens Faith, and the Iniquity of persecuting differing opinions. 1647.

Taylor, John. *All the Workes of Iohn Taylor The Water Poet Collected Into One Volum.* 1630. Facsimile reprint. London: The Scolar Press, 1973.

The Anatomy of the Separatists, alias, Brownists, the factious Brethren in these Times: wherein this seditious Sect is fairely dissected, and perspicuously discovered to the view of the World. 1642.

An apology for private preaching, in which those formes are warranted or rather justified, which the malignant sect contemme and daily by prophane pamphlets make ridiculous. 1642.

A Brown Dozen of Drunkards. 1648.

The Brownists Conventicle: Or an assemble of Brownists, Separatists, and Non-Conformists. 1641.

The Brownists Synagogue, or a late Discovery of their Conventicles, Assemblies, and places of meeting. 1641.

A Cluster of Coxcombes: or, A Cinquepace of Five Sorts of Knaves and Fooles: Namely, the Donatists, Publicans, Disciplinarians, Anabaptists, and Brownists. 1642.

The conversion, confession, contrition, coming to himselfe, & advise, of a mis-led, ill-bred, rebellious round-head. 1643.

Crop-Eare Curried, or, Tom Nash His Ghost. 1644.

The Decoy Duck: Together with the Discovery of the Knot in the Dragons Tayle. 1642.

A Description of the Round-Head and Rattle-Head. 1642.

The Devil Turn'd Round-head: or, Plvto becomes a Brownist. 1642.

The Diseases of the Times, Or, The Distempers of the Common-wealth. 1642.

The Divisions of the Church of England crept in at XV several doores. 1642.

An Exact Description of a Roundhead, and a Long-Head Shag-Poll: Taken ou[t]of the purest Antiquities and Records. 1642.

A Full and compleate Answer against the Writer of a late Volume set forth, entitled A Tale in a Tub, or a Tub lecture: with a Vindication of that ridiculous name called Round-Heads. 1642.

Grand Plvtoes Remonstrance, or, The Devill Horn-mad at Roundheads and Brownists. 1642.

Heads of all Fashions. Being, A Plaine Dissection or Definition of diverse, and sundry sorts of heads, Butting, Jetting, or pointing at vulgar opinion. And Allegorically shewing the Diversities of Religion in these distempered times. 1642.

Love one another: A Tvb Lectvre, Preached At Watford in Hartfordshire at a Conventicle on the 25. of December . . . by John Alexander, a Joyner. 1642.

Lucifer's Lackey, or the Devils new creature, being the true character of a dissembling Brownist. 1641.

Mad Fashions, Od [sic] Fashions, All out of all Fashions, or, The Emblem of these Distracted Times. 1642.

The Nest of Serpents. 1641.

New Preachers New. 1641.

Rebels Anathematized, and Anatomized: OR, A Satyricall Salutation to the Rabble of seditious, pestiferous Pulpit-praters, with their Brethren the Weekly Libellers, Railers, and Revilers. Oxford, 1645.

Religions Enemies, With a Brief and Ingenious Relation, as by Anabaptists, Brownists, Papists, Familists, Atheists, and Foolists, sawcily presuming to tosse Religion in a Blanquet. 1641.

Religions Lotterie, or the Churches Amazement. Wherein is declared how many sorts of Religions there is crept into the very bowels of this Kingdome, striving to shake the whole foundation and to destroy both Church and Kingdom. 1642.

A Reply as true as Steele to a Rusty, Rayling, Ridiculous, Lying Libell . . . called by the name of An Answer to a foolish Pamphlet Entituled, A Swarme of Sectaries and Schismatiques. 1641.

A Seasonable Lecture, or A most learned Oration: Disburthened from Henry VValker, a most judicious damn Iron monger, a late Pamphleteere and now (too late or too soon) a double diligent Preacher. 1642.

A Swarme of Sectaries, and Schismatiques. 1641.

A Tale in a Tub, or, A tub lecture. 1641.

The World turn'd upside down: or, A Briefe description of the ridiculous Fashions of these distracted Times. 1647.

A Testimony to the Truth of Jesus Christ, and to Our Solemn League and Covenant; as also against the Errours, Heresies and Blasphemies of these times, and the Toleration of them. 1648.

Thomason, William. *Regulated Zeal, or, An earnest request to all zealously affected Christians to seeke the desired reformation in a peaceable way.* 1641.

Thompson, Thomas. *A Diet for a Drvnkard.* 1612.

A Three-fold Discourse betweene three Neighbors, Algate, Bishopgate, and John Heyden, the late Cobler of Hounsditch, a professed Brownist. 1642.

A Threefold Preservative against three dangerous diseases of these latter times. 1610.

Tichell, John. *The bottomles pit smoaking in familisme.* Oxford, 1652.

Tilbury, Samuel. *Bloudy Newse from the North, and the Ranting Adamites Declaration.* 1650.

Tom Nash his Ghost. Written by Thomas Nash his Ghost, with Pap with a Hatchet, a little revived since the 30. Yeare of the late Qu. Elizabeths Reigne, when Martin Mar-prelate was as mad as any of his Tub-men are now. 1642.

Torshell, Samuel. *A Designe about Disposing the Bible into an Harmony. Or, an Essay, Concerning transposing the order of books and Chapters of the holy Scriptures for the reducting of all into a continued History.* 1647.

Travers, Walter. *A Directory of Church-government. Anciently contended for, and as farre as the Times would suffer, practiced by the first Non-conformists in the daies of Queen Elizabeth.* 1644.

A Treatise of Christian Renunciation. 1593.

A Treatise on the cohabitation of the faithful with the unfaithful. 1555.

A True and Perfect Picture of our present Reformation. 1648.

The True Emblem of Antichrist: Or, Schism Display'd. 1651.

Tub-preachers overturned. 1647.

Turner, Francis. *Animadversions upon a Late Pamphlet entituled the Naked Truth.* 1676.

Turner, William. *A Preservative agaynst the Poyson of Pelagius, lately renued by the Anabaptists.* n.p., 1551.

Twenty Lookes Over all the Rovnd-Heads that ever lived in the world. 1643.

Underhill, Thomas. *Hell broke loose, or, An history of the Quakers both old and new.* 1660.

Vernon, Jean. *A strong battery against the invocation of the saints.* 1562.

Vicars, John. *Coleman-street Conclave Visited, and, That Grand Impostor, the Schismaticks Cheater in Chief.* 1648.

The Schismatick Sifted. Or, the Picture of Independents, Freshly and Fairly Washt-over again. 1646.

The Vindication of the Separate Brethren of the Spirit. 1643.

Vines, Richard. *The Authours, Nature, and Danger of Hæresie.* 1647.

Vox populi, or the Peoples Cry against the clergy. 1646.

Walker, Henry. *An Answer to a Foolish Pamphlet entitvled A swarme of Sectaries & Schismaticks.* 1641.

The Modest Vindication of Henry Walker. In answer to certaine scandalous Pamphlets, forged and vented abroad in his name. 1642.

Walwyn, William. *A Whisper in the Eare of Mr. Thomas Edwards Minister.* 1645.

A Word More to Mr. Thomas Edwards Minister. 1644.

Ward, Nathaniel [Theodore de la Guard, pseud.]. *Mercurius Melancholicus. Mistris Parliament presented in her Bed, after the sore travaile and hard labour which she endured last week, in the Birth of her Monstrous Offspring, the Childe of Deformation.* 1648.

The Simple Cobbler of Aggavvam in America. 1646.

A Warning for England, Especially for London in the Famous History of the Frantick Anabaptists their wild Preachings and Practices in Germany. 1642.

Watson, Richard. *A Sermon Touching Schisme.* 1642.

Webb, John. *An Historical Essay Endeavoring a Probability that the Language of the Empire of China is the Primitive Language.* 1669.

Webbe, Thomas. *Mr. Edwards Pen No Slander: Or, The Gangræna once more searched.* 1646.

Webster, John. *Academiarum Examen, or, the Examination of the Academies.* 1654.

The Welsh Physitian. 1646.

White, Thomas. *A Discoverie of Brownisme: or, A briefe declaration of some of the errors and abhominations daily practiced and increased among the English company of the seperation remayning for the present at Amsterdam in Holland.* 1605.

Whitfeild, Thomas. *A Refutation of the Loose Opinions, and licentious tenets wherwith those Lay-preachers which wander up and downe the Kingdome, labour to seduce the simple people.* 1646.

Widdowes, Giles. *The schysmatical puritan.* Oxford, 1630.

Wilcock, James. *A Challenge Sent to Master E. B. a Semi-Separatist from the Church of England.* 1641.

Wilkinson, William. *A Confutation of Certaine Articles, Deliuered Vnto the Familye of Loue.* 1579. Facsimile reprint, Amsterdam: Theatrvm Orbis Terrarvm and New York: Da Capo Press, 1970.

Willis, H. *Times Whirligig.* 1646.

Wilson, Thomas. *A Christian Dictionary.* 1612.

Wing, John. *Saints Advantage, or, the Well-Fare of the Faithfull, in the worst times.* 1624.

A Worke for the Wisely Considerate. 1641.

Workman, Giles. *Private-men no Pulpit-men: or, A Modest Examination of Lay-Mens Preaching.* 1646.

Wortley, Francis. *Characters and Elegies.* 1646.

Wright, Leonard. *A Friendly Admonition to Martine Marprelate, and his Mates.* 1590.

Index

Compiled by Meg Davies
(Registered Indexer, Society of Indexers)